the losers: endgame

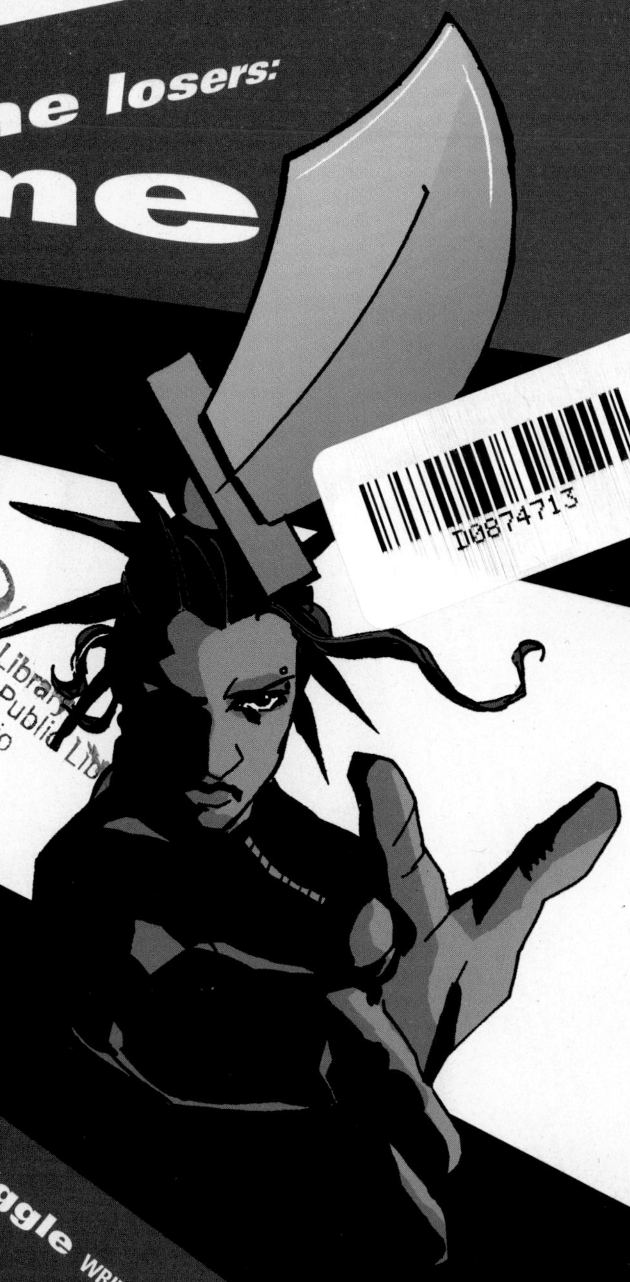

andy diggle WRITER
lee loughridge COLORIST
jock ORIGINAL SERIES COVERS
jock • colin wilson ARTISTS
clem robins LETTERER

KAREN BERGER, Senior VP-Executive Editor
RICHARD BRUNING, VP-Executive Editor   PORNSAK PICHETSHOTE, Editor-collected edition
ALISON GILL, VP-Manufacturing   PATRICK CALDON, Executive VP-Finance & Operations
JOHN NEE, VP-Business Development   GREGORY NOVECK, Senior VP-Creative Affairs

SCOTT NYBAKKEN, Editor-original series   PAUL LEVITZ, President & Publisher
PATRICK CALDON, Executive VP-Finance & Operations   ROBBIN BROSTERMAN, Senior Art Director
HANK KANALZ, VP-General Manager, WildStorm   JOHN CUNNINGHAM, VP-Marketing
CHRIS CARAMALIS, VP-Finance   JIM LEE, Editorial Director-WildStorm   TERRI CUNNINGHAM, VP-Managing Editor
LILLIAN LASERSON, Senior VP & General Counsel   PAULA LOWITT, Senior VP-Business Development, DC Direct
CHERYL RUBIN, Senior VP-Brand Management   JEFF TROJAN, VP-Business Development, DC Direct

GEORG BREWER, VP-Design & DC Direct Creative
STEPHANIE FIERMAN, Senior VP-Sales & Marketing
BOB WAYNE, VP-Sales   DAVID McKILLIPS, VP-Advertising & Custom Publishing

THE LOSERS: ENDGAME   Published by DC Comics. Cover, introduction and compilation copyright © 2006 DC Comics. All Rights Reserved. Originally published in single magazine form as THE LOSERS 26-32. Copyright © 2005,
2006 DC Comics. All Rights Reserved. All characters, their distinctive likenesses and related elements featured in this publication are trademarks of DC Comics. The stories, characters and incidents featured in this
publication are entirely fictional. DC Comics does not read or accept unsolicited submissions of ideas, stories or artwork. DC Comics, 1700 Broadway, New York, NY 10019. A Warner Bros. Entertainment Company.
Printed in Canada. First Printing.
ISBN: 1-4012-1004-X ISBN 13: 978-1-4012-1004-5.
Cover illustration by Jock.
Publication design by John J. Hill.

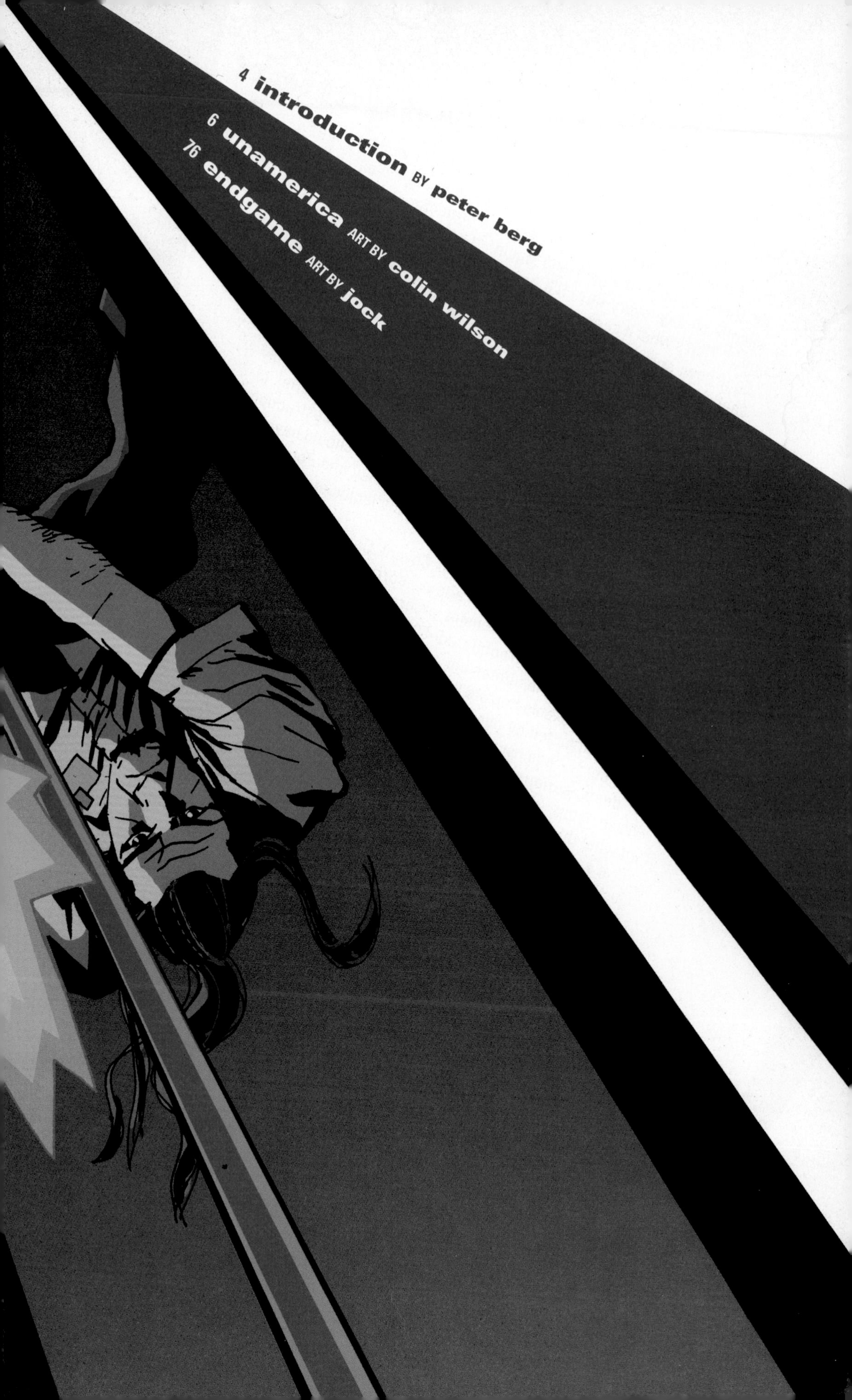

introduction

'Cause I like the idea of Cougar: dead quiet and ever vigilant, with deep eyes and a non-negotiable willingness to kill anyone who threatens those he loves. A true, selfless protector. One who will be there again and again and again. "Lean on me," he sings silently all day, every day. "I'll be your friend. I'll help you carry on..." That's what it seems to me we need more than anything else right now: someone who's willing to step down, lie back in the shadows, keep his mouth shut, and be there for his people — any time, any place.

I am a proud American, but as the father of a young boy I am truly starting to fear the darkness I see us moving towards: a series of explosions, detonations, gas releases, murders, and destruction unleashed against us by forces that could have — should have — been so much more manageable, if men like Clay and Pooch and Jensen and Cougar were just allowed a little legitimate access.

I've sat in dark, fish-fried pubs in Covent Garden and listened to Andy Diggle rave on about corruption and reverse assassinations and government programs so secret they exist only in shredded, graphite x5-6000 computer chips buried in triple-encased lead/titanium grab vaults. Deep secrets locked away. Unspeakable horrors that Diggle knows for a fact have and will be committed by our governments — hard and with extreme violence — against you, me and our Uncle Charlies. Diggle is dead serious. He knows there's something wrong in Washington, and he's fighting back. That's really at the core of what these black ops gangsters are all about: truth and justice. That's what Diggle and Jock are looking for: a little truth and justice — the American Way, served up by two sweet-smiling Brits deep outta the distant London suburbs. That's where these heroes come from, and God knows we need heroes.

Let these boys roll. I want my heroes smoking, fucking, fighting, laughing, suffering, and deeply aware of the stinging pain of real human anguish. I want my heroes to come back from the dark side with realtime experience of how black the eyes of the blood crow are as you travel deep up the river.

Clay knows. He's looked deep into those eyes.

Aisha knows. She's held that gaze.

They all have, and still do. They value human life. Still do. They push back. Still do. They rage against the dying of the light.

Andy Diggle and Jock have together created deeply flawed, badass, indestructible heroes whose hearts are as filled with light as their guns are filled with bullets.

— **Peter Berg**
2006

Peter Berg has worked in Hollywood for more than 15 years, where he has earned a reputation for taking on challenging material in a wide variety of creative roles. As an actor, he has starred in such films as The Last Seduction, Cop Land and Collateral, as well as the television series Chicago Hope and Alias. He directed the film The Rundown and wrote and directed Very Bad Things and the acclaimed Friday Night Lights. In addition, he created, wrote, produced and directed the ABC series Wonderland. Berg is currently directing The Kingdom, a thriller set in Saudi Arabia, and is in development to produce and direct his screenplay adaptation of THE LOSERS.

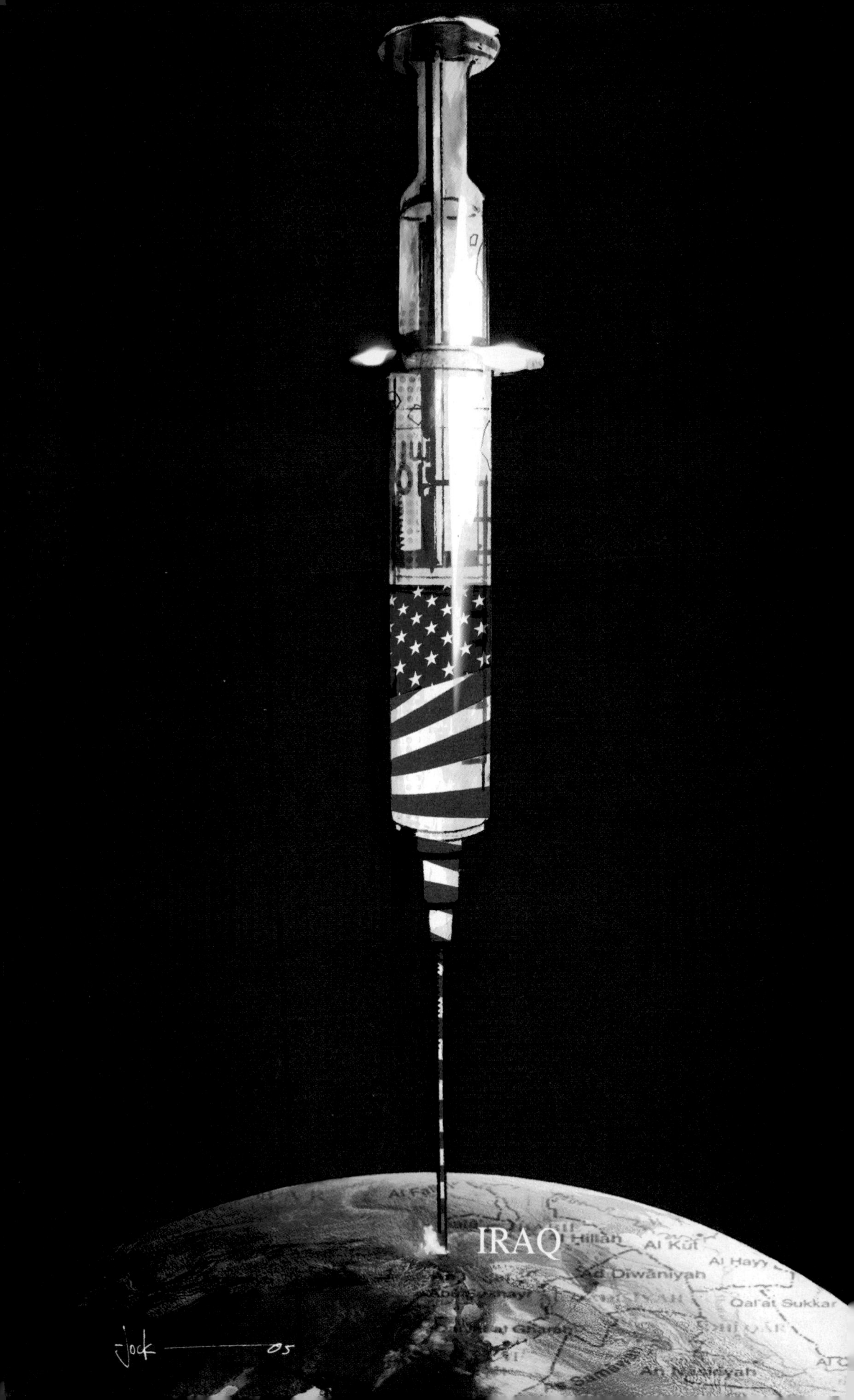
IRAQ
Hillah
Al Kut
Al Hayy
Ad Diwaniyah
Qal'at Sukkar
An Nasiriyah
jock 05

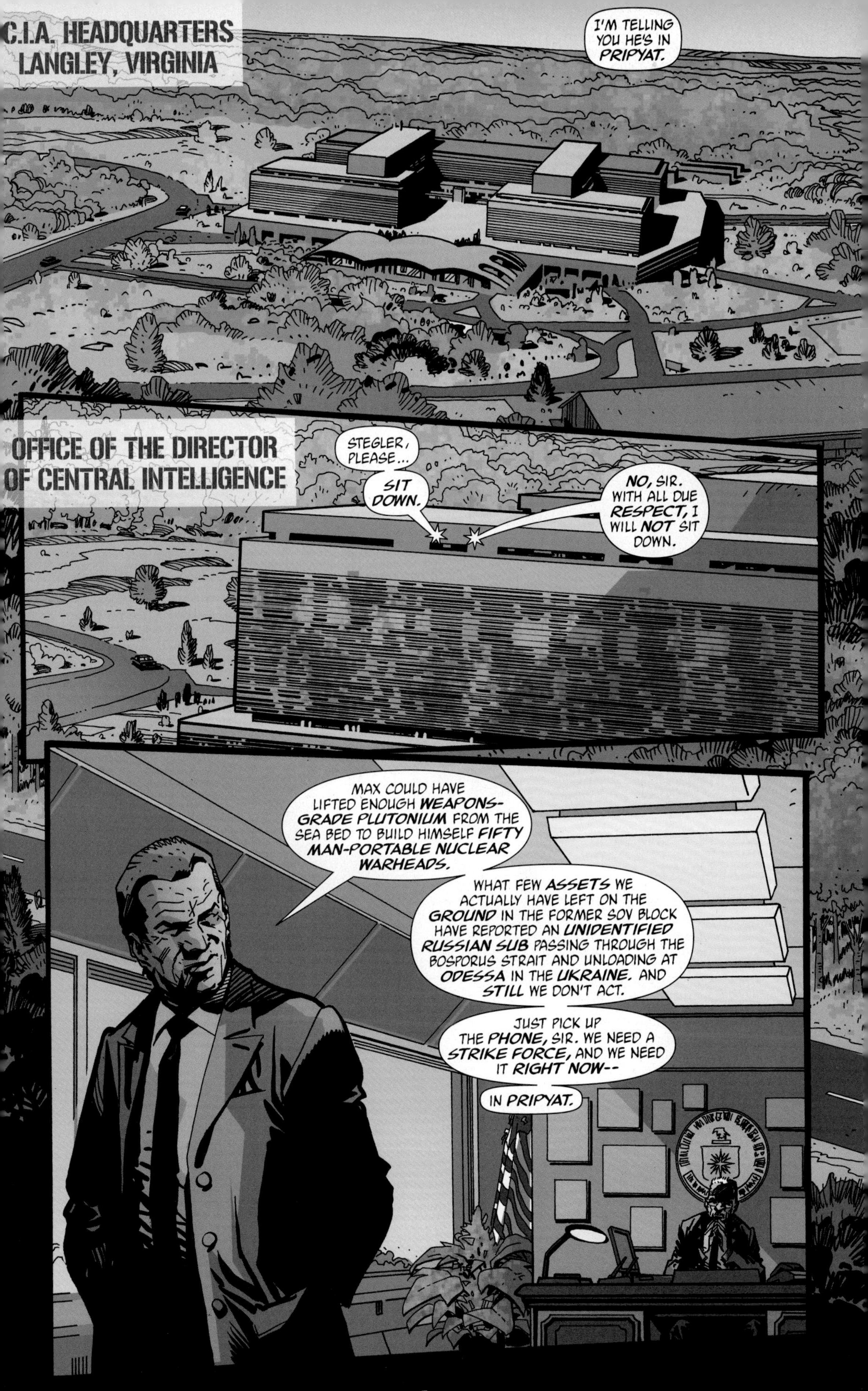
C.I.A. HEADQUARTERS
LANGLEY, VIRGINIA
I'M TELLING YOU HE'S IN PRIPYAT.
OFFICE OF THE DIRECTOR OF CENTRAL INTELLIGENCE
STEGLER, PLEASE...
SIT DOWN.
NO, SIR. WITH ALL DUE RESPECT, I WILL NOT SIT DOWN.
MAX COULD HAVE LIFTED ENOUGH WEAPONS-GRADE PLUTONIUM FROM THE SEA BED TO BUILD HIMSELF FIFTY MAN-PORTABLE NUCLEAR WARHEADS.
WHAT FEW ASSETS WE ACTUALLY HAVE LEFT ON THE GROUND IN THE FORMER SOV BLOCK HAVE REPORTED AN UNIDENTIFIED RUSSIAN SUB PASSING THROUGH THE BOSPORUS STRAIT AND UNLOADING AT ODESSA IN THE UKRAINE. AND STILL WE DON'T ACT.
JUST PICK UP THE PHONE, SIR. WE NEED A STRIKE FORCE, AND WE NEED IT RIGHT NOW--
IN PRIPYAT.

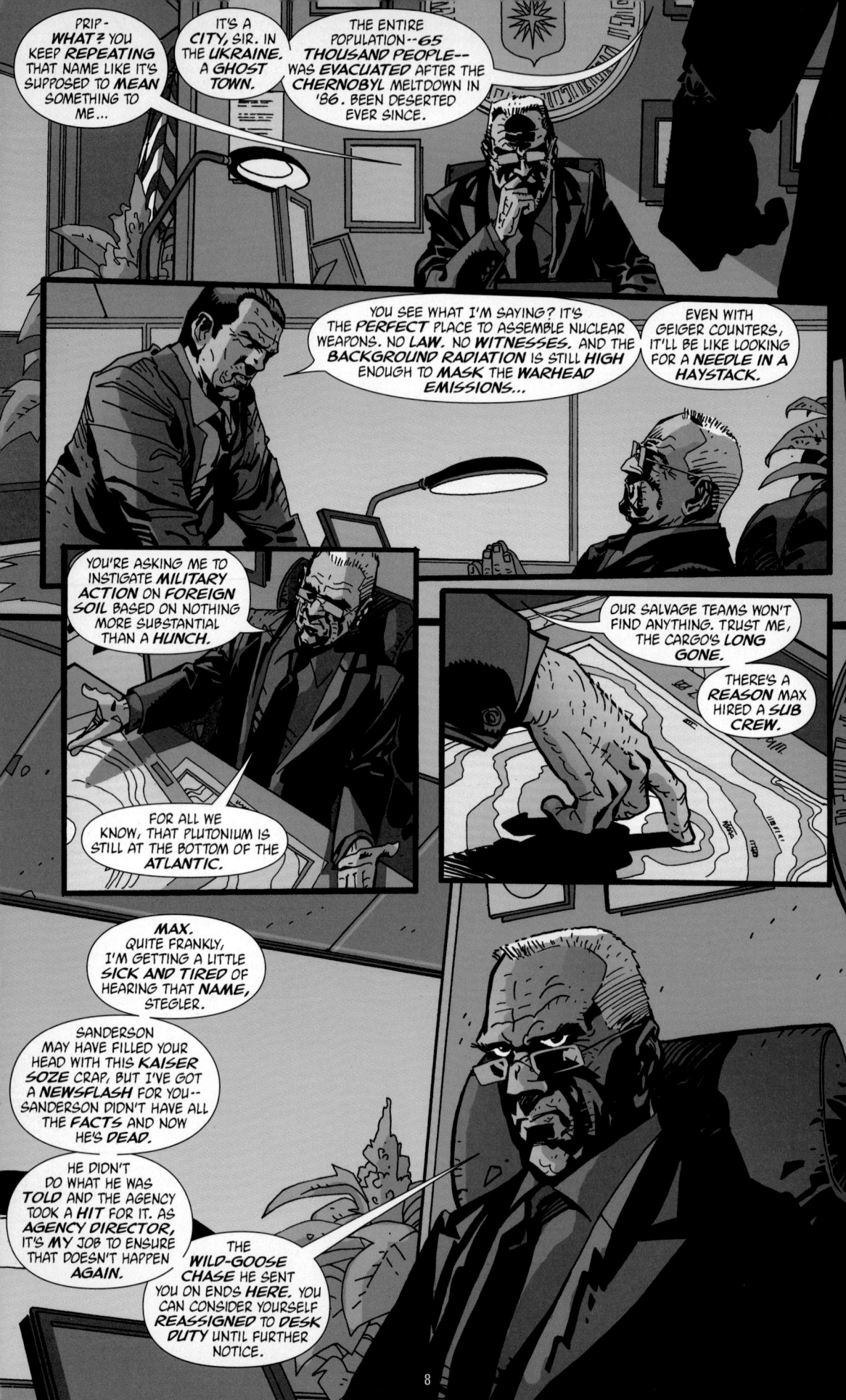

PRIP-- *WHAT?* YOU KEEP *REPEATING* THAT NAME LIKE IT'S SUPPOSED TO *MEAN* SOMETHING TO ME...

IT'S A *CITY,* SIR. IN THE *UKRAINE.* A *GHOST TOWN.*

THE ENTIRE POPULATION--*65 THOUSAND PEOPLE*-- WAS *EVACUATED* AFTER THE *CHERNOBYL* MELTDOWN IN '86. BEEN DESERTED EVER SINCE.

YOU SEE WHAT I'M SAYING? IT'S THE *PERFECT* PLACE TO ASSEMBLE NUCLEAR WEAPONS. NO *LAW.* NO *WITNESSES.* AND THE *BACKGROUND RADIATION* IS STILL *HIGH* ENOUGH TO *MASK* THE WARHEAD EMISSIONS...

EVEN WITH *GEIGER COUNTERS,* IT'LL BE LIKE LOOKING FOR A *NEEDLE* IN A *HAYSTACK.*

YOU'RE ASKING ME TO INSTIGATE *MILITARY ACTION* ON *FOREIGN SOIL* BASED ON NOTHING MORE SUBSTANTIAL THAN A *HUNCH.*

OUR SALVAGE TEAMS WON'T FIND ANYTHING. TRUST ME, THE CARGO'S *LONG GONE.*

THERE'S A *REASON* MAX HIRED A *SUB CREW.*

FOR ALL WE KNOW, THAT PLUTONIUM IS STILL AT THE BOTTOM OF THE *ATLANTIC.*

MAX. QUITE FRANKLY, I'M GETTING A LITTLE *SICK* AND *TIRED* OF HEARING THAT *NAME,* STEGLER.

SANDERSON MAY HAVE FILLED YOUR HEAD WITH THIS *KAISER SOZE* CRAP, BUT I'VE GOT A *NEWSFLASH* FOR YOU-- SANDERSON DIDN'T HAVE ALL THE *FACTS* AND NOW HE'S *DEAD.*

HE DIDN'T DO WHAT HE WAS *TOLD* AND THE AGENCY TOOK A *HIT* FOR IT. AS *AGENCY DIRECTOR,* IT'S *MY* JOB TO ENSURE THAT DOESN'T HAPPEN *AGAIN.*

THE *WILD-GOOSE CHASE* HE SENT YOU ON ENDS *HERE.* YOU CAN CONSIDER YOURSELF REASSIGNED TO *DESK DUTY* UNTIL FURTHER NOTICE.

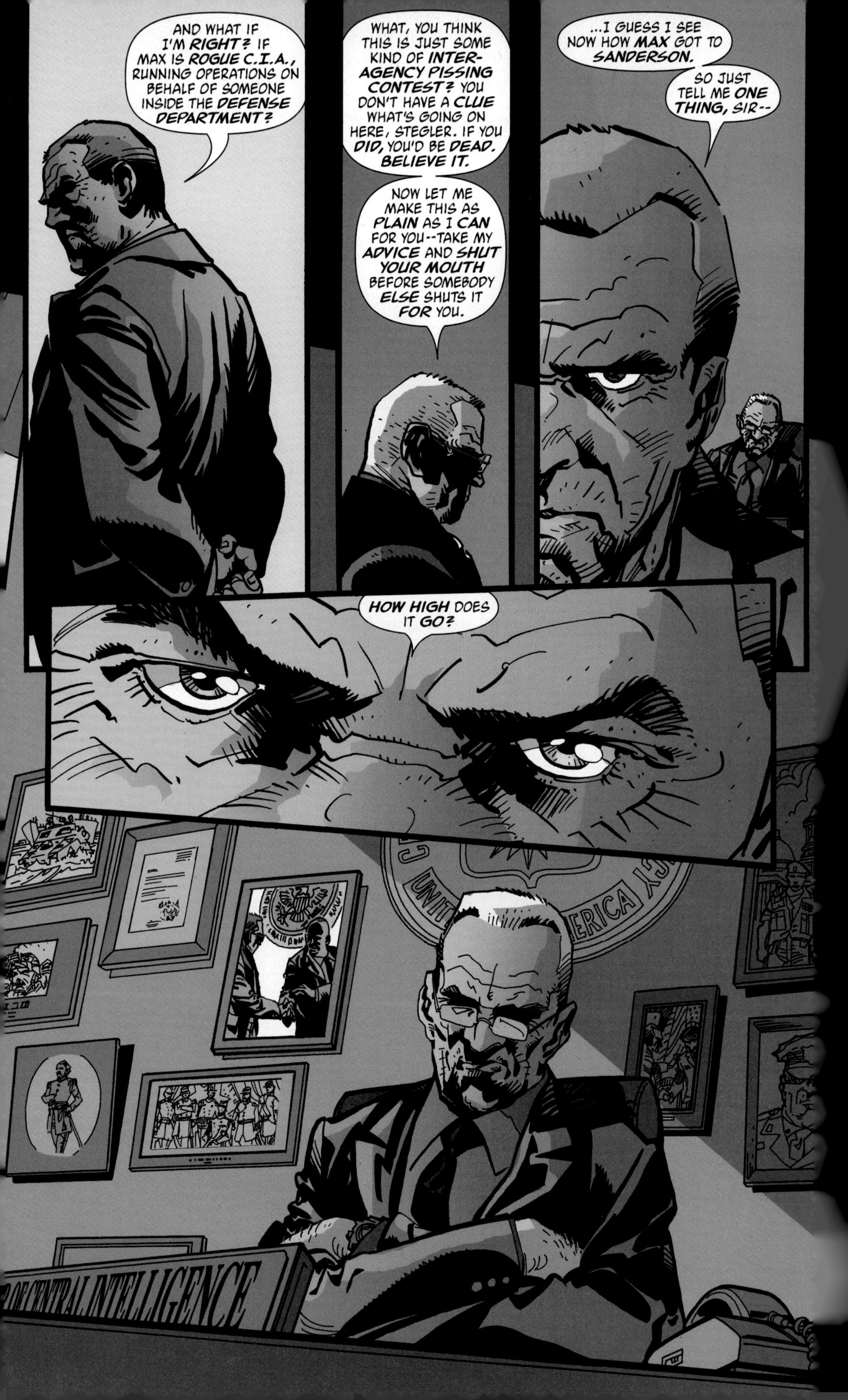
AND WHAT IF I'M RIGHT? IF MAX IS ROGUE C.I.A., RUNNING OPERATIONS ON BEHALF OF SOMEONE INSIDE THE DEFENSE DEPARTMENT?
WHAT, YOU THINK THIS IS JUST SOME KIND OF INTER-AGENCY PISSING CONTEST? YOU DON'T HAVE A CLUE WHAT'S GOING ON HERE, STEGLER. IF YOU DID, YOU'D BE DEAD. BELIEVE IT.
NOW LET ME MAKE THIS AS PLAIN AS I CAN FOR YOU--TAKE MY ADVICE AND SHUT YOUR MOUTH BEFORE SOMEBODY ELSE SHUTS IT FOR YOU.
...I GUESS I SEE NOW HOW MAX GOT TO SANDERSON.
SO JUST TELL ME ONE THING, SIR--
HOW HIGH DOES IT GO?
UNITED STATES OF AMERICA
OF CENTRAL INTELLIGENCE

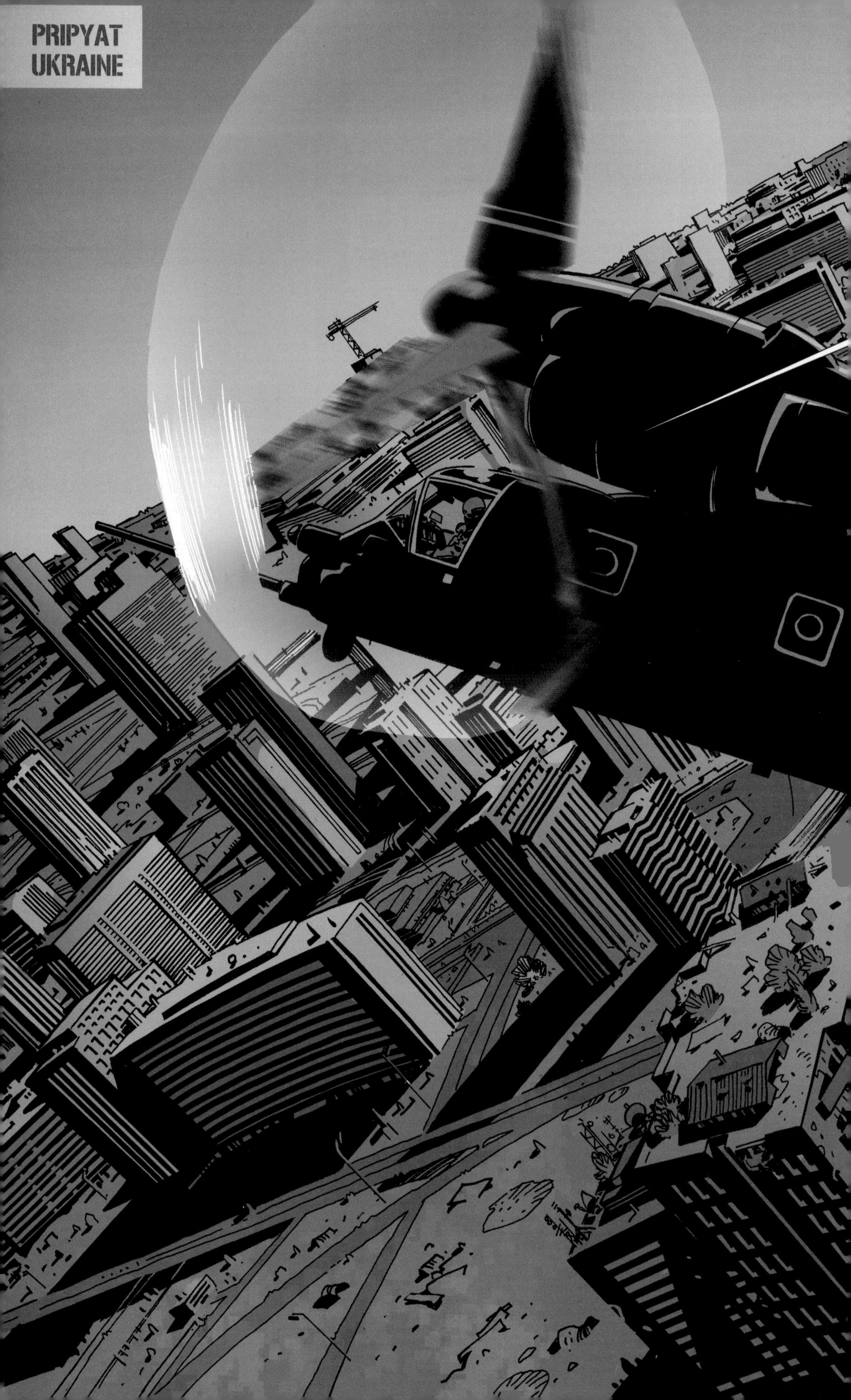
PRIPYAT
UKRAINE

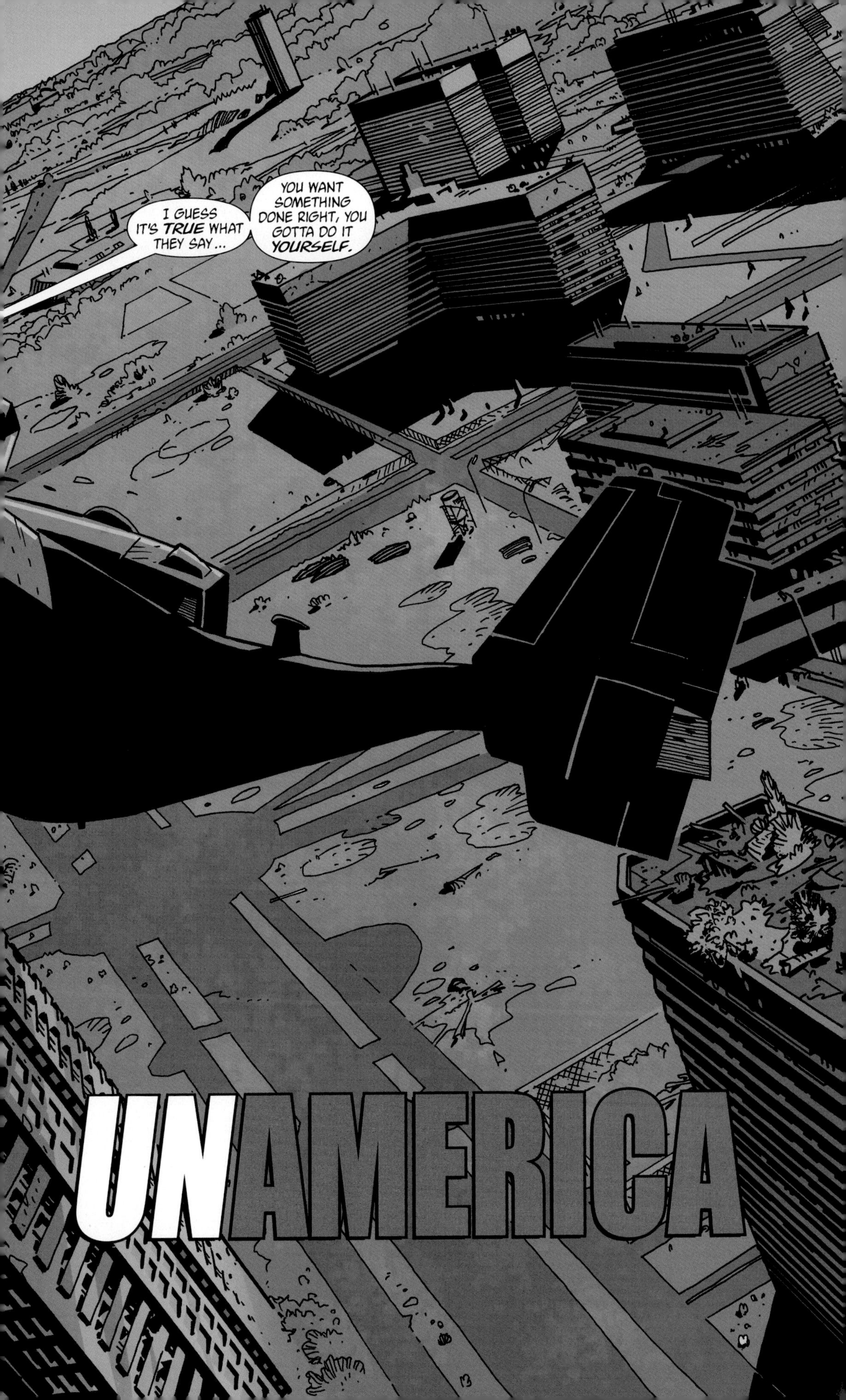
I GUESS IT'S TRUE WHAT THEY SAY...
YOU WANT SOMETHING DONE RIGHT, YOU GOTTA DO IT YOURSELF.
UNAMERICA

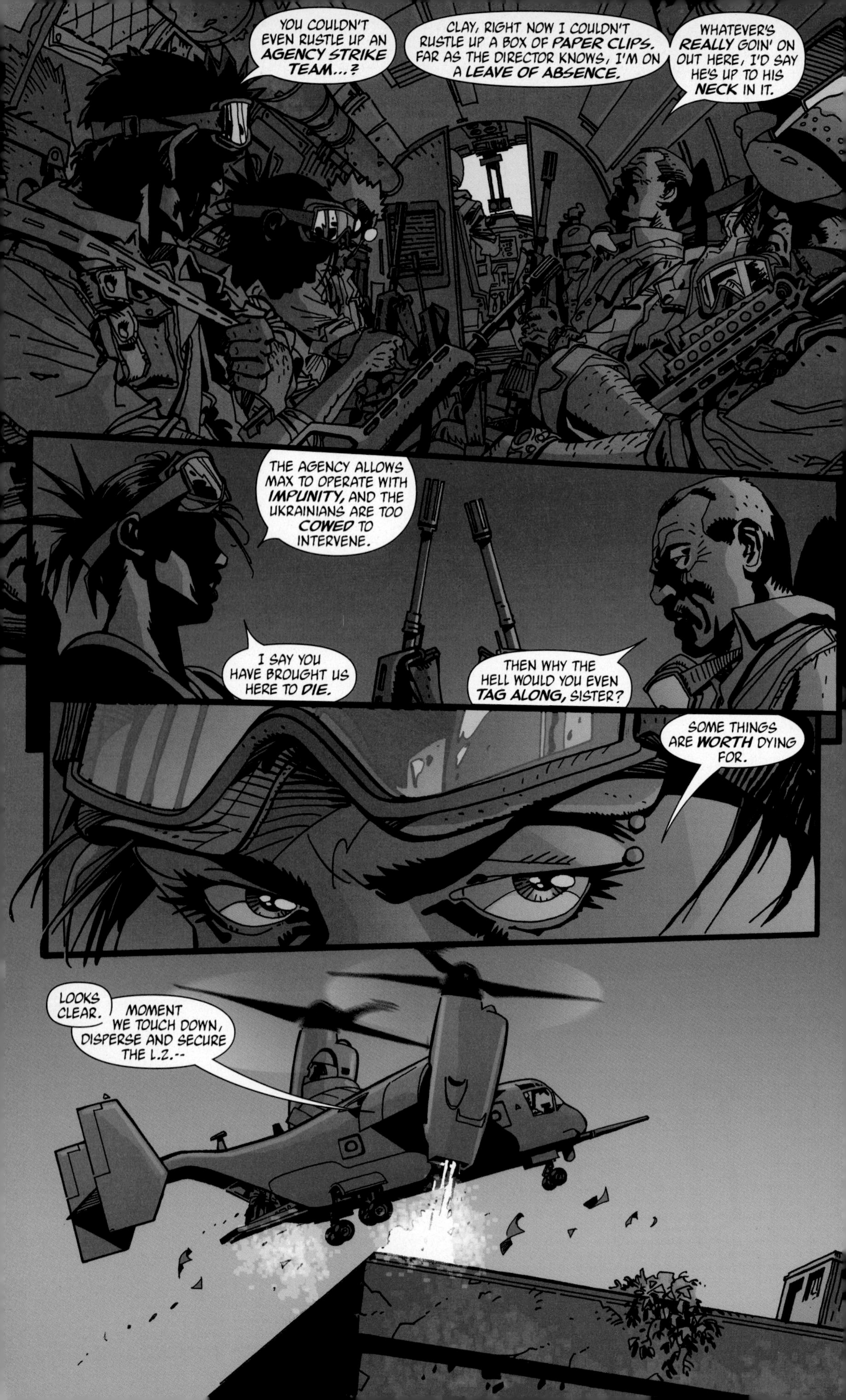
YOU COULDN'T EVEN RUSTLE UP AN AGENCY STRIKE TEAM...?
CLAY, RIGHT NOW I COULDN'T RUSTLE UP A BOX OF PAPER CLIPS. FAR AS THE DIRECTOR KNOWS, I'M ON A LEAVE OF ABSENCE.
WHATEVER'S REALLY GOIN' ON OUT HERE, I'D SAY HE'S UP TO HIS NECK IN IT.
THE AGENCY ALLOWS MAX TO OPERATE WITH IMPUNITY, AND THE UKRAINIANS ARE TOO COWED TO INTERVENE.
I SAY YOU HAVE BROUGHT US HERE TO DIE.
THEN WHY THE HELL WOULD YOU EVEN TAG ALONG, SISTER?
SOME THINGS ARE WORTH DYING FOR.
LOOKS CLEAR.
MOMENT WE TOUCH DOWN, DISPERSE AND SECURE THE L.Z.--

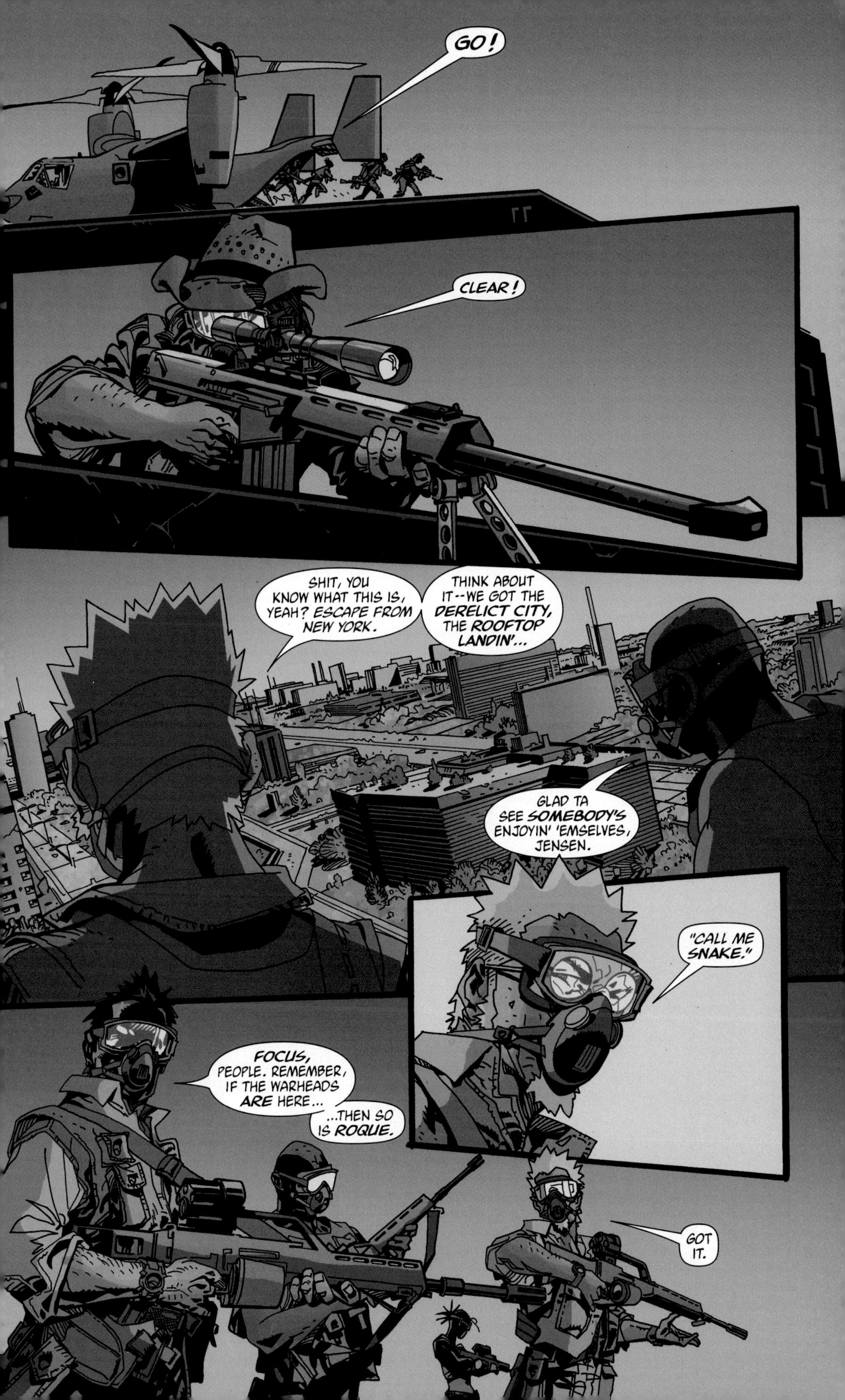
GO!
CLEAR!
SHIT, YOU KNOW WHAT THIS IS, YEAH? ESCAPE FROM NEW YORK.
THINK ABOUT IT--WE GOT THE DERELICT CITY, THE ROOFTOP LANDIN'...
GLAD TA SEE SOMEBODY'S ENJOYIN' 'EMSELVES, JENSEN.
"CALL ME SNAKE."
FOCUS, PEOPLE. REMEMBER, IF THE WARHEADS ARE HERE...
...THEN SO IS ROQUE.
GOT IT.

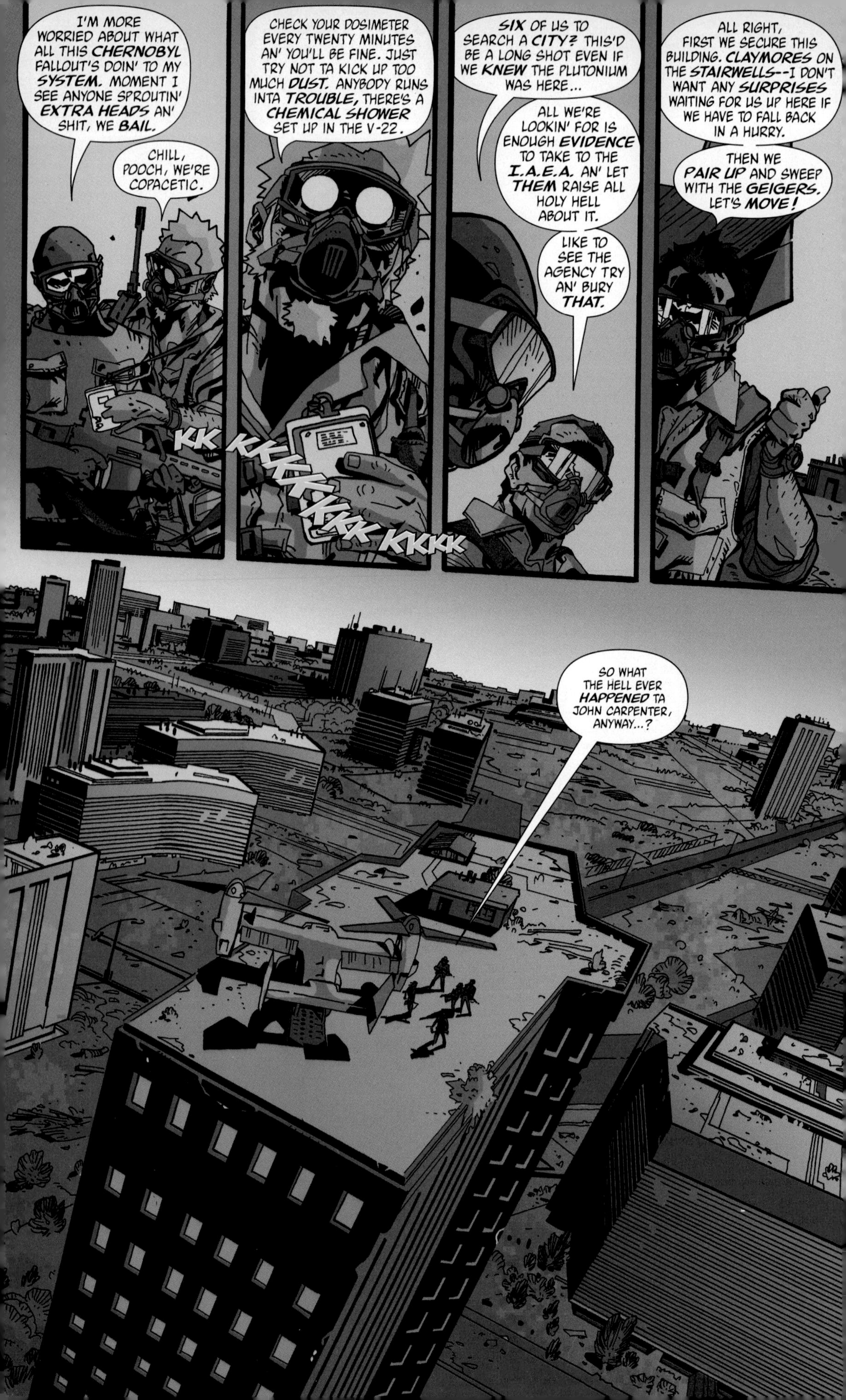
I'M MORE WORRIED ABOUT WHAT ALL THIS CHERNOBYL FALLOUT'S DOIN' TO MY SYSTEM. MOMENT I SEE ANYONE SPROUTIN' EXTRA HEADS AN' SHIT, WE BAIL.
CHILL, POOCH, WE'RE COPACETIC.
CHECK YOUR DOSIMETER EVERY TWENTY MINUTES AN' YOU'LL BE FINE. JUST TRY NOT TA KICK UP TOO MUCH DUST. ANYBODY RUNS INTA TROUBLE, THERE'S A CHEMICAL SHOWER SET UP IN THE V-22.
KK KKKKKKKKKKK KKKK
SIX OF US TO SEARCH A CITY? THIS'D BE A LONG SHOT EVEN IF WE KNEW THE PLUTONIUM WAS HERE...
ALL WE'RE LOOKIN' FOR IS ENOUGH EVIDENCE TO TAKE TO THE I.A.E.A. AN' LET THEM RAISE ALL HOLY HELL ABOUT IT.
LIKE TO SEE THE AGENCY TRY AN' BURY THAT.
ALL RIGHT, FIRST WE SECURE THIS BUILDING. CLAYMORES ON THE STAIRWELLS--I DON'T WANT ANY SURPRISES WAITING FOR US UP HERE IF WE HAVE TO FALL BACK IN A HURRY.
THEN WE PAIR UP AND SWEEP WITH THE GEIGERS. LET'S MOVE!
SO WHAT THE HELL EVER HAPPENED TA JOHN CARPENTER, ANYWAY...?

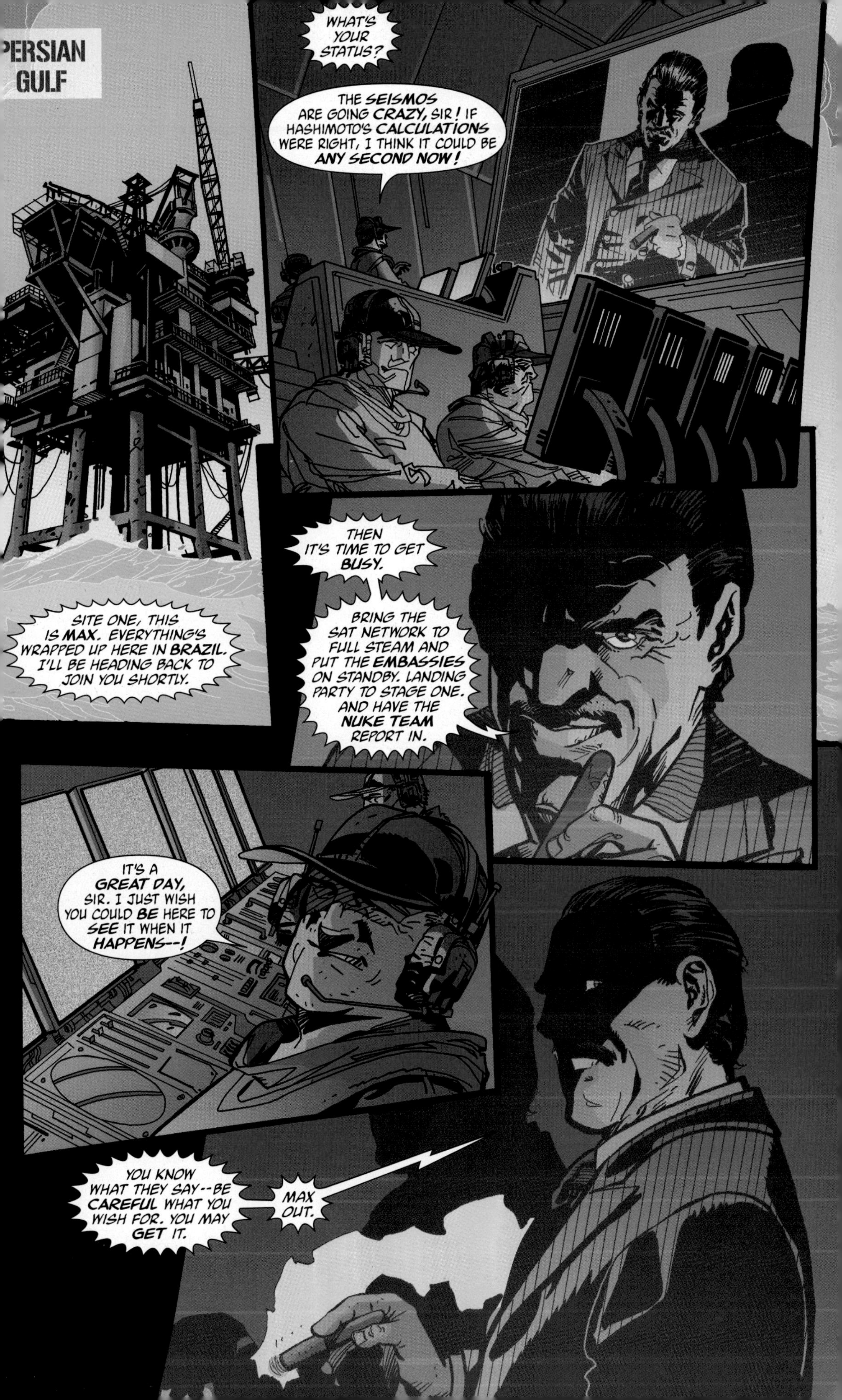
PERSIAN GULF
WHAT'S YOUR STATUS?
THE SEISMOS ARE GOING CRAZY, SIR! IF HASHIMOTO'S CALCULATIONS WERE RIGHT, I THINK IT COULD BE ANY SECOND NOW!
THEN IT'S TIME TO GET BUSY.
BRING THE SAT NETWORK TO FULL STEAM AND PUT THE EMBASSIES ON STANDBY. LANDING PARTY TO STAGE ONE. AND HAVE THE NUKE TEAM REPORT IN.
SITE ONE, THIS IS MAX. EVERYTHING'S WRAPPED UP HERE IN BRAZIL. I'LL BE HEADING BACK TO JOIN YOU SHORTLY.
IT'S A GREAT DAY, SIR. I JUST WISH YOU COULD BE HERE TO SEE IT WHEN IT HAPPENS--!
YOU KNOW WHAT THEY SAY--BE CAREFUL WHAT YOU WISH FOR. YOU MAY GET IT.
MAX OUT.

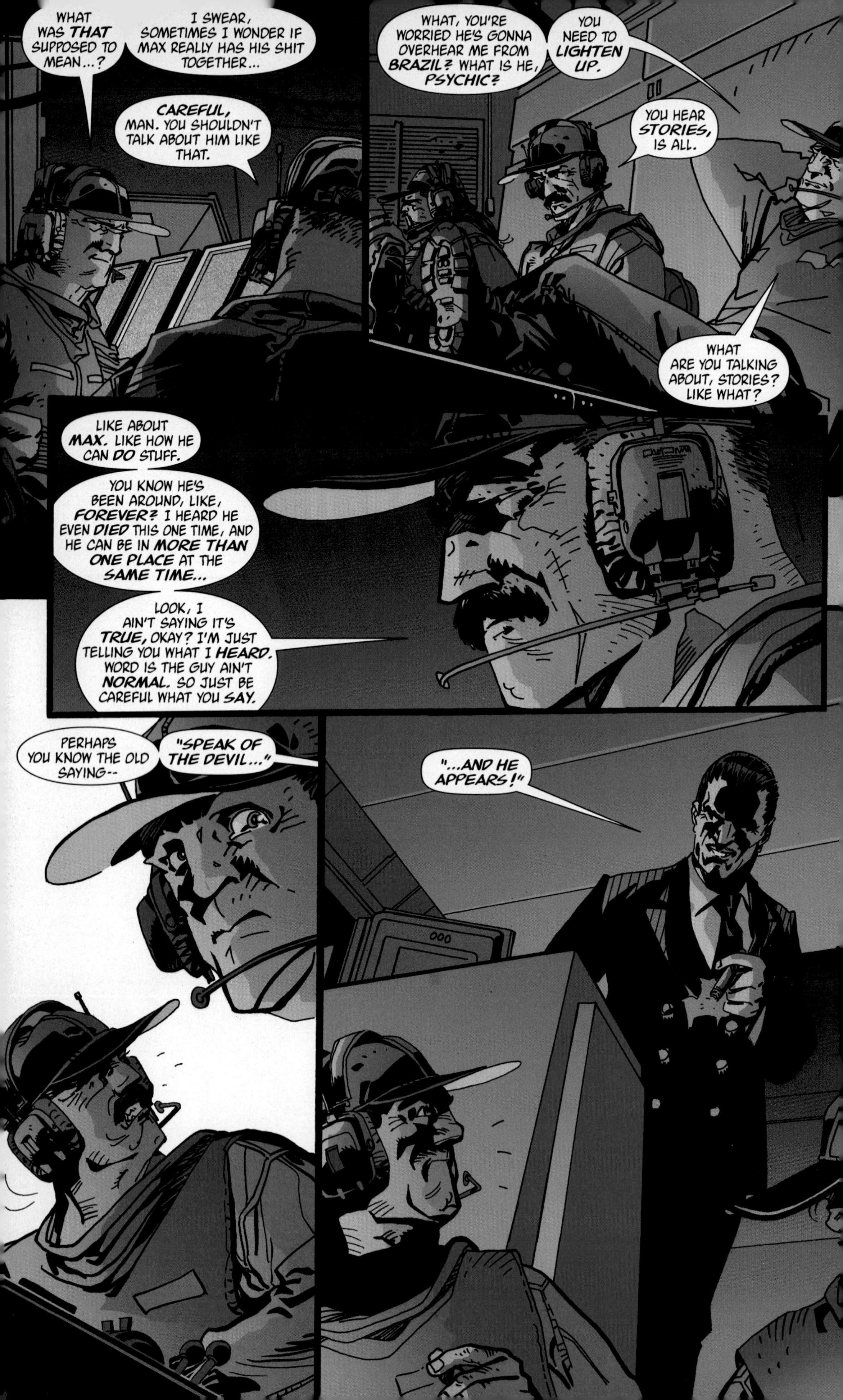

WHAT WAS THAT SUPPOSED TO MEAN...?
I SWEAR, SOMETIMES I WONDER IF MAX REALLY HAS HIS SHIT TOGETHER...
CAREFUL, MAN. YOU SHOULDN'T TALK ABOUT HIM LIKE THAT.
WHAT, YOU'RE WORRIED HE'S GONNA OVERHEAR ME FROM BRAZIL? WHAT IS HE, PSYCHIC?
YOU NEED TO LIGHTEN UP.
YOU HEAR STORIES, IS ALL.
WHAT ARE YOU TALKING ABOUT, STORIES? LIKE WHAT?
LIKE ABOUT MAX. LIKE HOW HE CAN DO STUFF.
YOU KNOW HE'S BEEN AROUND, LIKE, FOREVER? I HEARD HE EVEN DIED THIS ONE TIME, AND HE CAN BE IN MORE THAN ONE PLACE AT THE SAME TIME...
LOOK, I AIN'T SAYING IT'S TRUE, OKAY? I'M JUST TELLING YOU WHAT I HEARD. WORD IS THE GUY AIN'T NORMAL. SO JUST BE CAREFUL WHAT YOU SAY.
PERHAPS YOU KNOW THE OLD SAYING--
"SPEAK OF THE DEVIL..."
"...AND HE APPEARS!"

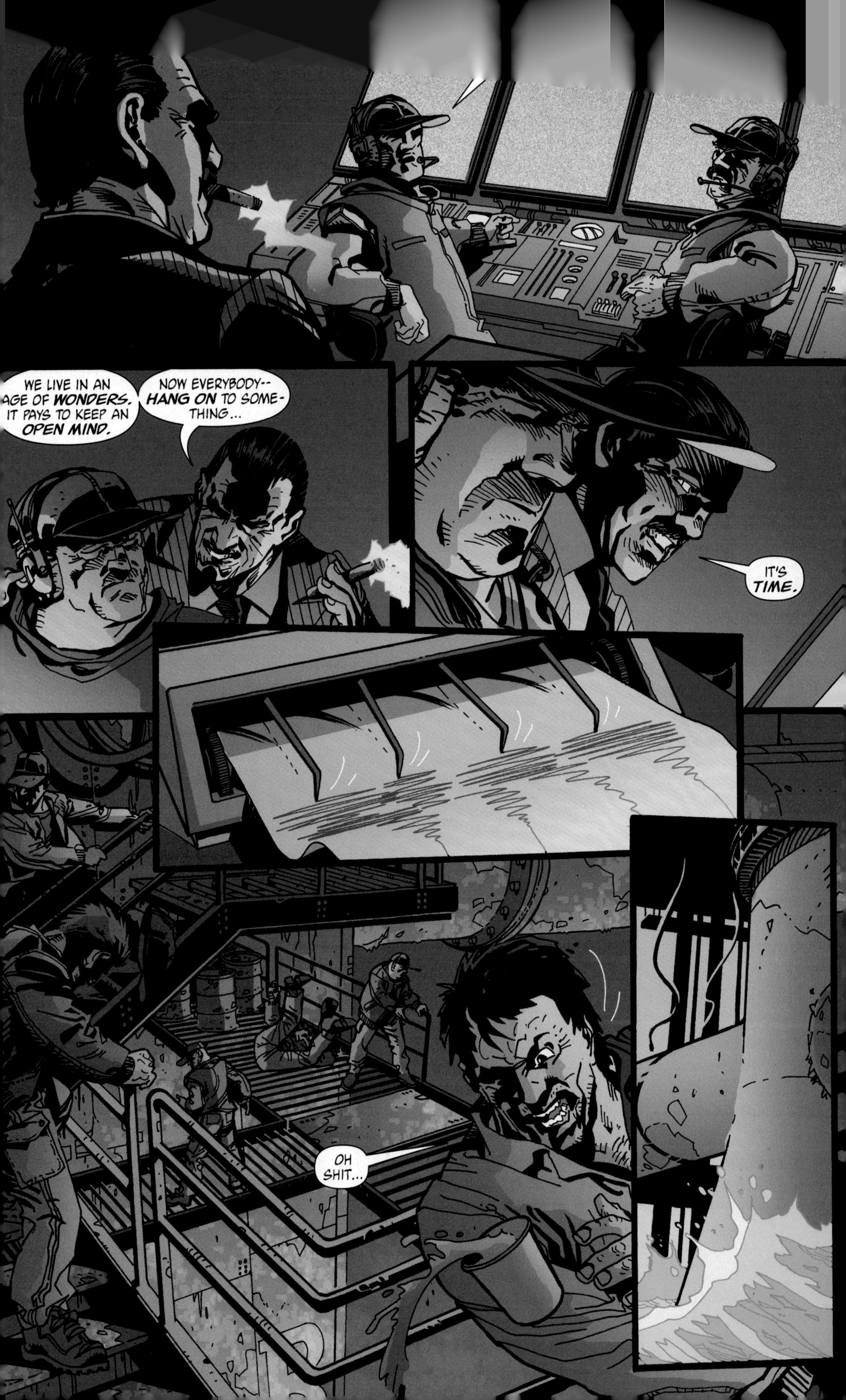
WE LIVE IN AN AGE OF WONDERS. IT PAYS TO KEEP AN OPEN MIND.
NOW EVERYBODY-- HANG ON TO SOMETHING...
IT'S TIME.
OH SHIT...

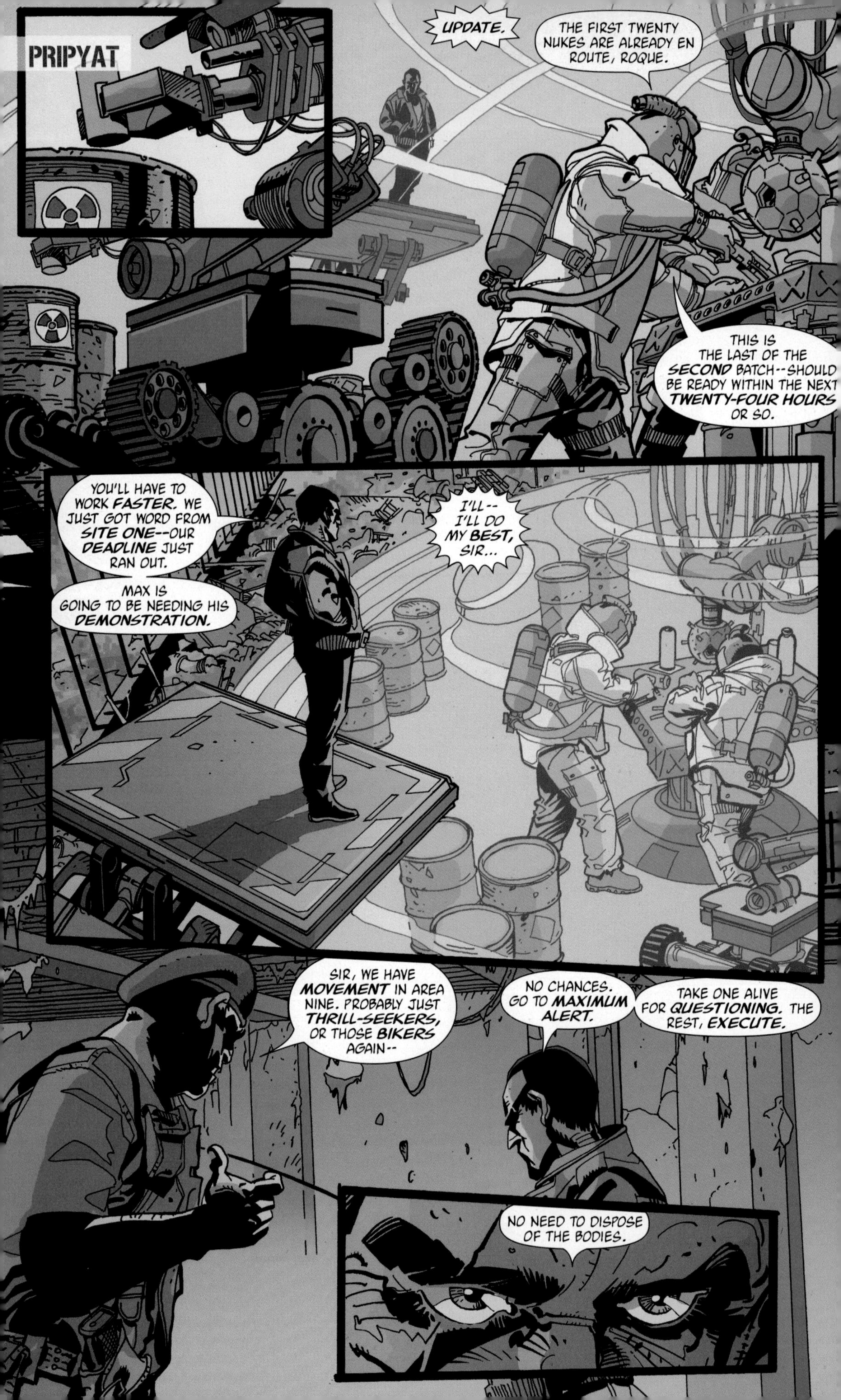
PRIPYAT
UPDATE.
THE FIRST TWENTY NUKES ARE ALREADY EN ROUTE, ROQUE.
THIS IS THE LAST OF THE SECOND BATCH--SHOULD BE READY WITHIN THE NEXT TWENTY-FOUR HOURS OR SO.
YOU'LL HAVE TO WORK FASTER. WE JUST GOT WORD FROM SITE ONE--OUR DEADLINE JUST RAN OUT.
MAX IS GOING TO BE NEEDING HIS DEMONSTRATION.
I'LL-- I'LL DO MY BEST, SIR...
SIR, WE HAVE MOVEMENT IN AREA NINE. PROBABLY JUST THRILL-SEEKERS, OR THOSE BIKERS AGAIN--
NO CHANCES. GO TO MAXIMUM ALERT.
TAKE ONE ALIVE FOR QUESTIONING. THE REST, EXECUTE.
NO NEED TO DISPOSE OF THE BODIES.

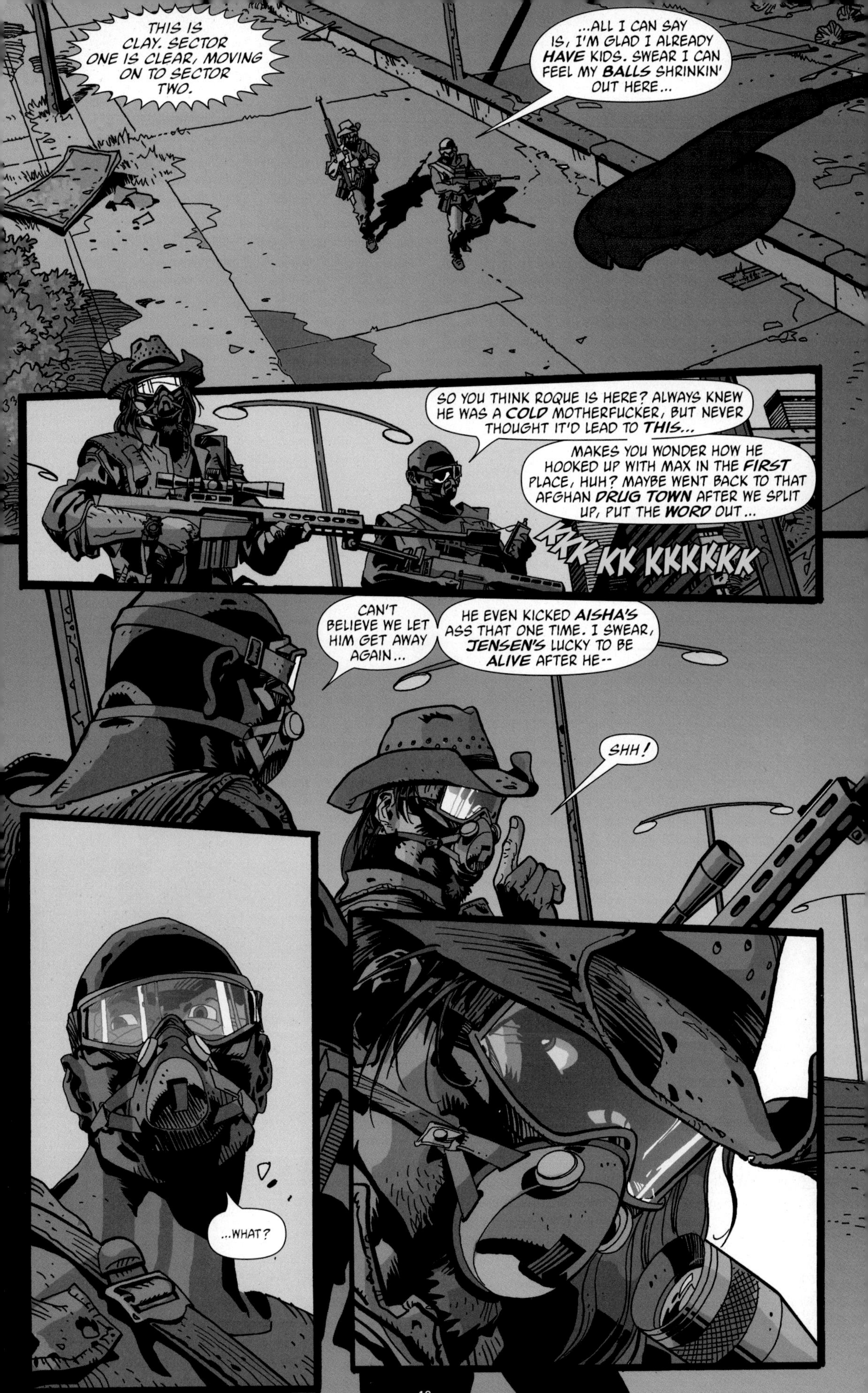

THIS IS CLAY. SECTOR ONE IS CLEAR, MOVING ON TO SECTOR TWO.
...ALL I CAN SAY IS, I'M GLAD I ALREADY HAVE KIDS. SWEAR I CAN FEEL MY BALLS SHRINKIN' OUT HERE...
SO YOU THINK ROQUE IS HERE? ALWAYS KNEW HE WAS A COLD MOTHERFUCKER, BUT NEVER THOUGHT IT'D LEAD TO THIS...
MAKES YOU WONDER HOW HE HOOKED UP WITH MAX IN THE FIRST PLACE, HUH? MAYBE WENT BACK TO THAT AFGHAN DRUG TOWN AFTER WE SPLIT UP, PUT THE WORD OUT...
KKK KK KKKKKK
CAN'T BELIEVE WE LET HIM GET AWAY AGAIN...
HE EVEN KICKED AISHA'S ASS THAT ONE TIME. I SWEAR, JENSEN'S LUCKY TO BE ALIVE AFTER HE--
SHH!
...WHAT?

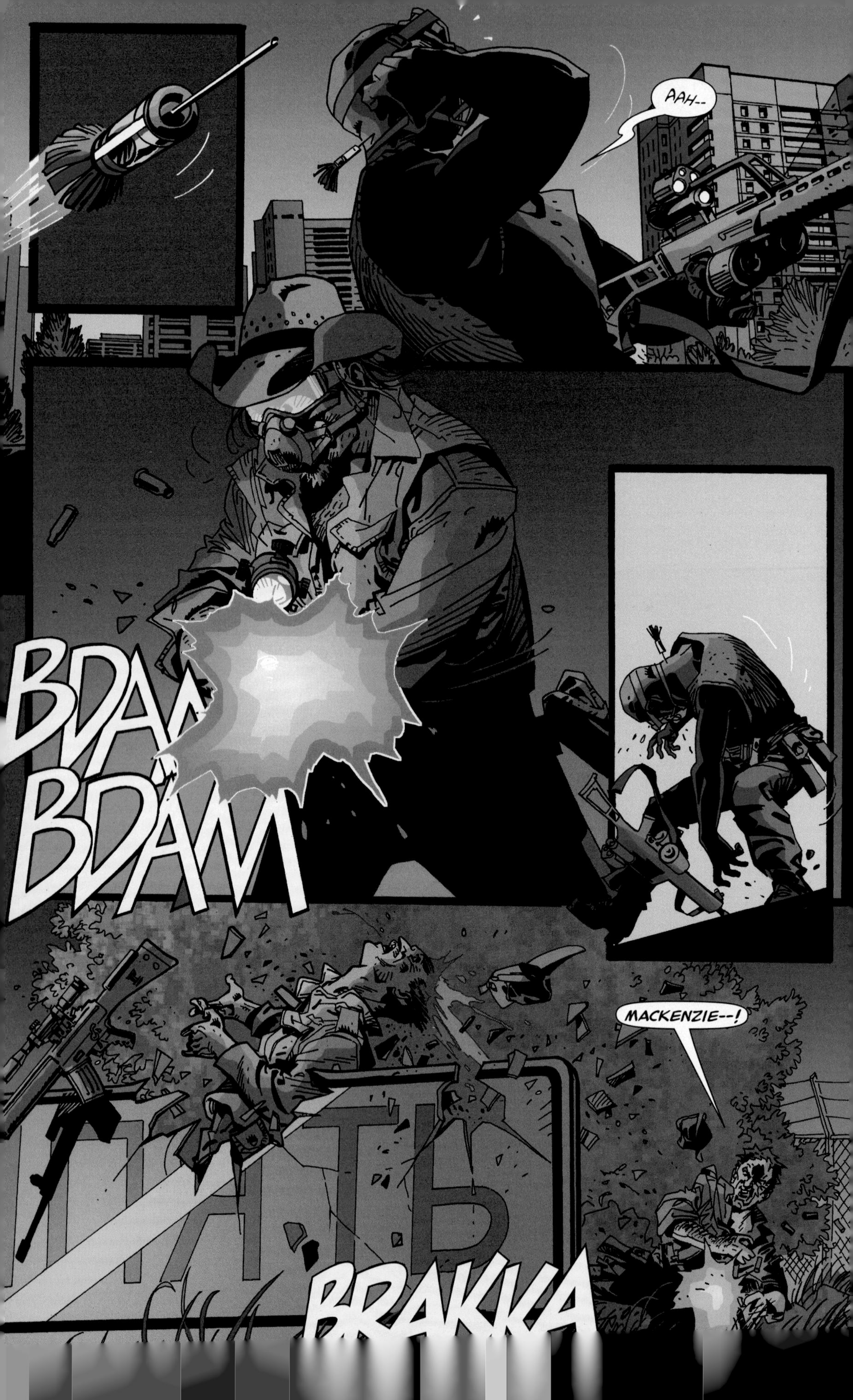
AAH--
BDAM
BDAM
MACKENZIE--!
BRAKKA

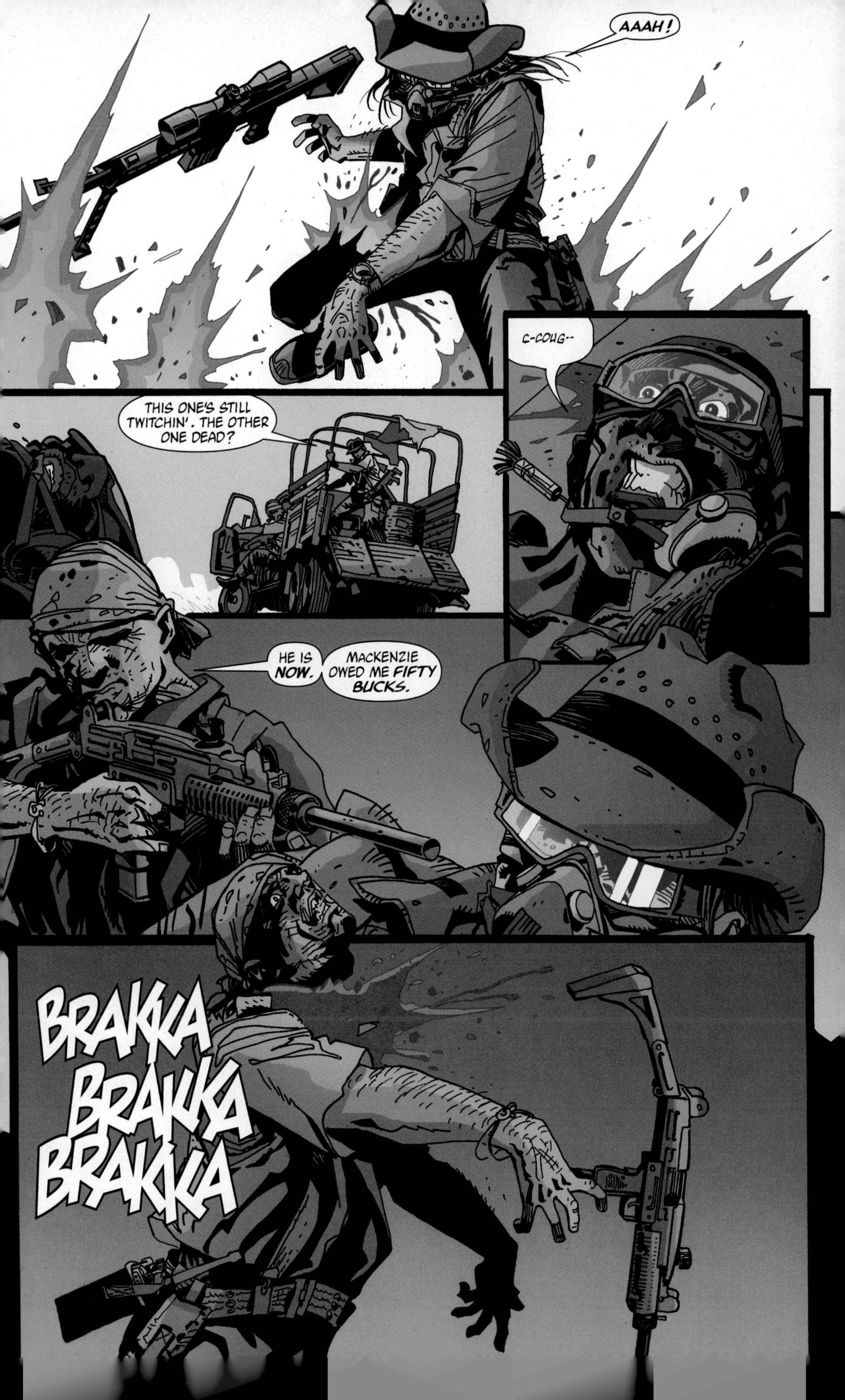
AAAH!
C-COUG--
THIS ONE'S STILL TWITCHIN'. THE OTHER ONE DEAD?
HE IS **NOW.**
MACKENZIE OWED ME **FIFTY BUCKS.**
BRAKKA
BRAKKA
BRAKKA

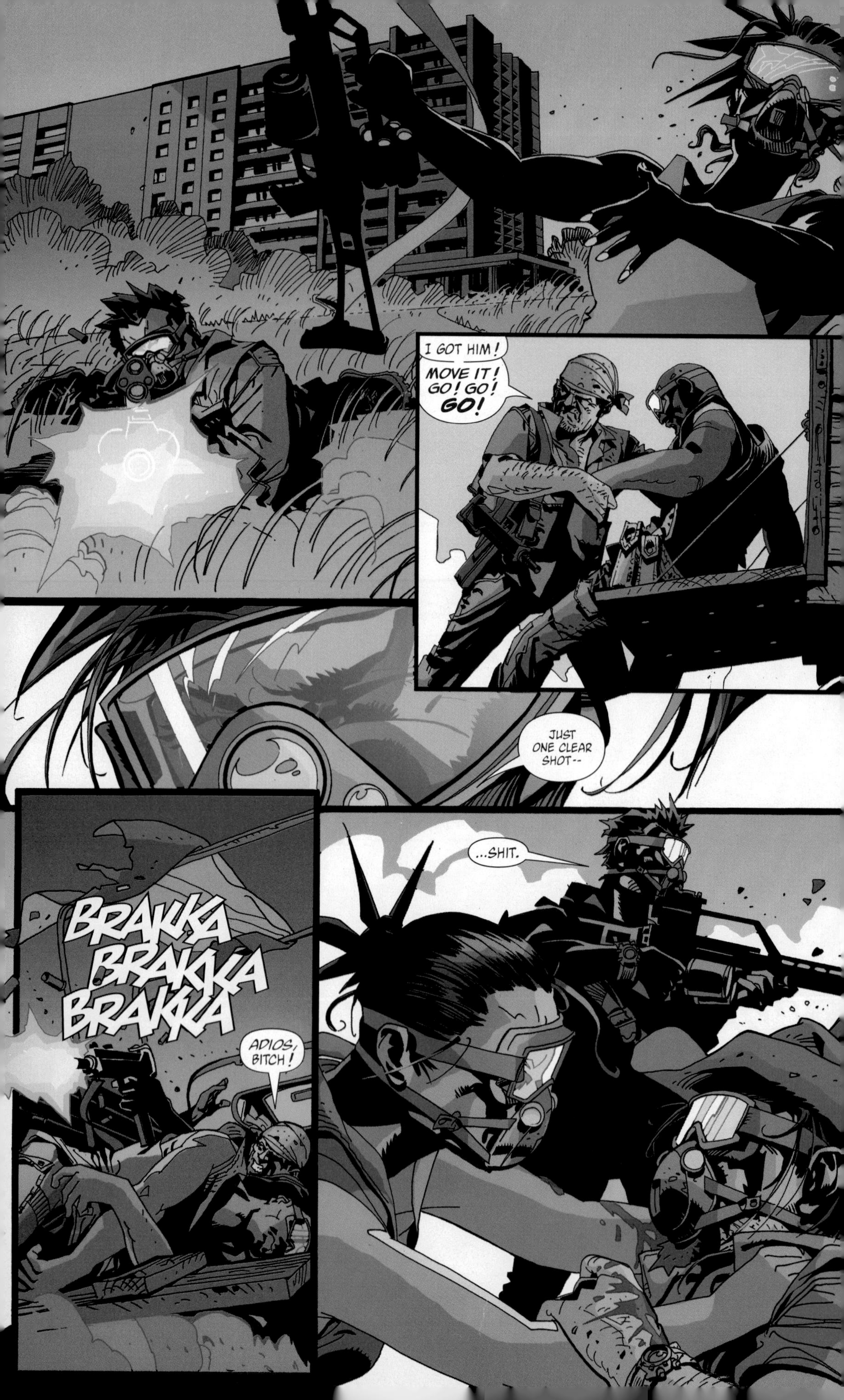
I GOT HIM!
MOVE IT! GO! GO! GO!
JUST ONE CLEAR SHOT--
BRAKKA BRAKKA BRAKKA
ADIOS, BITCH!
...SHIT.

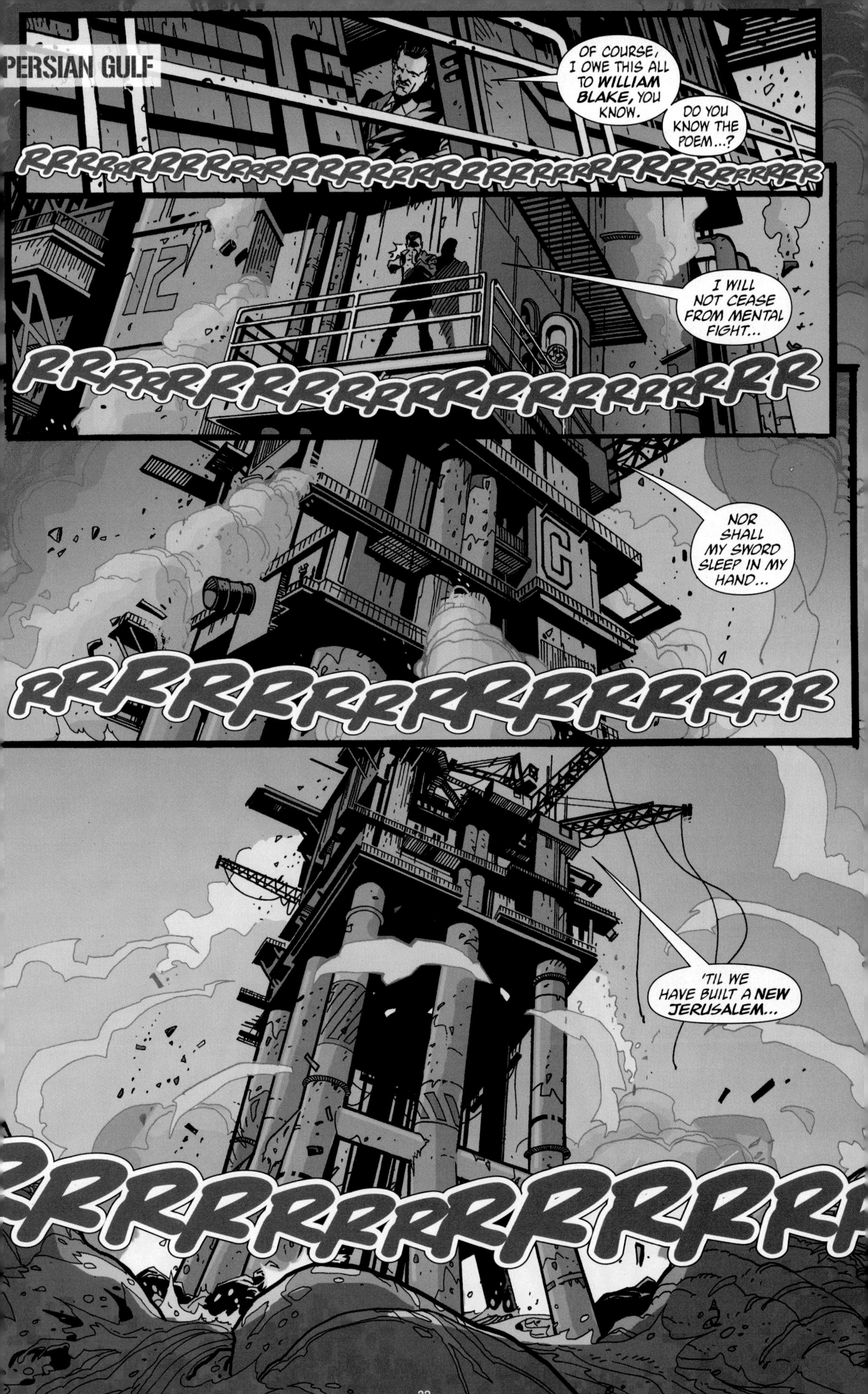
PERSIAN GULF
OF COURSE, I OWE THIS ALL TO WILLIAM BLAKE, YOU KNOW.
DO YOU KNOW THE POEM...?
RRRRRRRRRRRRRRRRRRRRRRRRRRRRRRRRRRRR
I WILL NOT CEASE FROM MENTAL FIGHT...
RRRRRRRRRRRRRRRRRRRRRRRRR
NOR SHALL MY SWORD SLEEP IN MY HAND...
RRRRRRRRRRRRRRRRRRRR
'TIL WE HAVE BUILT A NEW JERUSALEM...
RRRRRRRRRRRRRR

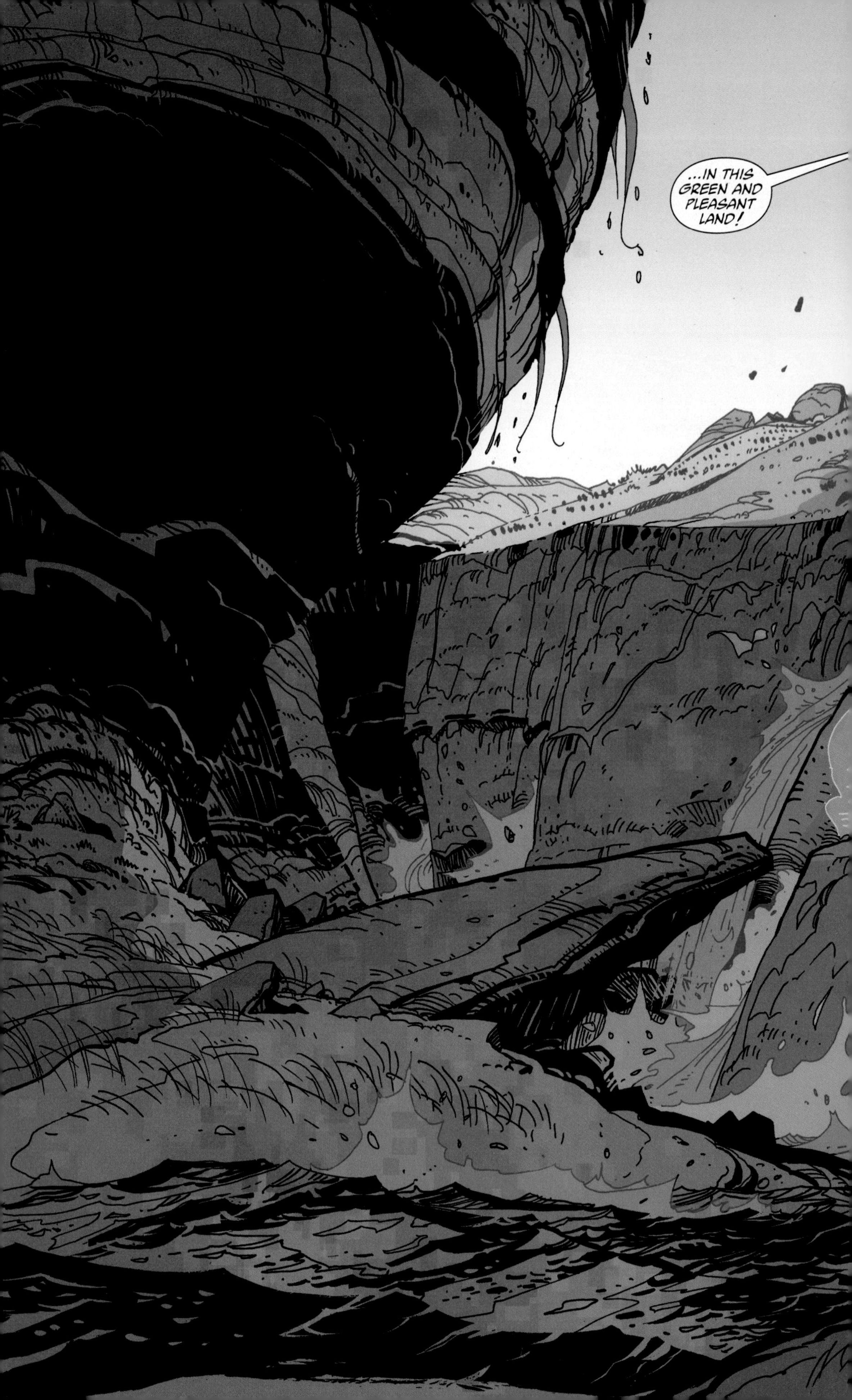
...IN THIS GREEN AND PLEASANT LAND!

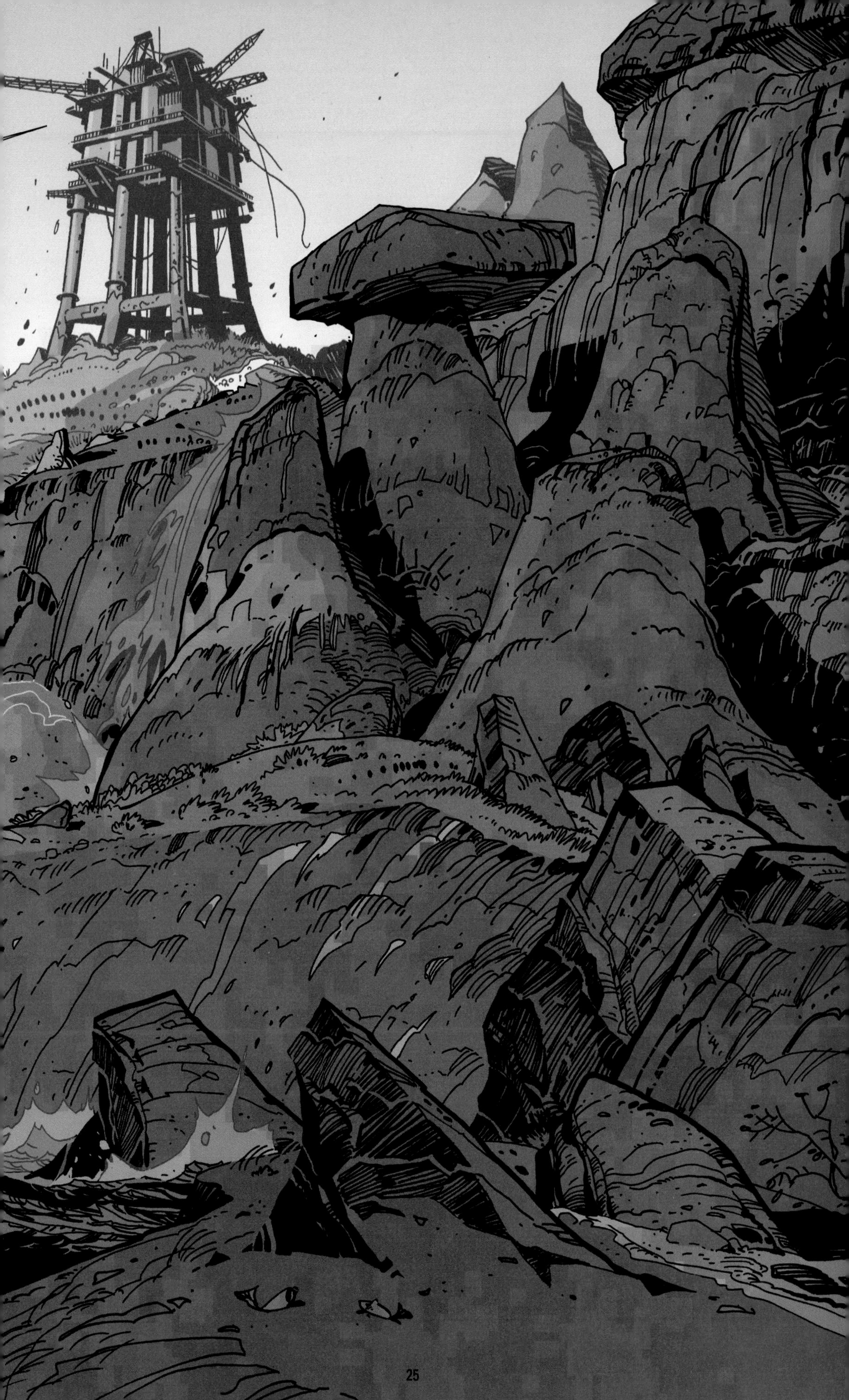

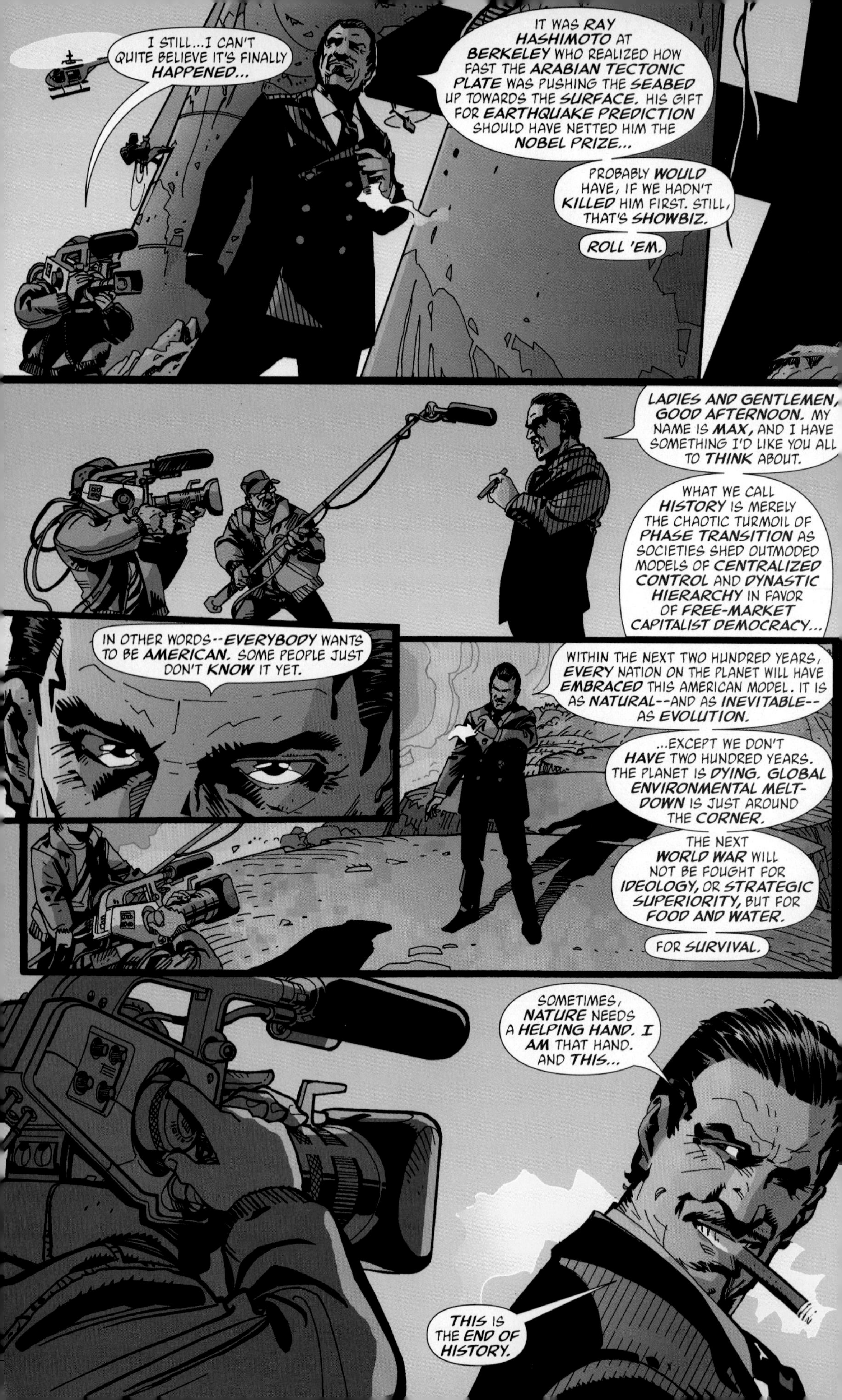
I STILL...I CAN'T QUITE BELIEVE IT'S FINALLY HAPPENED...
IT WAS RAY HASHIMOTO AT BERKELEY WHO REALIZED HOW FAST THE ARABIAN TECTONIC PLATE WAS PUSHING THE SEABED UP TOWARDS THE SURFACE. HIS GIFT FOR EARTHQUAKE PREDICTION SHOULD HAVE NETTED HIM THE NOBEL PRIZE...
PROBABLY WOULD HAVE, IF WE HADN'T KILLED HIM FIRST. STILL, THAT'S SHOWBIZ.
ROLL 'EM.
LADIES AND GENTLEMEN, GOOD AFTERNOON. MY NAME IS MAX, AND I HAVE SOMETHING I'D LIKE YOU ALL TO THINK ABOUT.
WHAT WE CALL HISTORY IS MERELY THE CHAOTIC TURMOIL OF PHASE TRANSITION AS SOCIETIES SHED OUTMODED MODELS OF CENTRALIZED CONTROL AND DYNASTIC HIERARCHY IN FAVOR OF FREE-MARKET CAPITALIST DEMOCRACY...
IN OTHER WORDS--EVERYBODY WANTS TO BE AMERICAN. SOME PEOPLE JUST DON'T KNOW IT YET.
WITHIN THE NEXT TWO HUNDRED YEARS, EVERY NATION ON THE PLANET WILL HAVE EMBRACED THIS AMERICAN MODEL. IT IS AS NATURAL--AND AS INEVITABLE--AS EVOLUTION.
...EXCEPT WE DON'T HAVE TWO HUNDRED YEARS. THE PLANET IS DYING. GLOBAL ENVIRONMENTAL MELT-DOWN IS JUST AROUND THE CORNER.
THE NEXT WORLD WAR WILL NOT BE FOUGHT FOR IDEOLOGY, OR STRATEGIC SUPERIORITY, BUT FOR FOOD AND WATER.
FOR SURVIVAL.
SOMETIMES, NATURE NEEDS A HELPING HAND. I AM THAT HAND. AND THIS...
THIS IS THE END OF HISTORY.

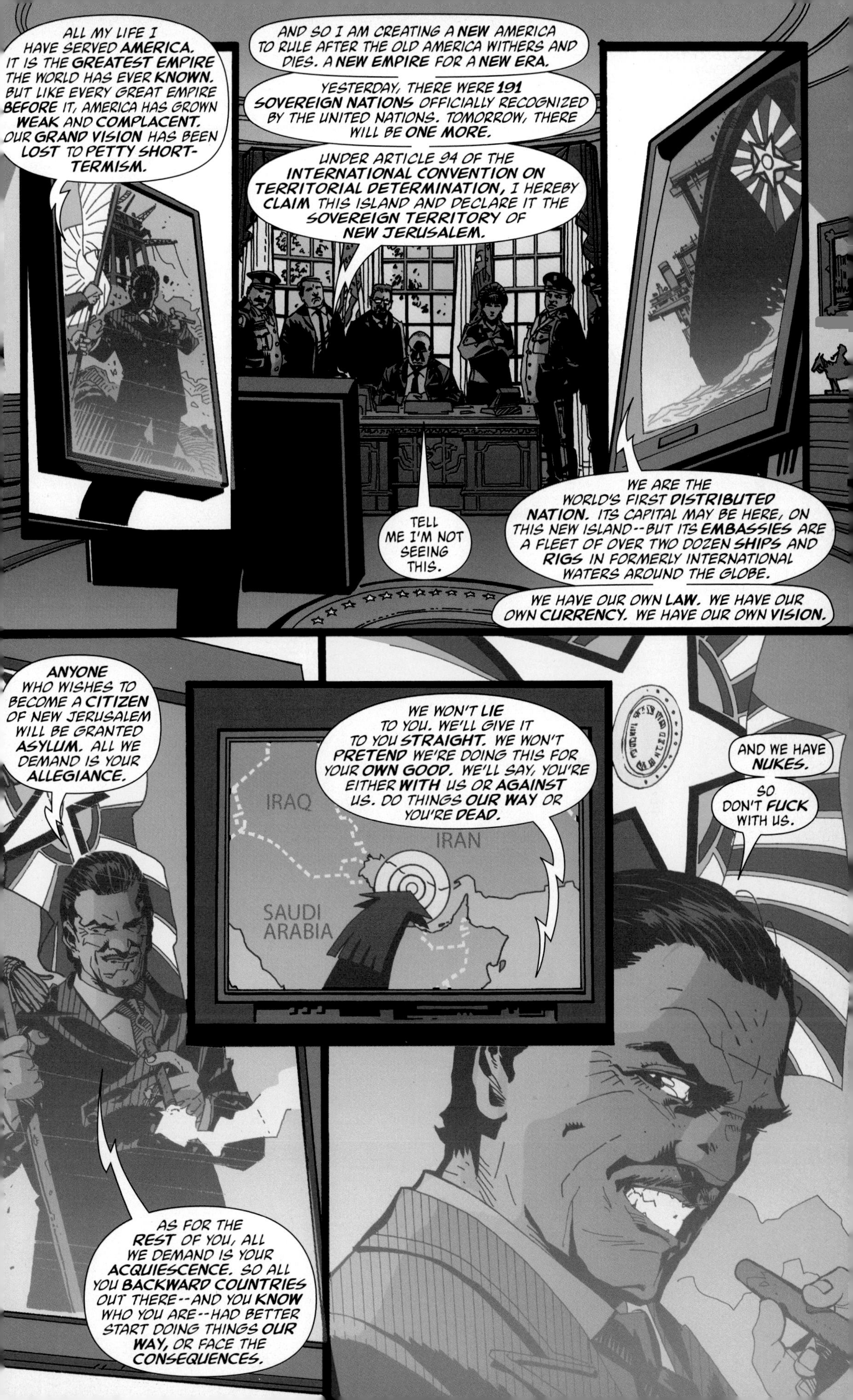

ALL MY LIFE I HAVE SERVED AMERICA. IT IS THE GREATEST EMPIRE THE WORLD HAS EVER KNOWN. BUT LIKE EVERY GREAT EMPIRE BEFORE IT, AMERICA HAS GROWN WEAK AND COMPLACENT. OUR GRAND VISION HAS BEEN LOST TO PETTY SHORT-TERMISM.
AND SO I AM CREATING A NEW AMERICA TO RULE AFTER THE OLD AMERICA WITHERS AND DIES. A NEW EMPIRE FOR A NEW ERA.
YESTERDAY, THERE WERE 191 SOVEREIGN NATIONS OFFICIALLY RECOGNIZED BY THE UNITED NATIONS. TOMORROW, THERE WILL BE ONE MORE.
UNDER ARTICLE 94 OF THE INTERNATIONAL CONVENTION ON TERRITORIAL DETERMINATION, I HEREBY CLAIM THIS ISLAND AND DECLARE IT THE SOVEREIGN TERRITORY OF NEW JERUSALEM.
TELL ME I'M NOT SEEING THIS.
WE ARE THE WORLD'S FIRST DISTRIBUTED NATION. ITS CAPITAL MAY BE HERE, ON THIS NEW ISLAND--BUT ITS EMBASSIES ARE A FLEET OF OVER TWO DOZEN SHIPS AND RIGS IN FORMERLY INTERNATIONAL WATERS AROUND THE GLOBE.
WE HAVE OUR OWN LAW. WE HAVE OUR OWN CURRENCY. WE HAVE OUR OWN VISION.
ANYONE WHO WISHES TO BECOME A CITIZEN OF NEW JERUSALEM WILL BE GRANTED ASYLUM. ALL WE DEMAND IS YOUR ALLEGIANCE.
WE WON'T LIE TO YOU. WE'LL GIVE IT TO YOU STRAIGHT. WE WON'T PRETEND WE'RE DOING THIS FOR YOUR OWN GOOD. WE'LL SAY, YOU'RE EITHER WITH US OR AGAINST US. DO THINGS OUR WAY OR YOU'RE DEAD.
IRAQ
IRAN
SAUDI ARABIA
AND WE HAVE NUKES.
SO DON'T FUCK WITH US.
AS FOR THE REST OF YOU, ALL WE DEMAND IS YOUR ACQUIESCENCE. SO ALL YOU BACKWARD COUNTRIES OUT THERE--AND YOU KNOW WHO YOU ARE--HAD BETTER START DOING THINGS OUR WAY, OR FACE THE CONSEQUENCES.

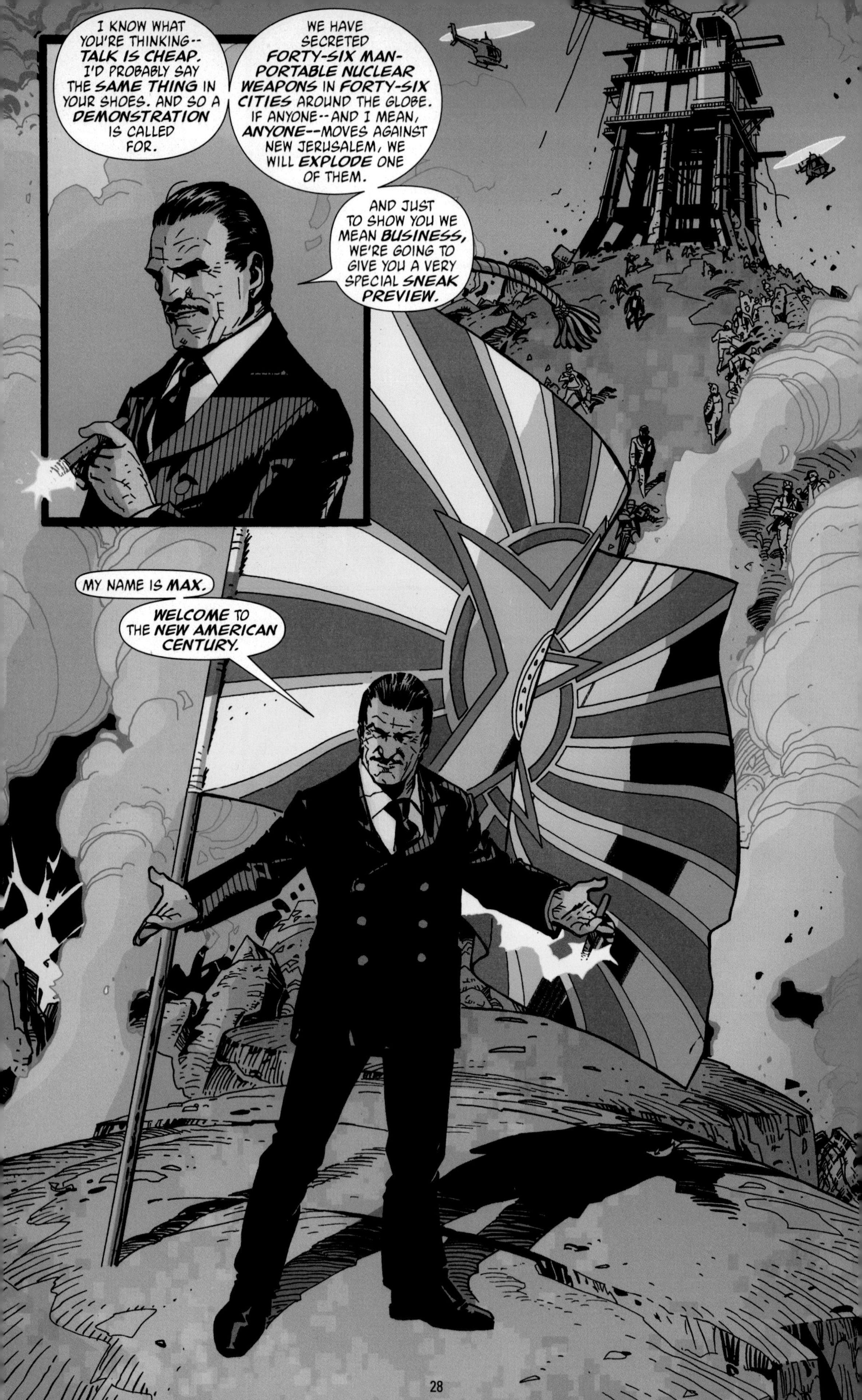
I KNOW WHAT YOU'RE THINKING-- TALK IS CHEAP. I'D PROBABLY SAY THE SAME THING IN YOUR SHOES. AND SO A DEMONSTRATION IS CALLED FOR.
WE HAVE SECRETED FORTY-SIX MAN-PORTABLE NUCLEAR WEAPONS IN FORTY-SIX CITIES AROUND THE GLOBE. IF ANYONE--AND I MEAN, ANYONE--MOVES AGAINST NEW JERUSALEM, WE WILL EXPLODE ONE OF THEM.
AND JUST TO SHOW YOU WE MEAN BUSINESS, WE'RE GOING TO GIVE YOU A VERY SPECIAL SNEAK PREVIEW.
MY NAME IS MAX.
WELCOME TO THE NEW AMERICAN CENTURY.

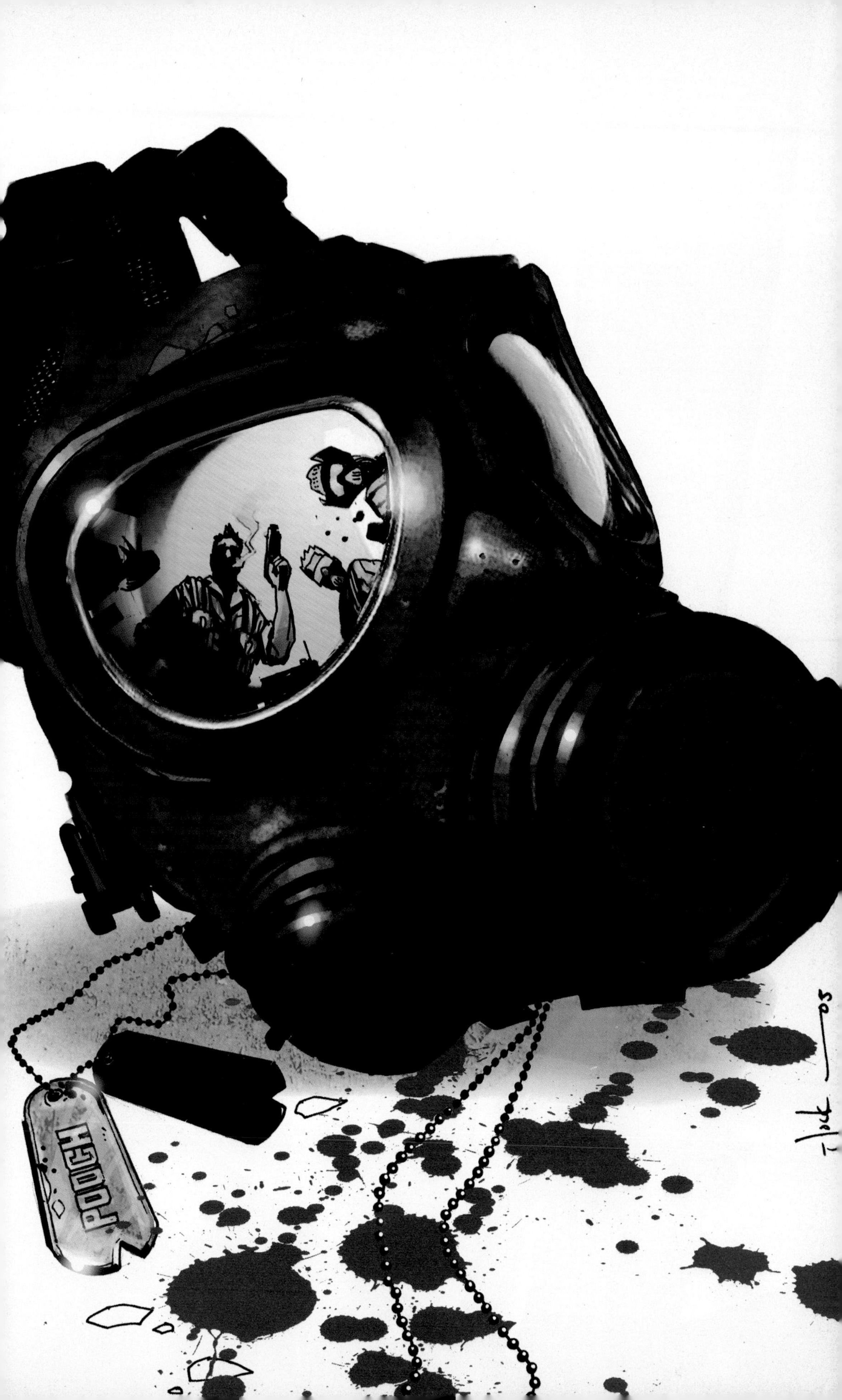
POOCH

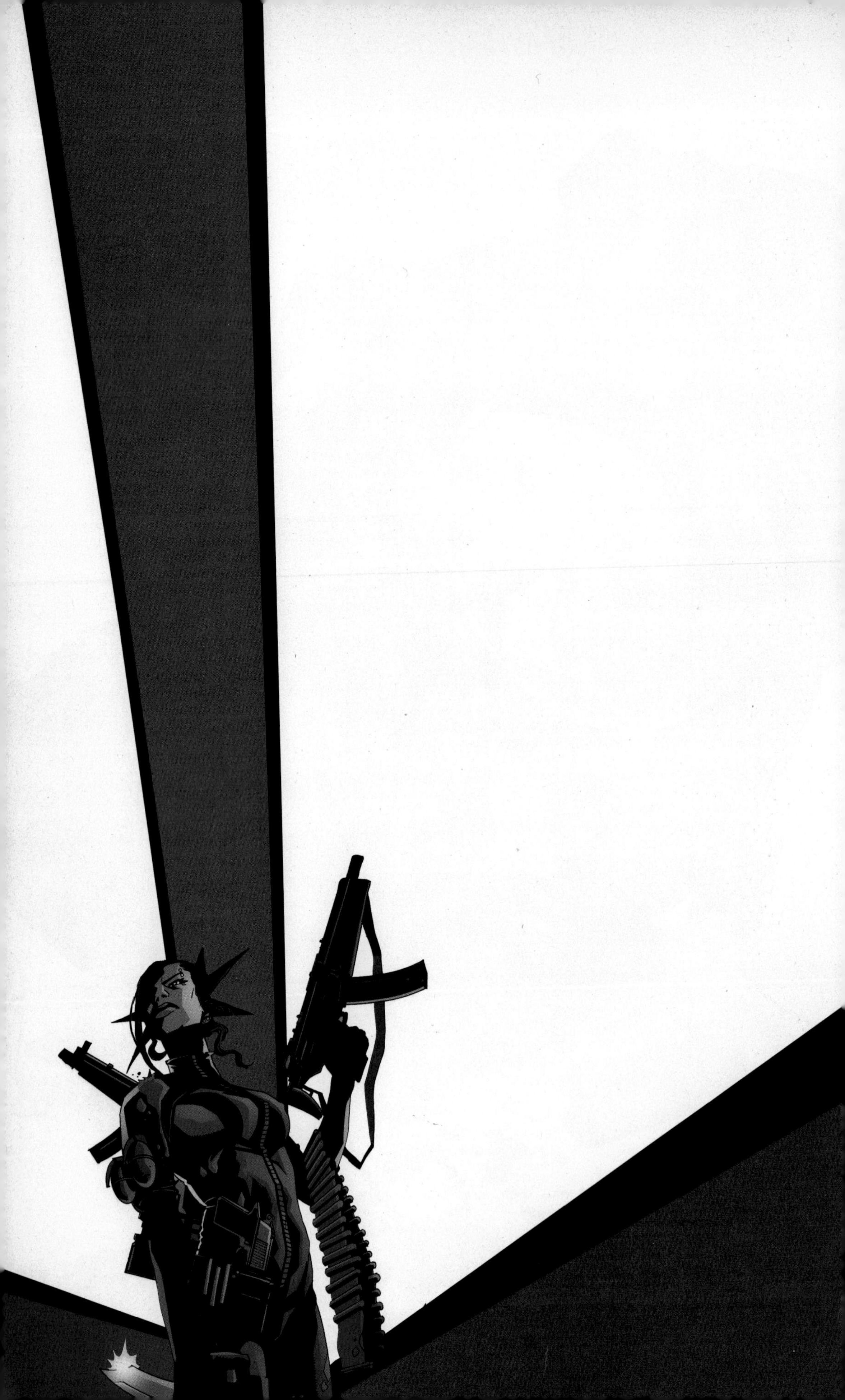

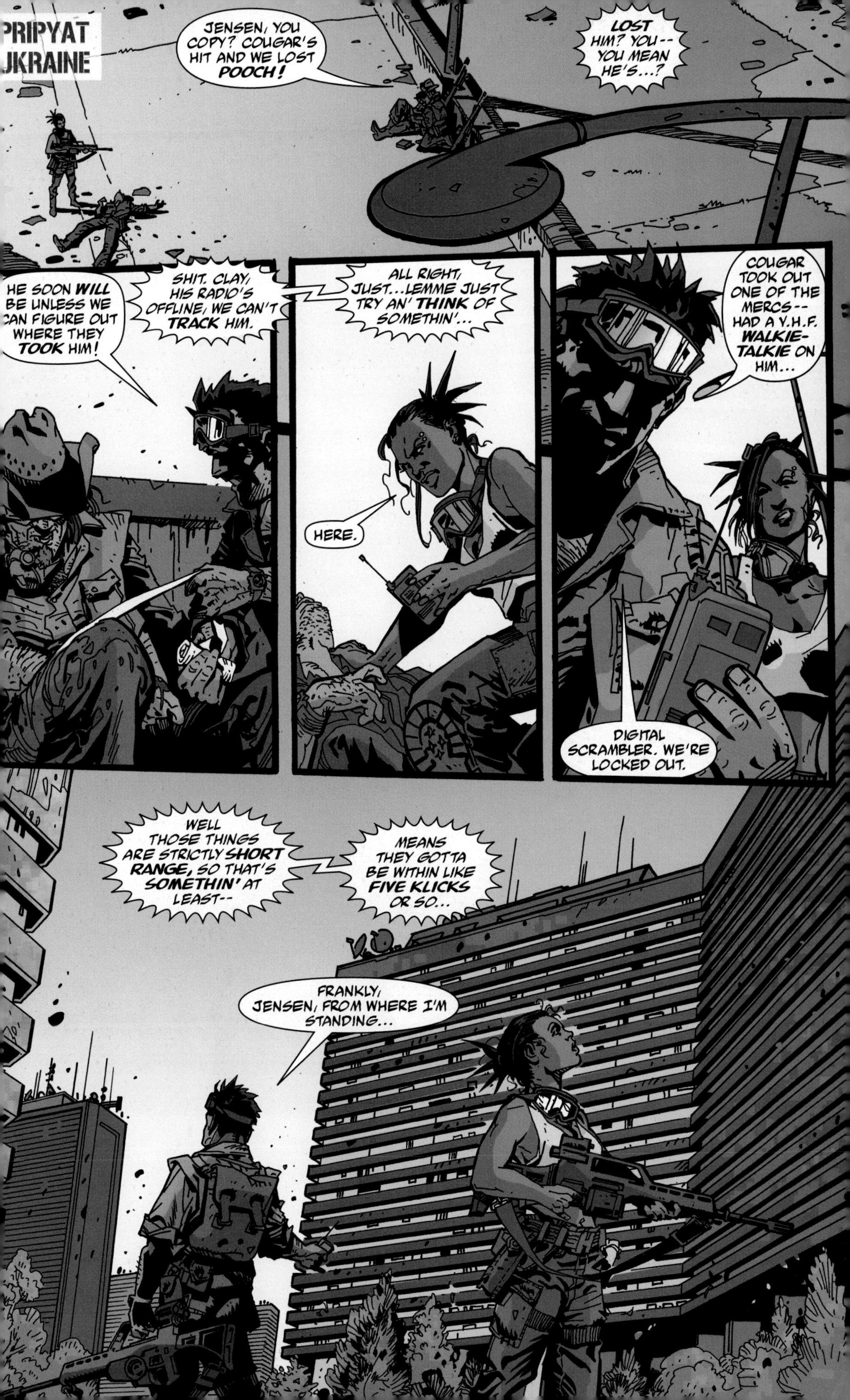

PRIPYAT
UKRAINE
JENSEN, YOU COPY? COUGAR'S HIT AND WE LOST POOCH!
LOST HIM? YOU-- YOU MEAN HE'S...?
HE SOON WILL BE UNLESS WE CAN FIGURE OUT WHERE THEY TOOK HIM!
SHIT. CLAY, HIS RADIO'S OFFLINE, WE CAN'T TRACK HIM.
ALL RIGHT, JUST...LEMME JUST TRY AN' THINK OF SOMETHIN'...
HERE.
COUGAR TOOK OUT ONE OF THE MERCS--HAD A V.H.F. WALKIE-TALKIE ON HIM...
DIGITAL SCRAMBLER. WE'RE LOCKED OUT.
WELL THOSE THINGS ARE STRICTLY SHORT RANGE, SO THAT'S SOMETHIN' AT LEAST--
MEANS THEY GOTTA BE WITHIN LIKE FIVE KLICKS OR SO...
FRANKLY, JENSEN, FROM WHERE I'M STANDING...

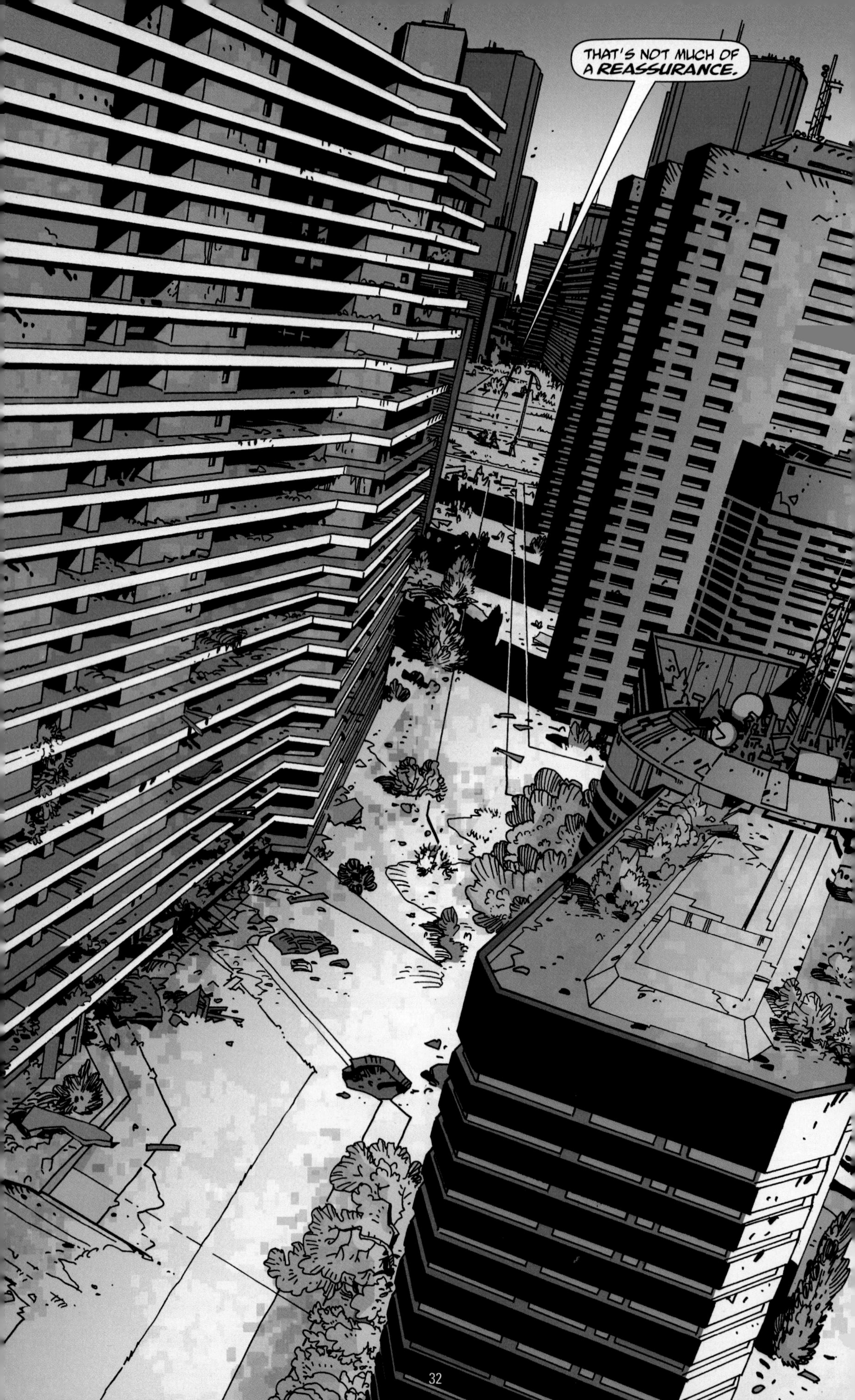
THAT'S NOT MUCH OF A REASSURANCE.

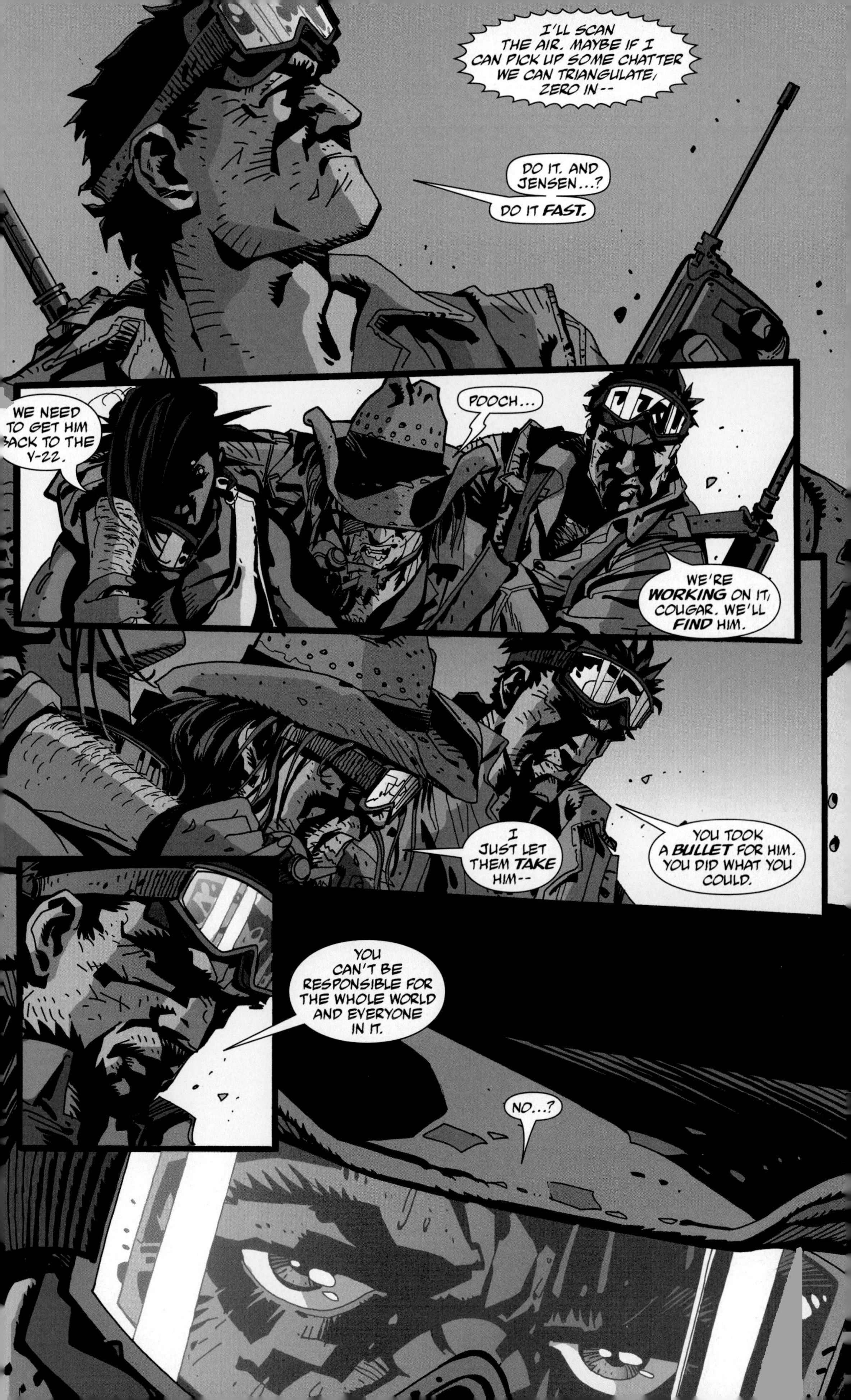
I'LL SCAN THE AIR. MAYBE IF I CAN PICK UP SOME CHATTER WE CAN TRIANGULATE, ZERO IN--
DO IT. AND JENSEN...?
DO IT FAST.
WE NEED TO GET HIM BACK TO THE V-22.
POOCH...
WE'RE WORKING ON IT, COUGAR. WE'LL FIND HIM.
I JUST LET THEM TAKE HIM--
YOU TOOK A BULLET FOR HIM. YOU DID WHAT YOU COULD.
YOU CAN'T BE RESPONSIBLE FOR THE WHOLE WORLD AND EVERYONE IN IT.
NO...?

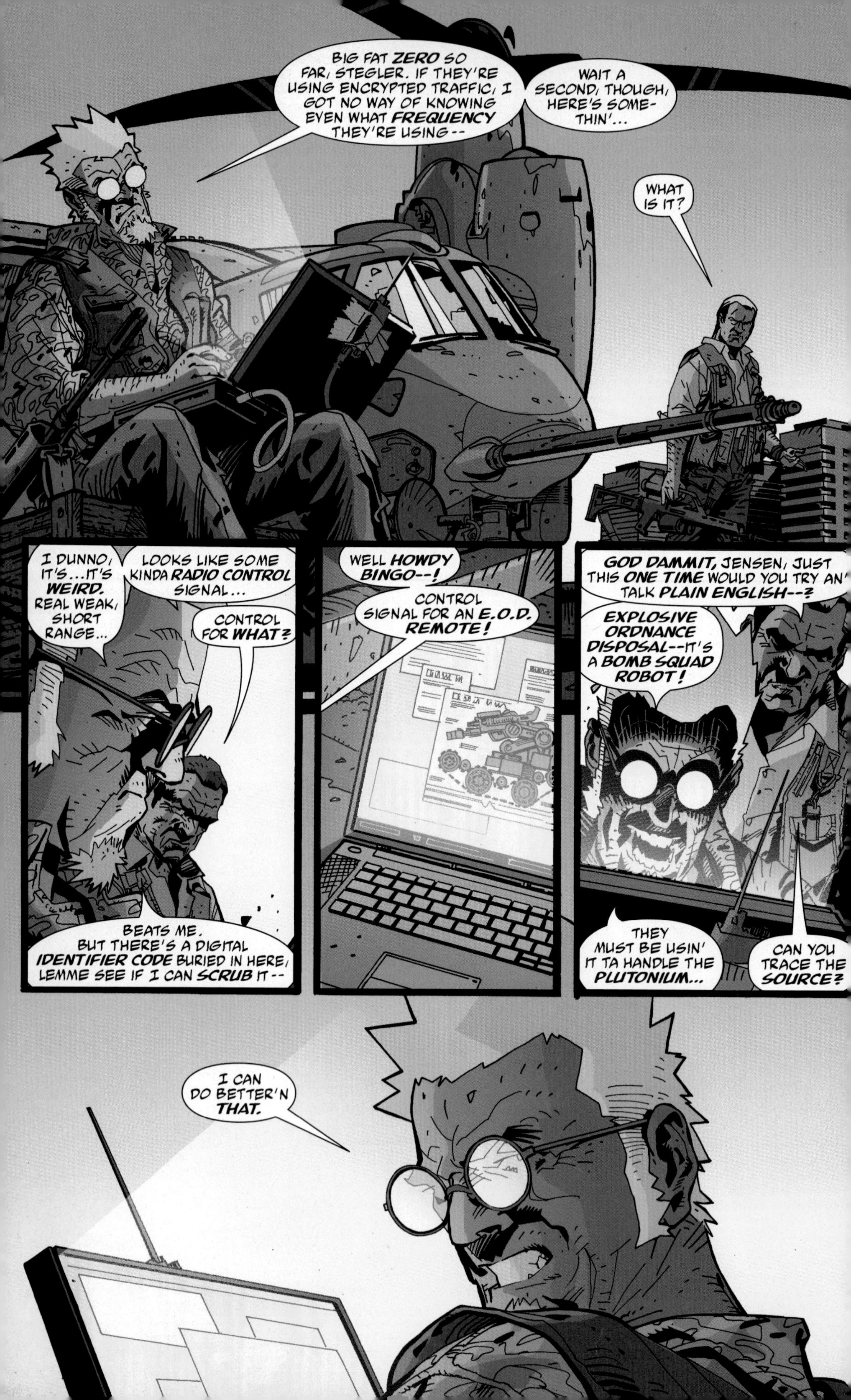
BIG FAT ZERO SO FAR, STEGLER. IF THEY'RE USING ENCRYPTED TRAFFIC, I GOT NO WAY OF KNOWING EVEN WHAT FREQUENCY THEY'RE USING--
WAIT A SECOND, THOUGH, HERE'S SOME-THIN'...
WHAT IS IT?
I DUNNO, IT'S...IT'S WEIRD. REAL WEAK, SHORT RANGE...
LOOKS LIKE SOME KINDA RADIO CONTROL SIGNAL...
CONTROL FOR WHAT?
BEATS ME. BUT THERE'S A DIGITAL IDENTIFIER CODE BURIED IN HERE, LEMME SEE IF I CAN SCRUB IT--
WELL HOWDY BINGO--!
CONTROL SIGNAL FOR AN E.O.D. REMOTE!
GOD DAMMIT, JENSEN, JUST THIS ONE TIME WOULD YOU TRY AN' TALK PLAIN ENGLISH--?
EXPLOSIVE ORDNANCE DISPOSAL--IT'S A BOMB SQUAD ROBOT!
THEY MUST BE USIN' IT TA HANDLE THE PLUTONIUM...
CAN YOU TRACE THE SOURCE?
I CAN DO BETTER'N THAT.

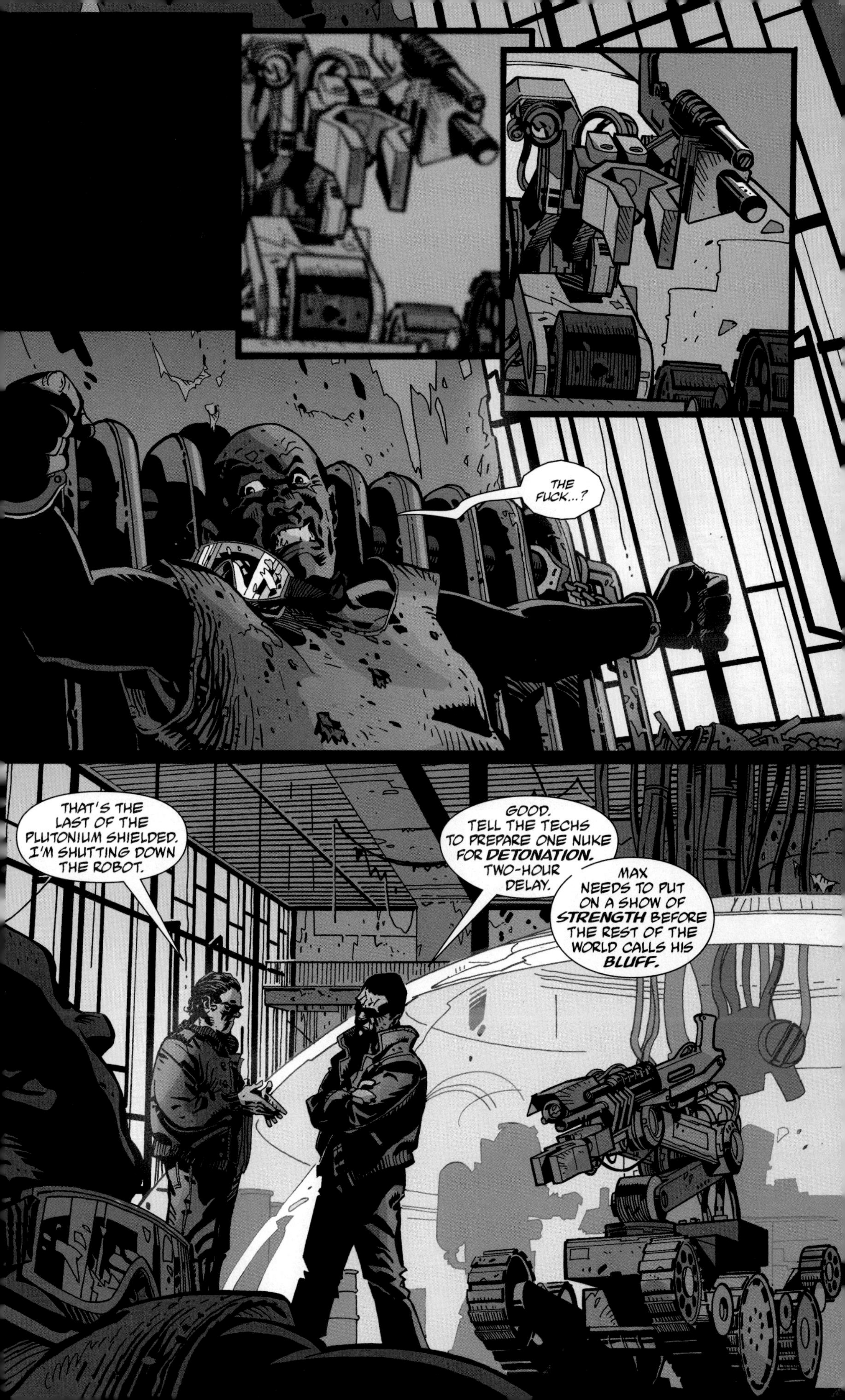
THE FUCK...?
THAT'S THE LAST OF THE PLUTONIUM SHIELDED. I'M SHUTTING DOWN THE ROBOT.
GOOD. TELL THE TECHS TO PREPARE ONE NUKE FOR DETONATION. TWO-HOUR DELAY.
MAX NEEDS TO PUT ON A SHOW OF STRENGTH BEFORE THE REST OF THE WORLD CALLS HIS BLUFF.

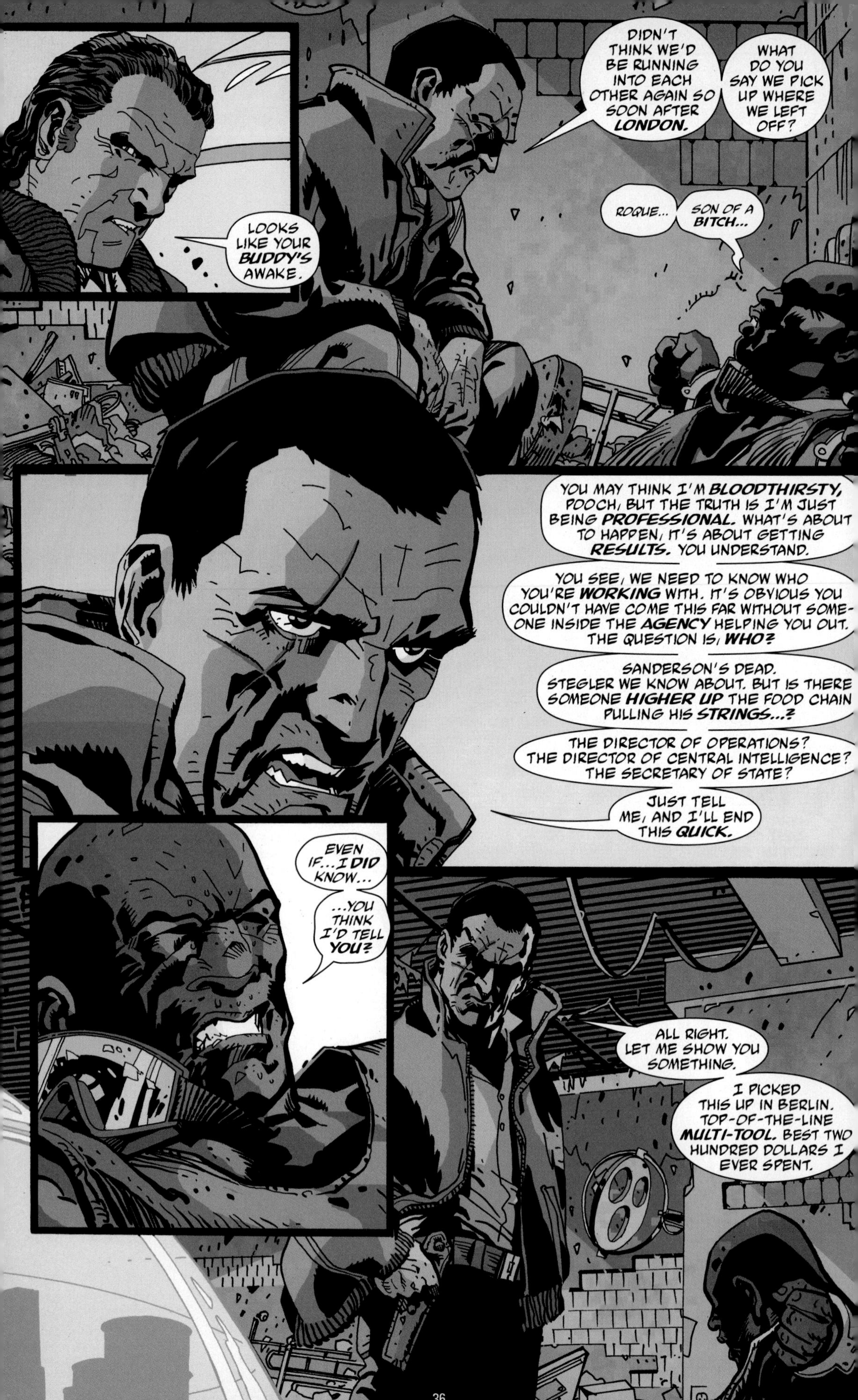

DIDN'T THINK WE'D BE RUNNING INTO EACH OTHER AGAIN SO SOON AFTER LONDON.
WHAT DO YOU SAY WE PICK UP WHERE WE LEFT OFF?
LOOKS LIKE YOUR BUDDY'S AWAKE.
ROQUE...
SON OF A BITCH...
YOU MAY THINK I'M BLOODTHIRSTY, POOCH, BUT THE TRUTH IS I'M JUST BEING PROFESSIONAL. WHAT'S ABOUT TO HAPPEN, IT'S ABOUT GETTING RESULTS. YOU UNDERSTAND.
YOU SEE, WE NEED TO KNOW WHO YOU'RE WORKING WITH. IT'S OBVIOUS YOU COULDN'T HAVE COME THIS FAR WITHOUT SOME-ONE INSIDE THE AGENCY HELPING YOU OUT. THE QUESTION IS, WHO?
SANDERSON'S DEAD. STEGLER WE KNOW ABOUT. BUT IS THERE SOMEONE HIGHER UP THE FOOD CHAIN PULLING HIS STRINGS...?
THE DIRECTOR OF OPERATIONS? THE DIRECTOR OF CENTRAL INTELLIGENCE? THE SECRETARY OF STATE?
JUST TELL ME, AND I'LL END THIS QUICK.
EVEN IF...I DID KNOW...
...YOU THINK I'D TELL YOU?
ALL RIGHT. LET ME SHOW YOU SOMETHING.
I PICKED THIS UP IN BERLIN. TOP-OF-THE-LINE MULTI-TOOL. BEST TWO HUNDRED DOLLARS I EVER SPENT.

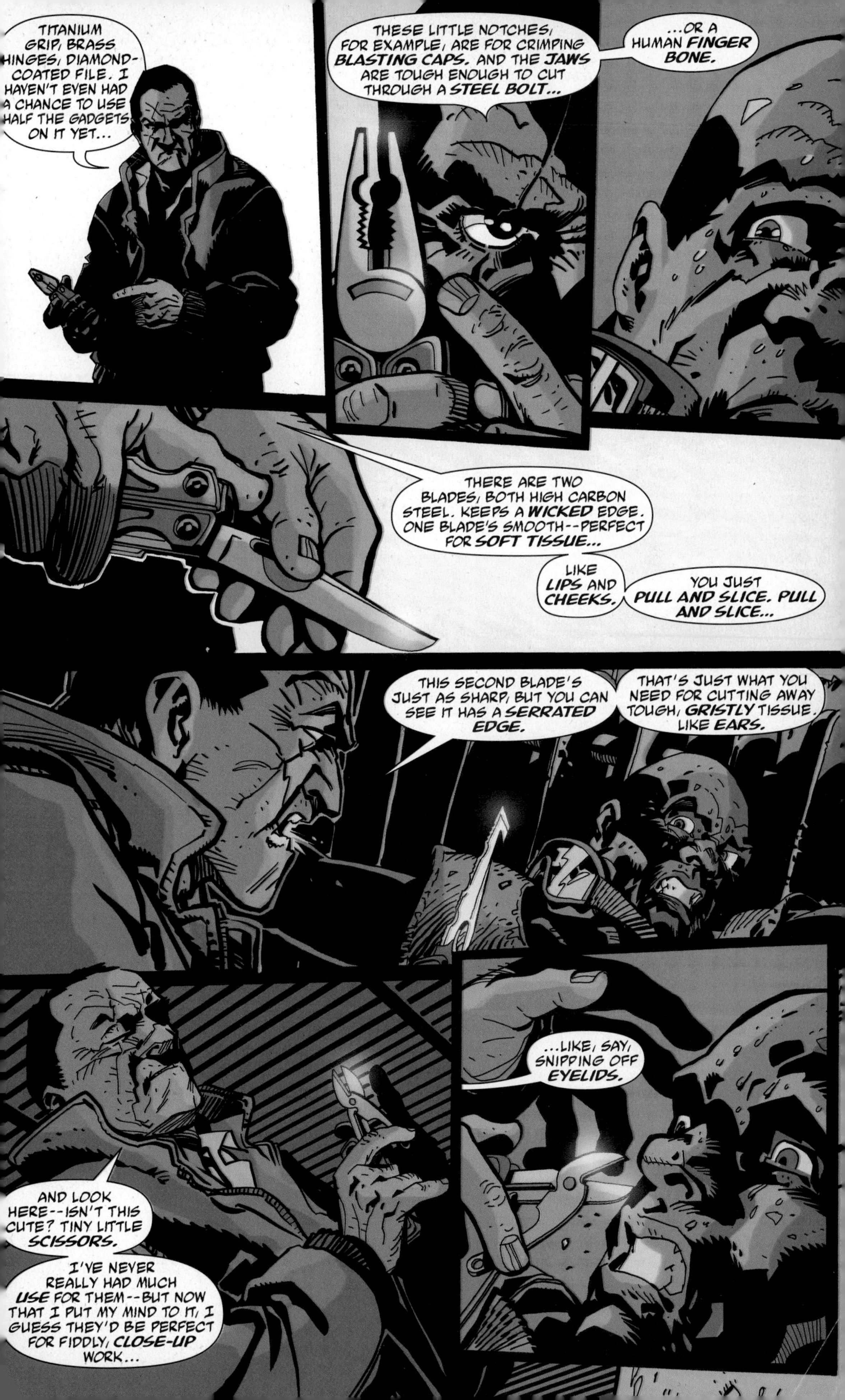
TITANIUM GRIP, BRASS HINGES, DIAMOND-COATED FILE. I HAVEN'T EVEN HAD A CHANCE TO USE HALF THE GADGETS ON IT YET...
THESE LITTLE NOTCHES, FOR EXAMPLE, ARE FOR CRIMPING BLASTING CAPS. AND THE JAWS ARE TOUGH ENOUGH TO CUT THROUGH A STEEL BOLT...
...OR A HUMAN FINGER BONE.
THERE ARE TWO BLADES, BOTH HIGH CARBON STEEL. KEEPS A WICKED EDGE. ONE BLADE'S SMOOTH--PERFECT FOR SOFT TISSUE...
LIKE LIPS AND CHEEKS.
YOU JUST PULL AND SLICE. PULL AND SLICE...
THIS SECOND BLADE'S JUST AS SHARP, BUT YOU CAN SEE IT HAS A SERRATED EDGE.
THAT'S JUST WHAT YOU NEED FOR CUTTING AWAY TOUGH, GRISTLY TISSUE. LIKE EARS.
AND LOOK HERE--ISN'T THIS CUTE? TINY LITTLE SCISSORS.
I'VE NEVER REALLY HAD MUCH USE FOR THEM--BUT NOW THAT I PUT MY MIND TO IT, I GUESS THEY'D BE PERFECT FOR FIDDLY, CLOSE-UP WORK...
...LIKE, SAY, SNIPPING OFF EYELIDS.

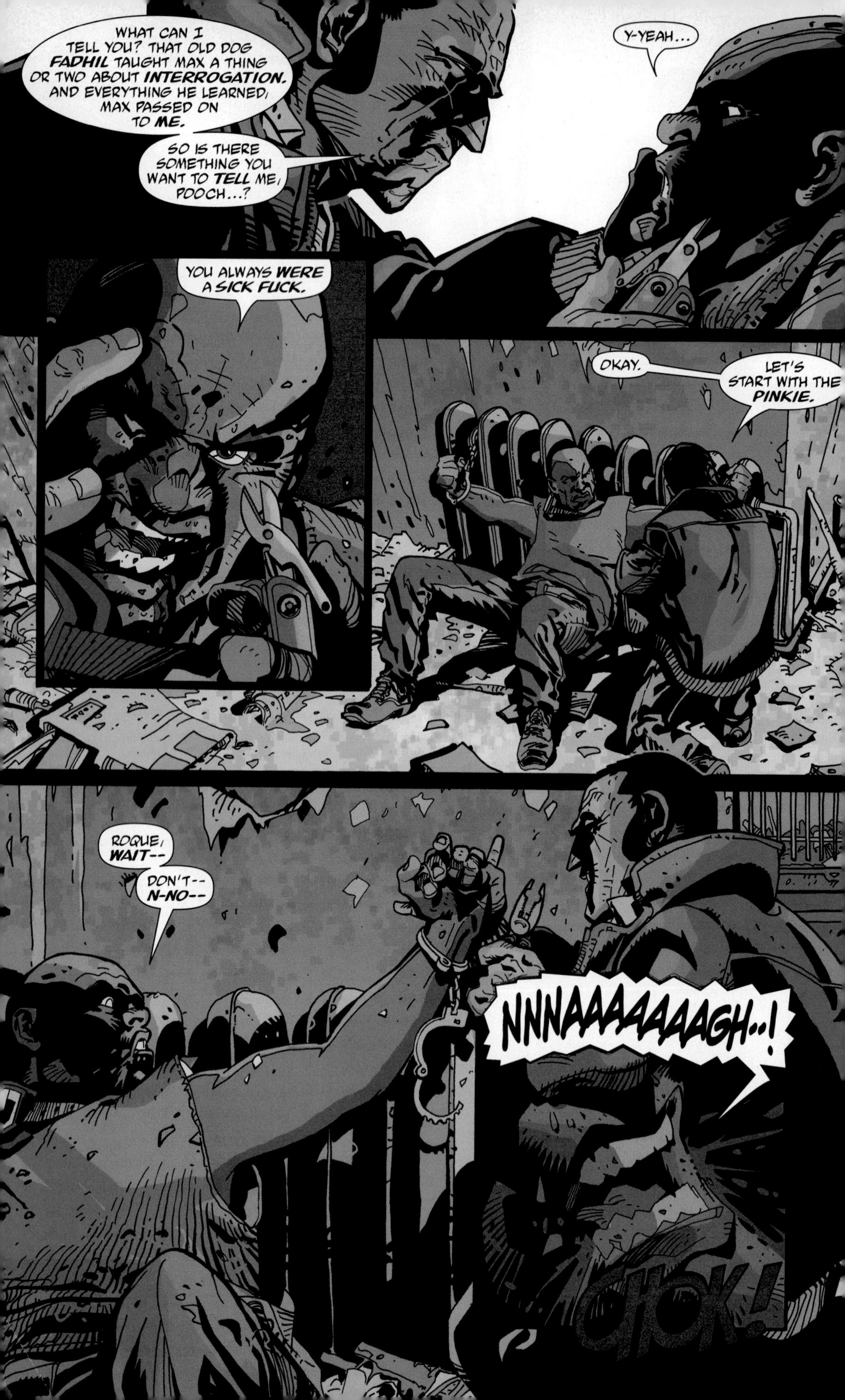
WHAT CAN I TELL YOU? THAT OLD DOG FADHIL TAUGHT MAX A THING OR TWO ABOUT INTERROGATION. AND EVERYTHING HE LEARNED, MAX PASSED ON TO ME.
SO IS THERE SOMETHING YOU WANT TO TELL ME, POOCH...?
Y-YEAH...
YOU ALWAYS WERE A SICK FUCK.
OKAY.
LET'S START WITH THE PINKIE.
ROQUE, WAIT--
DON'T-- N-NO--
NNNAAAAAAAAGH..!
CHOK!

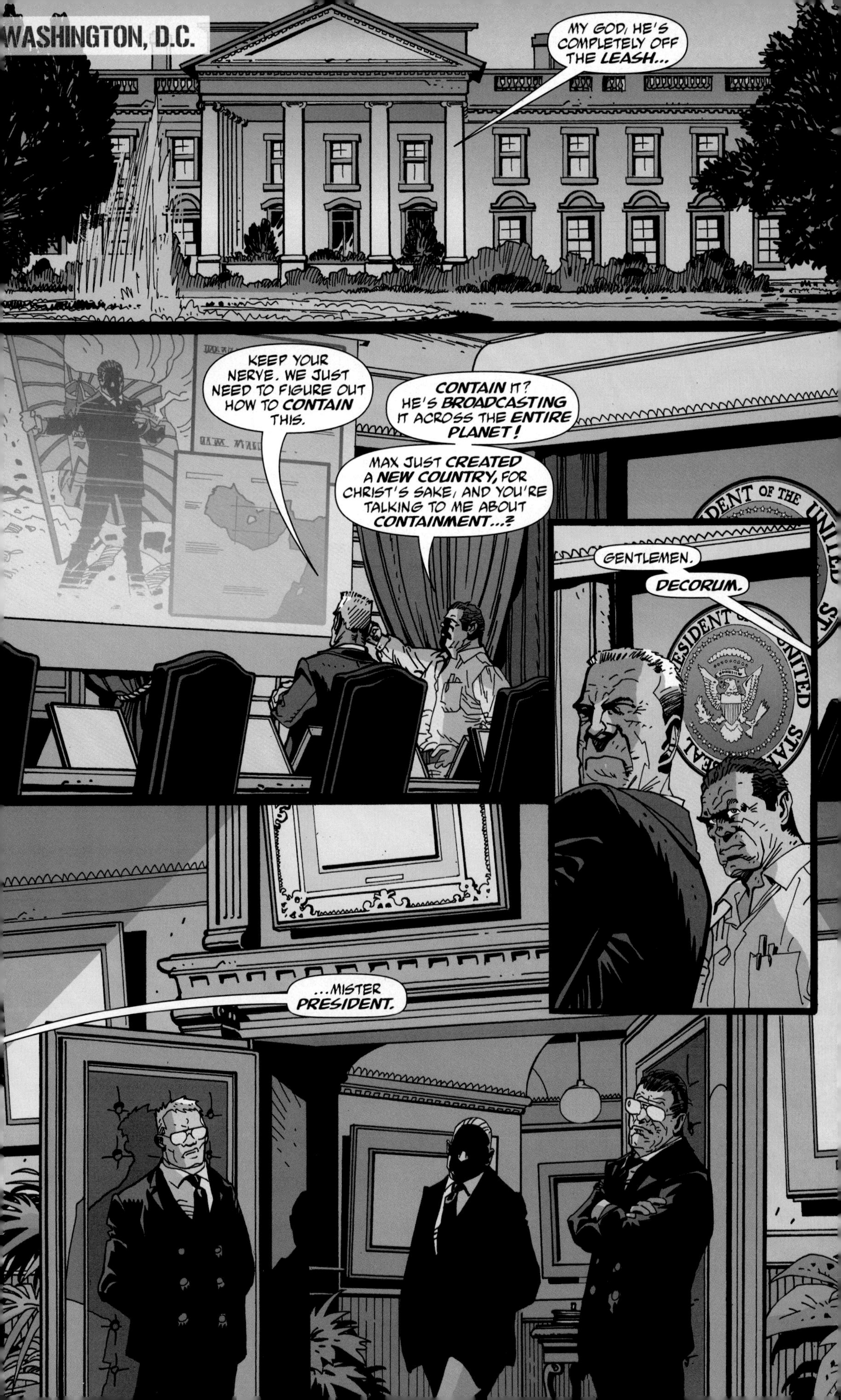

WASHINGTON, D.C.
MY GOD, HE'S COMPLETELY OFF THE LEASH...
KEEP YOUR NERVE. WE JUST NEED TO FIGURE OUT HOW TO CONTAIN THIS.
CONTAIN IT? HE'S BROADCASTING IT ACROSS THE ENTIRE PLANET!
MAX JUST CREATED A NEW COUNTRY, FOR CHRIST'S SAKE, AND YOU'RE TALKING TO ME ABOUT CONTAINMENT...?
GENTLEMEN.
DECORUM.
...MISTER PRESIDENT.

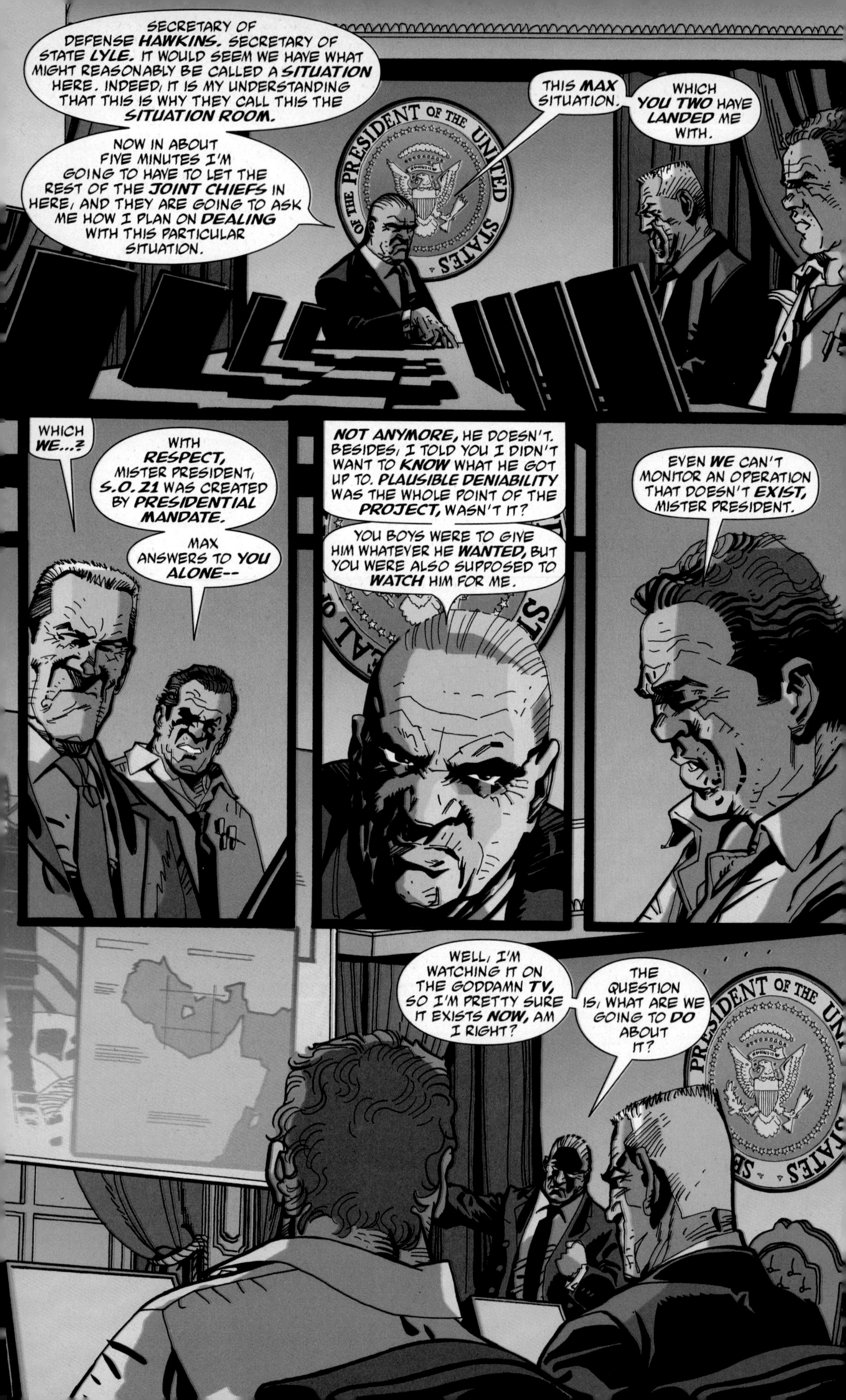

SECRETARY OF DEFENSE HAWKINS. SECRETARY OF STATE LYLE. IT WOULD SEEM WE HAVE WHAT MIGHT REASONABLY BE CALLED A SITUATION HERE. INDEED, IT IS MY UNDERSTANDING THAT THIS IS WHY THEY CALL THIS THE SITUATION ROOM.
NOW IN ABOUT FIVE MINUTES I'M GOING TO HAVE TO LET THE REST OF THE JOINT CHIEFS IN HERE, AND THEY ARE GOING TO ASK ME HOW I PLAN ON DEALING WITH THIS PARTICULAR SITUATION.
THIS MAX SITUATION.
WHICH YOU TWO HAVE LANDED ME WITH.
PRESIDENT OF THE UNITED STATES
WHICH WE...?
WITH RESPECT, MISTER PRESIDENT, S.O. 21 WAS CREATED BY PRESIDENTIAL MANDATE.
MAX ANSWERS TO YOU ALONE--
NOT ANYMORE, HE DOESN'T. BESIDES, I TOLD YOU I DIDN'T WANT TO KNOW WHAT HE GOT UP TO. PLAUSIBLE DENIABILITY WAS THE WHOLE POINT OF THE PROJECT, WASN'T IT?
YOU BOYS WERE TO GIVE HIM WHATEVER HE WANTED, BUT YOU WERE ALSO SUPPOSED TO WATCH HIM FOR ME.
EVEN WE CAN'T MONITOR AN OPERATION THAT DOESN'T EXIST, MISTER PRESIDENT.
WELL, I'M WATCHING IT ON THE GODDAMN TV, SO I'M PRETTY SURE IT EXISTS NOW, AM I RIGHT?
THE QUESTION IS, WHAT ARE WE GOING TO DO ABOUT IT?

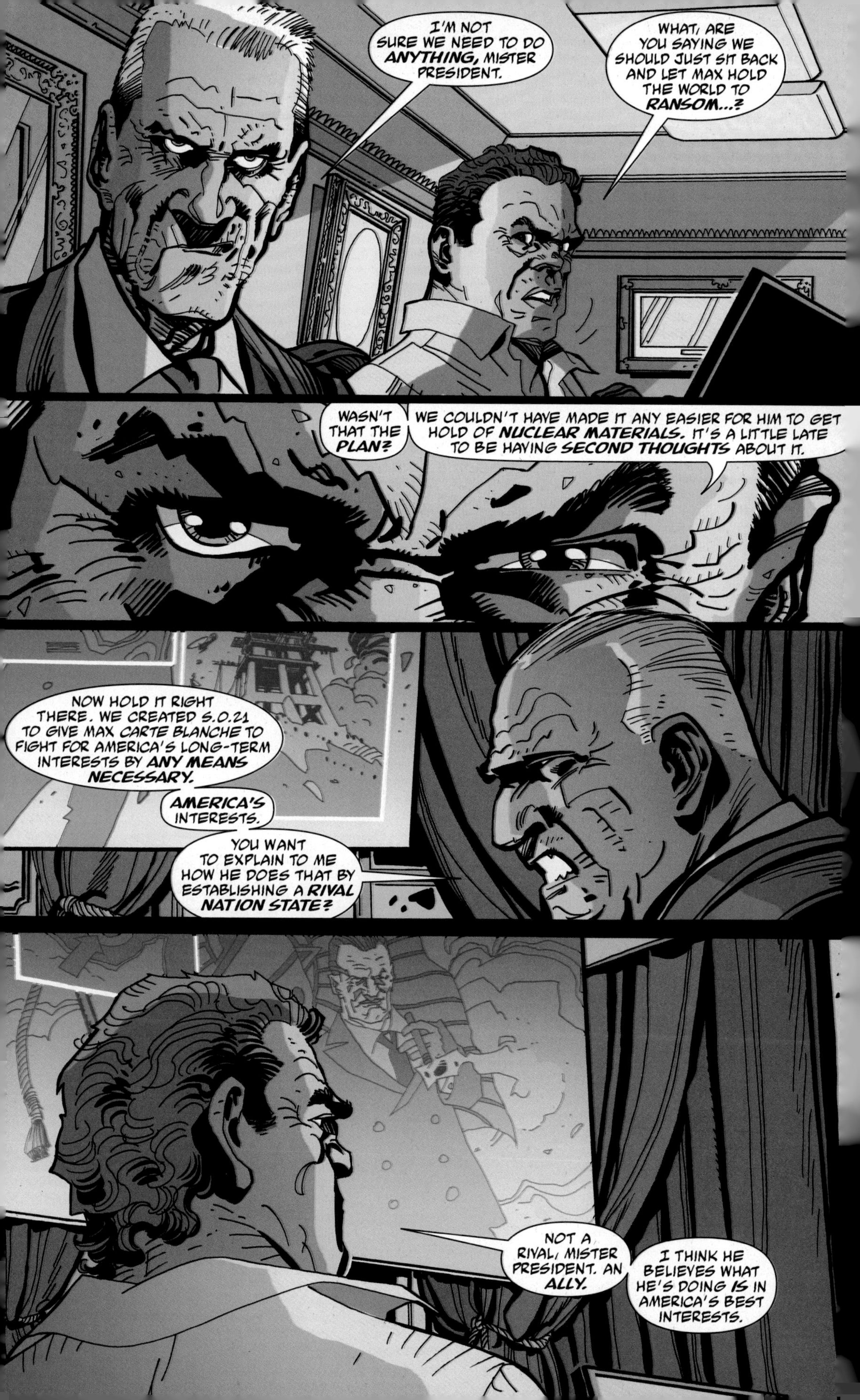
I'M NOT SURE WE NEED TO DO ANYTHING, MISTER PRESIDENT.
WHAT, ARE YOU SAYING WE SHOULD JUST SIT BACK AND LET MAX HOLD THE WORLD TO RANSOM...?
WASN'T THAT THE PLAN?
WE COULDN'T HAVE MADE IT ANY EASIER FOR HIM TO GET HOLD OF NUCLEAR MATERIALS. IT'S A LITTLE LATE TO BE HAVING SECOND THOUGHTS ABOUT IT.
NOW HOLD IT RIGHT THERE. WE CREATED S.O.21 TO GIVE MAX CARTE BLANCHE TO FIGHT FOR AMERICA'S LONG-TERM INTERESTS BY ANY MEANS NECESSARY.
AMERICA'S INTERESTS.
YOU WANT TO EXPLAIN TO ME HOW HE DOES THAT BY ESTABLISHING A RIVAL NATION STATE?
NOT A RIVAL, MISTER PRESIDENT. AN ALLY.
I THINK HE BELIEVES WHAT HE'S DOING IS IN AMERICA'S BEST INTERESTS.

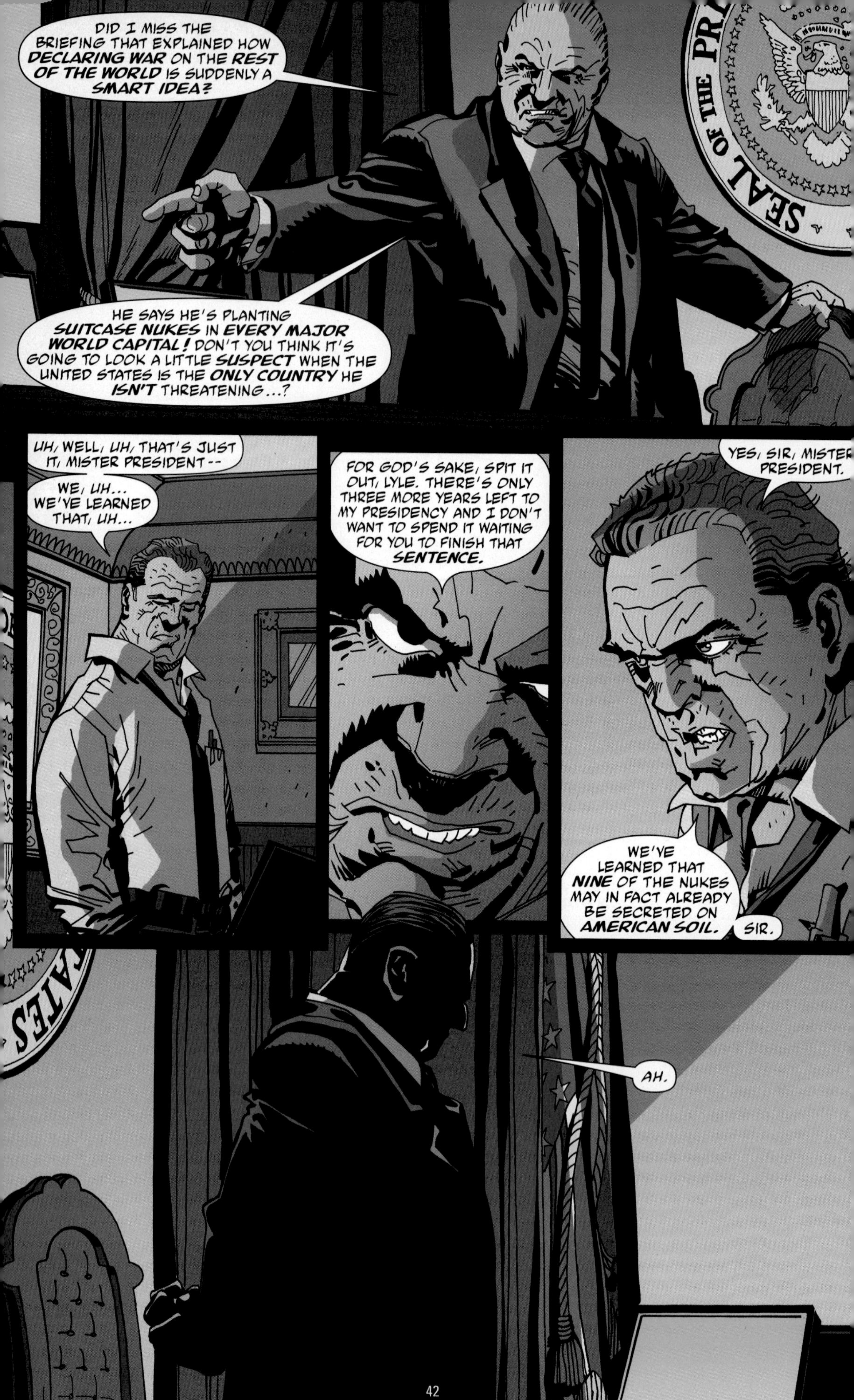
DID I MISS THE BRIEFING THAT EXPLAINED HOW DECLARING WAR ON THE REST OF THE WORLD IS SUDDENLY A SMART IDEA?
HE SAYS HE'S PLANTING SUITCASE NUKES IN EVERY MAJOR WORLD CAPITAL! DON'T YOU THINK IT'S GOING TO LOOK A LITTLE SUSPECT WHEN THE UNITED STATES IS THE ONLY COUNTRY HE ISN'T THREATENING...?
UH, WELL, UH, THAT'S JUST IT, MISTER PRESIDENT--
WE, UH... WE'VE LEARNED THAT, UH...
FOR GOD'S SAKE, SPIT IT OUT, LYLE. THERE'S ONLY THREE MORE YEARS LEFT TO MY PRESIDENCY AND I DON'T WANT TO SPEND IT WAITING FOR YOU TO FINISH THAT SENTENCE.
YES, SIR, MISTER PRESIDENT.
WE'VE LEARNED THAT NINE OF THE NUKES MAY IN FACT ALREADY BE SECRETED ON AMERICAN SOIL.
SIR.
AH.

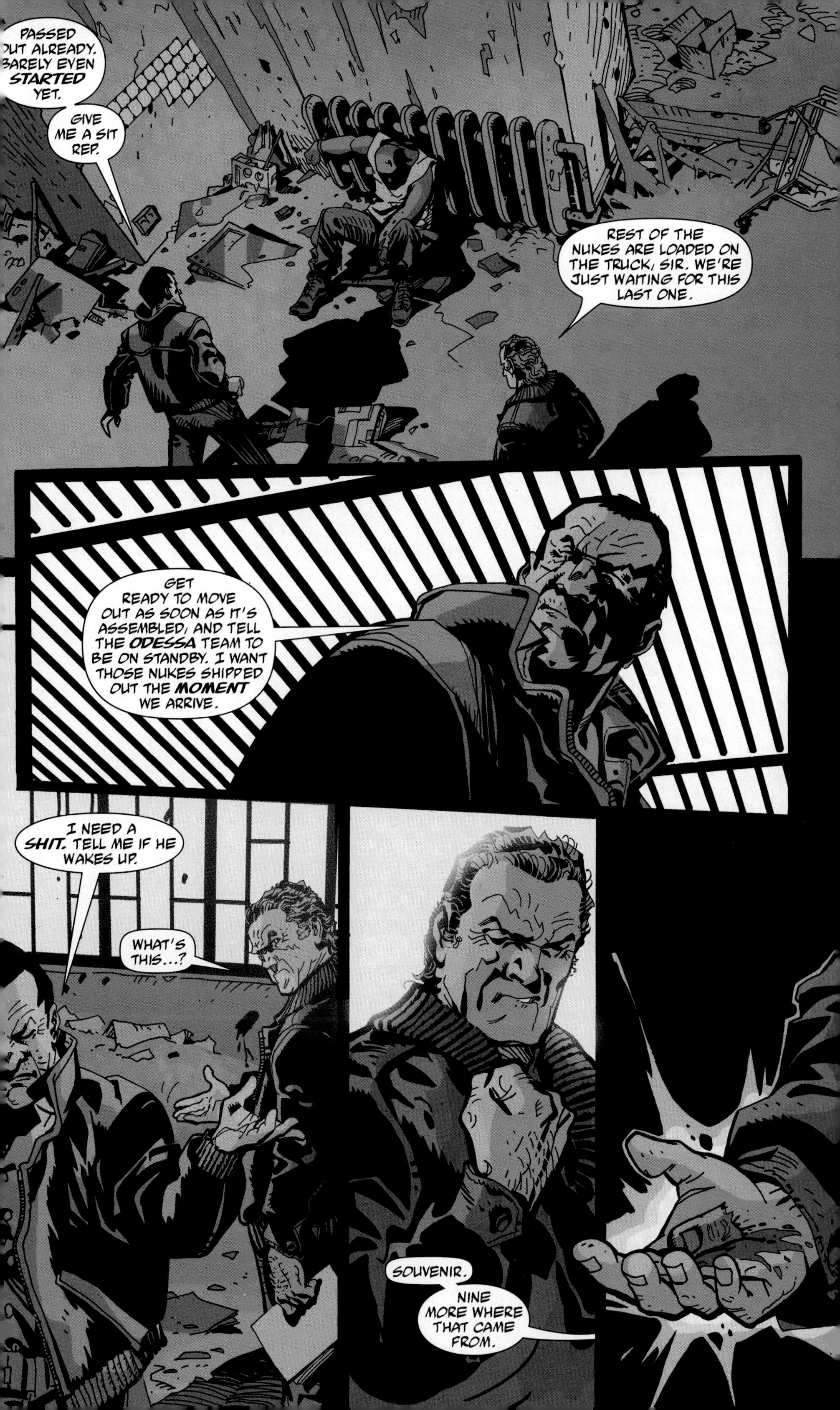

PASSED OUT ALREADY. BARELY EVEN STARTED YET.
GIVE ME A SIT REP.
REST OF THE NUKES ARE LOADED ON THE TRUCK, SIR. WE'RE JUST WAITING FOR THIS LAST ONE.
GET READY TO MOVE OUT AS SOON AS IT'S ASSEMBLED, AND TELL THE ODESSA TEAM TO BE ON STANDBY. I WANT THOSE NUKES SHIPPED OUT THE MOMENT WE ARRIVE.
I NEED A SHIT. TELL ME IF HE WAKES UP.
WHAT'S THIS...?
SOUVENIR.
NINE MORE WHERE THAT CAME FROM.

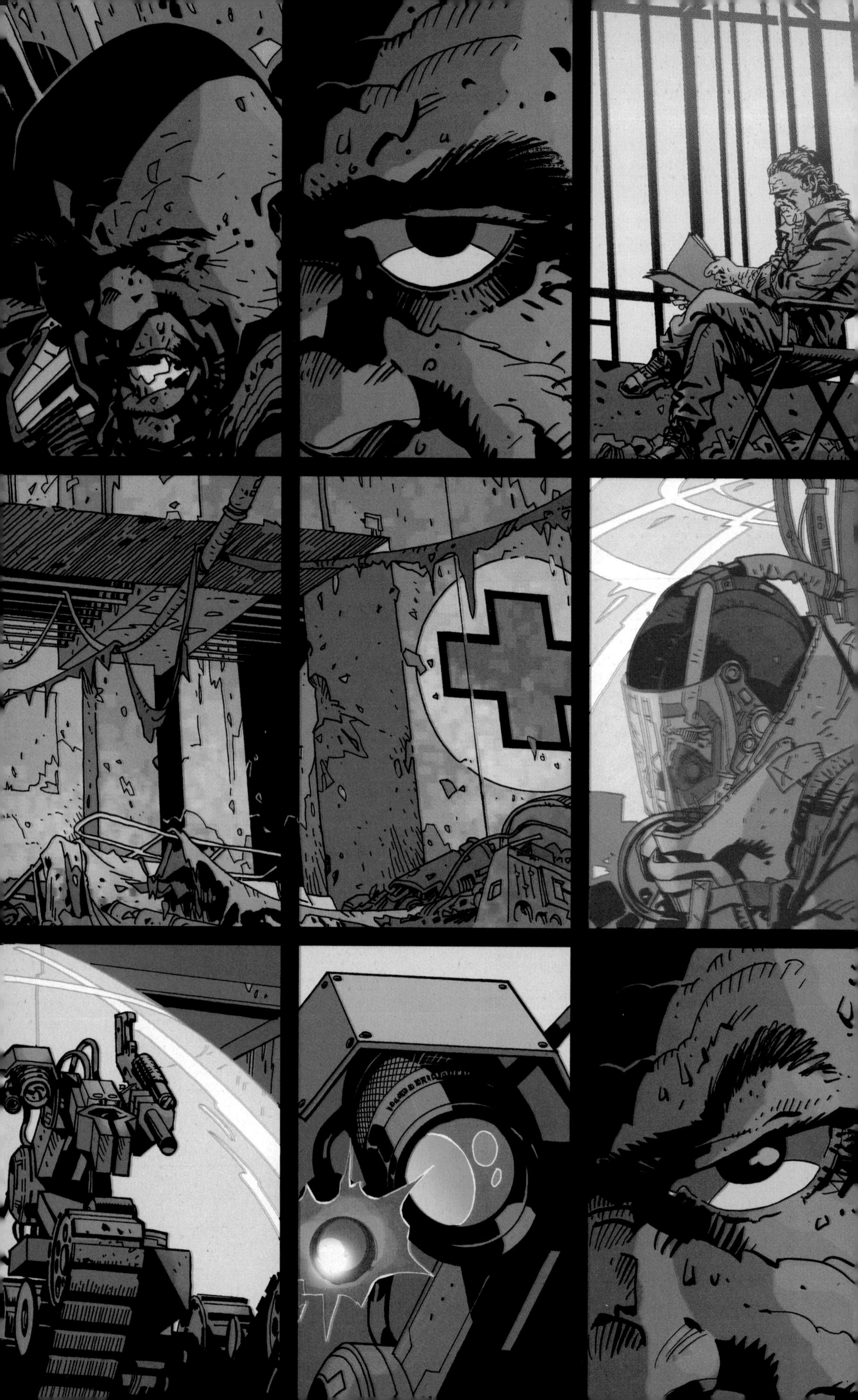

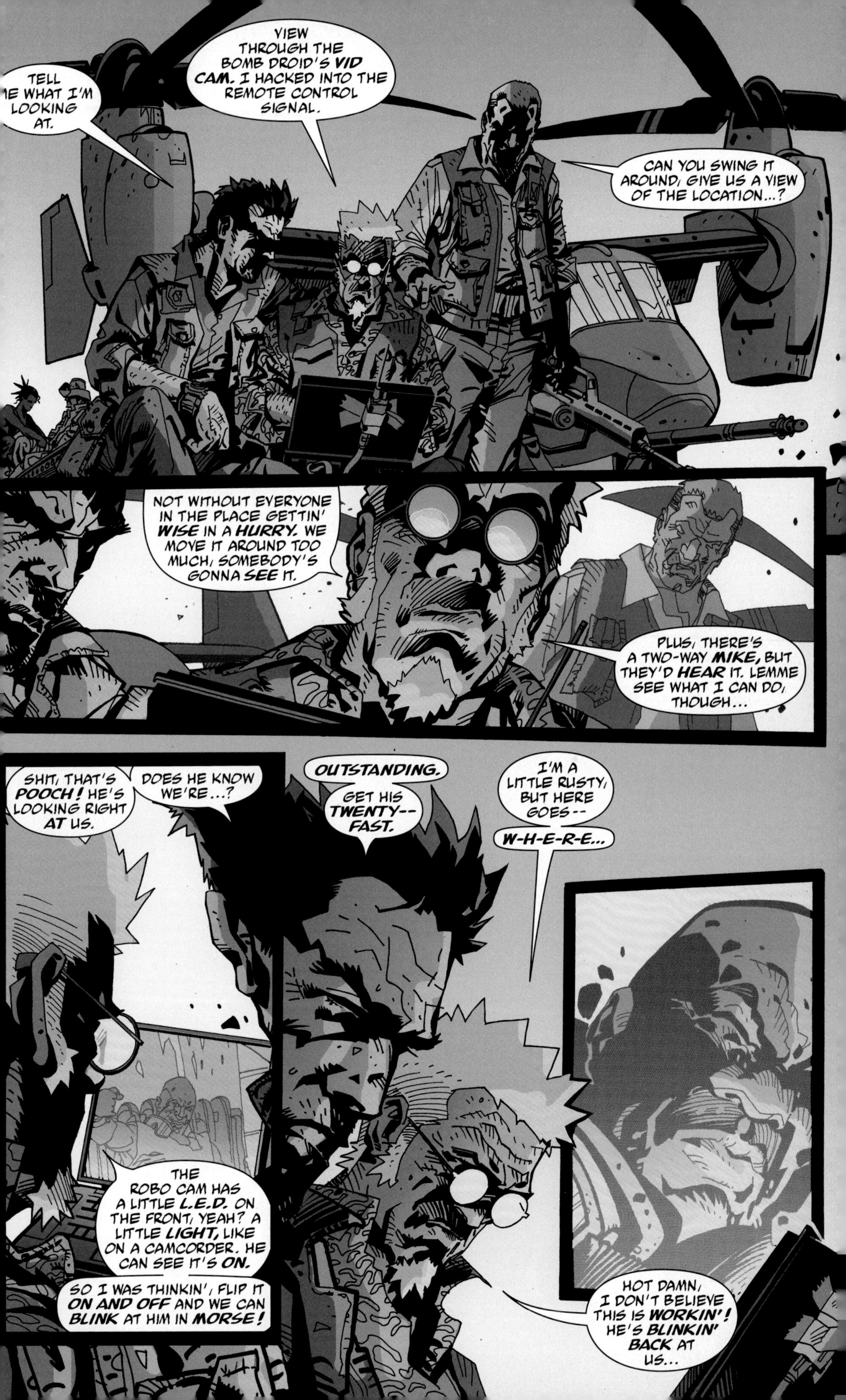
TELL ME WHAT I'M LOOKING AT.
VIEW THROUGH THE BOMB DROID'S **VID CAM.** I HACKED INTO THE REMOTE CONTROL SIGNAL.
CAN YOU SWING IT AROUND, GIVE US A VIEW OF THE LOCATION...?
NOT WITHOUT EVERYONE IN THE PLACE GETTIN' **WISE** IN A **HURRY.** WE MOVE IT AROUND TOO MUCH, SOMEBODY'S GONNA **SEE** IT.
PLUS, THERE'S A TWO-WAY **MIKE,** BUT THEY'D **HEAR** IT. LEMME SEE WHAT I CAN DO, THOUGH...
SHIT, THAT'S **POOCH!** HE'S LOOKING RIGHT **AT** US.
DOES HE KNOW WE'RE...?
OUTSTANDING.
GET HIS **TWENTY--FAST.**
I'M A LITTLE RUSTY, BUT HERE GOES--
W-H-E-R-E...
THE ROBO CAM HAS A LITTLE **L.E.D.** ON THE FRONT, YEAH? A LITTLE **LIGHT,** LIKE ON A CAMCORDER. HE CAN SEE IT'S **ON.**
SO I WAS THINKIN', FLIP IT **ON AND OFF** AND WE CAN **BLINK** AT HIM IN **MORSE!**
HOT DAMN, I DON'T BELIEVE THIS IS **WORKIN'!** HE'S **BLINKIN' BACK** AT US...

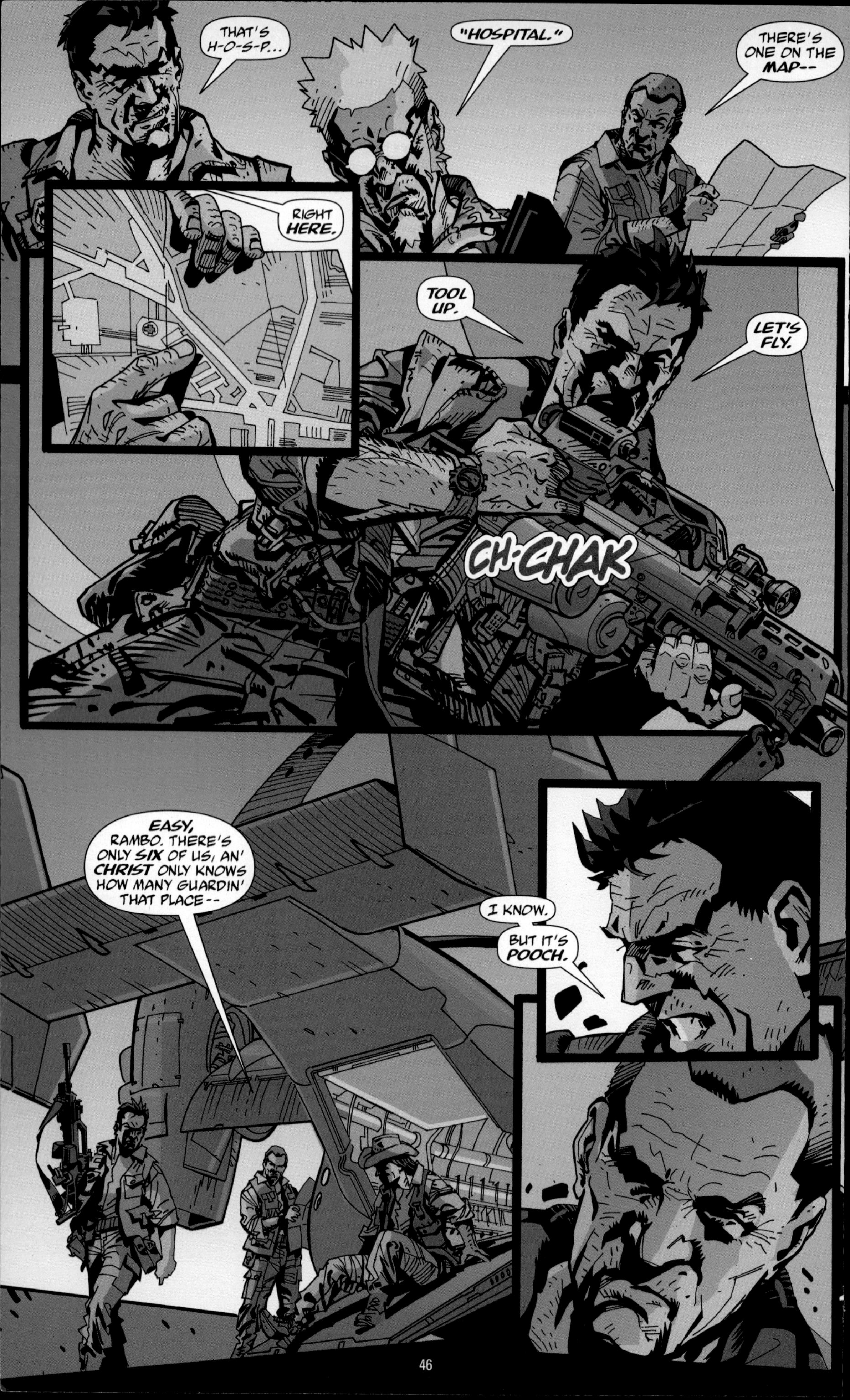
THAT'S H-O-S-P...
"HOSPITAL."
THERE'S ONE ON THE MAP--
RIGHT HERE.
TOOL UP.
LET'S FLY.
CH-CHAK
EASY, RAMBO. THERE'S ONLY SIX OF US, AN' CHRIST ONLY KNOWS HOW MANY GUARDIN' THAT PLACE--
I KNOW.
BUT IT'S POOCH.

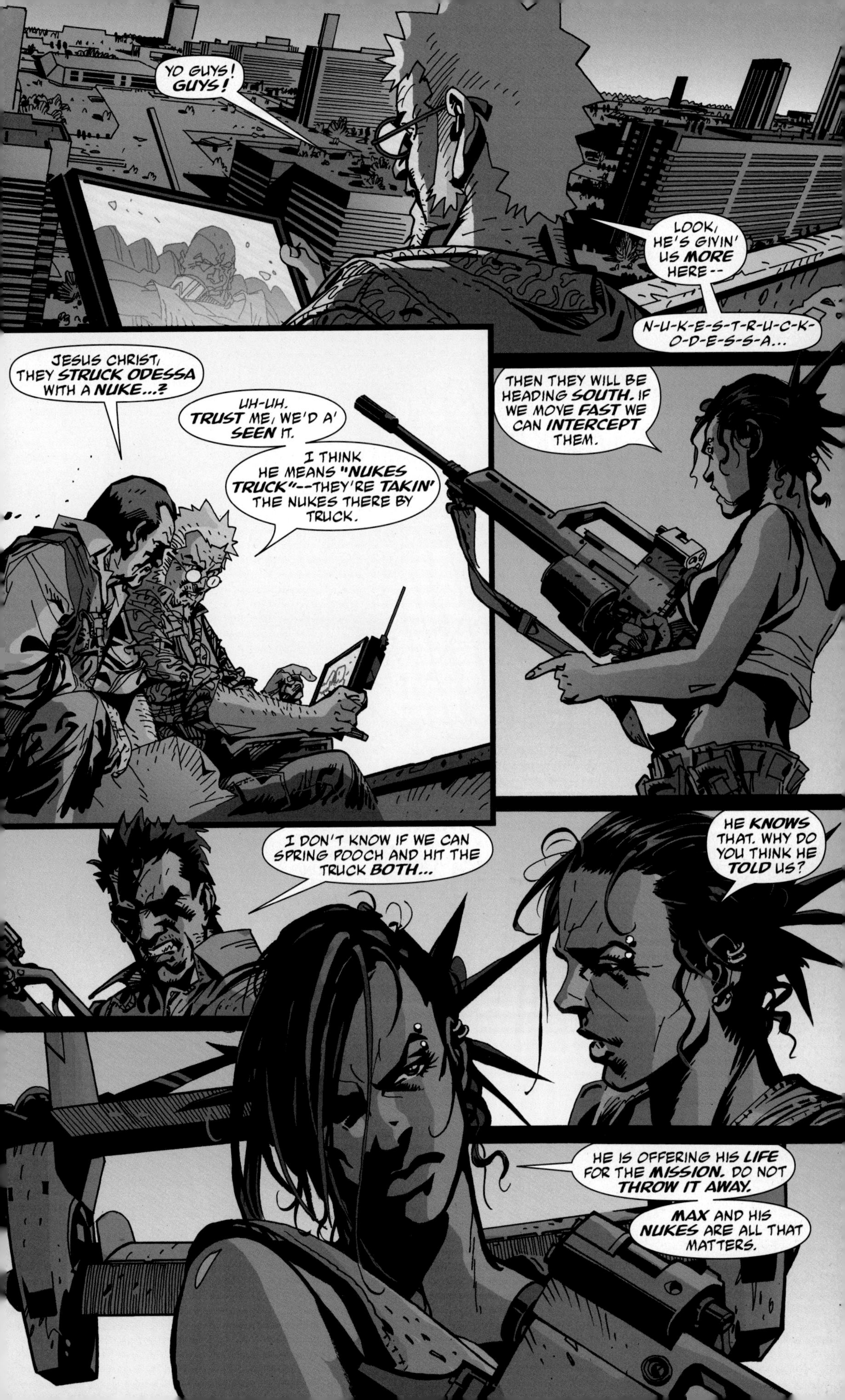
YO GUYS! GUYS!
LOOK, HE'S GIVIN' US MORE HERE--
N-U-K-E-S-T-R-U-C-K-O-D-E-S-S-A...
JESUS CHRIST, THEY STRUCK ODESSA WITH A NUKE...?
UH-UH. TRUST ME, WE'D A' SEEN IT.
I THINK HE MEANS "NUKES TRUCK"--THEY'RE TAKIN' THE NUKES THERE BY TRUCK.
THEN THEY WILL BE HEADING SOUTH. IF WE MOVE FAST WE CAN INTERCEPT THEM.
I DON'T KNOW IF WE CAN SPRING POOCH AND HIT THE TRUCK BOTH...
HE KNOWS THAT. WHY DO YOU THINK HE TOLD US?
HE IS OFFERING HIS LIFE FOR THE MISSION. DO NOT THROW IT AWAY.
MAX AND HIS NUKES ARE ALL THAT MATTERS.

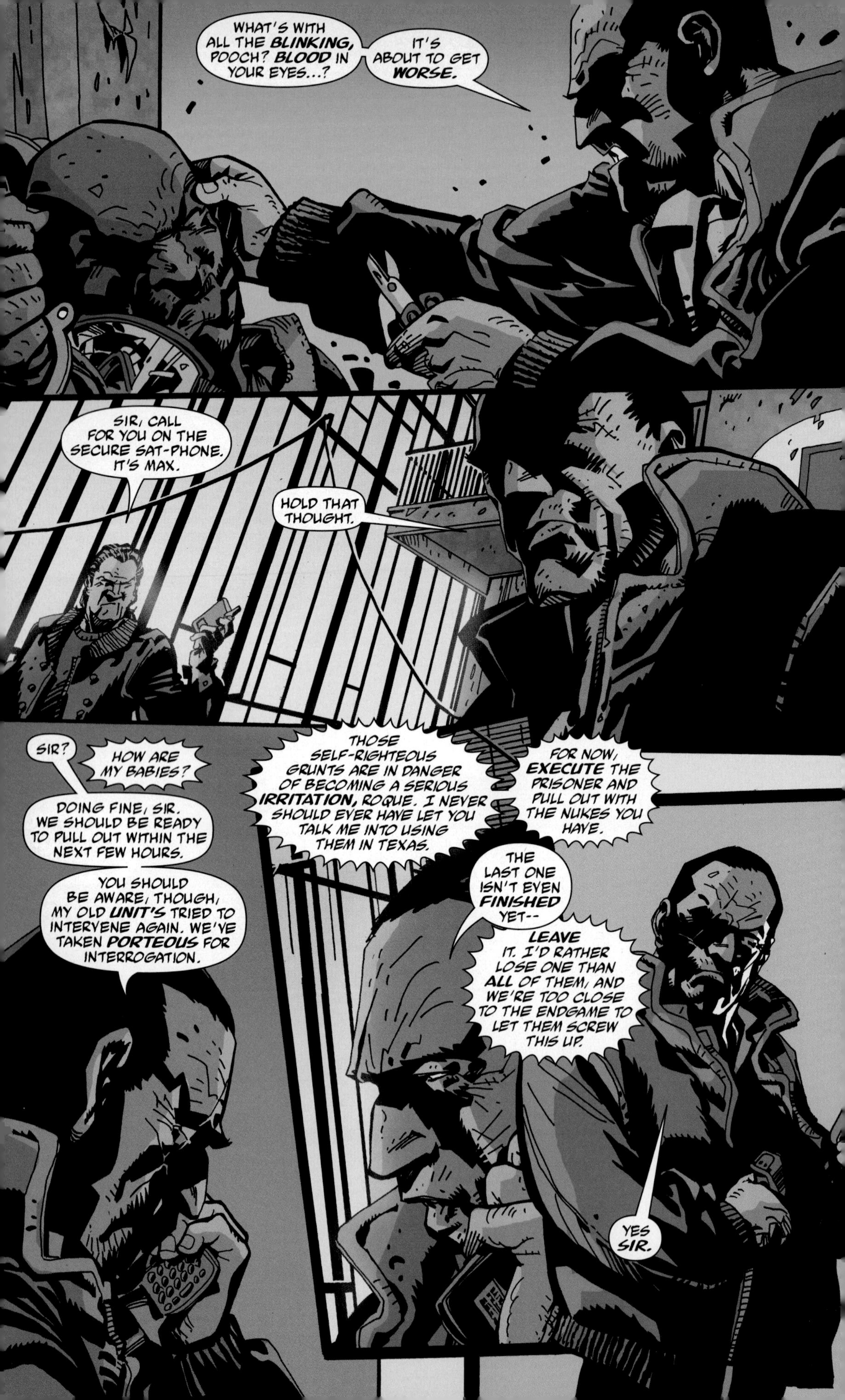
WHAT'S WITH ALL THE **BLINKING,** POOCH? **BLOOD** IN YOUR EYES...?
IT'S ABOUT TO GET **WORSE.**
SIR, CALL FOR YOU ON THE SECURE SAT-PHONE. IT'S MAX.
HOLD THAT THOUGHT.
SIR?
HOW ARE MY BABIES?
DOING FINE, SIR. WE SHOULD BE READY TO PULL OUT WITHIN THE NEXT FEW HOURS.
YOU SHOULD BE AWARE, THOUGH, MY OLD **UNIT'S** TRIED TO INTERVENE AGAIN. WE'VE TAKEN **PORTEOUS** FOR INTERROGATION.
THOSE SELF-RIGHTEOUS GRUNTS ARE IN DANGER OF BECOMING A SERIOUS **IRRITATION,** ROQUE. I NEVER SHOULD EVER HAVE LET YOU TALK ME INTO USING THEM IN TEXAS.
FOR NOW, **EXECUTE** THE PRISONER AND PULL OUT WITH THE NUKES YOU HAVE.
THE LAST ONE ISN'T EVEN **FINISHED** YET--
LEAVE IT. I'D RATHER LOSE ONE THAN **ALL** OF THEM, AND WE'RE TOO CLOSE TO THE ENDGAME TO LET THEM SCREW THIS UP.
YES **SIR.**

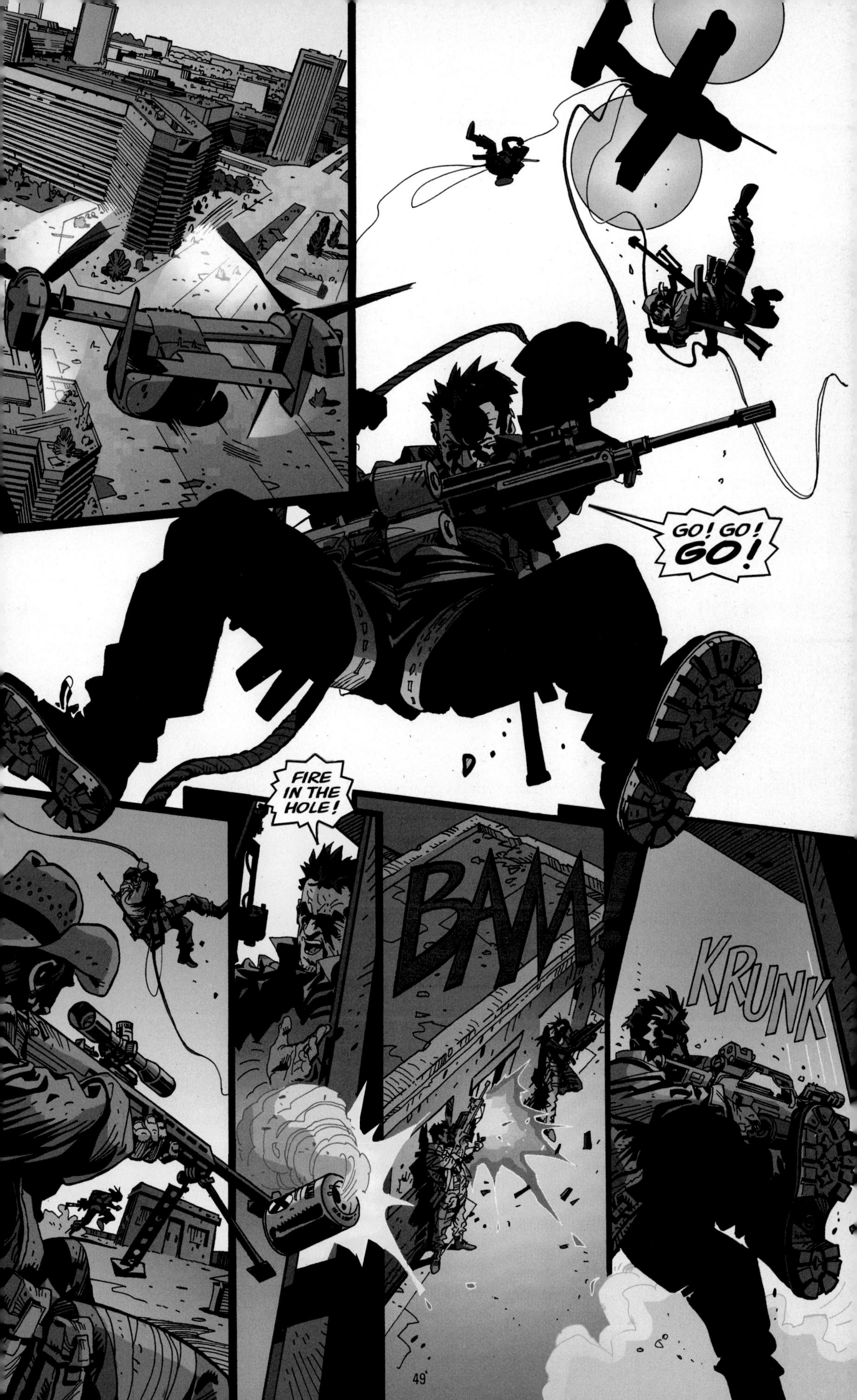
GO! GO! GO!
FIRE IN THE HOLE!
BAM!
KRUNK

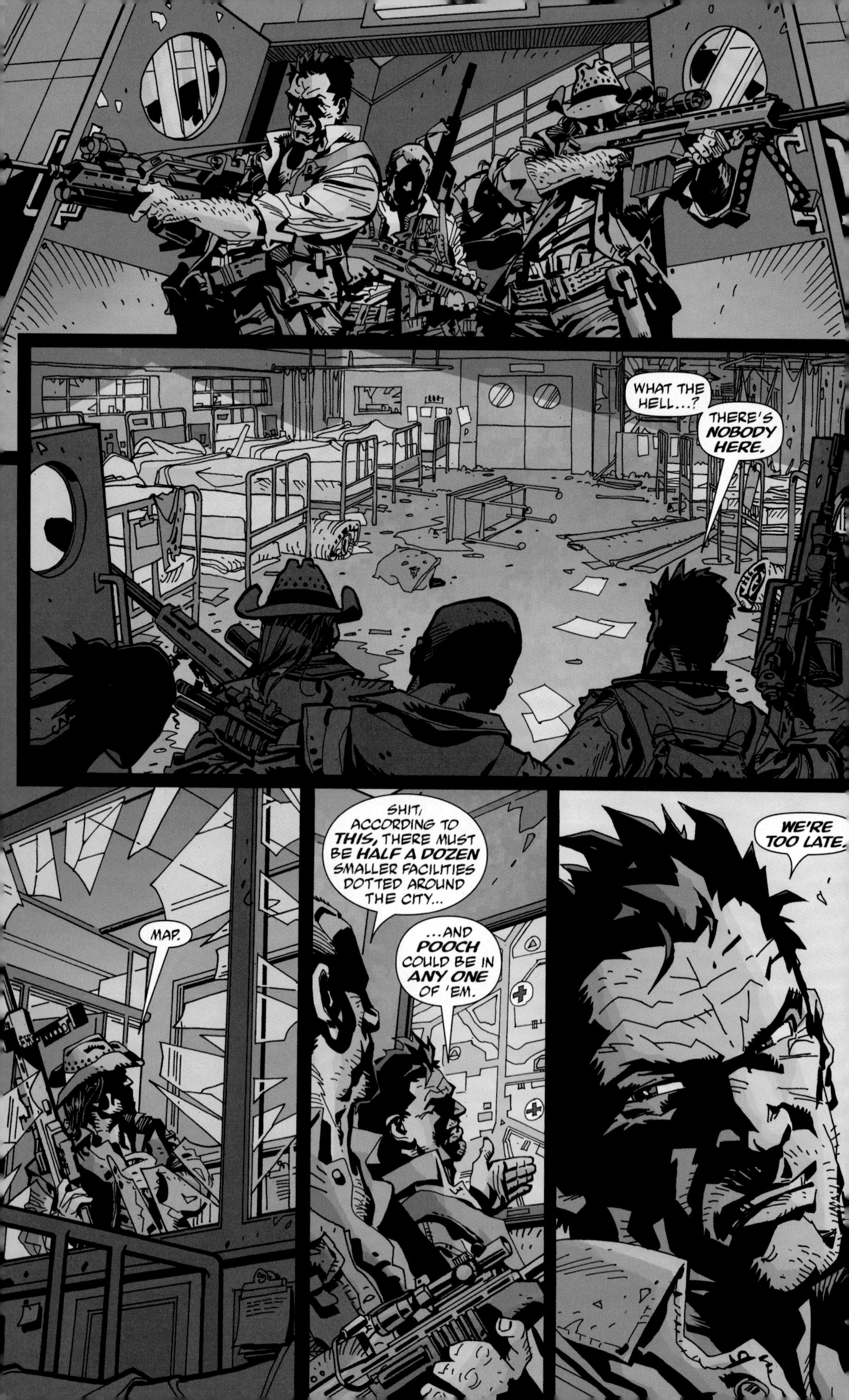
WHAT THE HELL...?
THERE'S NOBODY HERE.
MAP.
SHIT, ACCORDING TO THIS, THERE MUST BE HALF A DOZEN SMALLER FACILITIES DOTTED AROUND THE CITY...
...AND POOCH COULD BE IN ANY ONE OF 'EM.
WE'RE TOO LATE.

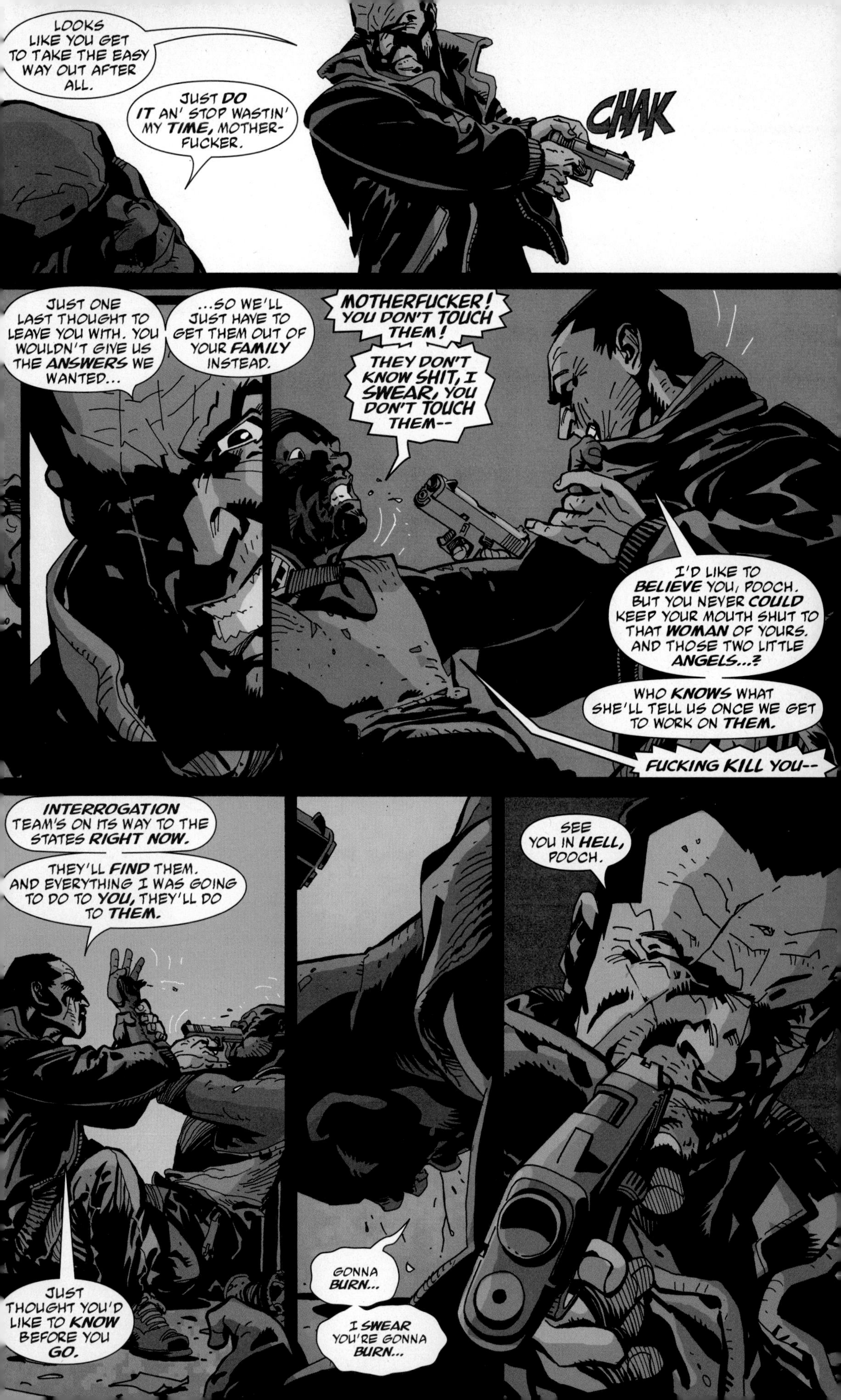
LOOKS LIKE YOU GET TO TAKE THE EASY WAY OUT AFTER ALL.
JUST DO IT AN' STOP WASTIN' MY TIME, MOTHER-FUCKER.
CHAK
JUST ONE LAST THOUGHT TO LEAVE YOU WITH. YOU WOULDN'T GIVE US THE ANSWERS WE WANTED...
...SO WE'LL JUST HAVE TO GET THEM OUT OF YOUR FAMILY INSTEAD.
MOTHERFUCKER! YOU DON'T TOUCH THEM!
THEY DON'T KNOW SHIT, I SWEAR, YOU DON'T TOUCH THEM--
I'D LIKE TO BELIEVE YOU, POOCH. BUT YOU NEVER COULD KEEP YOUR MOUTH SHUT TO THAT WOMAN OF YOURS. AND THOSE TWO LITTLE ANGELS...?
WHO KNOWS WHAT SHE'LL TELL US ONCE WE GET TO WORK ON THEM.
FUCKING KILL YOU--
INTERROGATION TEAM'S ON ITS WAY TO THE STATES RIGHT NOW.
THEY'LL FIND THEM. AND EVERYTHING I WAS GOING TO DO TO YOU, THEY'LL DO TO THEM.
JUST THOUGHT YOU'D LIKE TO KNOW BEFORE YOU GO.
GONNA BURN...
I SWEAR YOU'RE GONNA BURN...
SEE YOU IN HELL, POOCH.

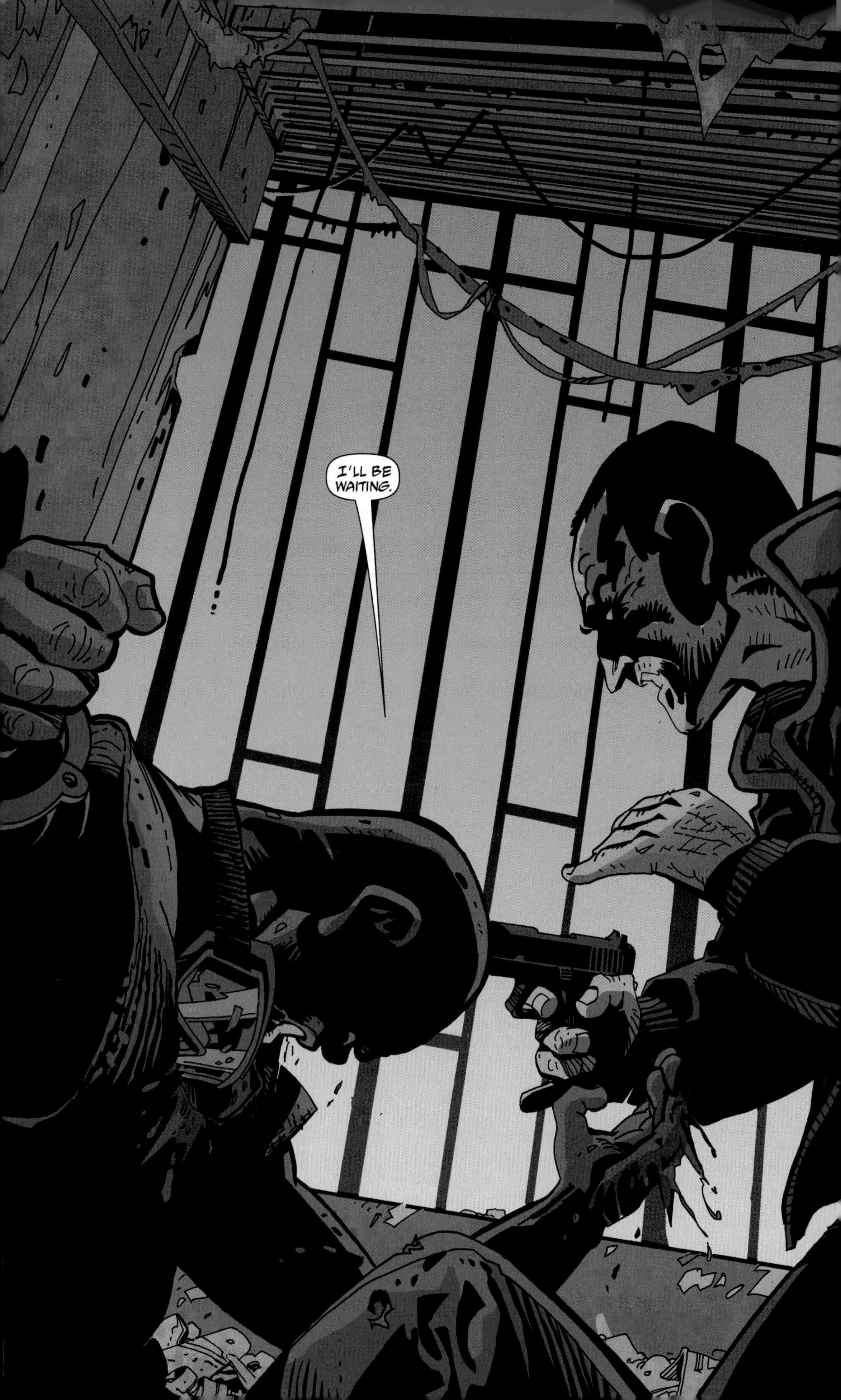
I'LL BE WAITING.

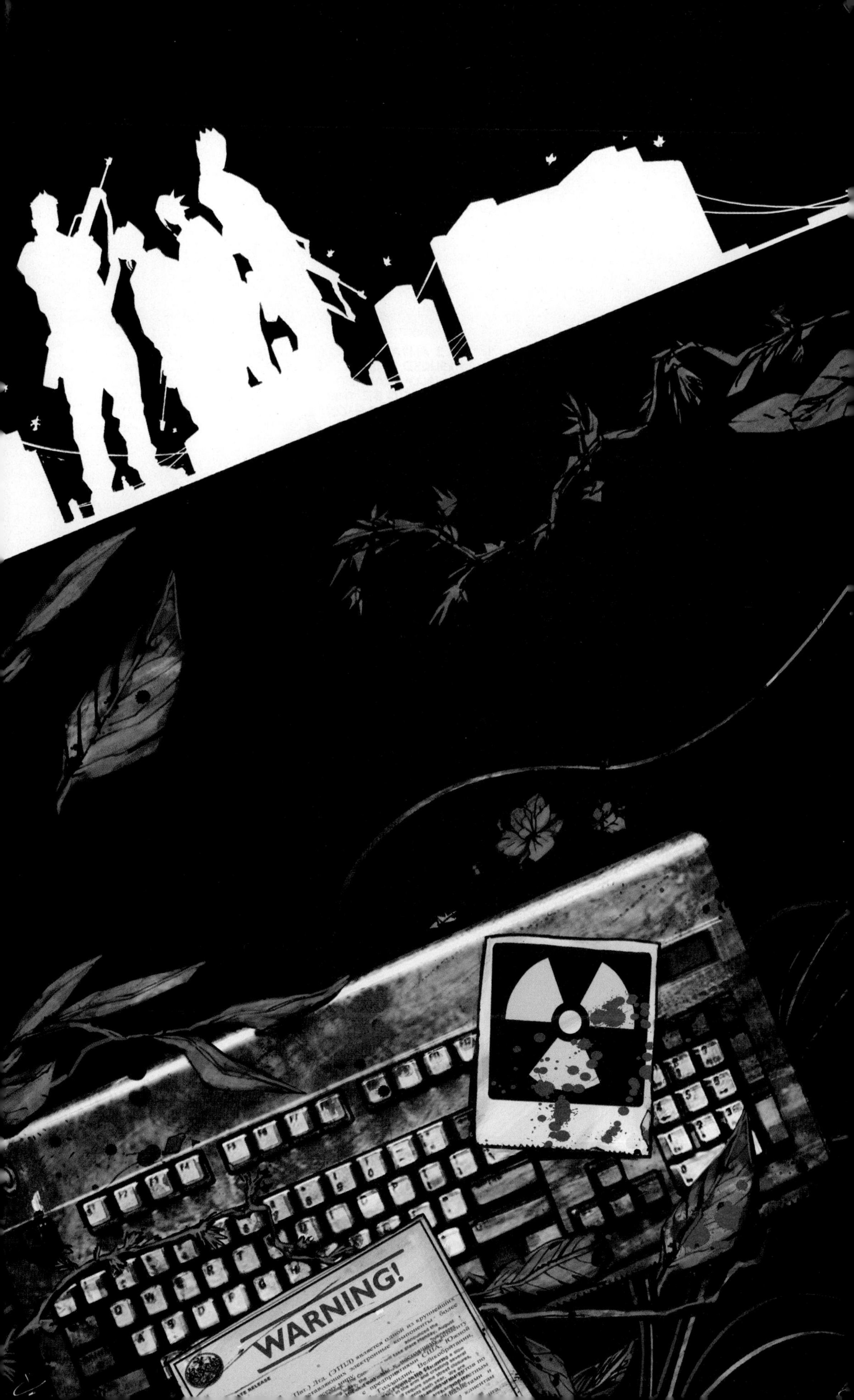
WARNING!

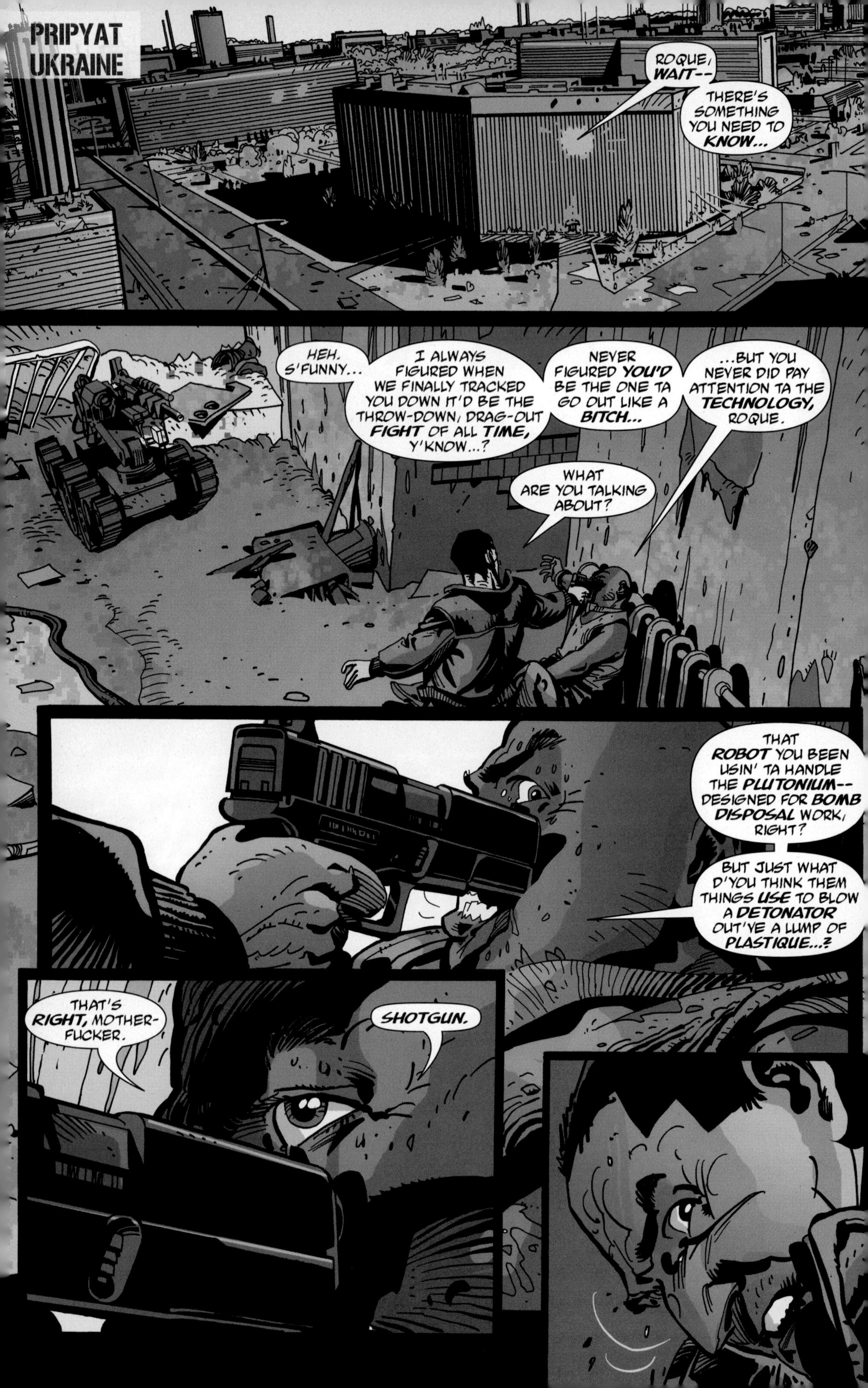
PRIPYAT UKRAINE
ROQUE, WAIT--
THERE'S SOMETHING YOU NEED TO KNOW...
HEH. S'FUNNY...
I ALWAYS FIGURED WHEN WE FINALLY TRACKED YOU DOWN IT'D BE THE THROW-DOWN, DRAG-OUT FIGHT OF ALL TIME, Y'KNOW...?
NEVER FIGURED YOU'D BE THE ONE TA GO OUT LIKE A BITCH...
...BUT YOU NEVER DID PAY ATTENTION TA THE TECHNOLOGY, ROQUE.
WHAT ARE YOU TALKING ABOUT?
THAT ROBOT YOU BEEN USIN' TA HANDLE THE PLUTONIUM-- DESIGNED FOR BOMB DISPOSAL WORK, RIGHT?
BUT JUST WHAT D'YOU THINK THEM THINGS USE TO BLOW A DETONATOR OUT'YE A LUMP OF PLASTIQUE...?
THAT'S RIGHT, MOTHER-FUCKER.
SHOTGUN.

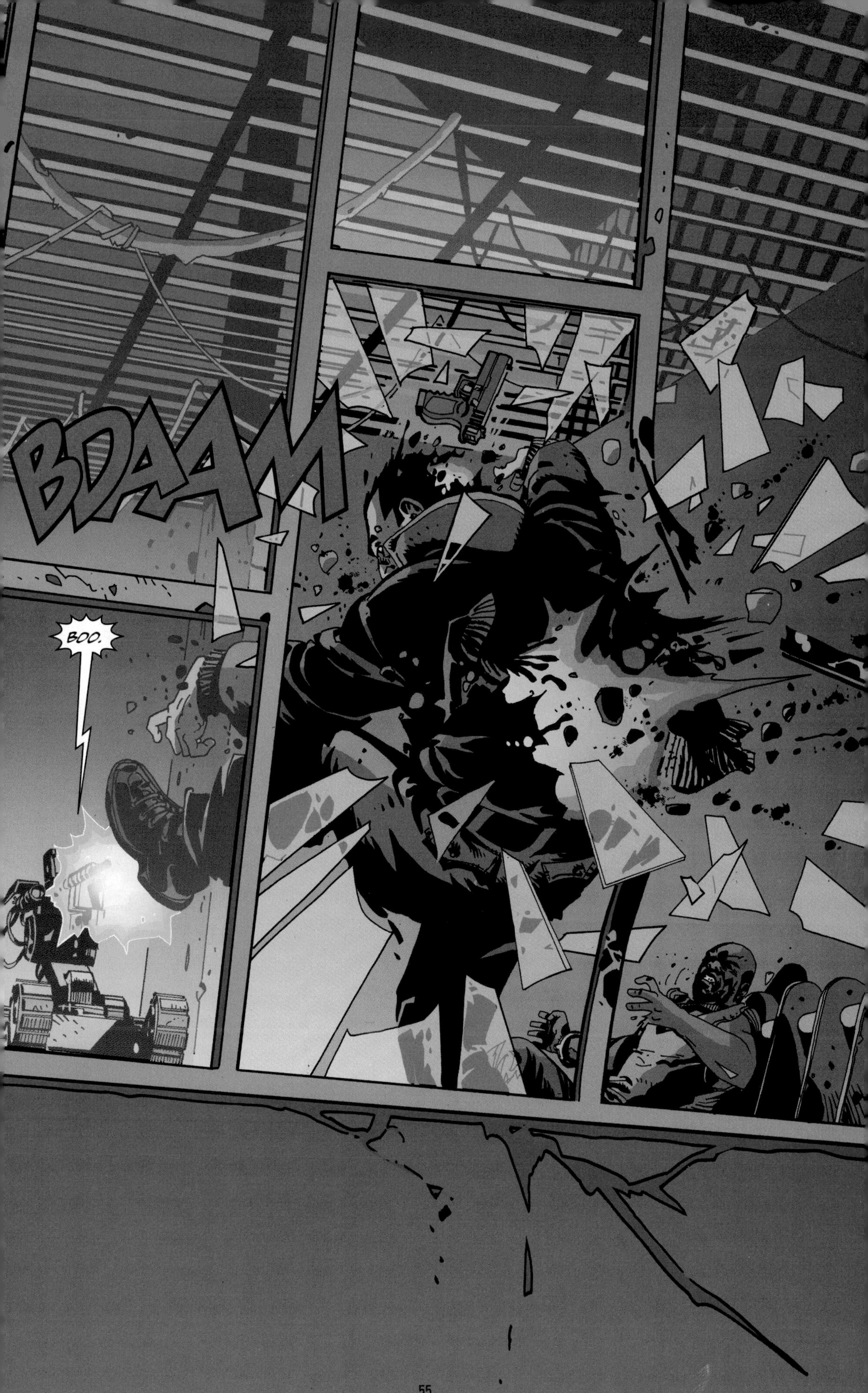
BDAAM
BOO.

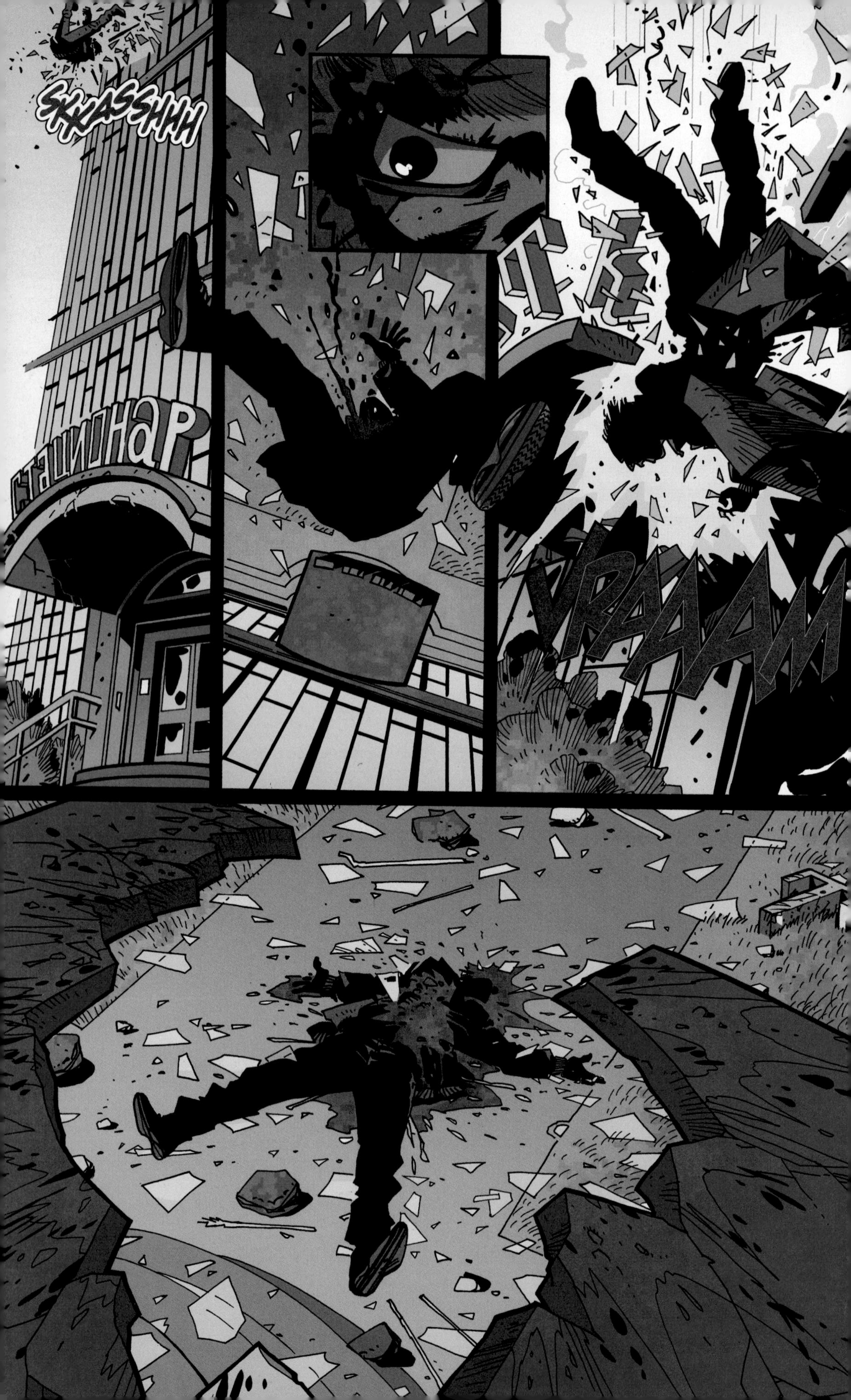
SKKASSHHH
СТАЦИОНАР
VRAAAM

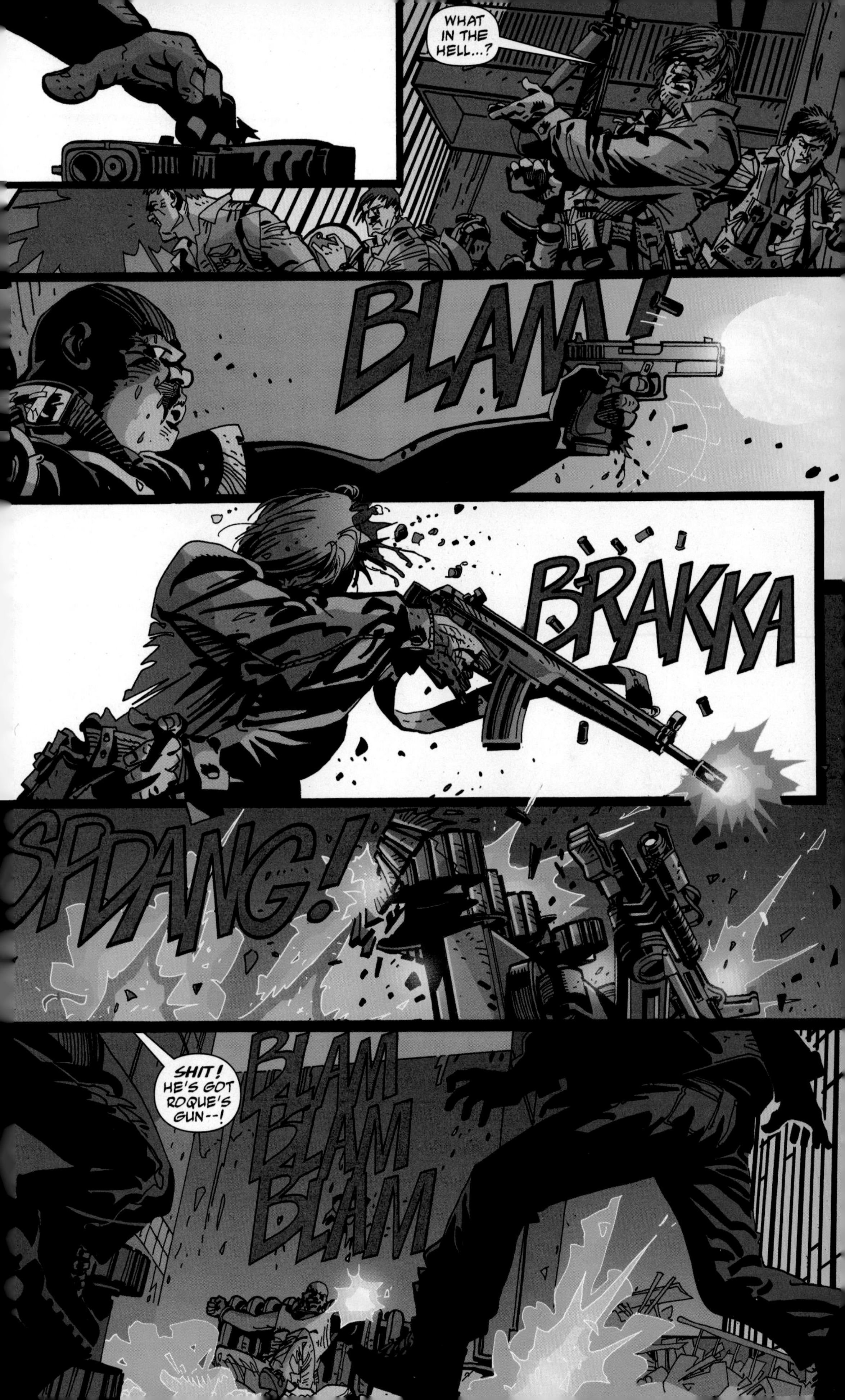
WHAT IN THE HELL...?
BLAM!
BRAKKA
SPDANG!
SHIT! HE'S GOT ROQUE'S GUN--!
BLAM
BLAM
BLAM

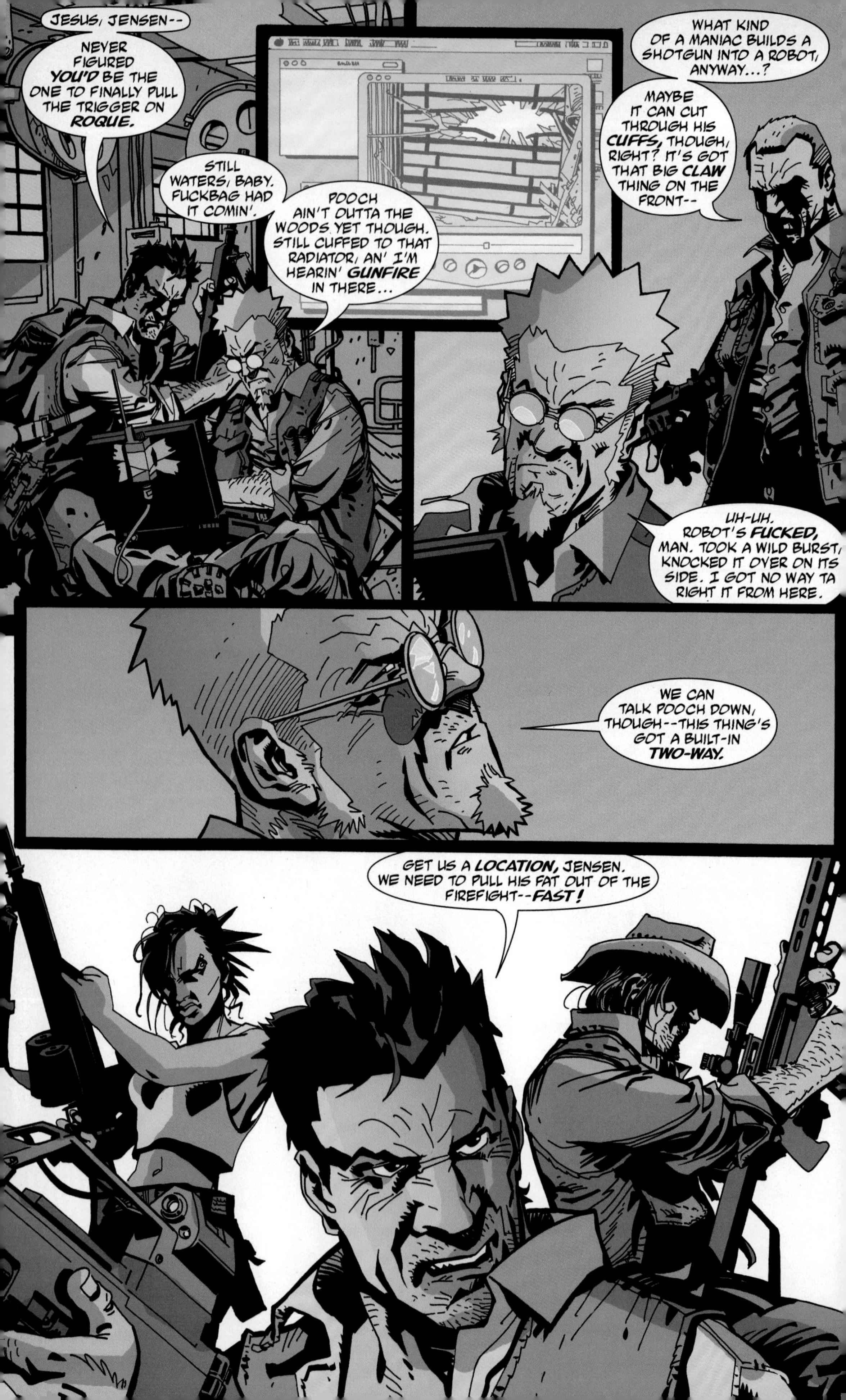
JESUS, JENSEN--
NEVER FIGURED YOU'D BE THE ONE TO FINALLY PULL THE TRIGGER ON ROQUE.
STILL WATERS, BABY. FUCKBAG HAD IT COMIN'.
POOCH AIN'T OUTTA THE WOODS YET THOUGH. STILL CUFFED TO THAT RADIATOR, AN' I'M HEARIN' GUNFIRE IN THERE...
WHAT KIND OF A MANIAC BUILDS A SHOTGUN INTO A ROBOT, ANYWAY...?
MAYBE IT CAN CUT THROUGH HIS CUFFS, THOUGH, RIGHT? IT'S GOT THAT BIG CLAW THING ON THE FRONT--
UH-UH. ROBOT'S FUCKED, MAN. TOOK A WILD BURST, KNOCKED IT OVER ON ITS SIDE. I GOT NO WAY TA RIGHT IT FROM HERE.
WE CAN TALK POOCH DOWN, THOUGH--THIS THING'S GOT A BUILT-IN TWO-WAY.
GET US A LOCATION, JENSEN. WE NEED TO PULL HIS FAT OUT OF THE FIREFIGHT--FAST!

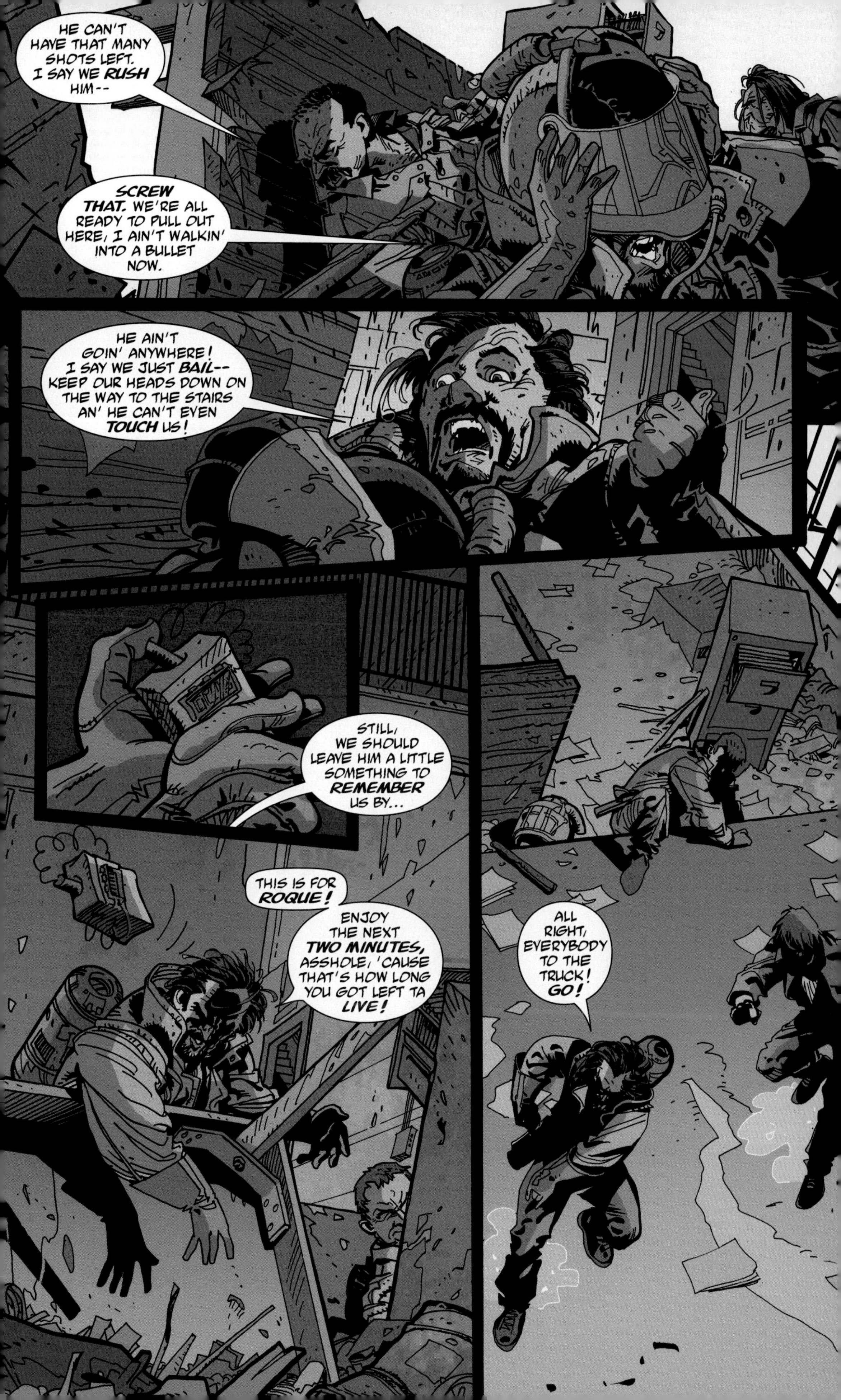
HE CAN'T HAVE THAT MANY SHOTS LEFT. I SAY WE RUSH HIM--
SCREW THAT. WE'RE ALL READY TO PULL OUT HERE, I AIN'T WALKIN' INTO A BULLET NOW.
HE AIN'T GOIN' ANYWHERE! I SAY WE JUST BAIL-- KEEP OUR HEADS DOWN ON THE WAY TO THE STAIRS AN' HE CAN'T EVEN TOUCH US!
STILL, WE SHOULD LEAVE HIM A LITTLE SOMETHING TO REMEMBER US BY...
THIS IS FOR ROQUE!
ENJOY THE NEXT TWO MINUTES, ASSHOLE, 'CAUSE THAT'S HOW LONG YOU GOT LEFT TA LIVE!
ALL RIGHT, EVERYBODY TO THE TRUCK! GO!

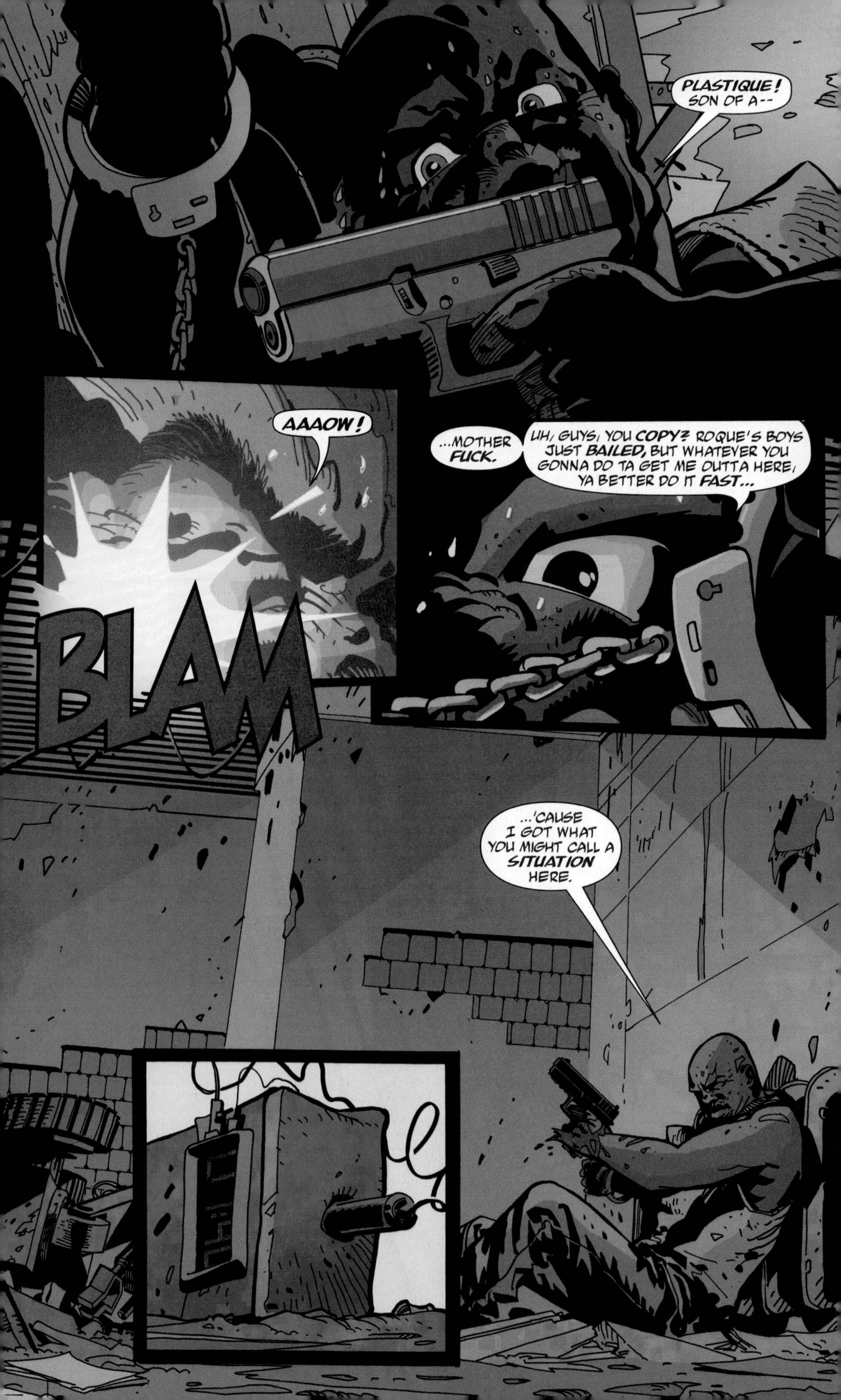
PLASTIQUE! SON OF A--
AAAOW!
BLAM
...MOTHER FUCK.
UH, GUYS, YOU COPY? ROQUE'S BOYS JUST BAILED, BUT WHATEVER YOU GONNA DO TA GET ME OUTTA HERE, YA BETTER DO IT FAST...
...'CAUSE I GOT WHAT YOU MIGHT CALL A SITUATION HERE.

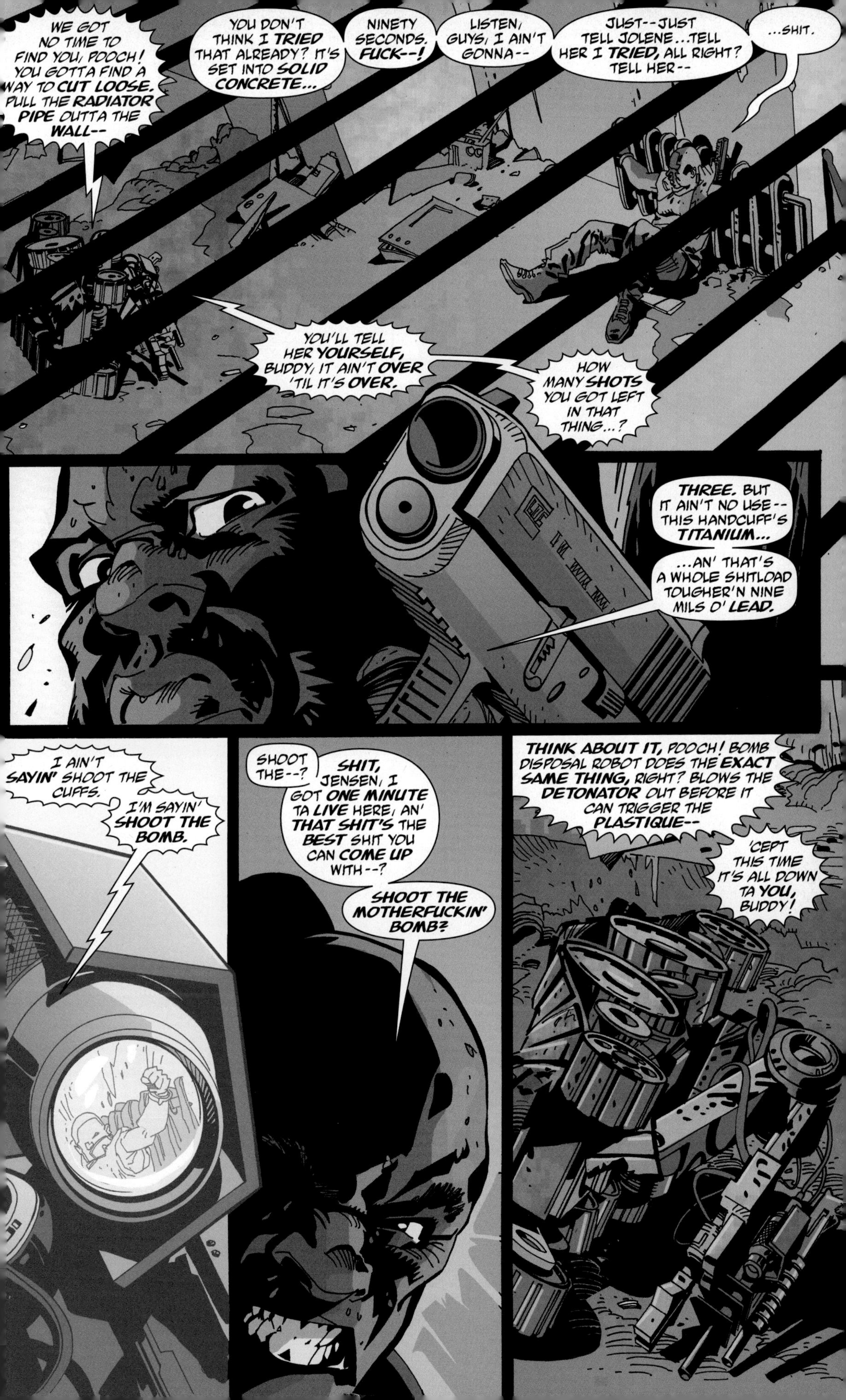
WE GOT NO TIME TO FIND YOU, POOCH! YOU GOTTA FIND A WAY TO CUT LOOSE. PULL THE RADIATOR PIPE OUTTA THE WALL--
YOU DON'T THINK I TRIED THAT ALREADY? IT'S SET INTO SOLID CONCRETE...
NINETY SECONDS. FUCK--!
LISTEN, GUYS, I AIN'T GONNA--
JUST--JUST TELL JOLENE...TELL HER I TRIED, ALL RIGHT? TELL HER--
...SHIT.
YOU'LL TELL HER YOURSELF, BUDDY, IT AIN'T OVER 'TIL IT'S OVER.
HOW MANY SHOTS YOU GOT LEFT IN THAT THING...?
THREE. BUT IT AIN'T NO USE-- THIS HANDCUFF'S TITANIUM...
...AN' THAT'S A WHOLE SHITLOAD TOUGHER'N NINE MILS O' LEAD.
I AIN'T SAYIN' SHOOT THE CUFFS.
I'M SAYIN' SHOOT THE BOMB.
SHOOT THE--?
SHIT, JENSEN, I GOT ONE MINUTE TA LIVE HERE, AN' THAT SHIT'S THE BEST SHIT YOU CAN COME UP WITH--?
SHOOT THE MOTHERFUCKIN' BOMB?
THINK ABOUT IT, POOCH! BOMB DISPOSAL ROBOT DOES THE EXACT SAME THING, RIGHT? BLOWS THE DETONATOR OUT BEFORE IT CAN TRIGGER THE PLASTIQUE--
'CEPT THIS TIME IT'S ALL DOWN TA YOU, BUDDY!

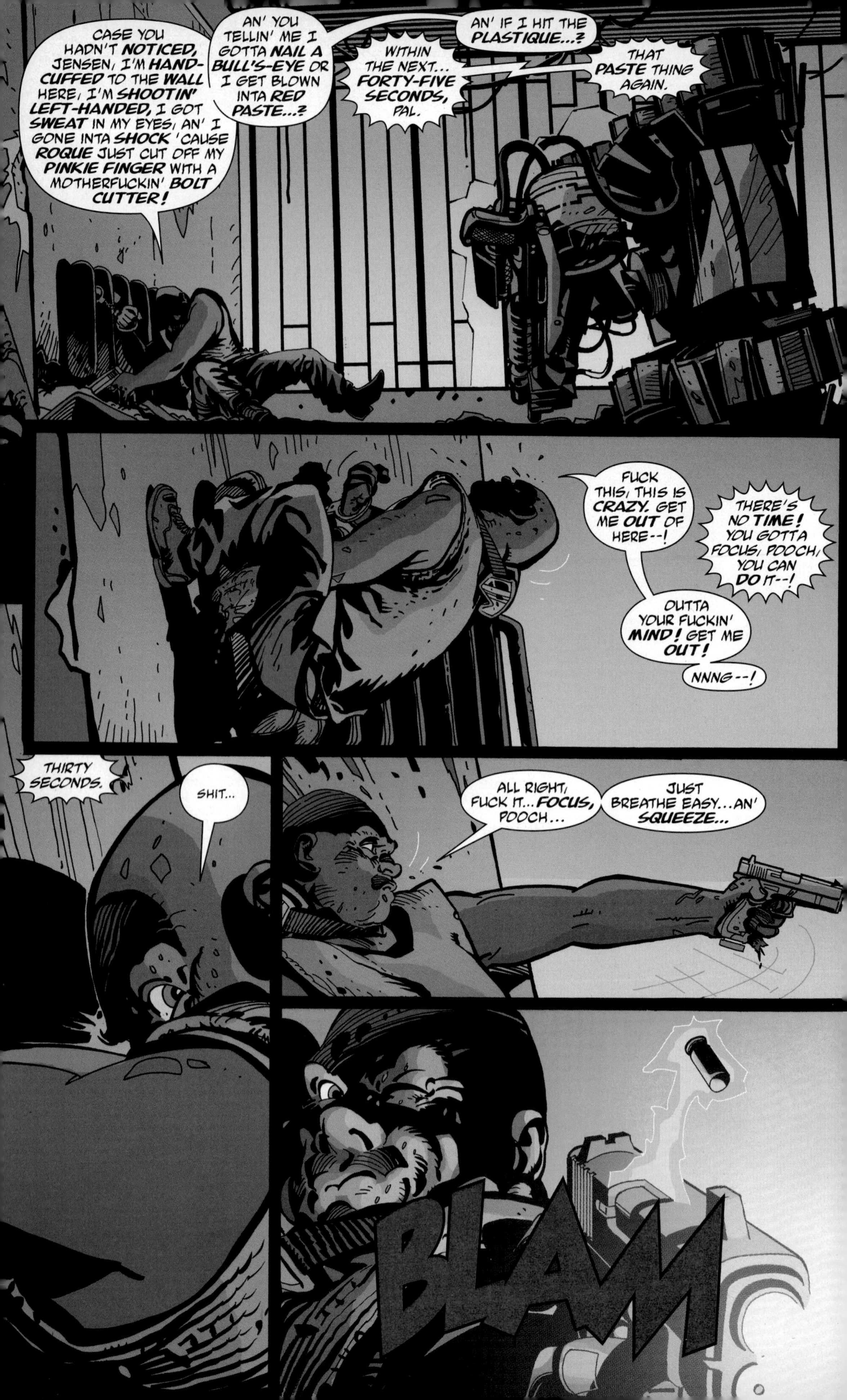
CASE YOU HADN'T NOTICED, JENSEN, I'M HAND-CUFFED TO THE WALL HERE, I'M SHOOTIN' LEFT-HANDED, I GOT SWEAT IN MY EYES, AN' I GONE INTA SHOCK 'CAUSE ROQUE JUST CUT OFF MY PINKIE FINGER WITH A MOTHERFUCKIN' BOLT CUTTER!
AN' YOU TELLIN' ME I GOTTA NAIL A BULL'S-EYE OR I GET BLOWN INTA RED PASTE...?
WITHIN THE NEXT... FORTY-FIVE SECONDS, PAL.
AN' IF I HIT THE PLASTIQUE...?
THAT PASTE THING AGAIN.
FUCK THIS, THIS IS CRAZY. GET ME OUT OF HERE--!
THERE'S NO TIME! YOU GOTTA FOCUS, POOCH, YOU CAN DO IT--!
OUTTA YOUR FUCKIN' MIND! GET ME OUT!
NNNG--!
THIRTY SECONDS.
SHIT...
ALL RIGHT, FUCK IT... FOCUS, POOCH...
JUST BREATHE EASY... AN' SQUEEZE...
BLAM

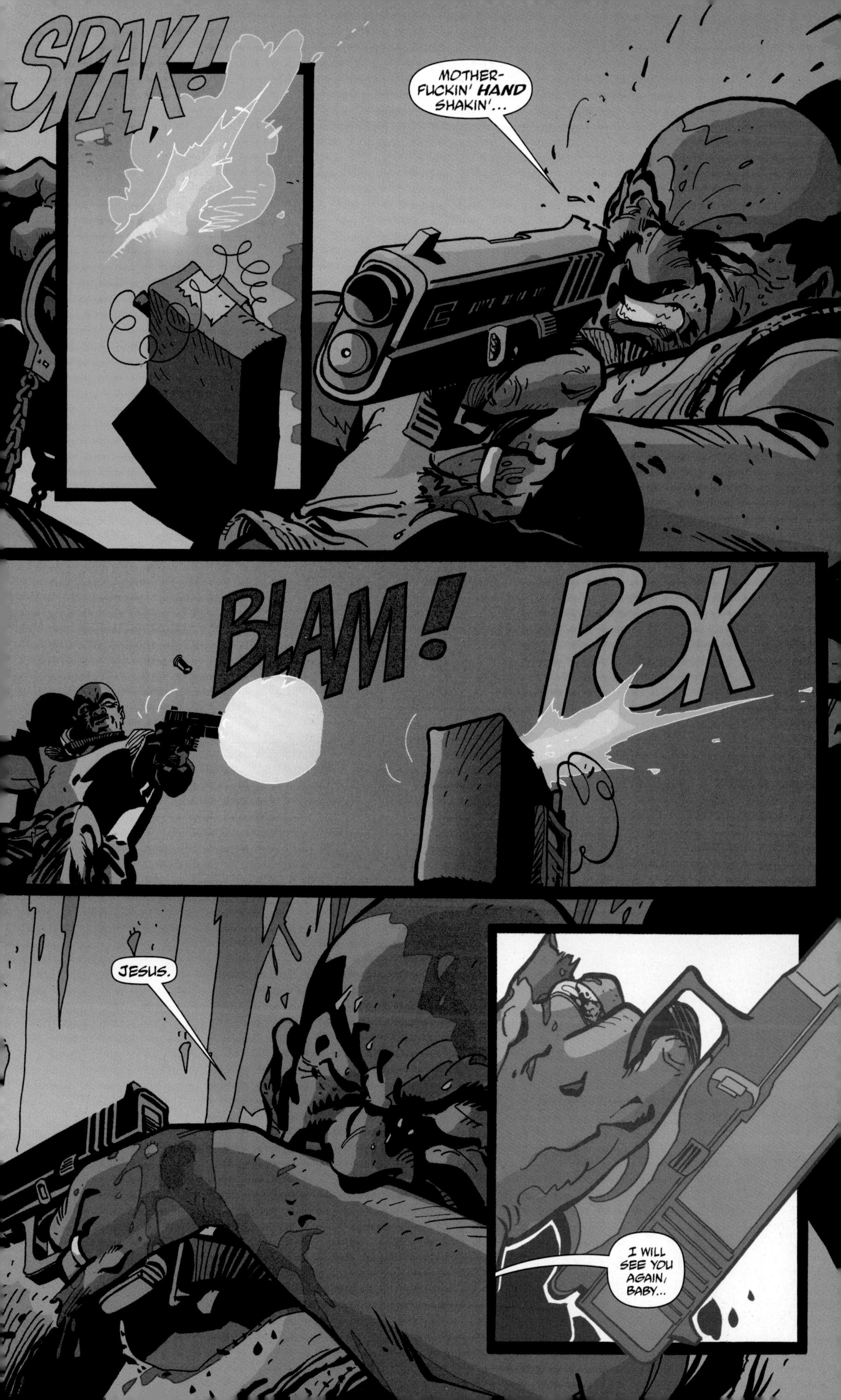
SPAK!
MOTHER-FUCKIN' HAND SHAKIN'...
BLAM!
POK
JESUS.
I WILL SEE YOU AGAIN, BABY...

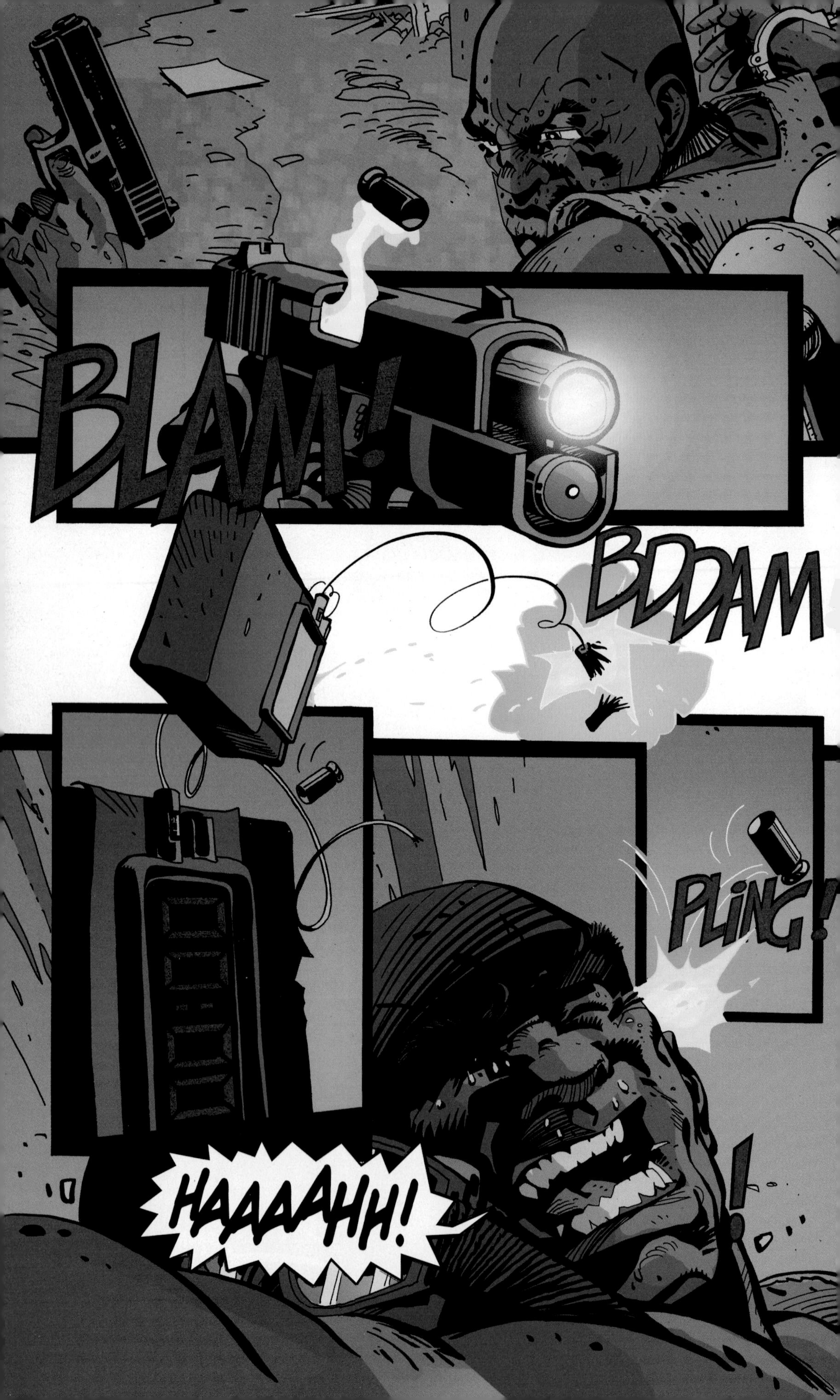
BLAM!
BDDAM
PLING!
HAAAAHH!

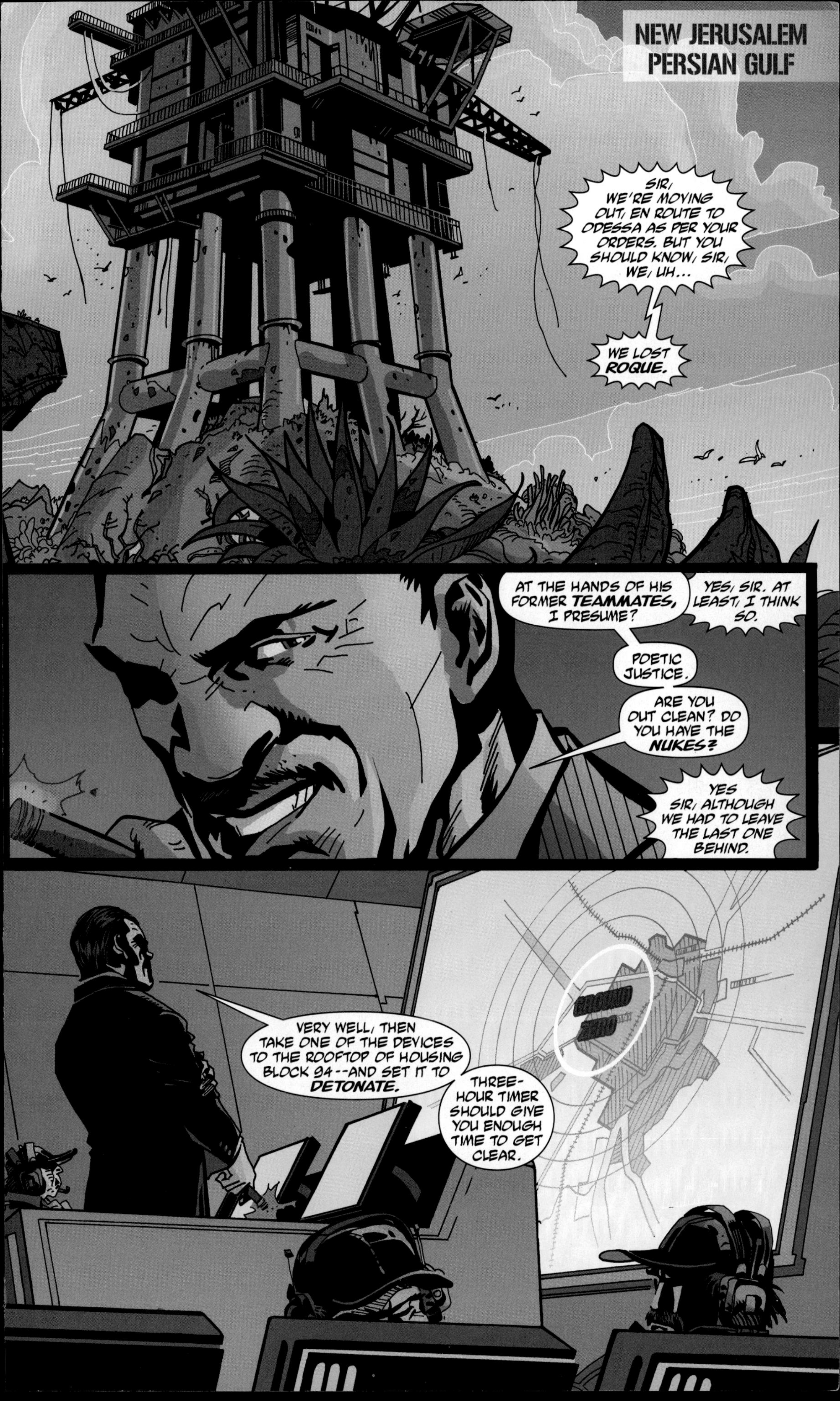
NEW JERUSALEM
PERSIAN GULF
SIR, WE'RE MOVING OUT, EN ROUTE TO ODESSA AS PER YOUR ORDERS. BUT YOU SHOULD KNOW, SIR, WE, UH...
WE LOST ROGUE.
AT THE HANDS OF HIS FORMER TEAMMATES, I PRESUME?
YES, SIR. AT LEAST, I THINK SO.
POETIC JUSTICE.
ARE YOU OUT CLEAN? DO YOU HAVE THE NUKES?
YES SIR, ALTHOUGH WE HAD TO LEAVE THE LAST ONE BEHIND.
VERY WELL, THEN TAKE ONE OF THE DEVICES TO THE ROOFTOP OF HOUSING BLOCK 94--AND SET IT TO DETONATE.
THREE-HOUR TIMER SHOULD GIVE YOU ENOUGH TIME TO GET CLEAR.
GROUND ZERO

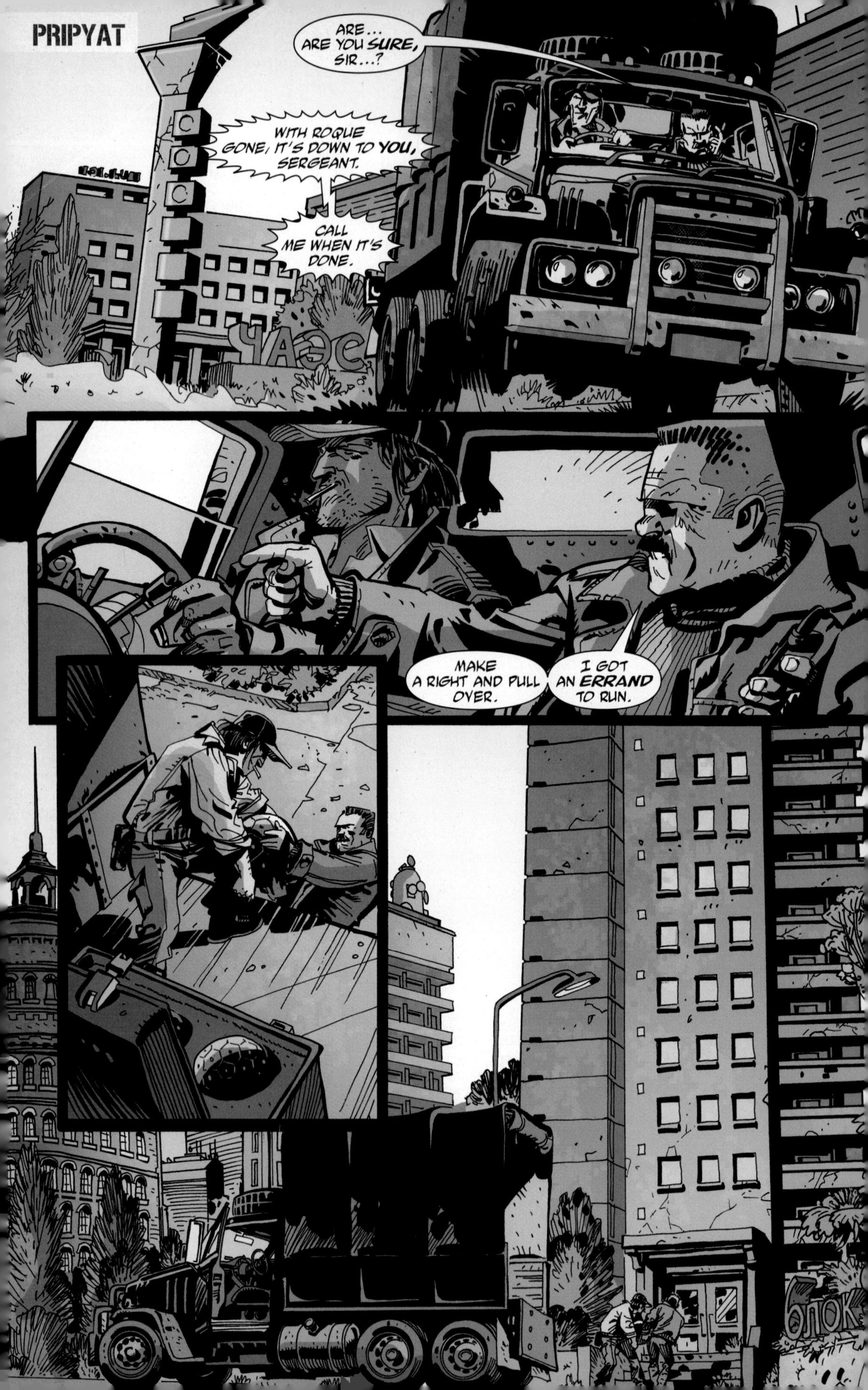
PRIPYAT
ARE... ARE YOU SURE, SIR...?
WITH ROQUE GONE, IT'S DOWN TO YOU, SERGEANT.
CALL ME WHEN IT'S DONE.
MAKE A RIGHT AND PULL OVER.
I GOT AN ERRAND TO RUN.

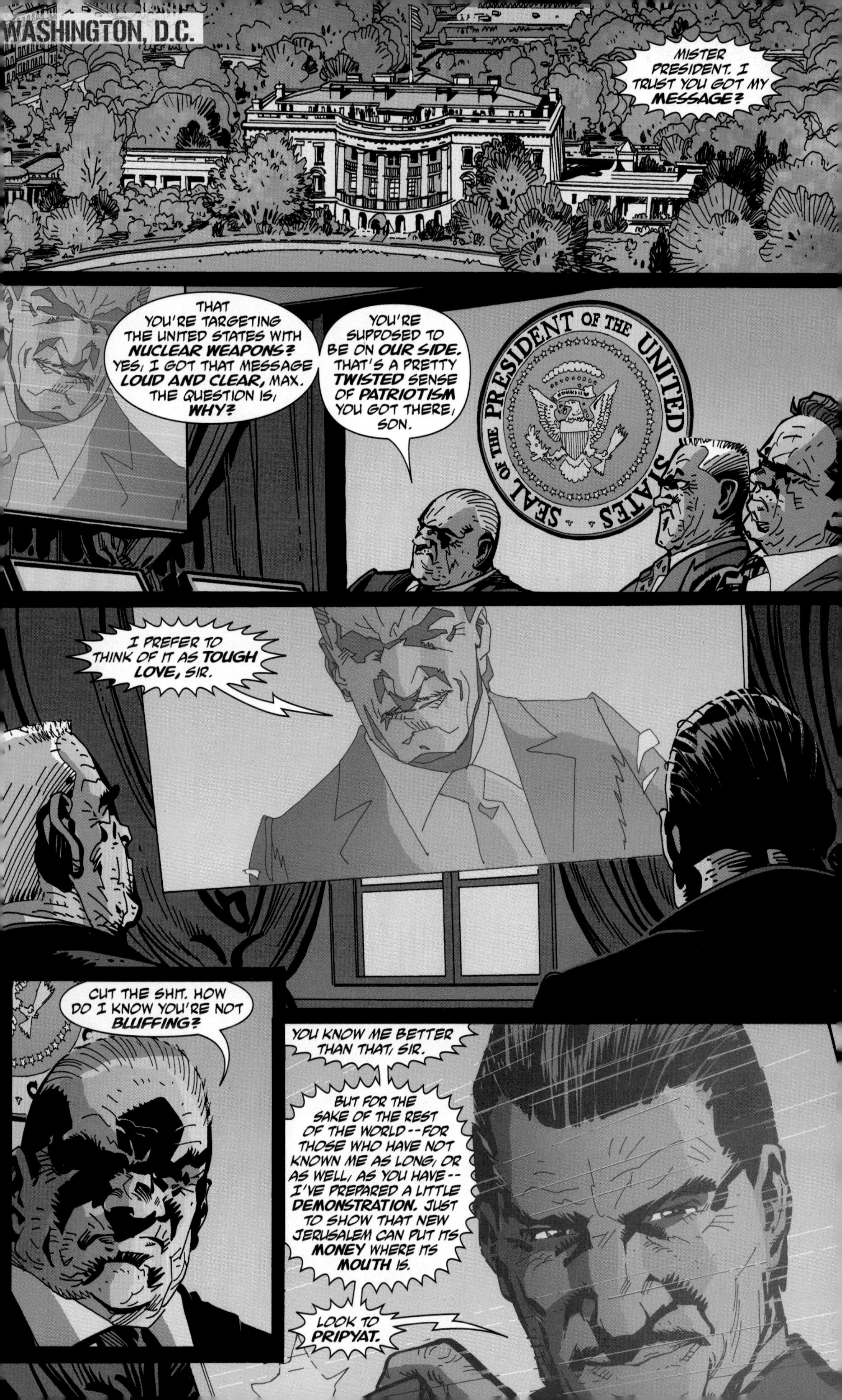
WASHINGTON, D.C.
MISTER PRESIDENT. I TRUST YOU GOT MY MESSAGE?
THAT YOU'RE TARGETING THE UNITED STATES WITH NUCLEAR WEAPONS? YES, I GOT THAT MESSAGE LOUD AND CLEAR, MAX. THE QUESTION IS, WHY?
YOU'RE SUPPOSED TO BE ON OUR SIDE. THAT'S A PRETTY TWISTED SENSE OF PATRIOTISM YOU GOT THERE, SON.
SEAL OF THE PRESIDENT OF THE UNITED STATES
I PREFER TO THINK OF IT AS TOUGH LOVE, SIR.
CUT THE SHIT. HOW DO I KNOW YOU'RE NOT BLUFFING?
YOU KNOW ME BETTER THAN THAT, SIR.
BUT FOR THE SAKE OF THE REST OF THE WORLD--FOR THOSE WHO HAVE NOT KNOWN ME AS LONG, OR AS WELL, AS YOU HAVE--I'VE PREPARED A LITTLE DEMONSTRATION. JUST TO SHOW THAT NEW JERUSALEM CAN PUT ITS MONEY WHERE ITS MOUTH IS.
LOOK TO PRIPYAT.

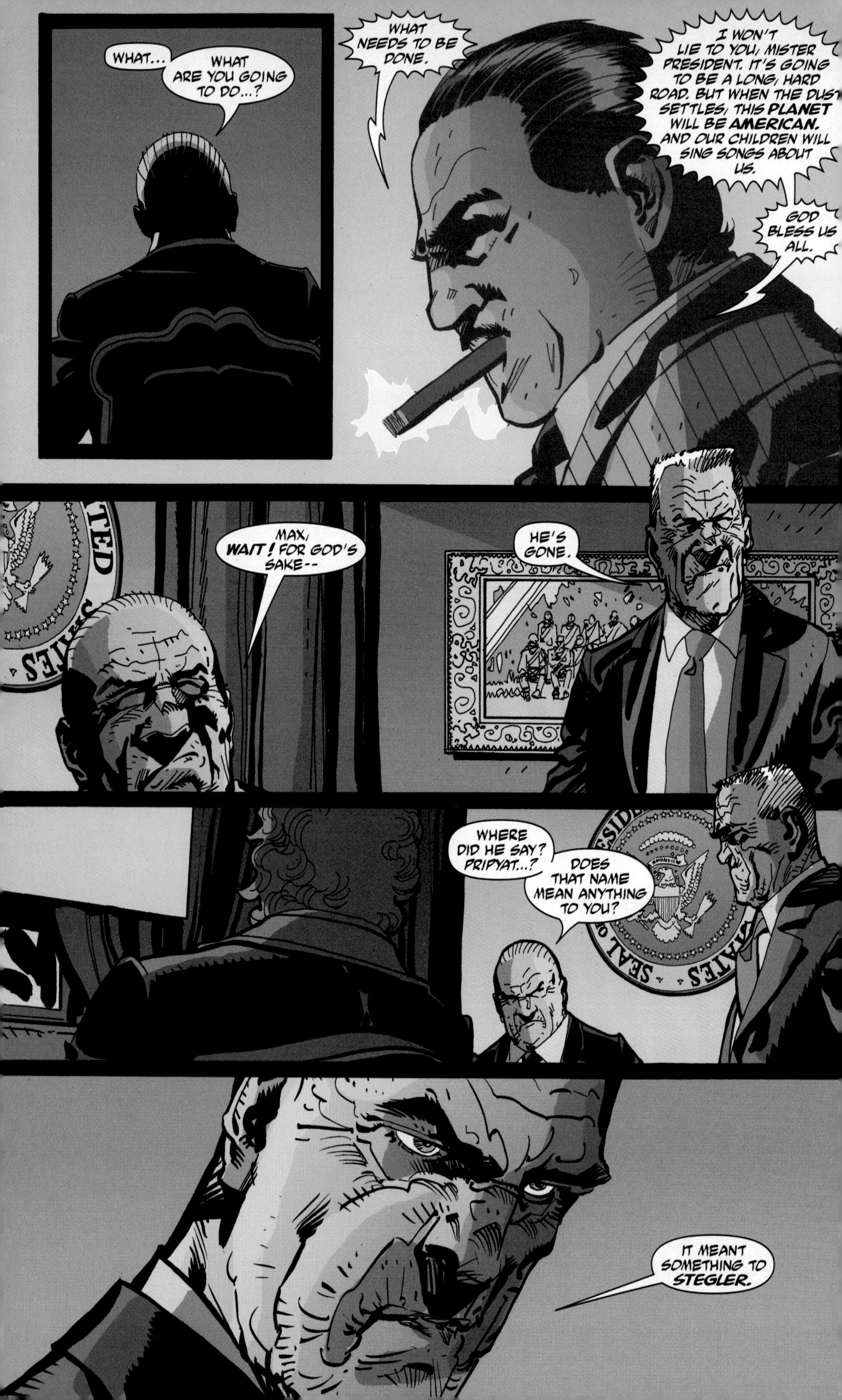

WHAT...
WHAT ARE YOU GOING TO DO...?
WHAT NEEDS TO BE DONE.
I WON'T LIE TO YOU, MISTER PRESIDENT. IT'S GOING TO BE A LONG, HARD ROAD. BUT WHEN THE DUST SETTLES, THIS PLANET WILL BE AMERICAN. AND OUR CHILDREN WILL SING SONGS ABOUT US.
GOD BLESS US ALL.
MAX, WAIT! FOR GOD'S SAKE--
HE'S GONE.
WHERE DID HE SAY? PRIPYAT...?
DOES THAT NAME MEAN ANYTHING TO YOU?
IT MEANT SOMETHING TO STEGLER.

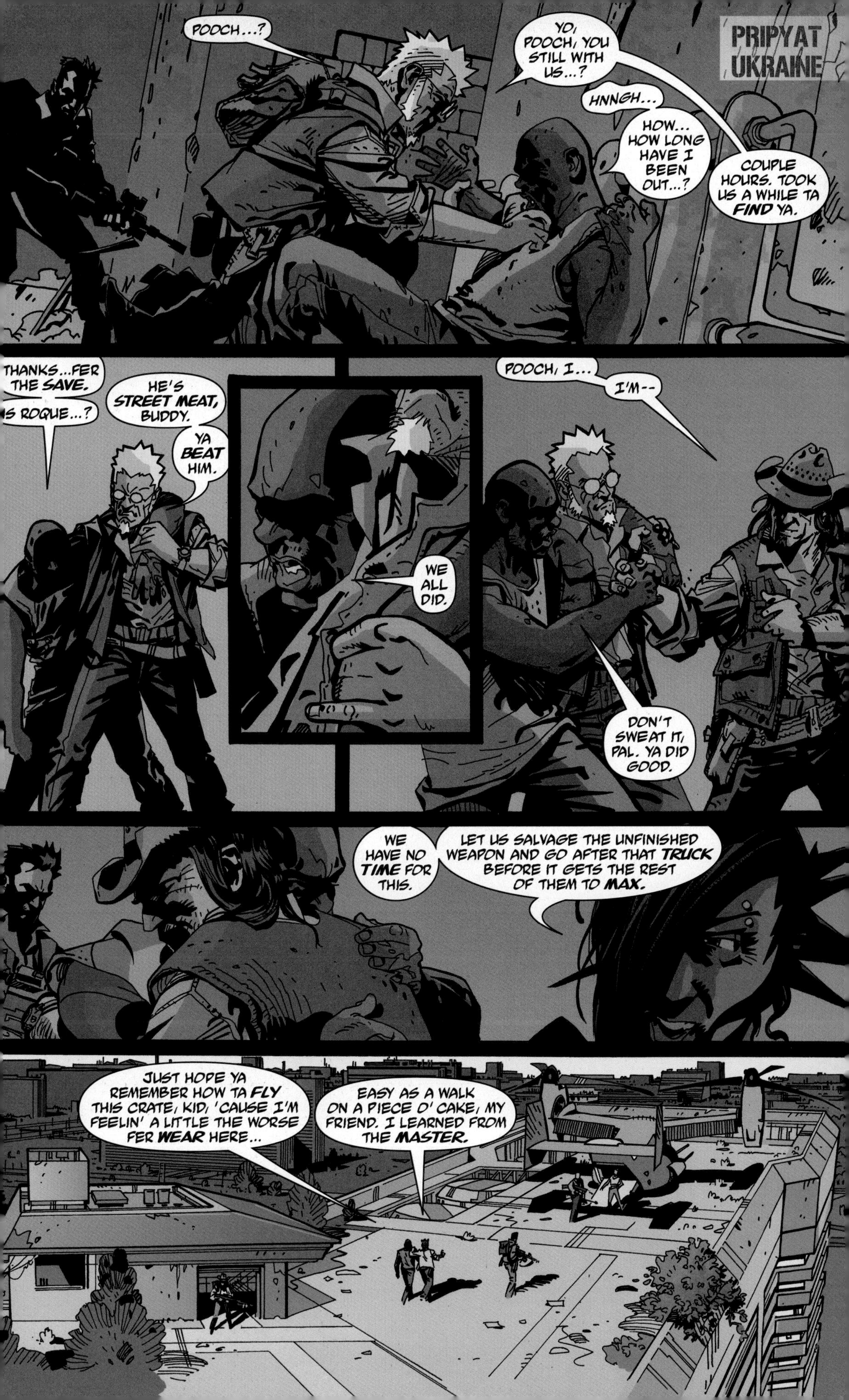
PRIPYAT UKRAINE
POOCH...?
YO, POOCH, YOU STILL WITH US...?
HNNGH...
HOW... HOW LONG HAVE I BEEN OUT...?
COUPLE HOURS. TOOK US A WHILE TA FIND YA.
THANKS...FER THE SAVE.
S ROQUE...?
HE'S STREET MEAT, BUDDY.
YA BEAT HIM.
WE ALL DID.
POOCH, I...
I'M--
DON'T SWEAT IT, PAL. YA DID GOOD.
WE HAVE NO TIME FOR THIS.
LET US SALVAGE THE UNFINISHED WEAPON AND GO AFTER THAT TRUCK BEFORE IT GETS THE REST OF THEM TO MAX.
JUST HOPE YA REMEMBER HOW TA FLY THIS CRATE, KID, 'CAUSE I'M FEELIN' A LITTLE THE WORSE FER WEAR HERE...
EASY AS A WALK ON A PIECE O' CAKE, MY FRIEND. I LEARNED FROM THE MASTER.

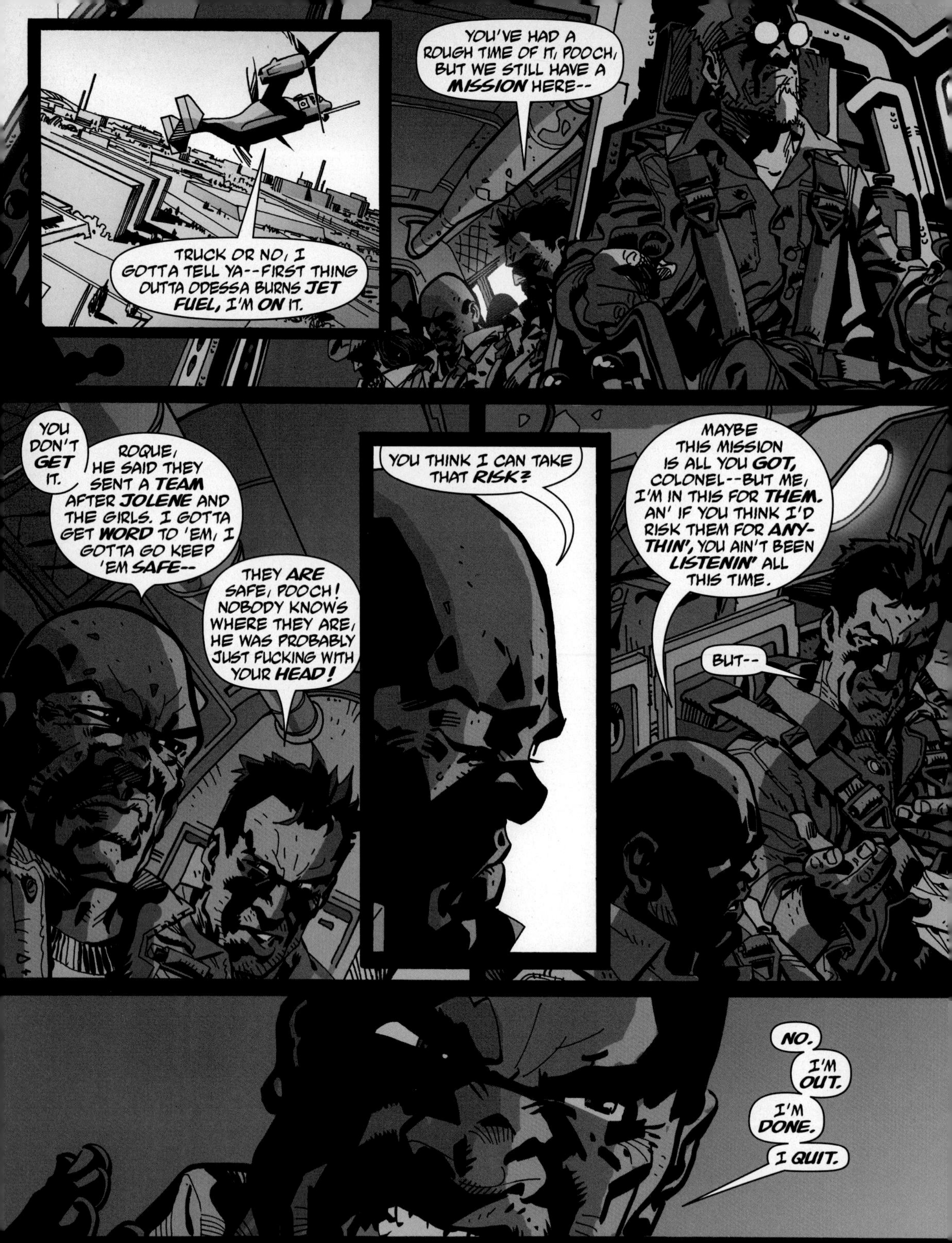
YOU'VE HAD A ROUGH TIME OF IT, POOCH, BUT WE STILL HAVE A MISSION HERE--
TRUCK OR NO, I GOTTA TELL YA--FIRST THING OUTTA ODESSA BURNS JET FUEL, I'M ON IT.
YOU DON'T GET IT.
ROQUE, HE SAID THEY SENT A TEAM AFTER JOLENE AND THE GIRLS. I GOTTA GET WORD TO 'EM, I GOTTA GO KEEP 'EM SAFE--
THEY ARE SAFE, POOCH! NOBODY KNOWS WHERE THEY ARE, HE WAS PROBABLY JUST FUCKING WITH YOUR HEAD!
YOU THINK I CAN TAKE THAT RISK?
MAYBE THIS MISSION IS ALL YOU GOT, COLONEL--BUT ME, I'M IN THIS FOR THEM. AN' IF YOU THINK I'D RISK THEM FOR ANYTHIN', YOU AIN'T BEEN LISTENIN' ALL THIS TIME.
BUT--
NO.
I'M OUT.
I'M DONE.
I QUIT.

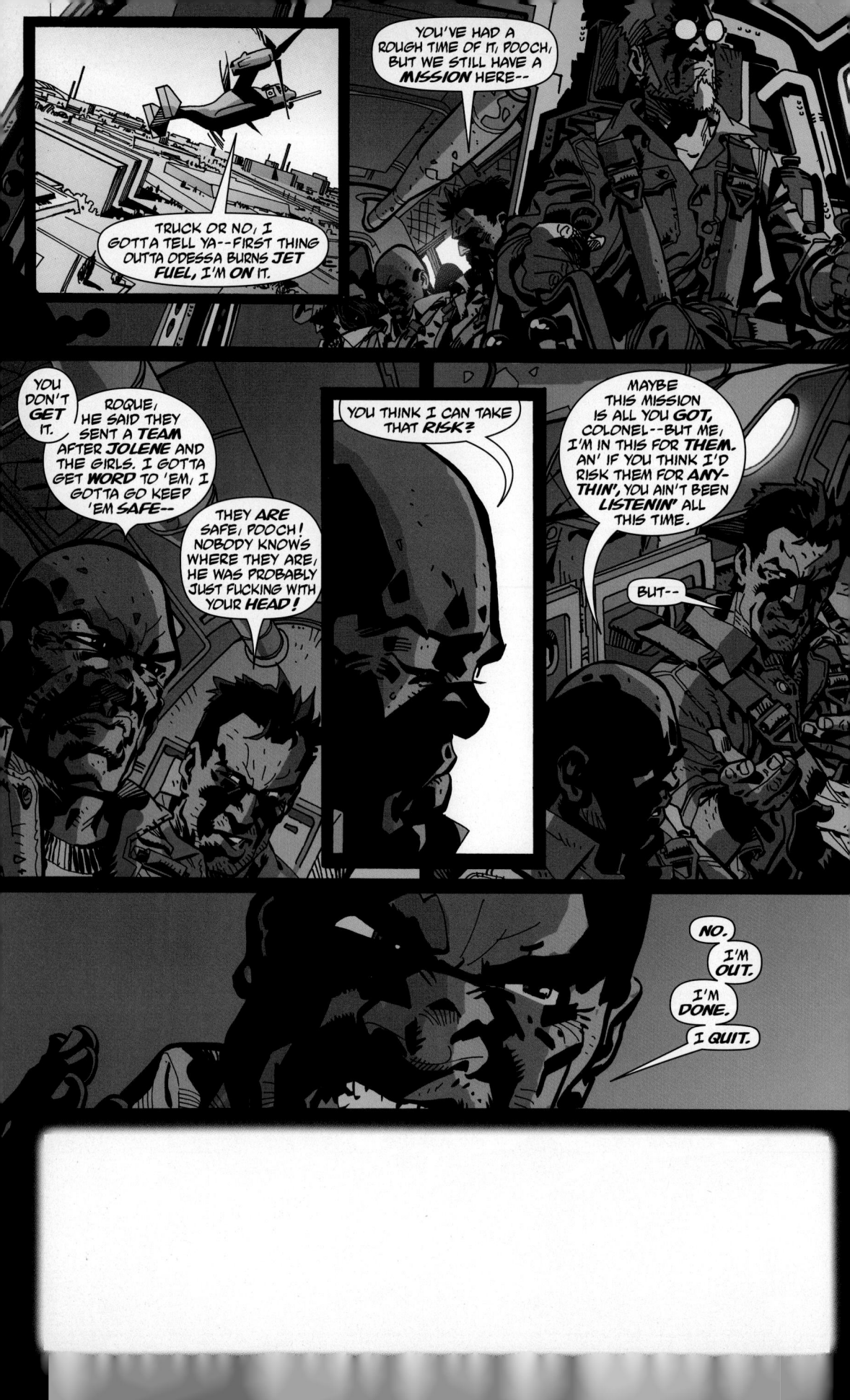

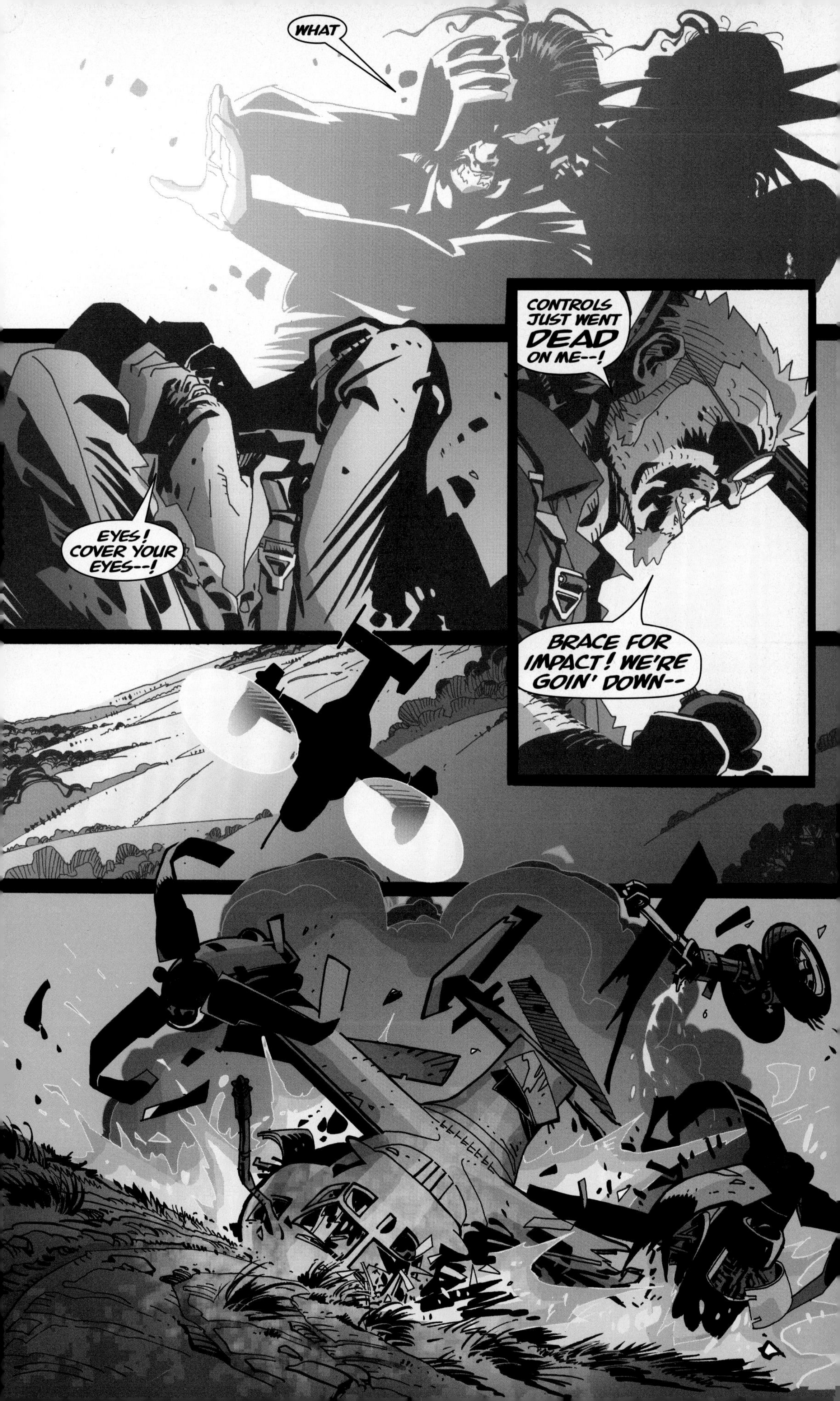
WHAT
CONTROLS JUST WENT DEAD ON ME--!
EYES! COVER YOUR EYES--!
BRACE FOR IMPACT! WE'RE GOIN' DOWN--

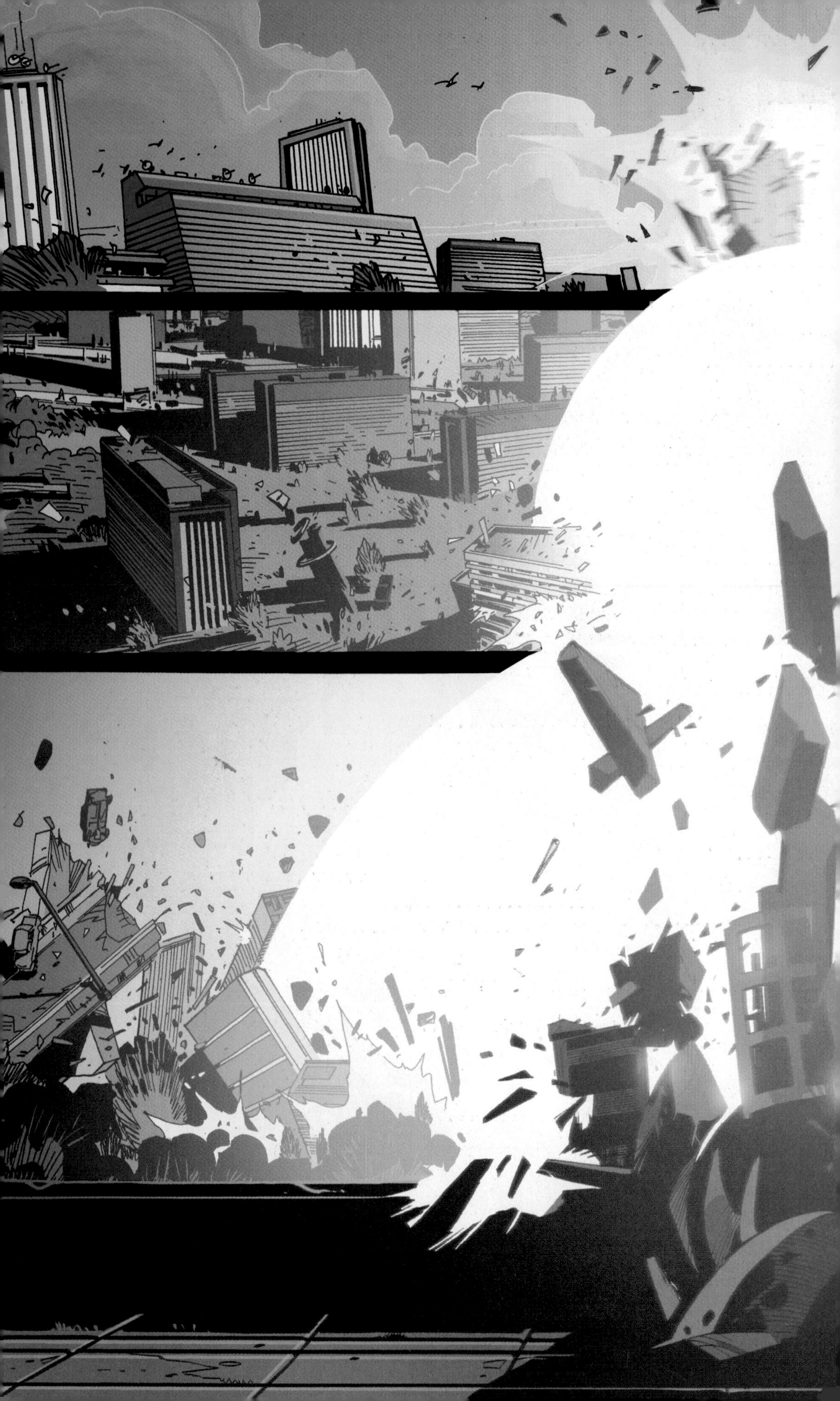

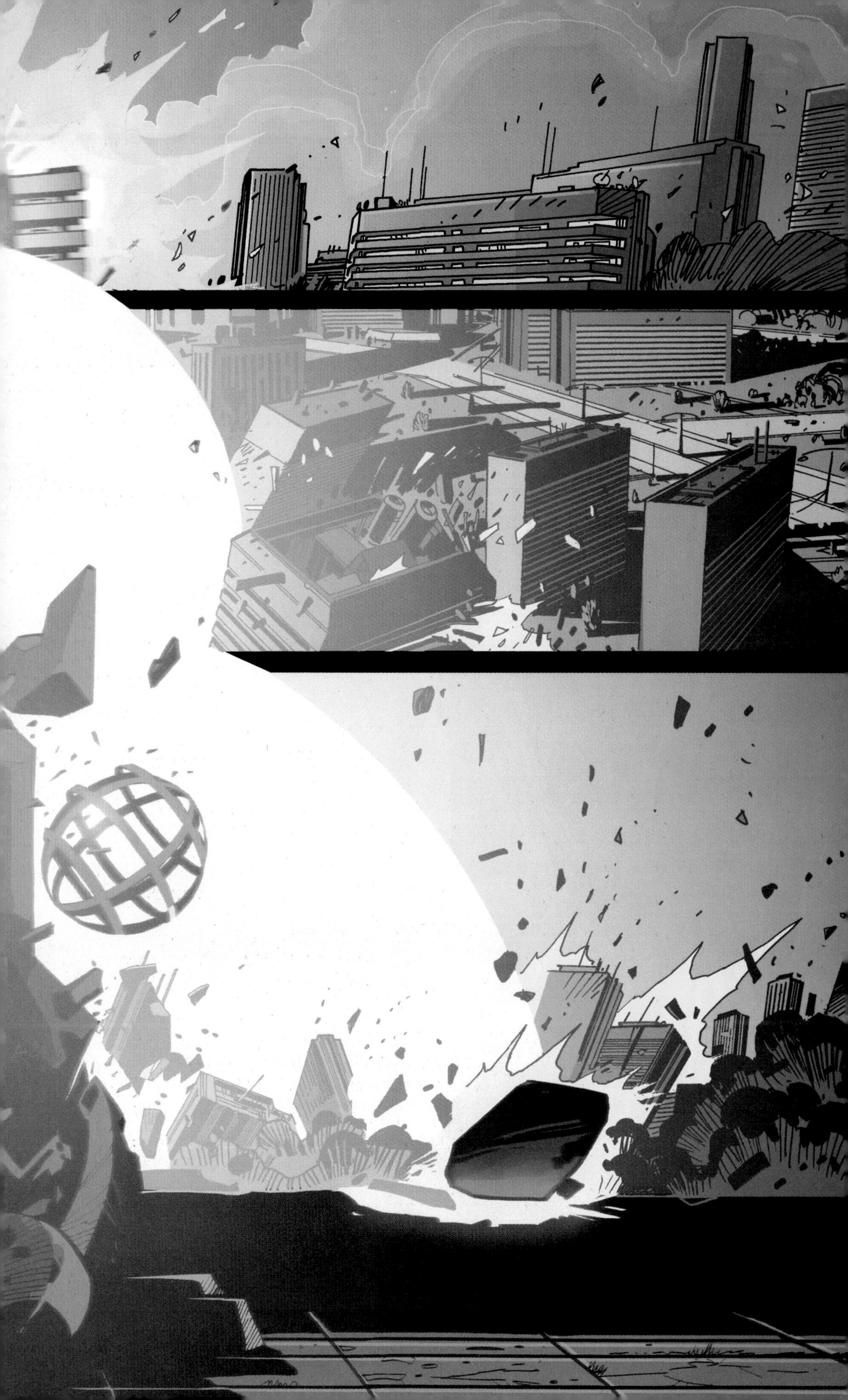

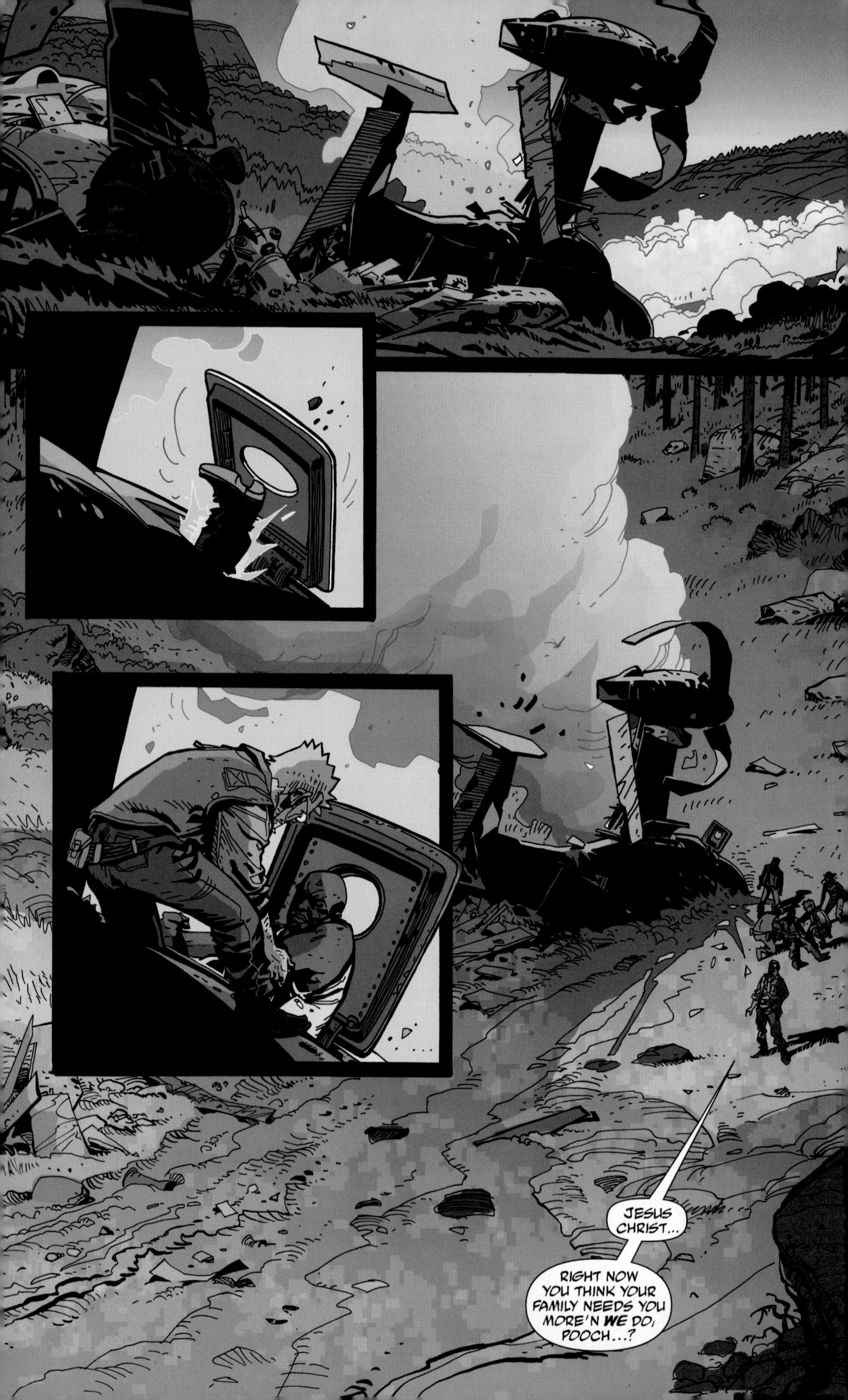
JESUS CHRIST...
RIGHT NOW YOU THINK YOUR FAMILY NEEDS YOU MORE'N WE DO, POOCH...?

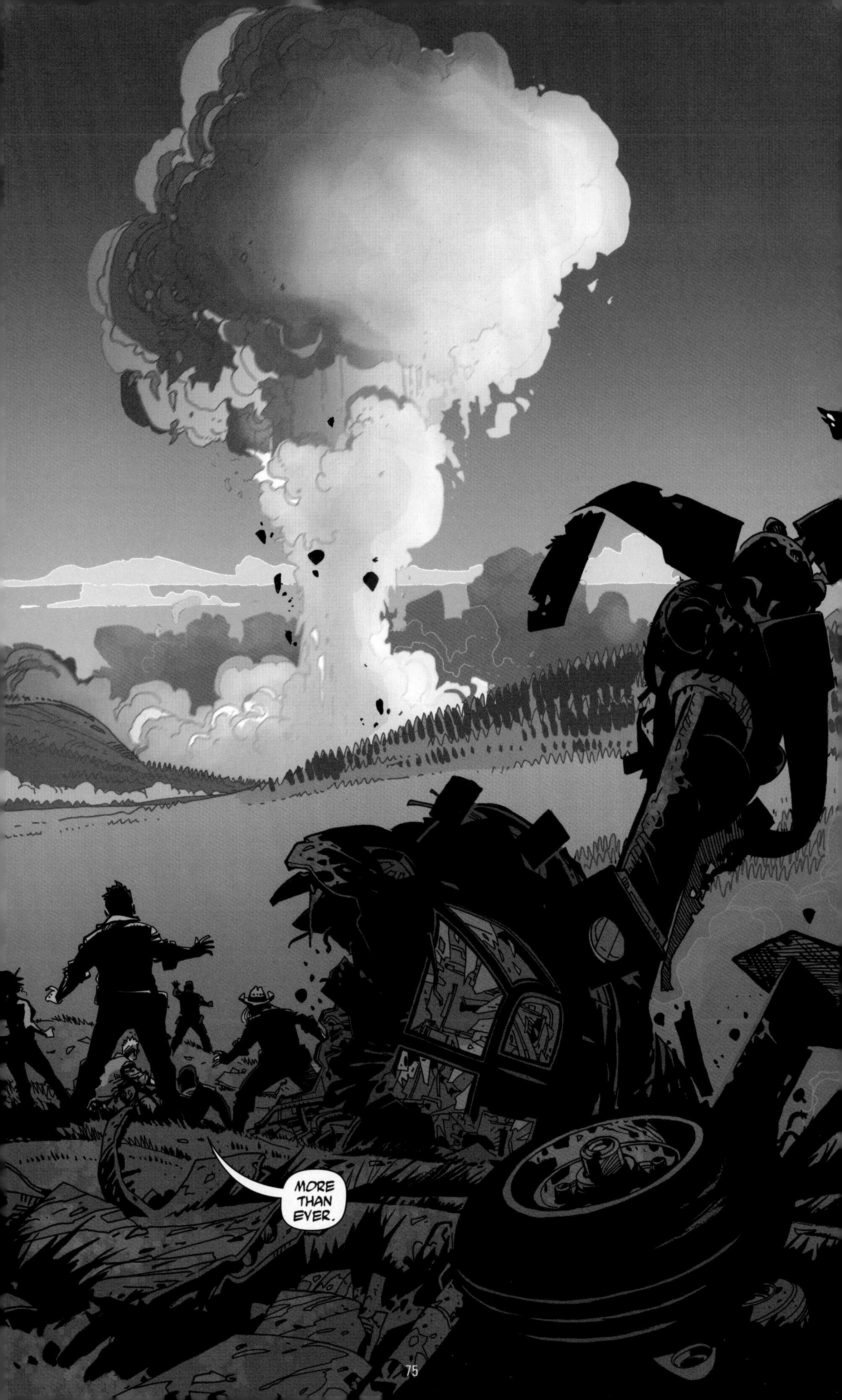
MORE THAN EVER.

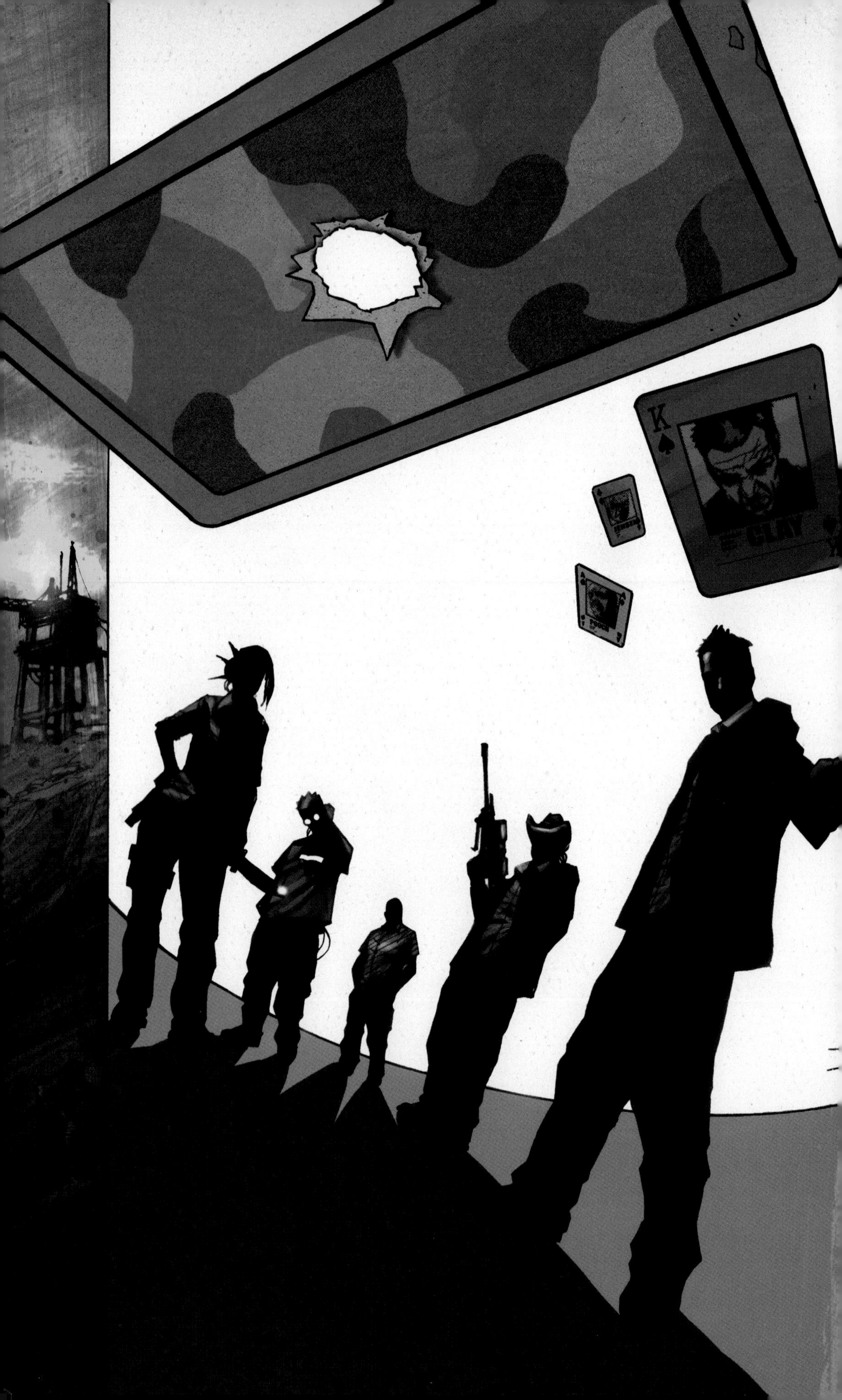

K
CLAY
JENSEN
POOCH

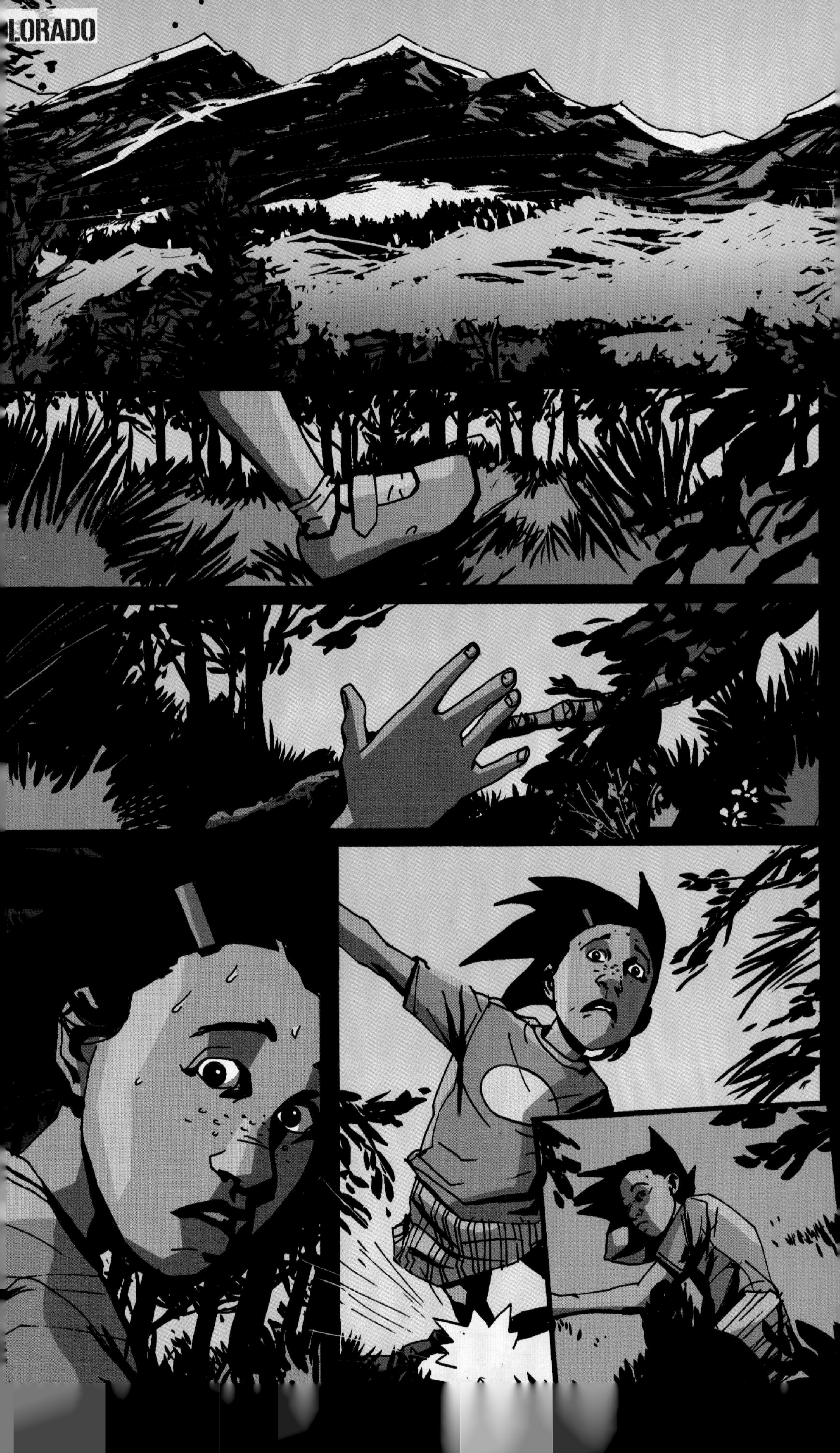
LORADO

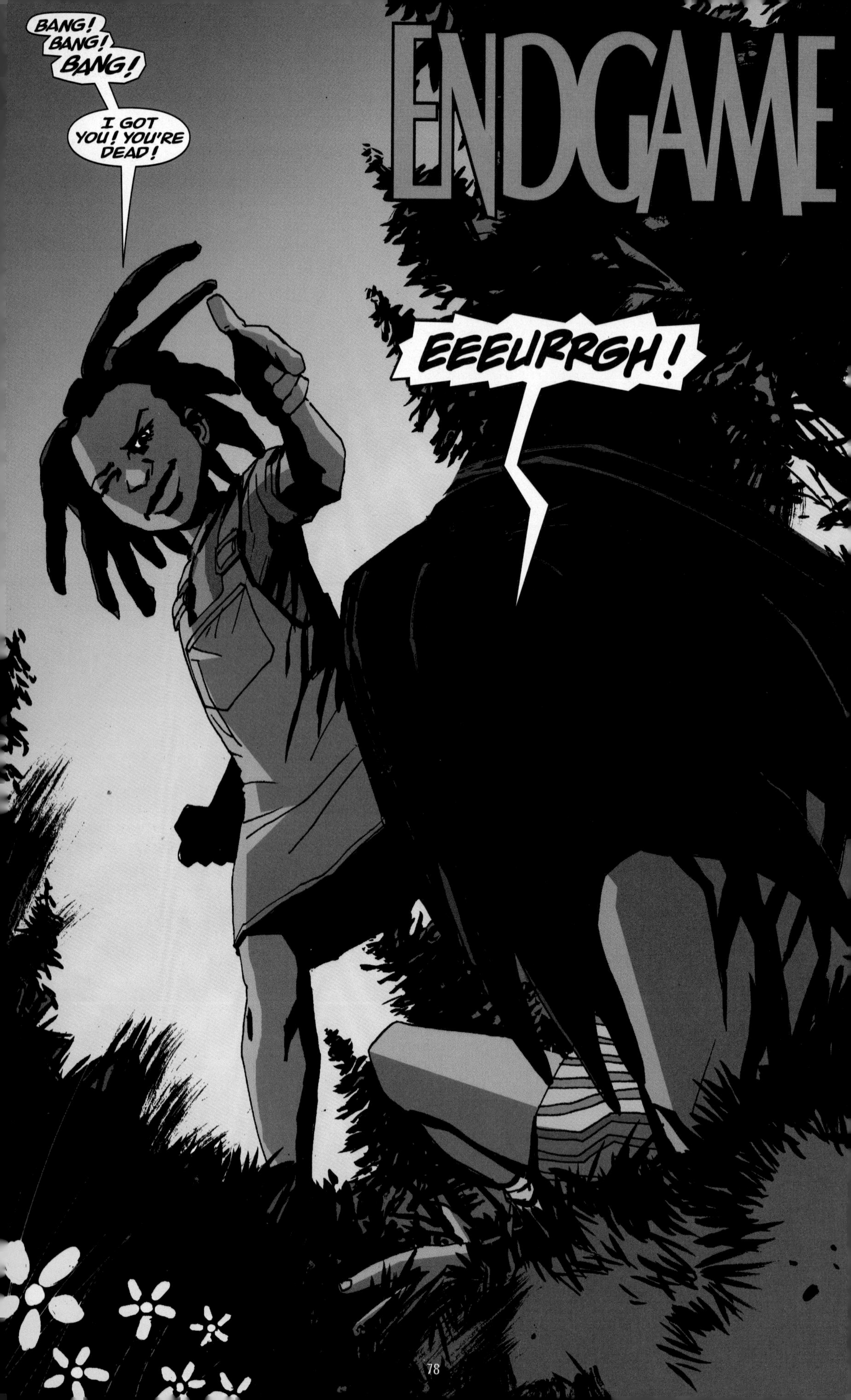
ENDGAME
BANG! BANG! BANG!
I GOT YOU! YOU'RE DEAD!
EEEURRGH!

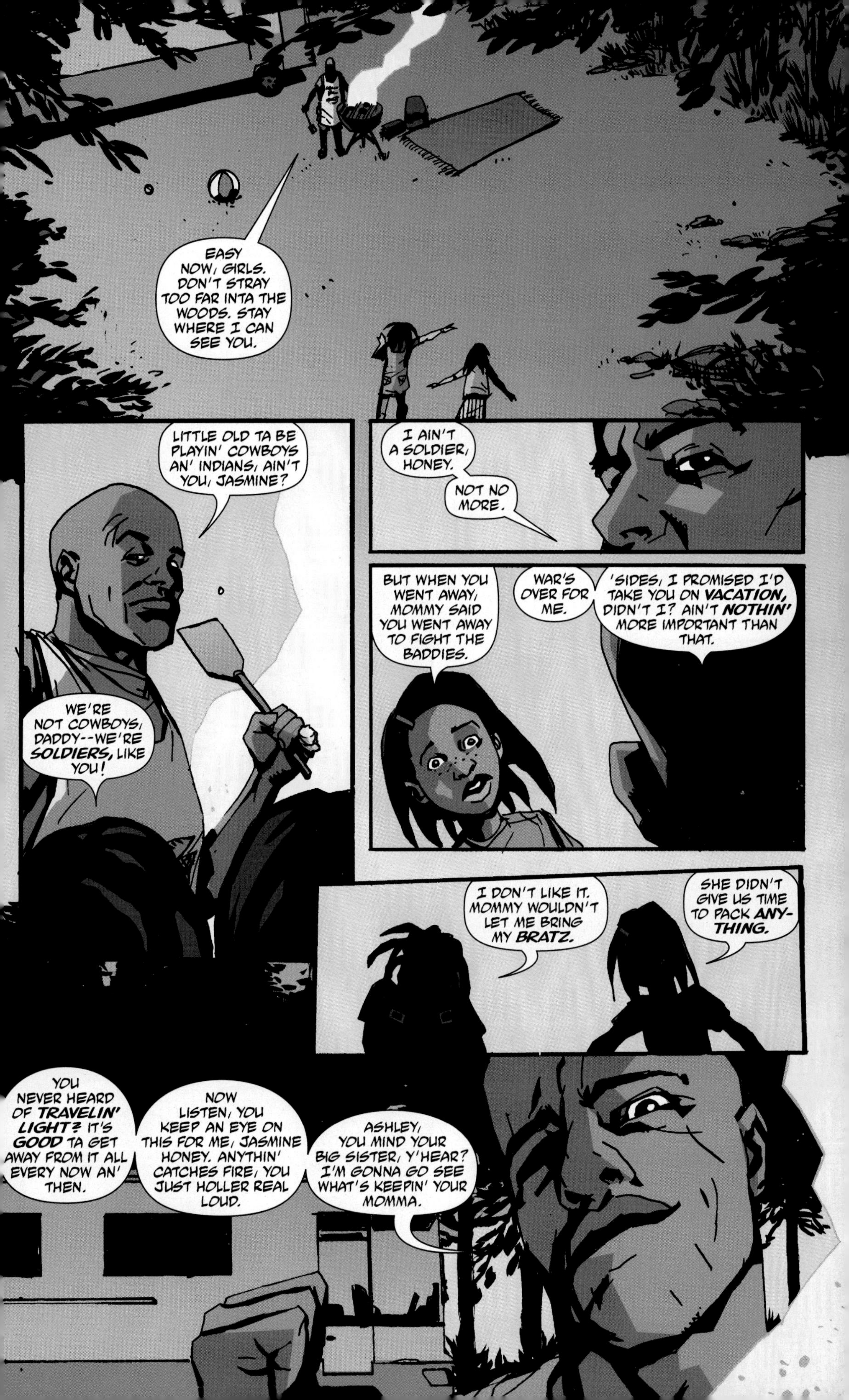
EASY NOW, GIRLS. DON'T STRAY TOO FAR INTA THE WOODS. STAY WHERE I CAN SEE YOU.
LITTLE OLD TA BE PLAYIN' COWBOYS AN' INDIANS, AIN'T YOU, JASMINE?
WE'RE NOT COWBOYS, DADDY--WE'RE SOLDIERS, LIKE YOU!
I AIN'T A SOLDIER, HONEY.
NOT NO MORE.
BUT WHEN YOU WENT AWAY, MOMMY SAID YOU WENT AWAY TO FIGHT THE BADDIES.
WAR'S OVER FOR ME.
'SIDES, I PROMISED I'D TAKE YOU ON VACATION, DIDN'T I? AIN'T NOTHIN' MORE IMPORTANT THAN THAT.
I DON'T LIKE IT. MOMMY WOULDN'T LET ME BRING MY BRATZ.
SHE DIDN'T GIVE US TIME TO PACK ANY-THING.
YOU NEVER HEARD OF TRAVELIN' LIGHT? IT'S GOOD TA GET AWAY FROM IT ALL EVERY NOW AN' THEN.
NOW LISTEN, YOU KEEP AN EYE ON THIS FOR ME, JASMINE HONEY. ANYTHIN' CATCHES FIRE, YOU JUST HOLLER REAL LOUD.
ASHLEY, YOU MIND YOUR BIG SISTER, Y'HEAR? I'M GONNA GO SEE WHAT'S KEEPIN' YOUR MOMMA.

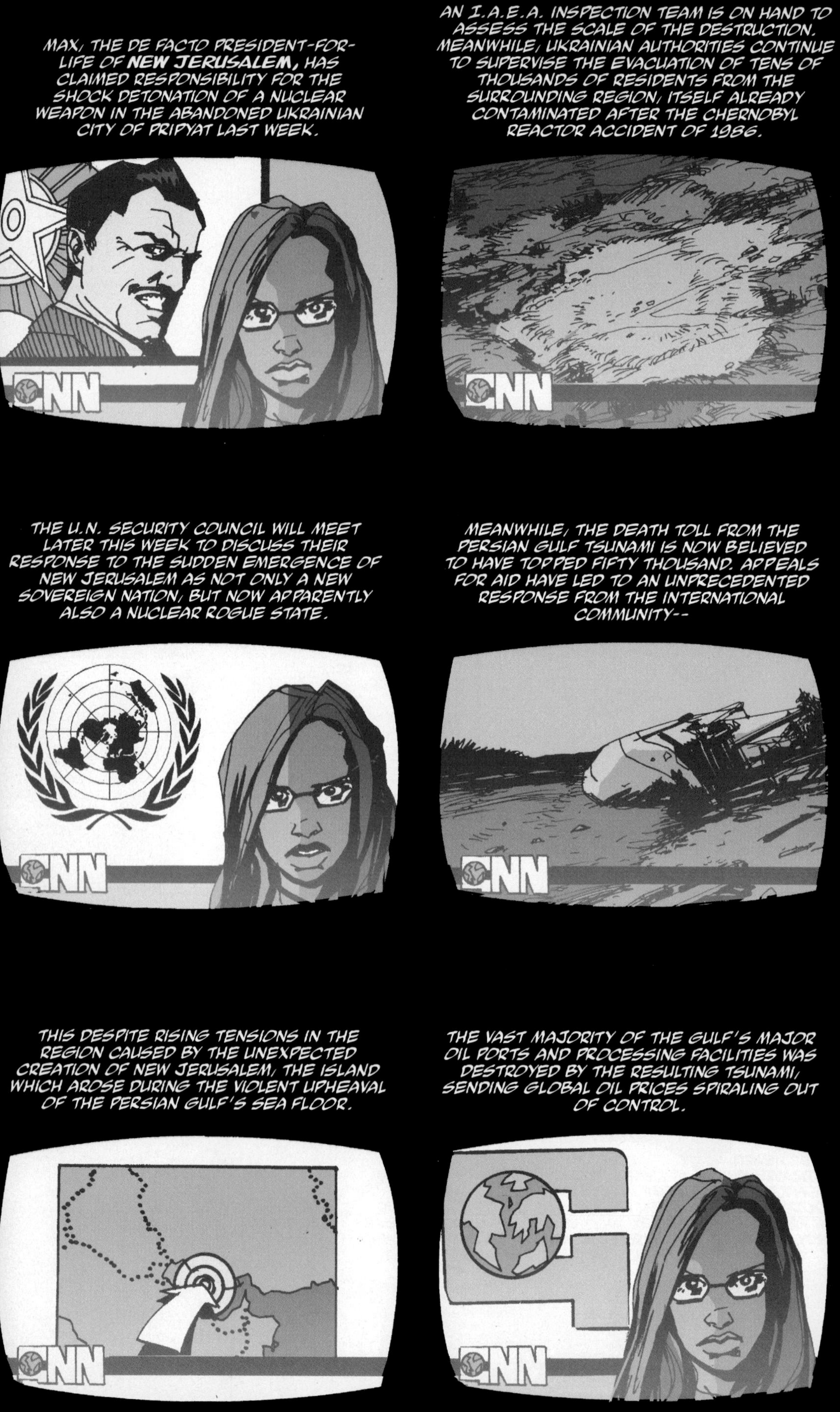
MAX, THE DE FACTO PRESIDENT-FOR-LIFE OF **NEW JERUSALEM,** HAS CLAIMED RESPONSIBILITY FOR THE SHOCK DETONATION OF A NUCLEAR WEAPON IN THE ABANDONED UKRAINIAN CITY OF PRIPYAT LAST WEEK.
AN I.A.E.A. INSPECTION TEAM IS ON HAND TO ASSESS THE SCALE OF THE DESTRUCTION. MEANWHILE, UKRAINIAN AUTHORITIES CONTINUE TO SUPERVISE THE EVACUATION OF TENS OF THOUSANDS OF RESIDENTS FROM THE SURROUNDING REGION, ITSELF ALREADY CONTAMINATED AFTER THE CHERNOBYL REACTOR ACCIDENT OF 1986.
THE U.N. SECURITY COUNCIL WILL MEET LATER THIS WEEK TO DISCUSS THEIR RESPONSE TO THE SUDDEN EMERGENCE OF NEW JERUSALEM AS NOT ONLY A NEW SOVEREIGN NATION, BUT NOW APPARENTLY ALSO A NUCLEAR ROGUE STATE.
MEANWHILE, THE DEATH TOLL FROM THE PERSIAN GULF TSUNAMI IS NOW BELIEVED TO HAVE TOPPED FIFTY THOUSAND. APPEALS FOR AID HAVE LED TO AN UNPRECEDENTED RESPONSE FROM THE INTERNATIONAL COMMUNITY--
THIS DESPITE RISING TENSIONS IN THE REGION CAUSED BY THE UNEXPECTED CREATION OF NEW JERUSALEM, THE ISLAND WHICH AROSE DURING THE VIOLENT UPHEAVAL OF THE PERSIAN GULF'S SEA FLOOR.
THE VAST MAJORITY OF THE GULF'S MAJOR OIL PORTS AND PROCESSING FACILITIES WAS DESTROYED BY THE RESULTING TSUNAMI, SENDING GLOBAL OIL PRICES SPIRALING OUT OF CONTROL.

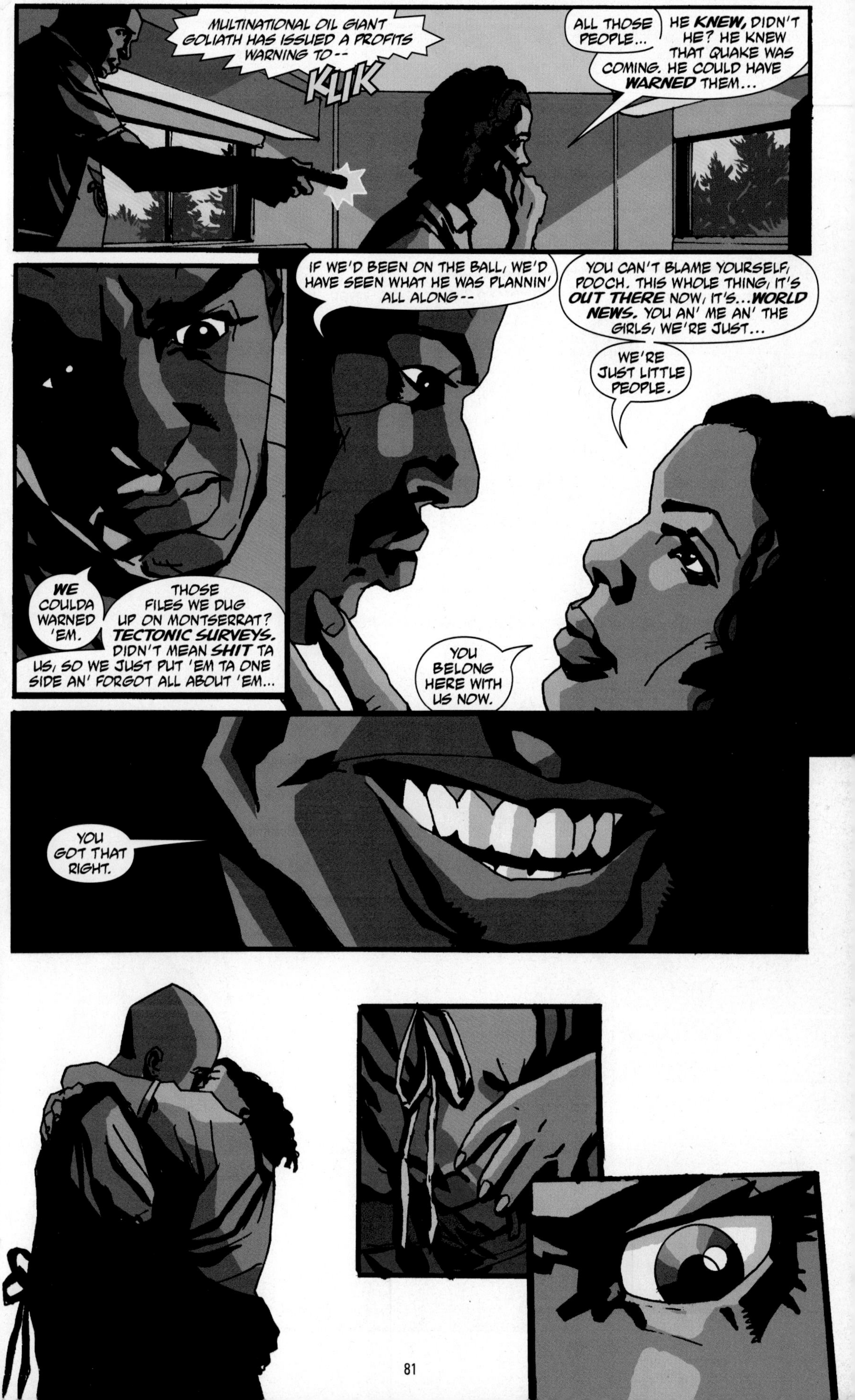
MULTINATIONAL OIL GIANT GOLIATH HAS ISSUED A PROFITS WARNING TO--
KLIK
ALL THOSE PEOPLE...
HE KNEW, DIDN'T HE? HE KNEW THAT QUAKE WAS COMING. HE COULD HAVE WARNED THEM...
IF WE'D BEEN ON THE BALL, WE'D HAVE SEEN WHAT HE WAS PLANNIN' ALL ALONG--
WE COULDA WARNED 'EM.
THOSE FILES WE DUG UP ON MONTSERRAT? TECTONIC SURVEYS. DIDN'T MEAN SHIT TA US, SO WE JUST PUT 'EM TA ONE SIDE AN' FORGOT ALL ABOUT 'EM...
YOU CAN'T BLAME YOURSELF, POOCH. THIS WHOLE THING, IT'S OUT THERE NOW, IT'S...WORLD NEWS. YOU AN' ME AN' THE GIRLS, WE'RE JUST...
WE'RE JUST LITTLE PEOPLE.
YOU BELONG HERE WITH US NOW.
YOU GOT THAT RIGHT.

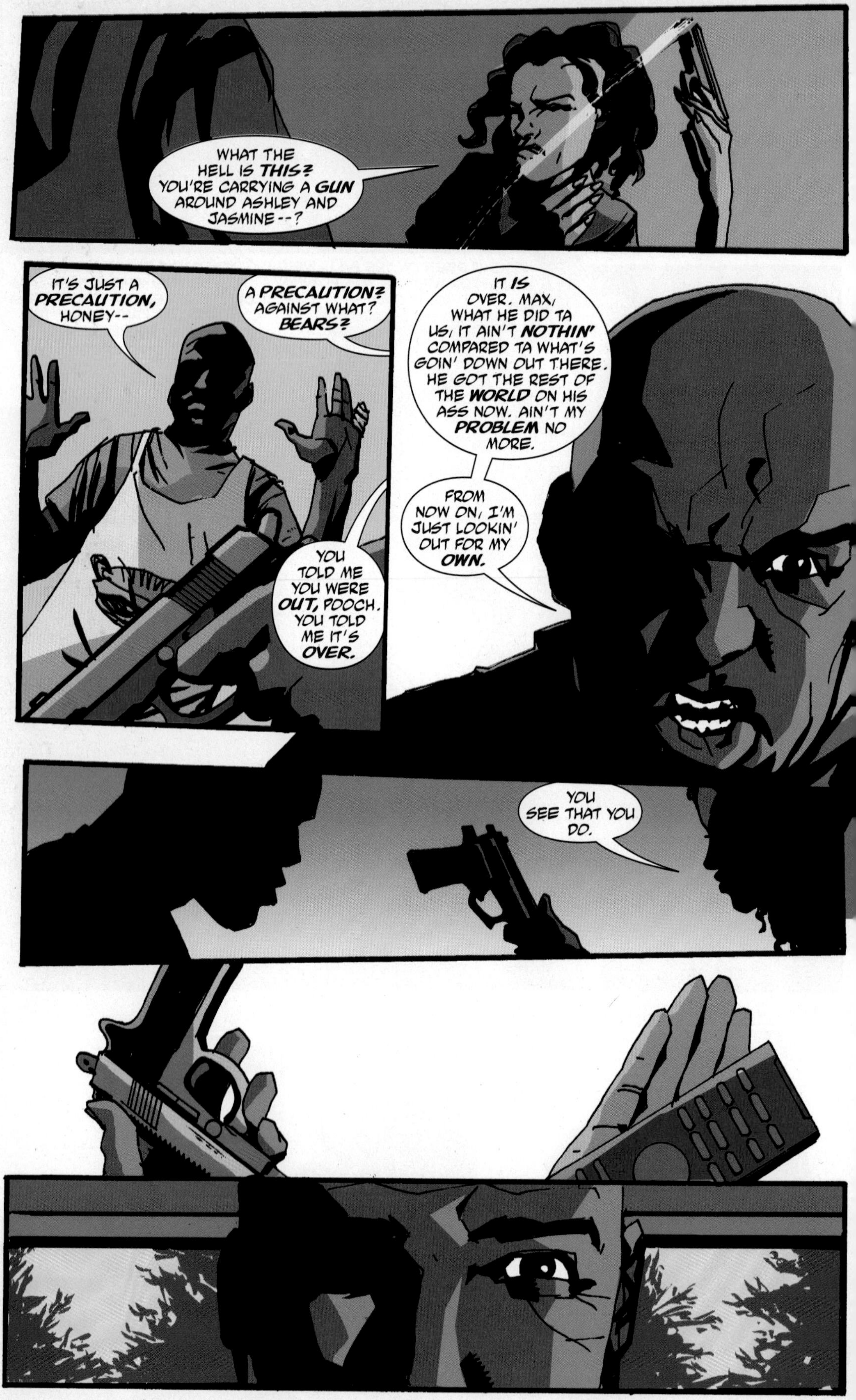
WHAT THE HELL IS THIS? YOU'RE CARRYING A GUN AROUND ASHLEY AND JASMINE--?
IT'S JUST A PRECAUTION, HONEY--
A PRECAUTION? AGAINST WHAT? BEARS?
YOU TOLD ME YOU WERE OUT, POOCH. YOU TOLD ME IT'S OVER.
IT IS OVER. MAX, WHAT HE DID TA US, IT AIN'T NOTHIN' COMPARED TA WHAT'S GOIN' DOWN OUT THERE. HE GOT THE REST OF THE WORLD ON HIS ASS NOW. AIN'T MY PROBLEM NO MORE.
FROM NOW ON, I'M JUST LOOKIN' OUT FOR MY OWN.
YOU SEE THAT YOU DO.

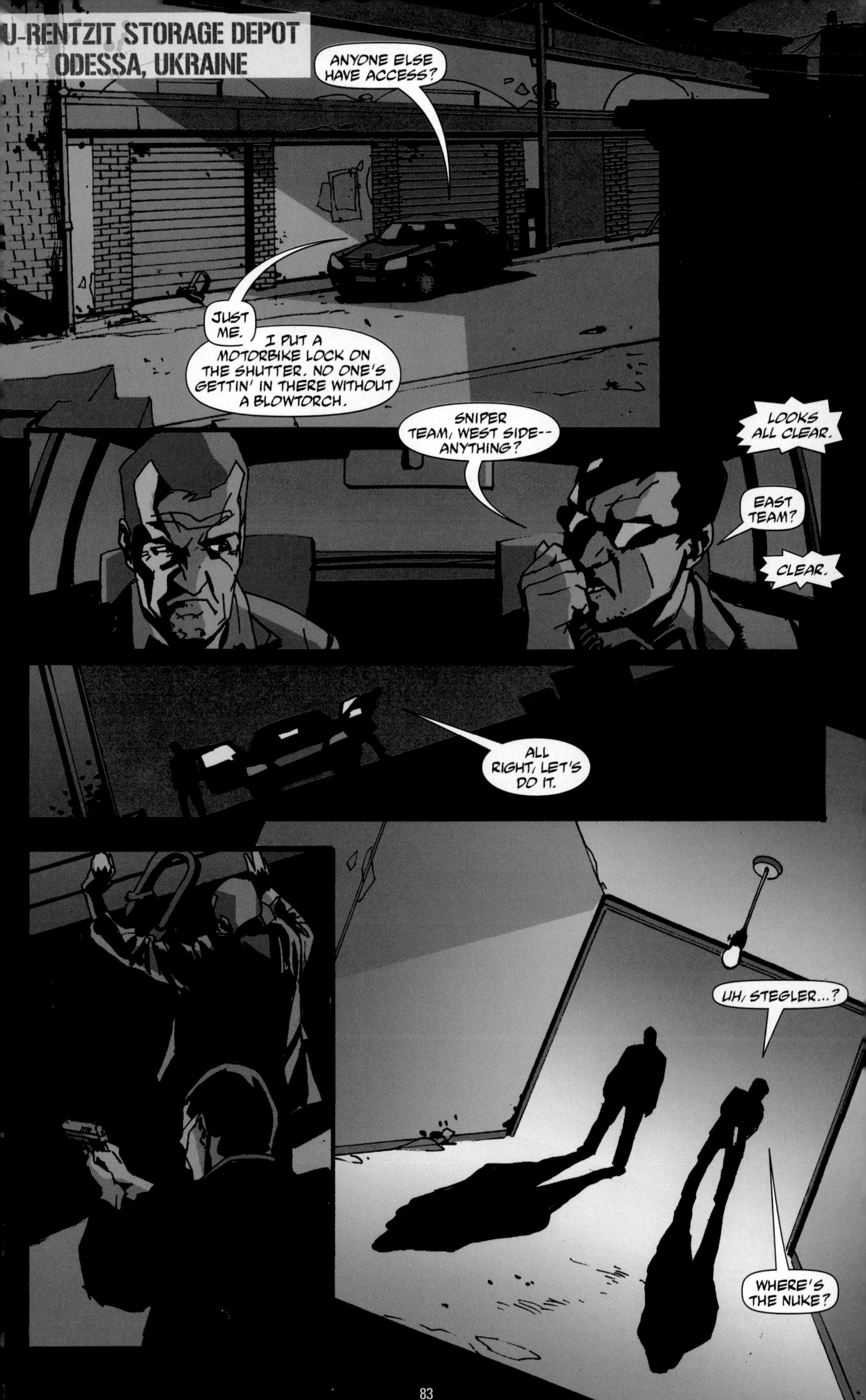
U-RENTZIT STORAGE DEPOT
ODESSA, UKRAINE
ANYONE ELSE HAVE ACCESS?
JUST ME.
I PUT A MOTORBIKE LOCK ON THE SHUTTER. NO ONE'S GETTIN' IN THERE WITHOUT A BLOWTORCH.
SNIPER TEAM, WEST SIDE--ANYTHING?
LOOKS ALL CLEAR.
EAST TEAM?
CLEAR.
ALL RIGHT, LET'S DO IT.
UH, STEGLER...?
WHERE'S THE NUKE?

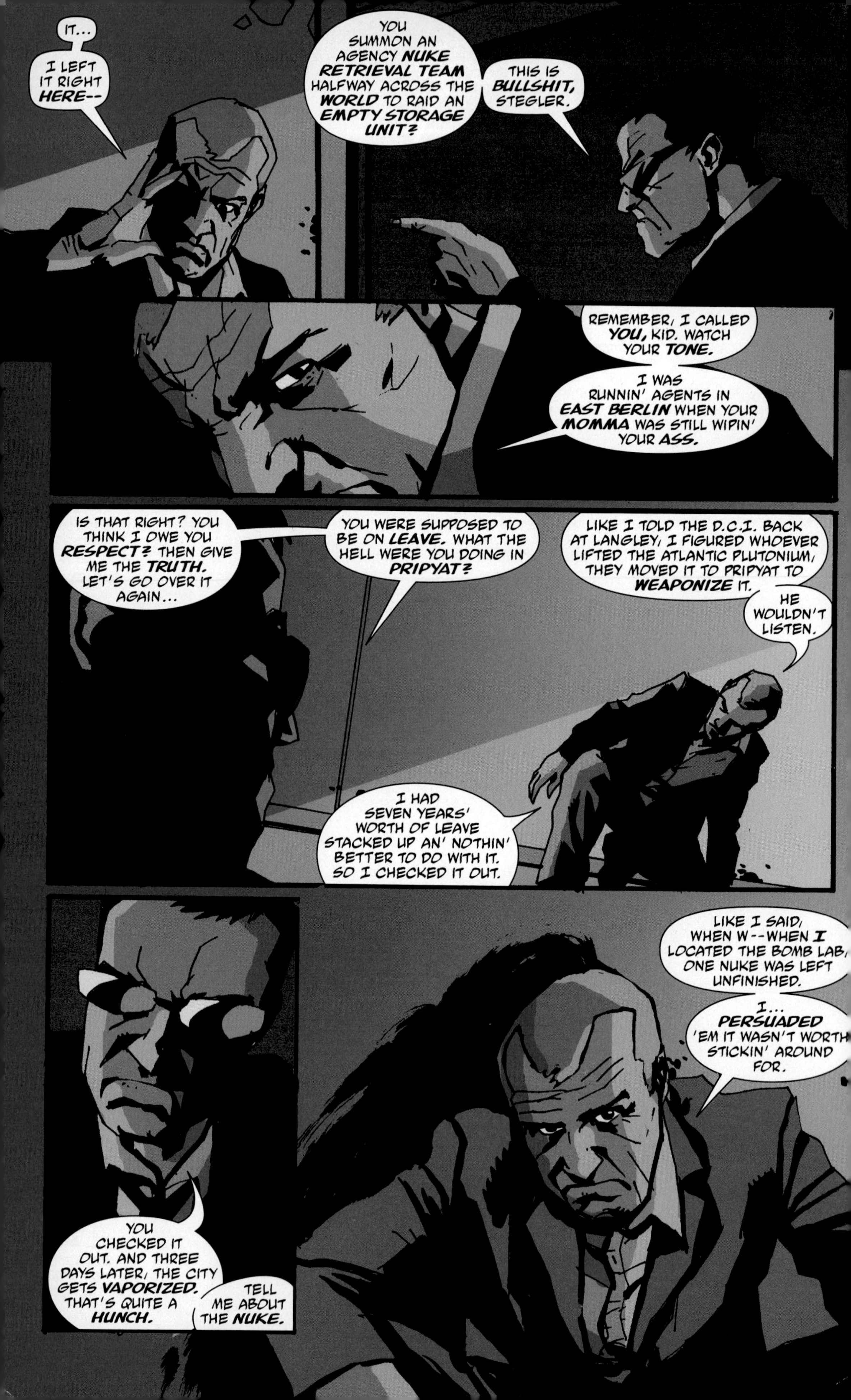
IT...
I LEFT IT RIGHT HERE--
YOU SUMMON AN AGENCY NUKE RETRIEVAL TEAM HALFWAY ACROSS THE WORLD TO RAID AN EMPTY STORAGE UNIT?
THIS IS BULLSHIT, STEGLER.
REMEMBER, I CALLED YOU, KID. WATCH YOUR TONE.
I WAS RUNNIN' AGENTS IN EAST BERLIN WHEN YOUR MOMMA WAS STILL WIPIN' YOUR ASS.
IS THAT RIGHT? YOU THINK I OWE YOU RESPECT? THEN GIVE ME THE TRUTH. LET'S GO OVER IT AGAIN...
YOU WERE SUPPOSED TO BE ON LEAVE. WHAT THE HELL WERE YOU DOING IN PRIPYAT?
LIKE I TOLD THE D.C.I. BACK AT LANGLEY, I FIGURED WHOEVER LIFTED THE ATLANTIC PLUTONIUM, THEY MOVED IT TO PRIPYAT TO WEAPONIZE IT.
HE WOULDN'T LISTEN.
I HAD SEVEN YEARS' WORTH OF LEAVE STACKED UP AN' NOTHIN' BETTER TO DO WITH IT. SO I CHECKED IT OUT.
LIKE I SAID, WHEN W--WHEN I LOCATED THE BOMB LAB, ONE NUKE WAS LEFT UNFINISHED.
I... PERSUADED 'EM IT WASN'T WORTH STICKIN' AROUND FOR.
YOU CHECKED IT OUT. AND THREE DAYS LATER, THE CITY GETS VAPORIZED. THAT'S QUITE A HUNCH.
TELL ME ABOUT THE NUKE.

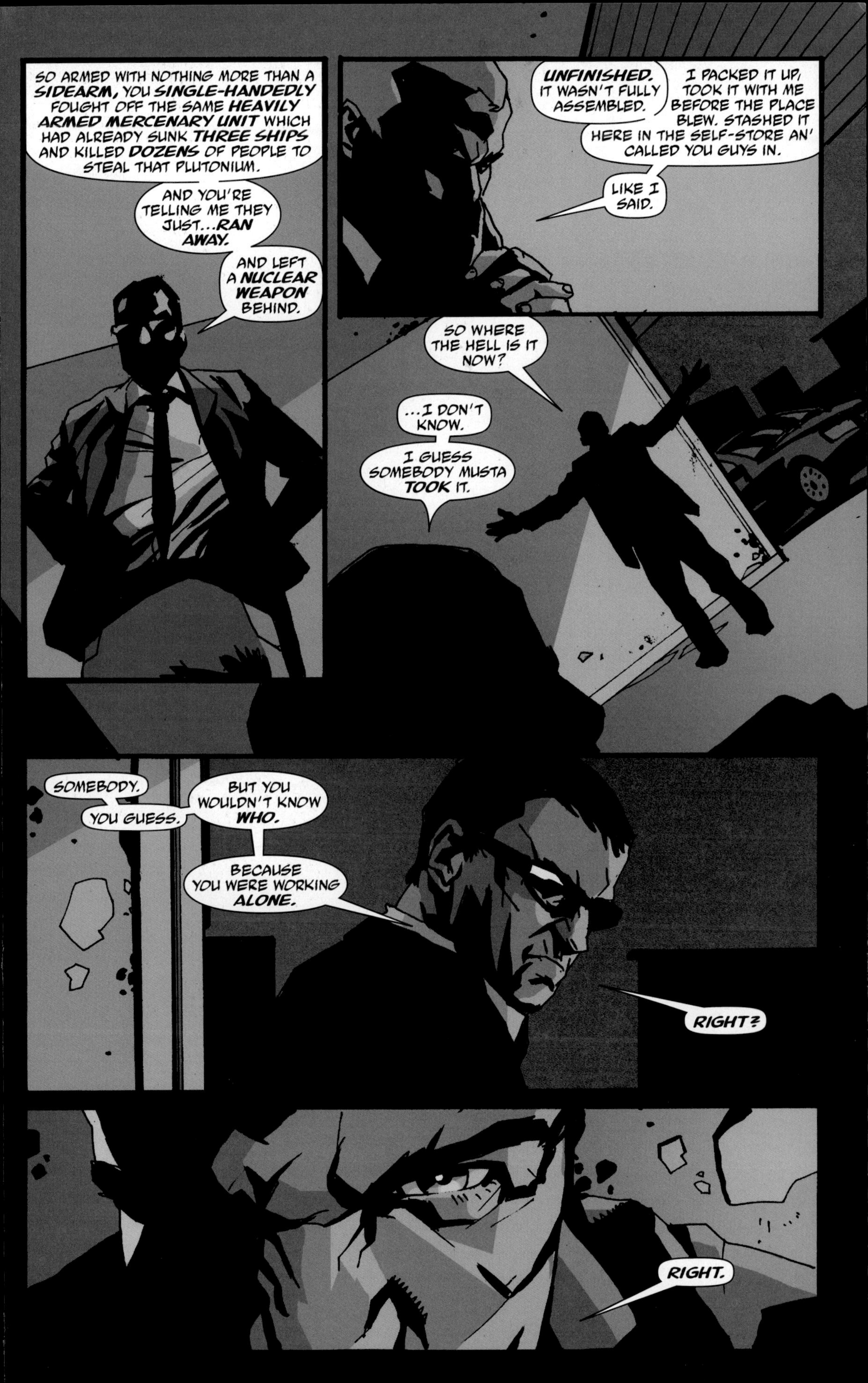

SO ARMED WITH NOTHING MORE THAN A SIDEARM, YOU SINGLE-HANDEDLY FOUGHT OFF THE SAME HEAVILY ARMED MERCENARY UNIT WHICH HAD ALREADY SUNK THREE SHIPS AND KILLED DOZENS OF PEOPLE TO STEAL THAT PLUTONIUM.
AND YOU'RE TELLING ME THEY JUST...RAN AWAY.
AND LEFT A NUCLEAR WEAPON BEHIND.
UNFINISHED. IT WASN'T FULLY ASSEMBLED.
I PACKED IT UP, TOOK IT WITH ME BEFORE THE PLACE BLEW. STASHED IT HERE IN THE SELF-STORE AN' CALLED YOU GUYS IN.
LIKE I SAID.
SO WHERE THE HELL IS IT NOW?
...I DON'T KNOW.
I GUESS SOMEBODY MUSTA TOOK IT.
SOMEBODY.
YOU GUESS.
BUT YOU WOULDN'T KNOW WHO.
BECAUSE YOU WERE WORKING ALONE.
RIGHT?
RIGHT.

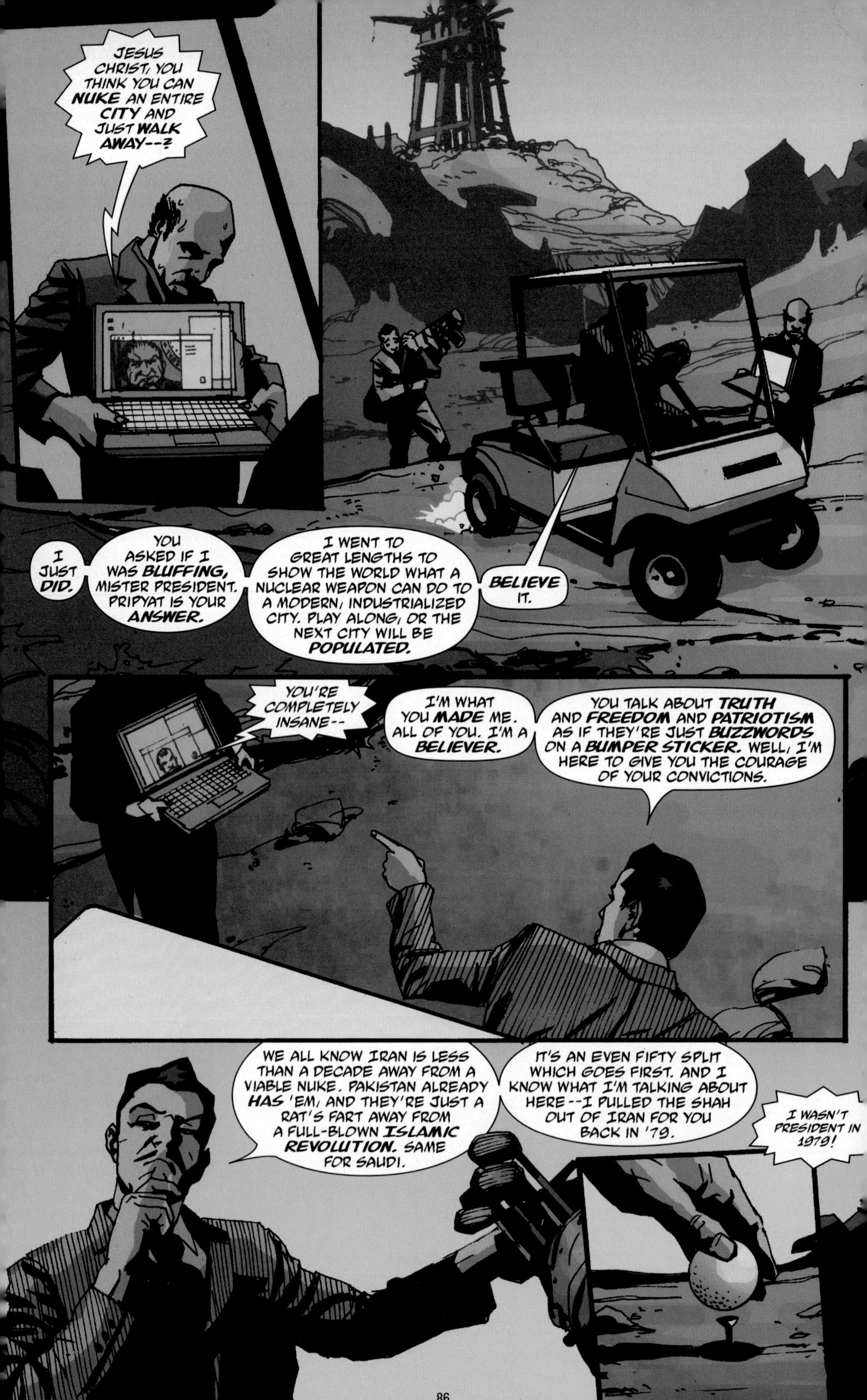
JESUS CHRIST, YOU THINK YOU CAN NUKE AN ENTIRE CITY AND JUST WALK AWAY--?
I JUST DID.
YOU ASKED IF I WAS BLUFFING, MISTER PRESIDENT. PRIPYAT IS YOUR ANSWER.
I WENT TO GREAT LENGTHS TO SHOW THE WORLD WHAT A NUCLEAR WEAPON CAN DO TO A MODERN, INDUSTRIALIZED CITY. PLAY ALONG, OR THE NEXT CITY WILL BE POPULATED.
BELIEVE IT.
YOU'RE COMPLETELY INSANE--
I'M WHAT YOU MADE ME. ALL OF YOU. I'M A BELIEVER.
YOU TALK ABOUT TRUTH AND FREEDOM AND PATRIOTISM AS IF THEY'RE JUST BUZZWORDS ON A BUMPER STICKER. WELL, I'M HERE TO GIVE YOU THE COURAGE OF YOUR CONVICTIONS.
WE ALL KNOW IRAN IS LESS THAN A DECADE AWAY FROM A VIABLE NUKE. PAKISTAN ALREADY HAS 'EM, AND THEY'RE JUST A RAT'S FART AWAY FROM A FULL-BLOWN ISLAMIC REVOLUTION. SAME FOR SAUDI.
IT'S AN EVEN FIFTY SPLIT WHICH GOES FIRST. AND I KNOW WHAT I'M TALKING ABOUT HERE--I PULLED THE SHAH OUT OF IRAN FOR YOU BACK IN '79.
I WASN'T PRESIDENT IN 1979!

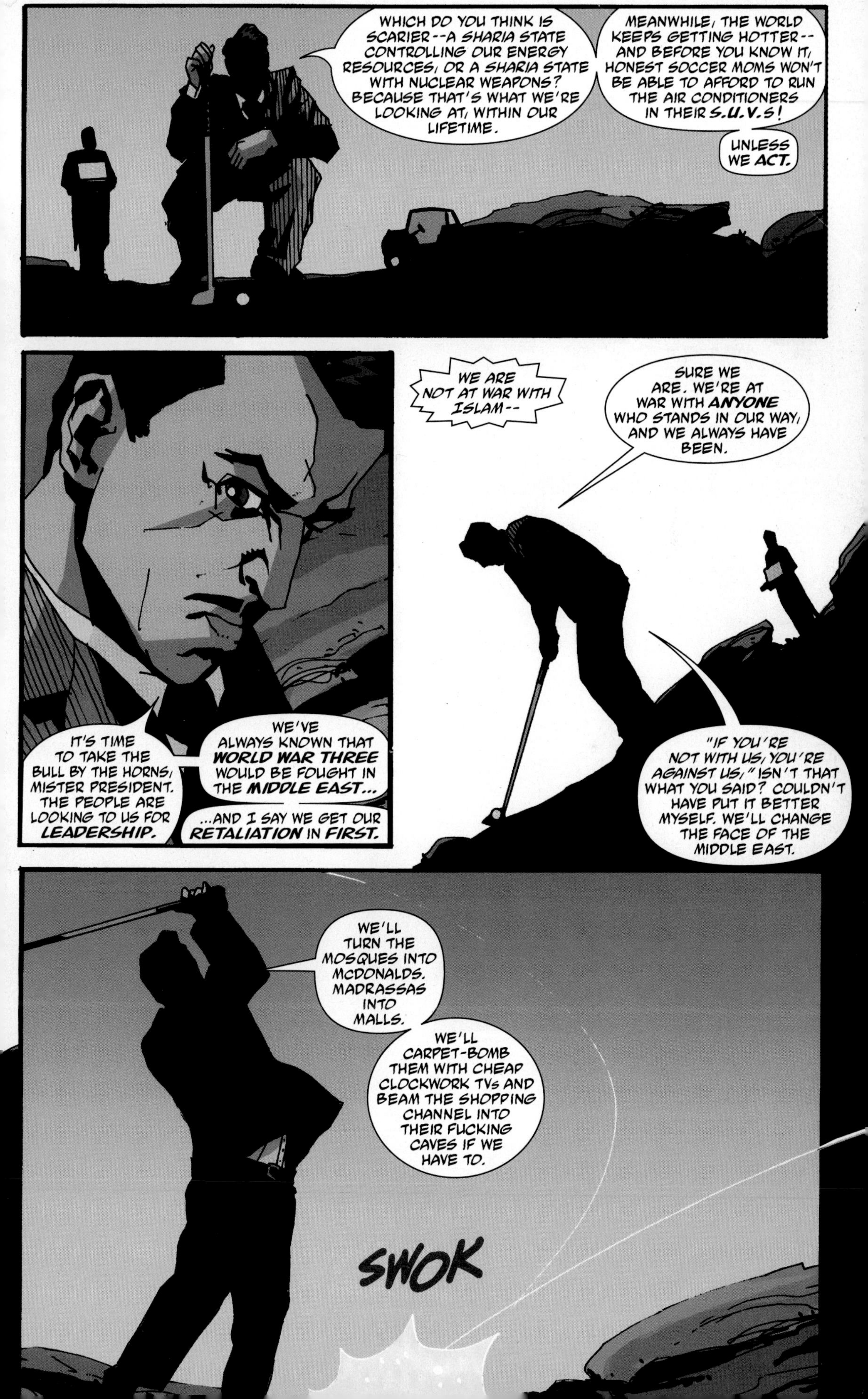
WHICH DO YOU THINK IS SCARIER--A SHARIA STATE CONTROLLING OUR ENERGY RESOURCES, OR A SHARIA STATE WITH NUCLEAR WEAPONS? BECAUSE THAT'S WHAT WE'RE LOOKING AT, WITHIN OUR LIFETIME.
MEANWHILE, THE WORLD KEEPS GETTING HOTTER--AND BEFORE YOU KNOW IT, HONEST SOCCER MOMS WON'T BE ABLE TO AFFORD TO RUN THE AIR CONDITIONERS IN THEIR S.U.V.S!
UNLESS WE ACT.
WE'VE ALWAYS KNOWN THAT WORLD WAR THREE WOULD BE FOUGHT IN THE MIDDLE EAST...
IT'S TIME TO TAKE THE BULL BY THE HORNS, MISTER PRESIDENT. THE PEOPLE ARE LOOKING TO US FOR LEADERSHIP.
...AND I SAY WE GET OUR RETALIATION IN FIRST.
WE ARE NOT AT WAR WITH ISLAM--
SURE WE ARE. WE'RE AT WAR WITH ANYONE WHO STANDS IN OUR WAY, AND WE ALWAYS HAVE BEEN.
"IF YOU'RE NOT WITH US, YOU'RE AGAINST US," ISN'T THAT WHAT YOU SAID? COULDN'T HAVE PUT IT BETTER MYSELF. WE'LL CHANGE THE FACE OF THE MIDDLE EAST.
WE'LL TURN THE MOSQUES INTO McDONALDS. MADRASSAS INTO MALLS.
WE'LL CARPET-BOMB THEM WITH CHEAP CLOCKWORK TVs AND BEAM THE SHOPPING CHANNEL INTO THEIR FUCKING CAVES IF WE HAVE TO.
SWOK

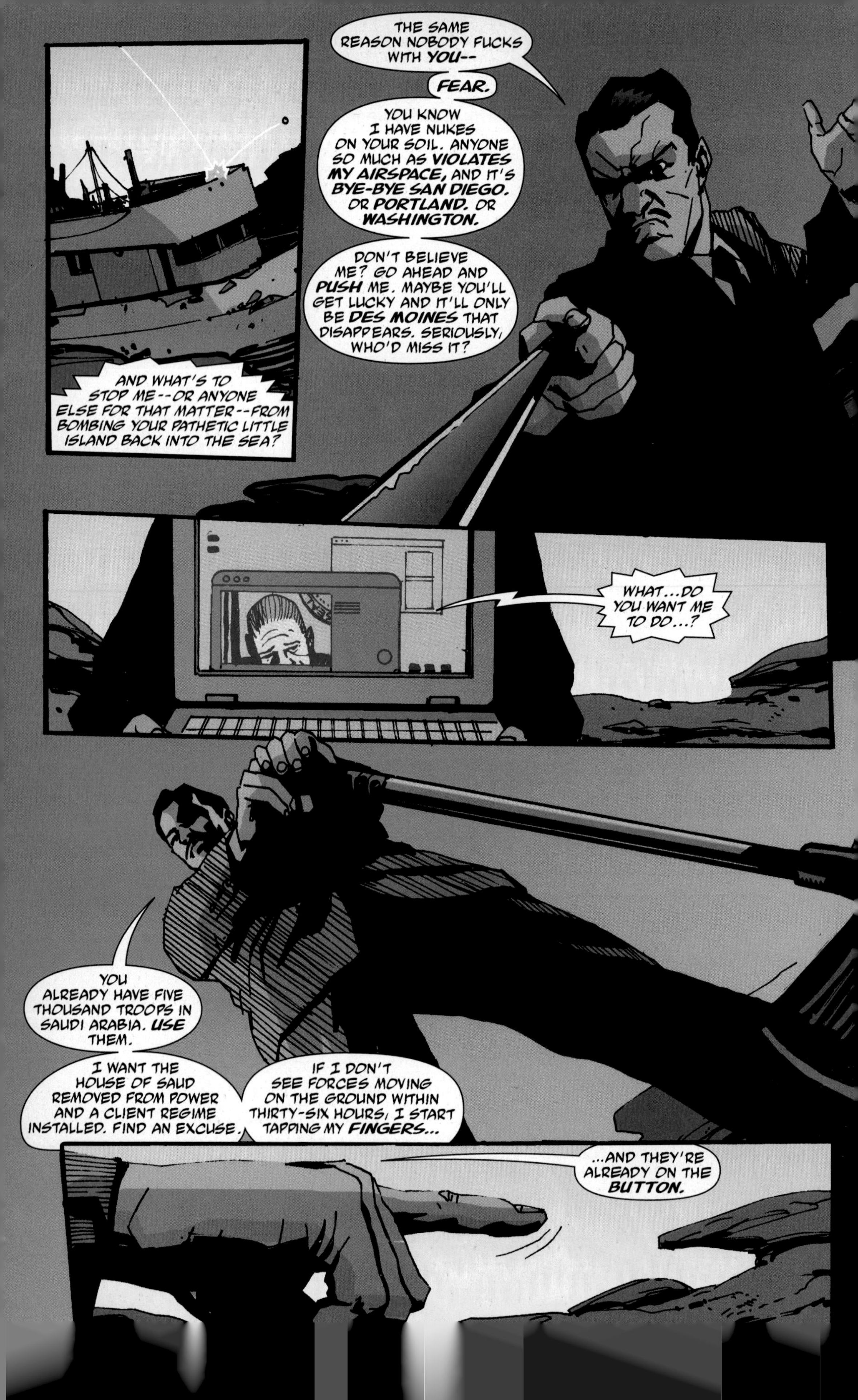
THE SAME REASON NOBODY FUCKS WITH YOU--
FEAR.
YOU KNOW I HAVE NUKES ON YOUR SOIL. ANYONE SO MUCH AS VIOLATES MY AIRSPACE, AND IT'S BYE-BYE SAN DIEGO. OR PORTLAND. OR WASHINGTON.
DON'T BELIEVE ME? GO AHEAD AND PUSH ME. MAYBE YOU'LL GET LUCKY AND IT'LL ONLY BE DES MOINES THAT DISAPPEARS. SERIOUSLY, WHO'D MISS IT?
AND WHAT'S TO STOP ME--OR ANYONE ELSE FOR THAT MATTER--FROM BOMBING YOUR PATHETIC LITTLE ISLAND BACK INTO THE SEA?
WHAT...DO YOU WANT ME TO DO...?
YOU ALREADY HAVE FIVE THOUSAND TROOPS IN SAUDI ARABIA. USE THEM.
I WANT THE HOUSE OF SAUD REMOVED FROM POWER AND A CLIENT REGIME INSTALLED. FIND AN EXCUSE.
IF I DON'T SEE FORCES MOVING ON THE GROUND WITHIN THIRTY-SIX HOURS, I START TAPPING MY FINGERS...
...AND THEY'RE ALREADY ON THE BUTTON.

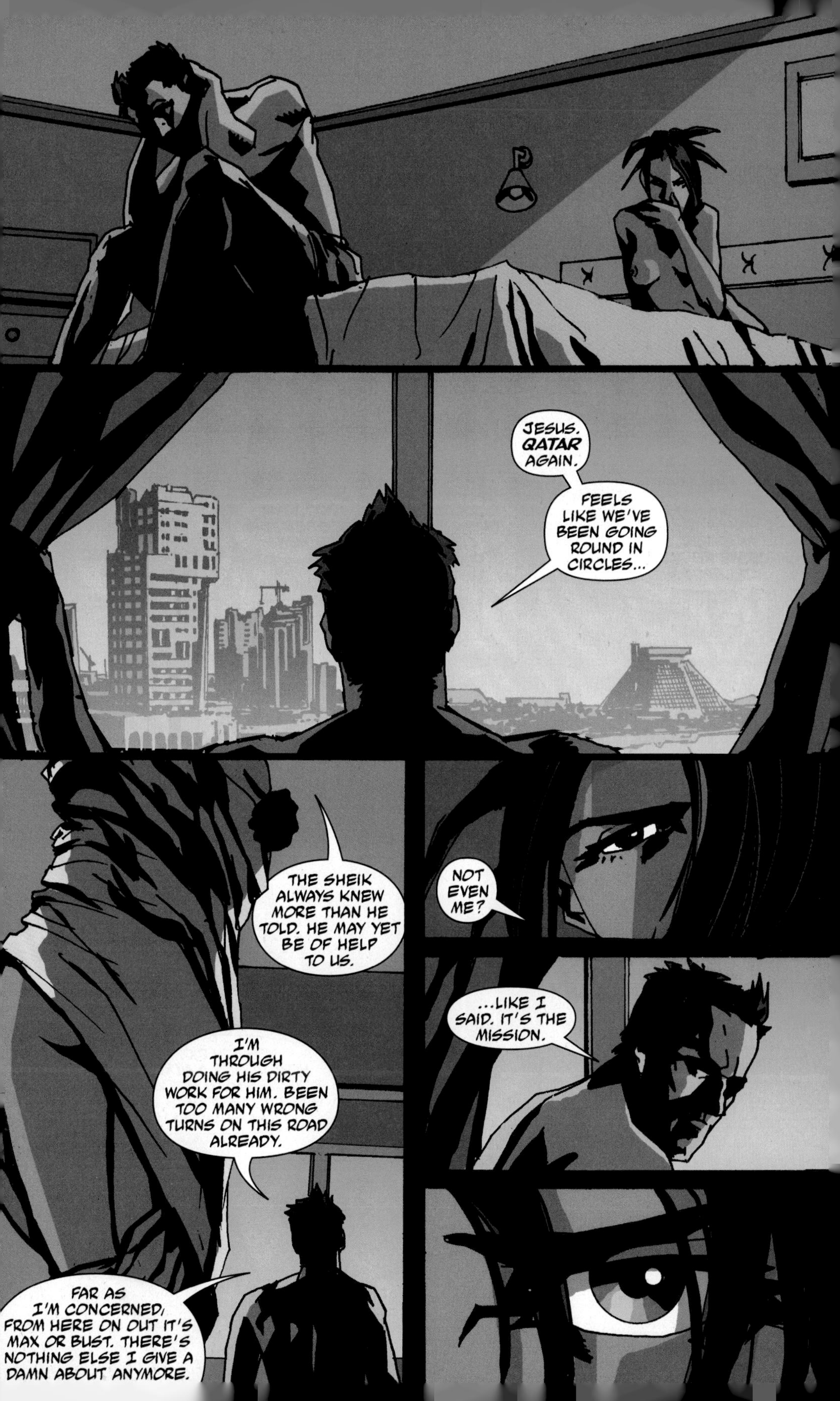
JESUS. QATAR AGAIN.
FEELS LIKE WE'VE BEEN GOING ROUND IN CIRCLES...
THE SHEIK ALWAYS KNEW MORE THAN HE TOLD. HE MAY YET BE OF HELP TO US.
NOT EVEN ME?
...LIKE I SAID. IT'S THE MISSION.
I'M THROUGH DOING HIS DIRTY WORK FOR HIM. BEEN TOO MANY WRONG TURNS ON THIS ROAD ALREADY.
FAR AS I'M CONCERNED, FROM HERE ON OUT IT'S MAX OR BUST. THERE'S NOTHING ELSE I GIVE A DAMN ABOUT ANYMORE.

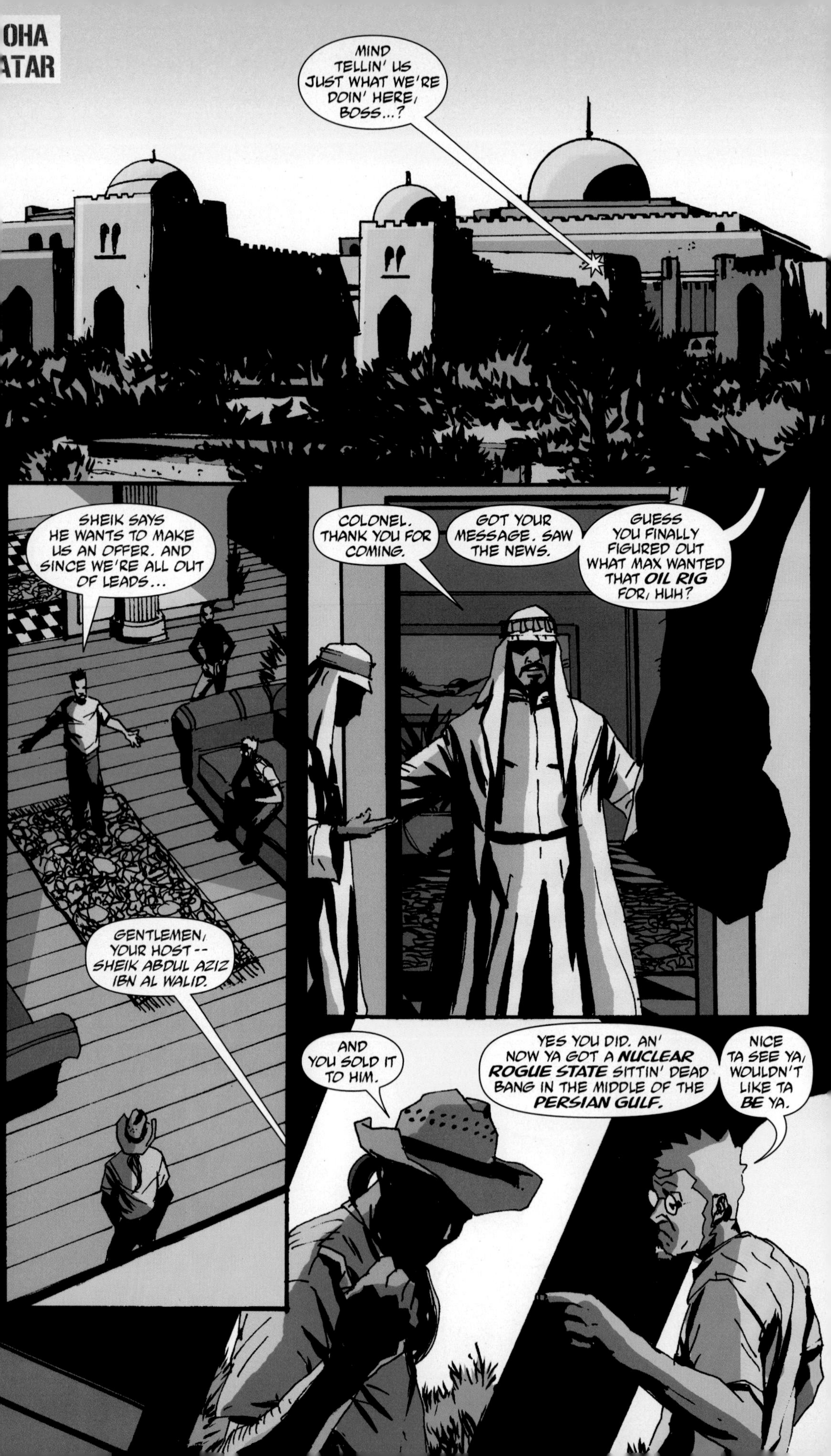

OHA
ATAR
MIND TELLIN' US JUST WHAT WE'RE DOIN' HERE, BOSS...?
SHEIK SAYS HE WANTS TO MAKE US AN OFFER. AND SINCE WE'RE ALL OUT OF LEADS...
GENTLEMEN, YOUR HOST -- SHEIK ABDUL AZIZ IBN AL WALID.
COLONEL. THANK YOU FOR COMING.
GOT YOUR MESSAGE. SAW THE NEWS.
GUESS YOU FINALLY FIGURED OUT WHAT MAX WANTED THAT OIL RIG FOR, HUH?
AND YOU SOLD IT TO HIM.
YES YOU DID. AN' NOW YA GOT A NUCLEAR ROGUE STATE SITTIN' DEAD BANG IN THE MIDDLE OF THE PERSIAN GULF.
NICE TA SEE YA, WOULDN'T LIKE TA BE YA.

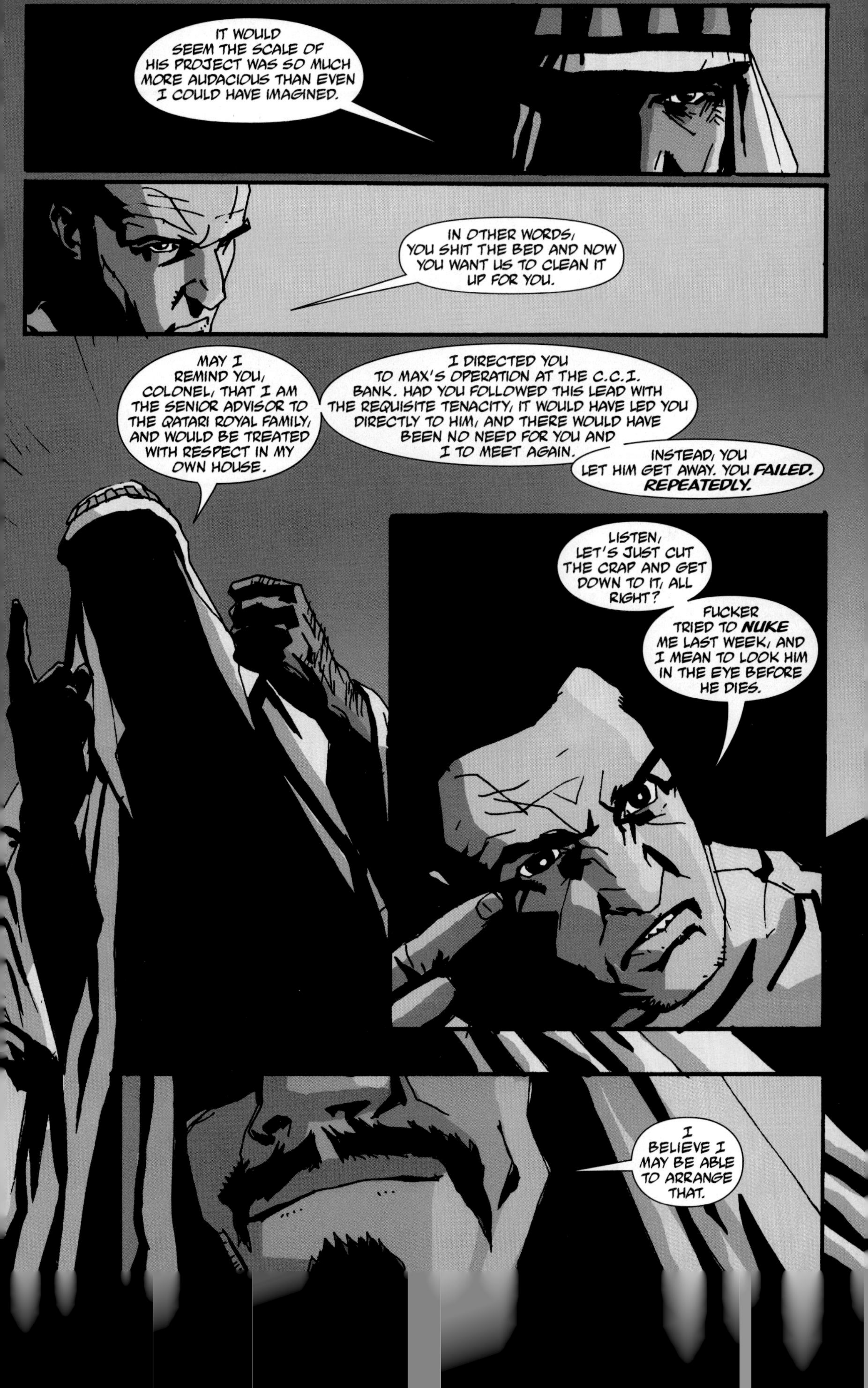
IT WOULD SEEM THE SCALE OF HIS PROJECT WAS SO MUCH MORE AUDACIOUS THAN EVEN I COULD HAVE IMAGINED.
IN OTHER WORDS, YOU SHIT THE BED AND NOW YOU WANT US TO CLEAN IT UP FOR YOU.
MAY I REMIND YOU, COLONEL, THAT I AM THE SENIOR ADVISOR TO THE QATARI ROYAL FAMILY, AND WOULD BE TREATED WITH RESPECT IN MY OWN HOUSE.
I DIRECTED YOU TO MAX'S OPERATION AT THE C.C.I. BANK. HAD YOU FOLLOWED THIS LEAD WITH THE REQUISITE TENACITY, IT WOULD HAVE LED YOU DIRECTLY TO HIM, AND THERE WOULD HAVE BEEN NO NEED FOR YOU AND I TO MEET AGAIN.
INSTEAD, YOU LET HIM GET AWAY. YOU ***FAILED. REPEATEDLY.***
LISTEN, LET'S JUST CUT THE CRAP AND GET DOWN TO IT, ALL RIGHT?
FUCKER TRIED TO ***NUKE*** ME LAST WEEK, AND I MEAN TO LOOK HIM IN THE EYE BEFORE HE DIES.
I BELIEVE I MAY BE ABLE TO ARRANGE THAT.

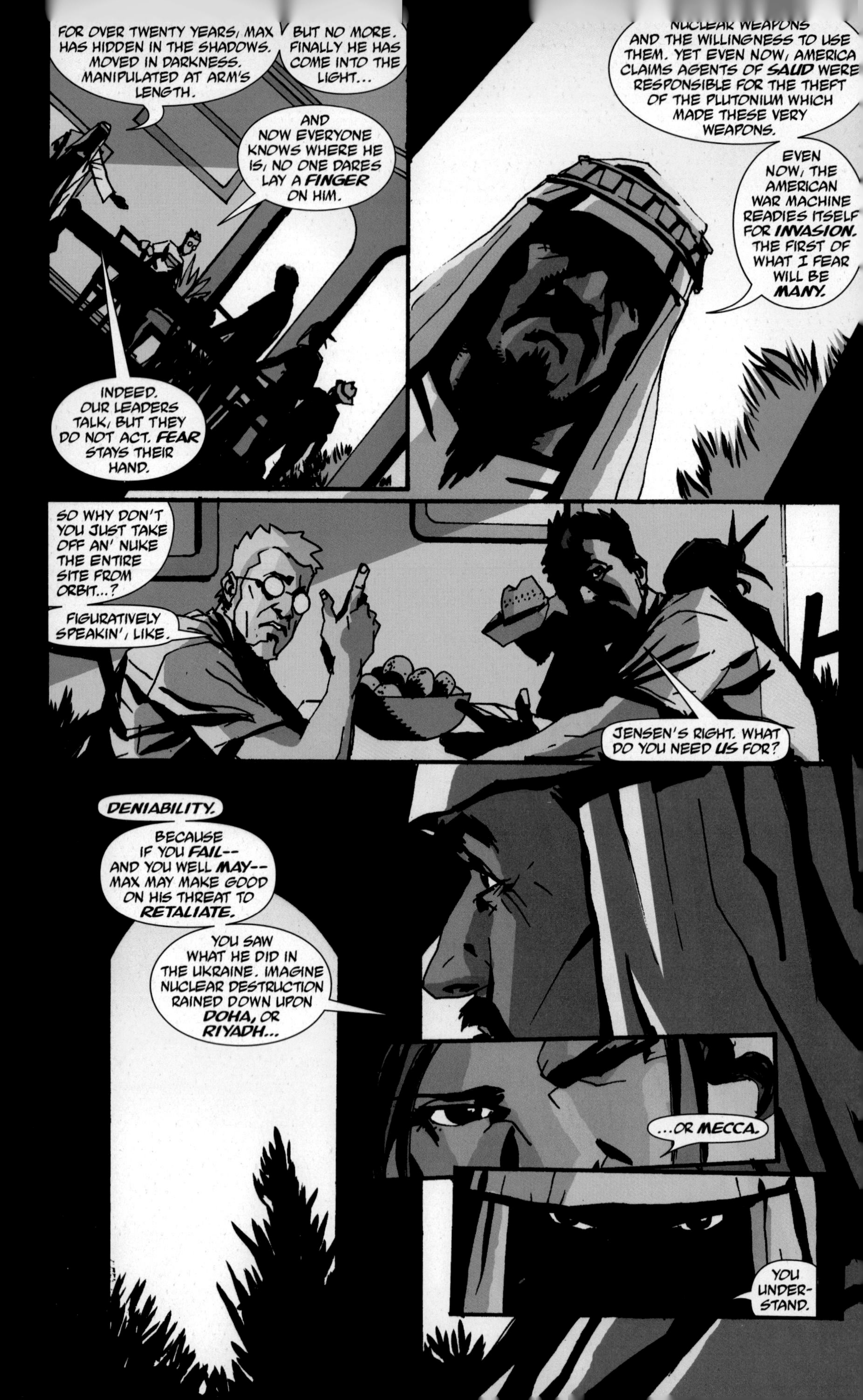
FOR OVER TWENTY YEARS, MAX HAS HIDDEN IN THE SHADOWS. MOVED IN DARKNESS. MANIPULATED AT ARM'S LENGTH.
BUT NO MORE. FINALLY HE HAS COME INTO THE LIGHT...
AND NOW EVERYONE KNOWS WHERE HE IS, NO ONE DARES LAY A FINGER ON HIM.
INDEED. OUR LEADERS TALK, BUT THEY DO NOT ACT. FEAR STAYS THEIR HAND.
NUCLEAR WEAPONS AND THE WILLINGNESS TO USE THEM. YET EVEN NOW, AMERICA CLAIMS AGENTS OF SAUD WERE RESPONSIBLE FOR THE THEFT OF THE PLUTONIUM WHICH MADE THESE VERY WEAPONS.
EVEN NOW, THE AMERICAN WAR MACHINE READIES ITSELF FOR INVASION. THE FIRST OF WHAT I FEAR WILL BE MANY.
SO WHY DON'T YOU JUST TAKE OFF AN' NUKE THE ENTIRE SITE FROM ORBIT...?
FIGURATIVELY SPEAKIN', LIKE.
JENSEN'S RIGHT. WHAT DO YOU NEED US FOR?
DENIABILITY.
BECAUSE IF YOU FAIL-- AND YOU WELL MAY-- MAX MAY MAKE GOOD ON HIS THREAT TO RETALIATE.
YOU SAW WHAT HE DID IN THE UKRAINE. IMAGINE NUCLEAR DESTRUCTION RAINED DOWN UPON DOHA, OR RIYADH...
...OR MECCA.
YOU UNDER-STAND.

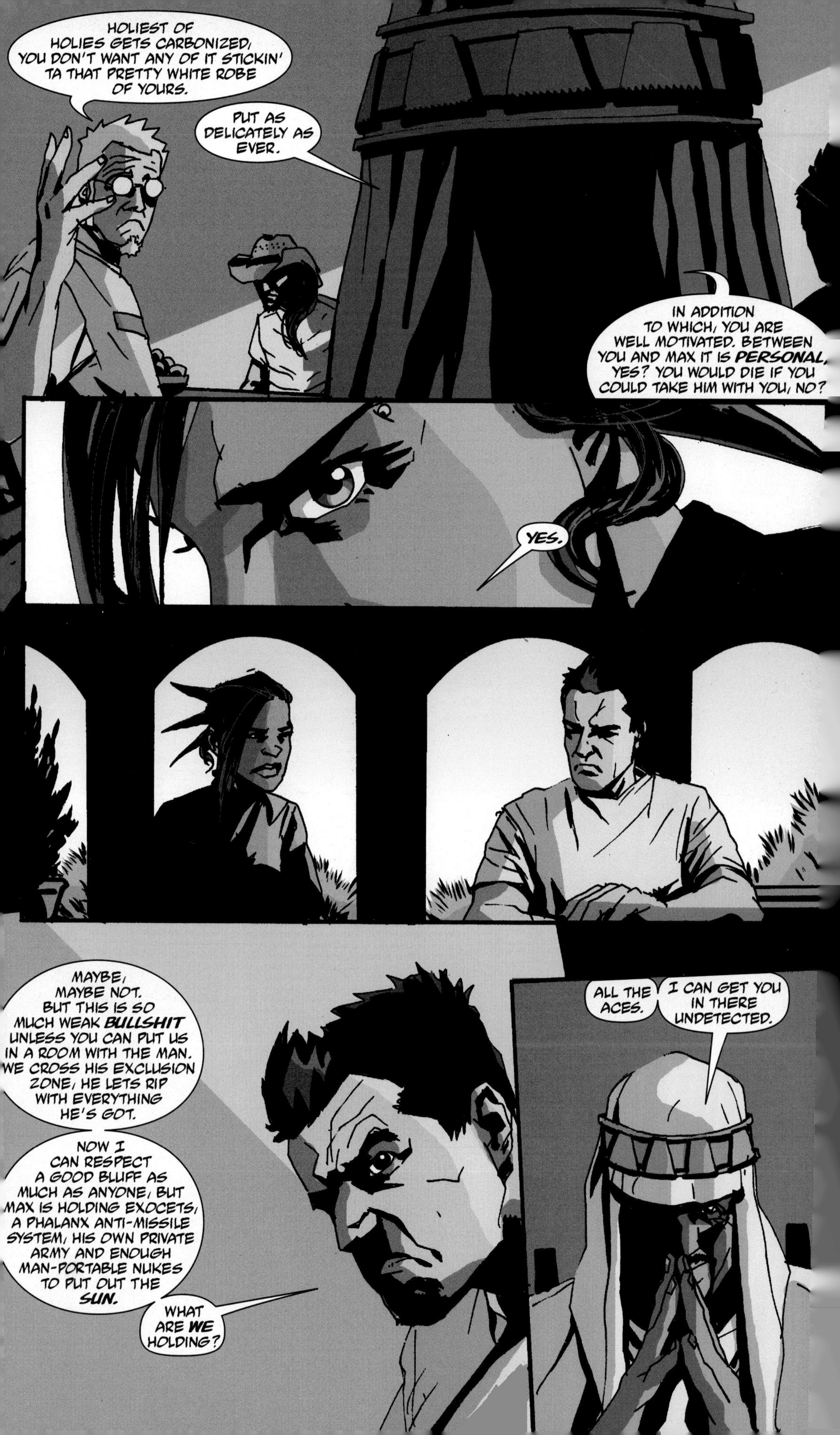
HOLIEST OF HOLIES GETS CARBONIZED, YOU DON'T WANT ANY OF IT STICKIN' TA THAT PRETTY WHITE ROBE OF YOURS.
PUT AS DELICATELY AS EVER.
IN ADDITION TO WHICH, YOU ARE WELL MOTIVATED. BETWEEN YOU AND MAX IT IS PERSONAL, YES? YOU WOULD DIE IF YOU COULD TAKE HIM WITH YOU, NO?
YES.
MAYBE, MAYBE NOT. BUT THIS IS SO MUCH WEAK BULLSHIT UNLESS YOU CAN PUT US IN A ROOM WITH THE MAN. WE CROSS HIS EXCLUSION ZONE, HE LETS RIP WITH EVERYTHING HE'S GOT.
NOW I CAN RESPECT A GOOD BLUFF AS MUCH AS ANYONE, BUT MAX IS HOLDING EXOCETS, A PHALANX ANTI-MISSILE SYSTEM, HIS OWN PRIVATE ARMY AND ENOUGH MAN-PORTABLE NUKES TO PUT OUT THE SUN.
WHAT ARE WE HOLDING?
ALL THE ACES.
I CAN GET YOU IN THERE UNDETECTED.

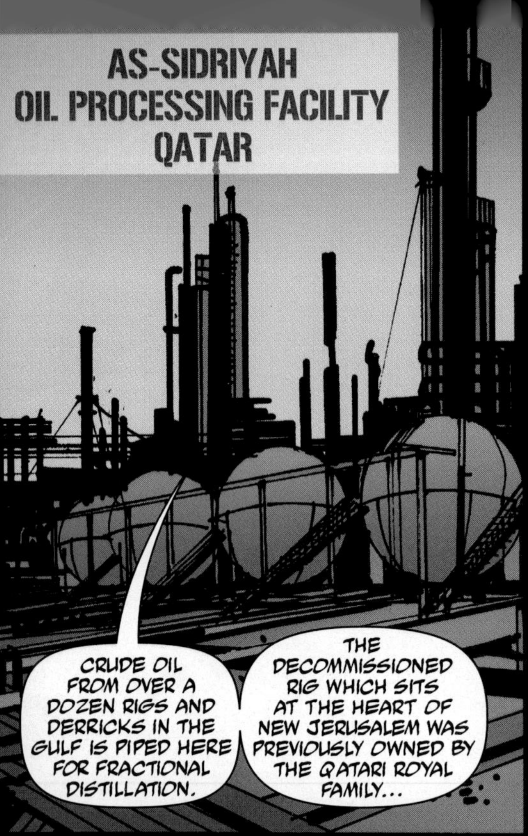
AS-SIDRIYAH
OIL PROCESSING FACILITY
QATAR
CRUDE OIL FROM OVER A DOZEN RIGS AND DERRICKS IN THE GULF IS PIPED HERE FOR FRACTIONAL DISTILLATION.
THE DECOMMISSIONED RIG WHICH SITS AT THE HEART OF NEW JERUSALEM WAS PREVIOUSLY OWNED BY THE QATARI ROYAL FAMILY...

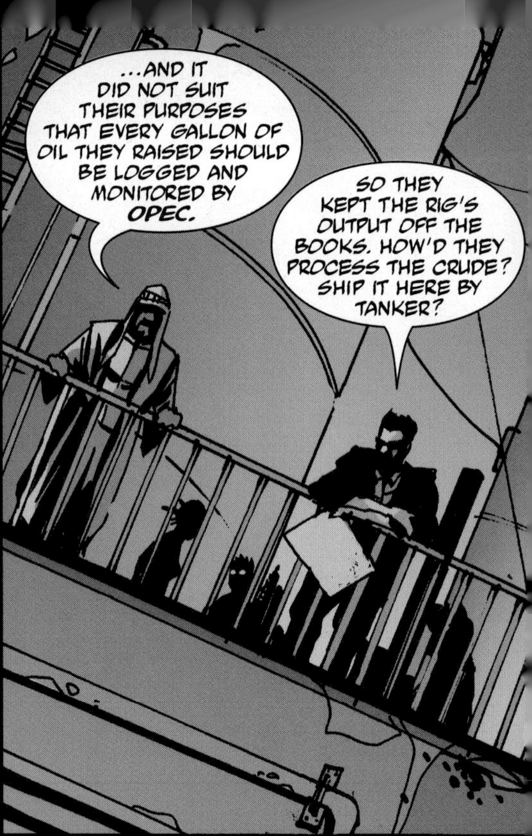
...AND IT DID NOT SUIT THEIR PURPOSES THAT EVERY GALLON OF OIL THEY RAISED SHOULD BE LOGGED AND MONITORED BY **OPEC.**
SO THEY KEPT THE RIG'S OUTPUT OFF THE BOOKS. HOW'D THEY PROCESS THE CRUDE? SHIP IT HERE BY TANKER?

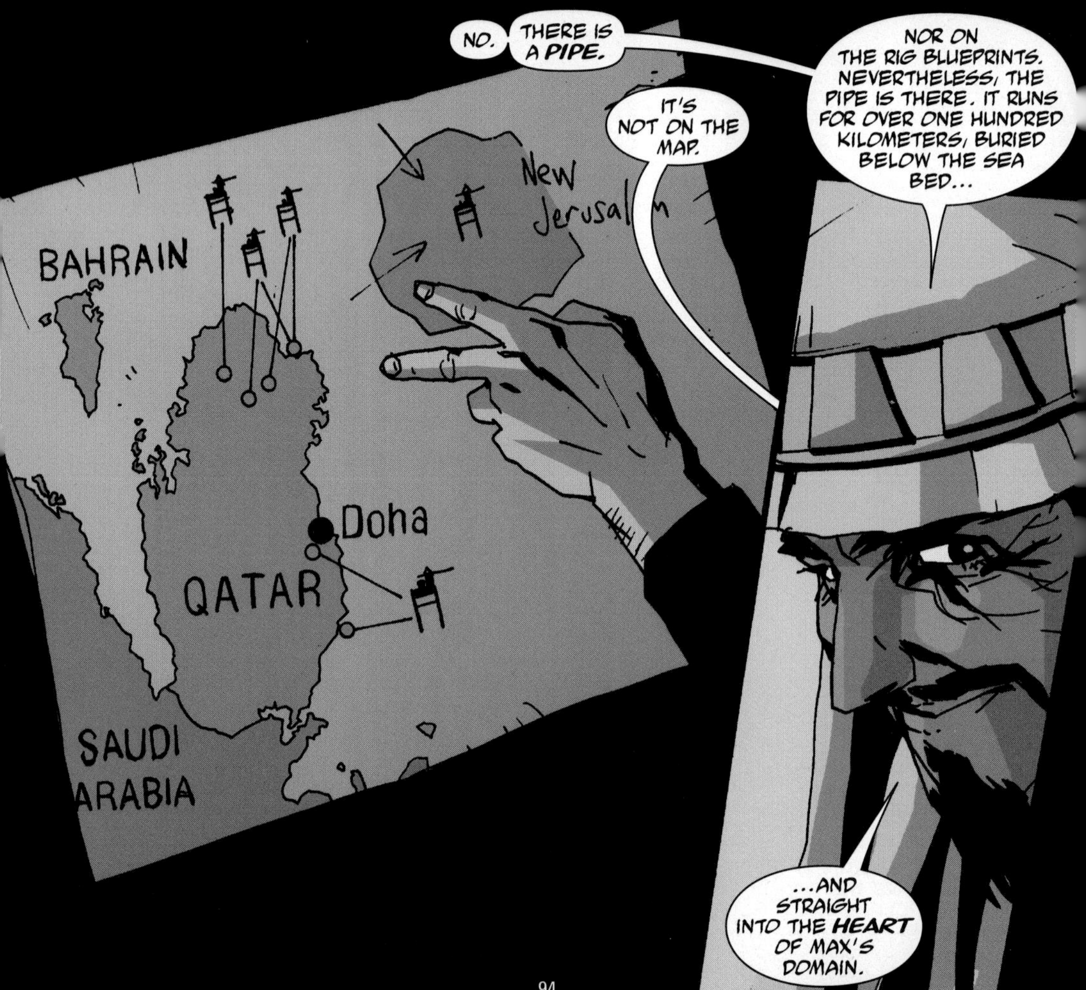
NO.
THERE IS A **PIPE.**
IT'S NOT ON THE MAP.
NOR ON THE RIG BLUEPRINTS. NEVERTHELESS, THE PIPE IS THERE. IT RUNS FOR OVER ONE HUNDRED KILOMETERS, BURIED BELOW THE SEA BED...
BAHRAIN
New Jerusalem
Doha
QATAR
SAUDI ARABIA
...AND STRAIGHT INTO THE **HEART** OF MAX'S DOMAIN.

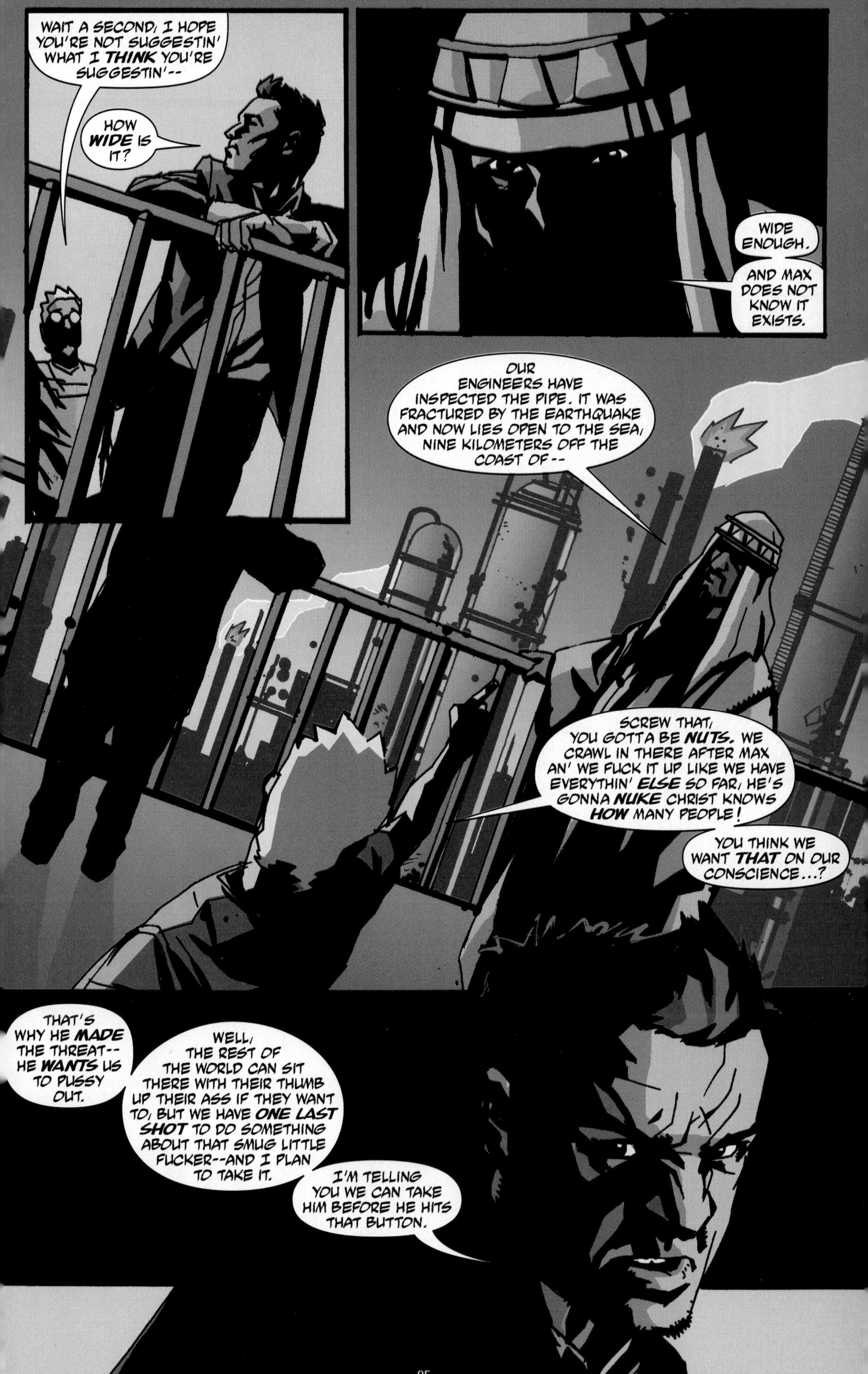

WAIT A SECOND, I HOPE YOU'RE NOT SUGGESTIN' WHAT I THINK YOU'RE SUGGESTIN'--
HOW WIDE IS IT?
WIDE ENOUGH.
AND MAX DOES NOT KNOW IT EXISTS.
OUR ENGINEERS HAVE INSPECTED THE PIPE. IT WAS FRACTURED BY THE EARTHQUAKE AND NOW LIES OPEN TO THE SEA, NINE KILOMETERS OFF THE COAST OF--
SCREW THAT, YOU GOTTA BE NUTS. WE CRAWL IN THERE AFTER MAX AN' WE FUCK IT UP LIKE WE HAVE EVERYTHIN' ELSE SO FAR, HE'S GONNA NUKE CHRIST KNOWS HOW MANY PEOPLE!
YOU THINK WE WANT THAT ON OUR CONSCIENCE...?
THAT'S WHY HE MADE THE THREAT-- HE WANTS US TO PUSSY OUT.
WELL, THE REST OF THE WORLD CAN SIT THERE WITH THEIR THUMB UP THEIR ASS IF THEY WANT TO, BUT WE HAVE ONE LAST SHOT TO DO SOMETHING ABOUT THAT SMUG LITTLE FUCKER--AND I PLAN TO TAKE IT.
I'M TELLING YOU WE CAN TAKE HIM BEFORE HE HITS THAT BUTTON.

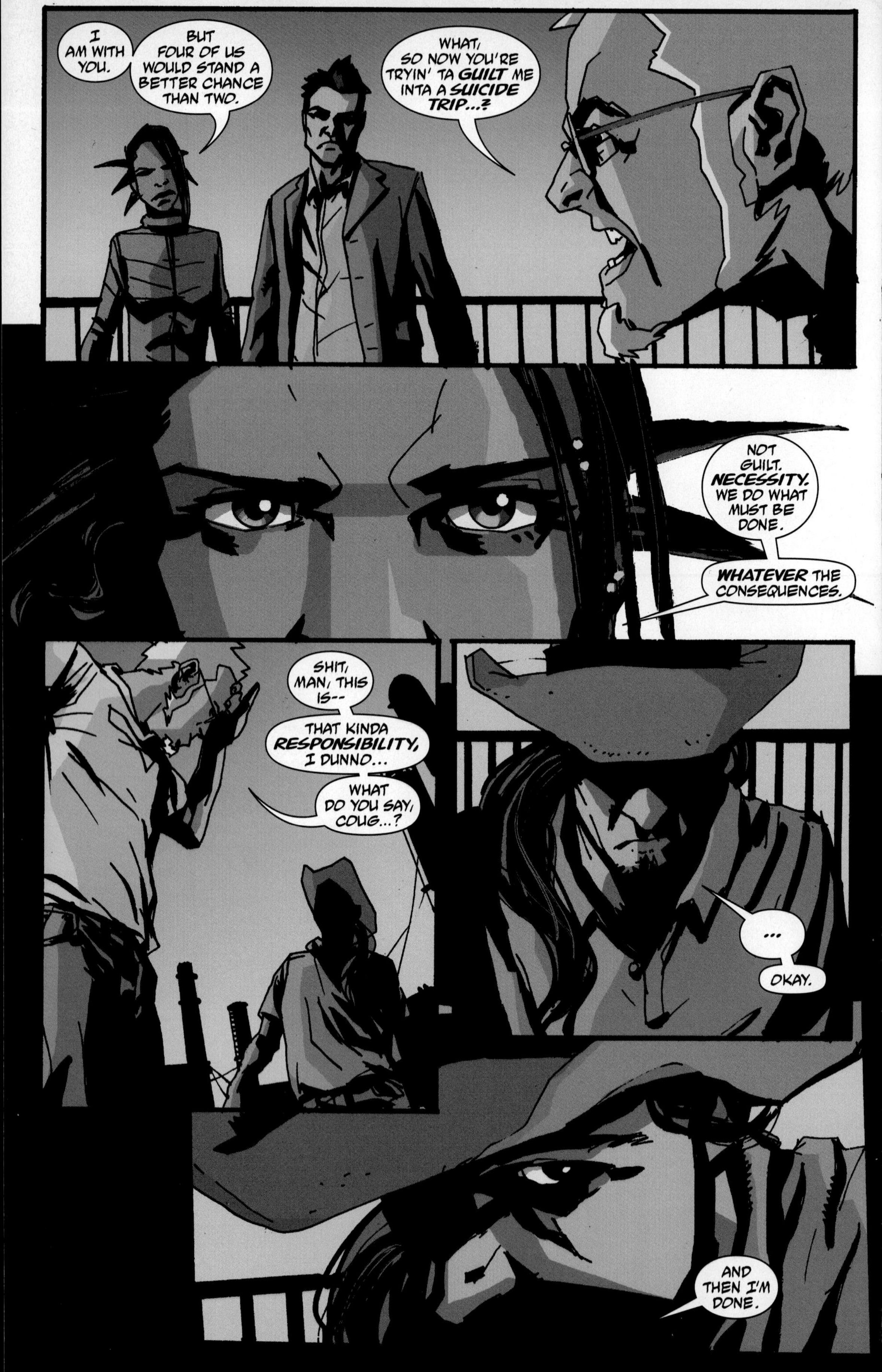
I AM WITH YOU.
BUT FOUR OF US WOULD STAND A BETTER CHANCE THAN TWO.
WHAT, SO NOW YOU'RE TRYIN' TA GUILT ME INTA A SUICIDE TRIP...?
NOT GUILT. NECESSITY. WE DO WHAT MUST BE DONE.
WHATEVER THE CONSEQUENCES.
SHIT, MAN, THIS IS--
THAT KINDA RESPONSIBILITY, I DUNNO...
WHAT DO YOU SAY, COUG...?
...
OKAY.
AND THEN I'M DONE.

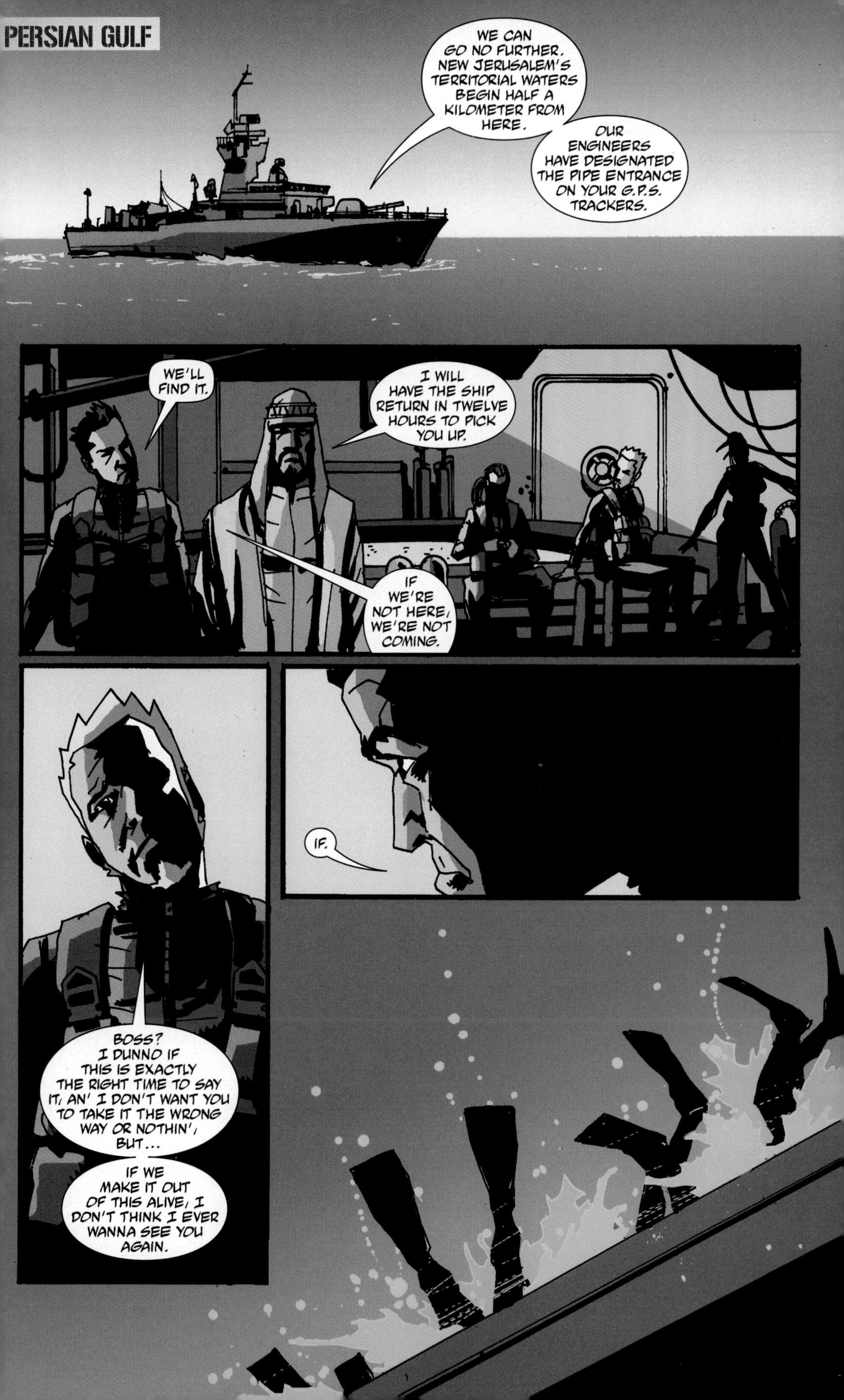
PERSIAN GULF
WE CAN GO NO FURTHER. NEW JERUSALEM'S TERRITORIAL WATERS BEGIN HALF A KILOMETER FROM HERE.
OUR ENGINEERS HAVE DESIGNATED THE PIPE ENTRANCE ON YOUR G.P.S. TRACKERS.
WE'LL FIND IT.
I WILL HAVE THE SHIP RETURN IN TWELVE HOURS TO PICK YOU UP.
IF WE'RE NOT HERE, WE'RE NOT COMING.
IF.
BOSS? I DUNNO IF THIS IS EXACTLY THE RIGHT TIME TO SAY IT, AN' I DON'T WANT YOU TO TAKE IT THE WRONG WAY OR NOTHIN', BUT...
IF WE MAKE IT OUT OF THIS ALIVE, I DON'T THINK I EVER WANNA SEE YOU AGAIN.

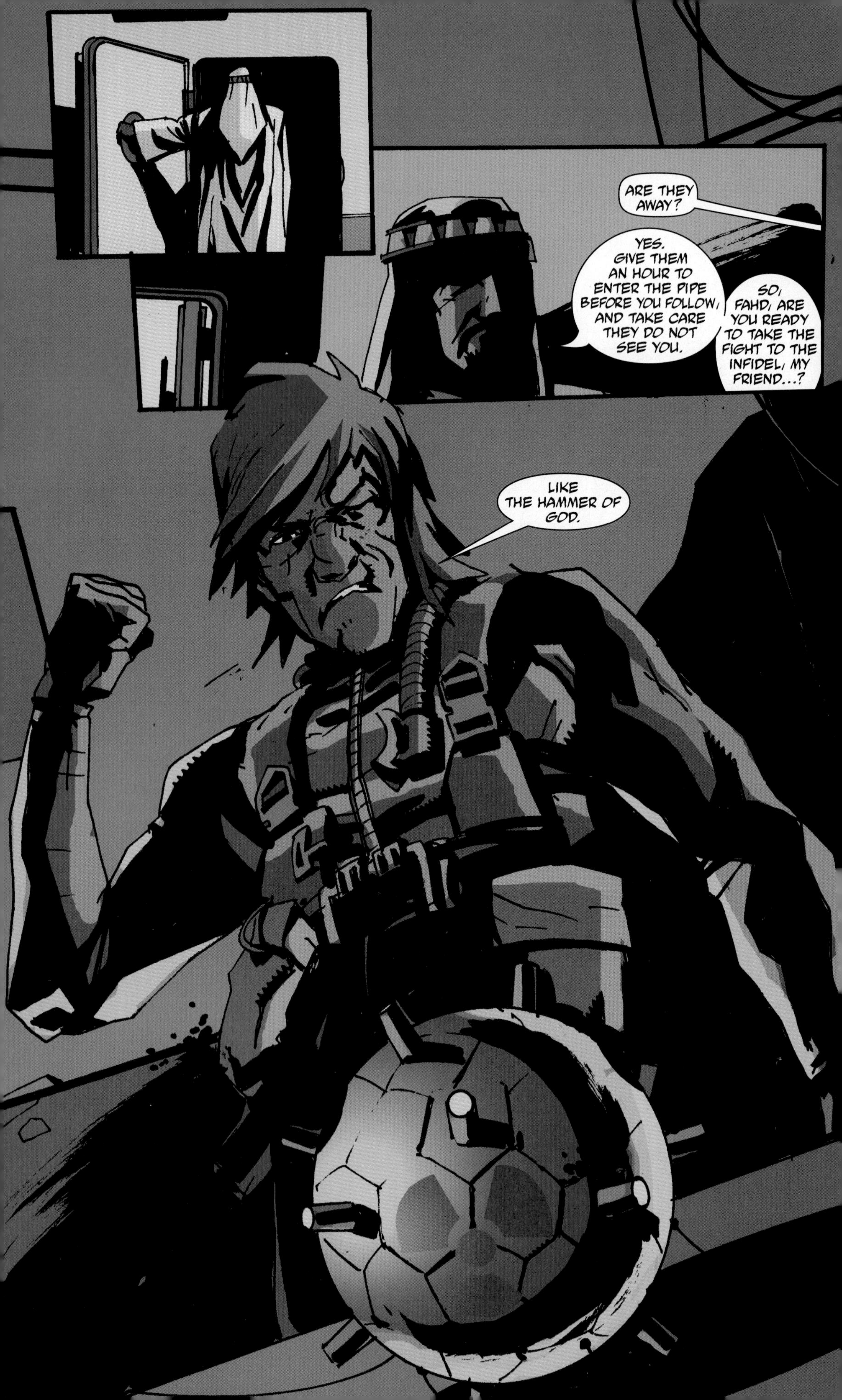
ARE THEY AWAY?
YES. GIVE THEM AN HOUR TO ENTER THE PIPE BEFORE YOU FOLLOW, AND TAKE CARE THEY DO NOT SEE YOU.
SO, FAHD, ARE YOU READY TO TAKE THE FIGHT TO THE INFIDEL, MY FRIEND...?
LIKE THE HAMMER OF GOD.

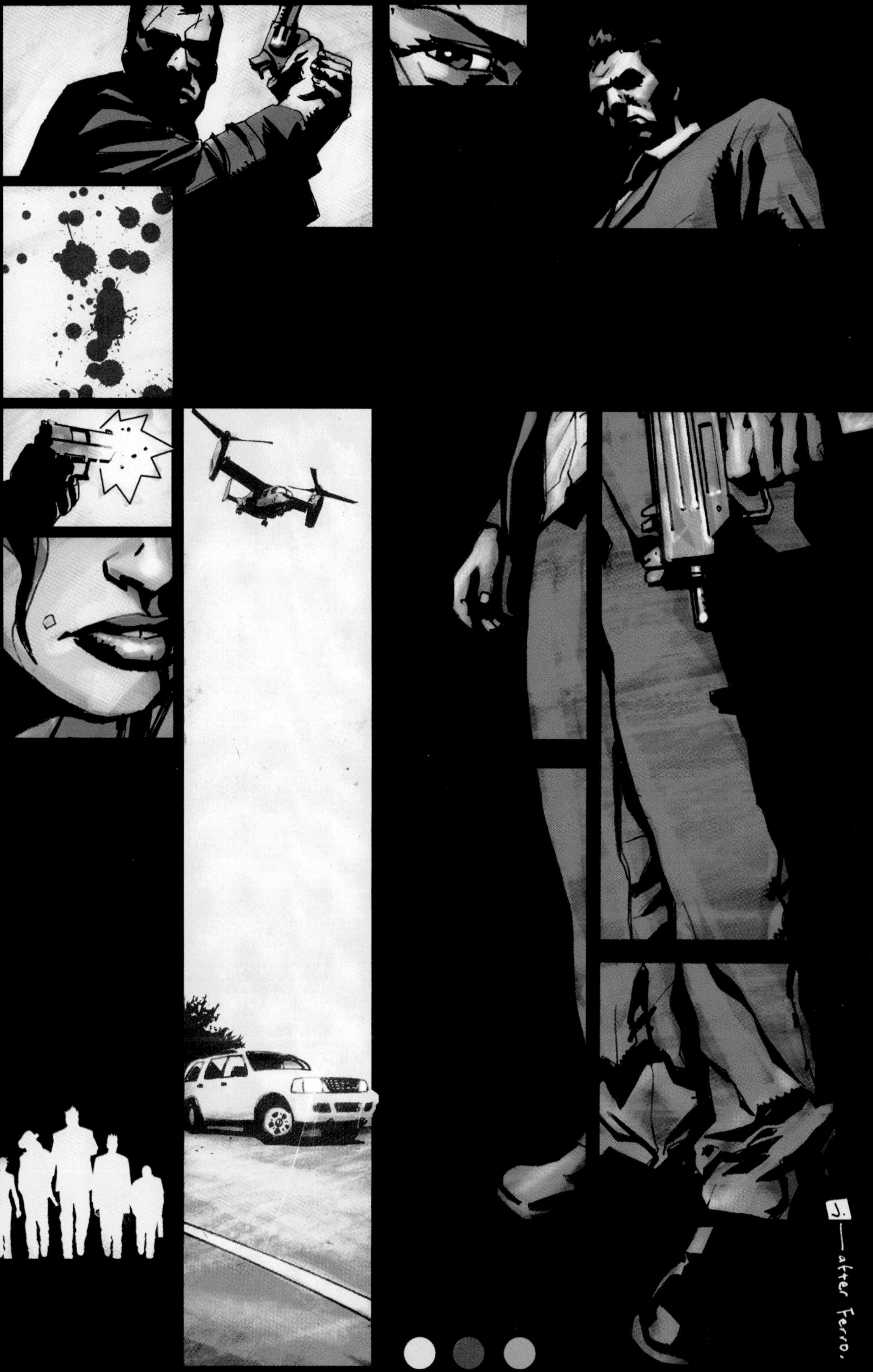
J.
—after Ferro.

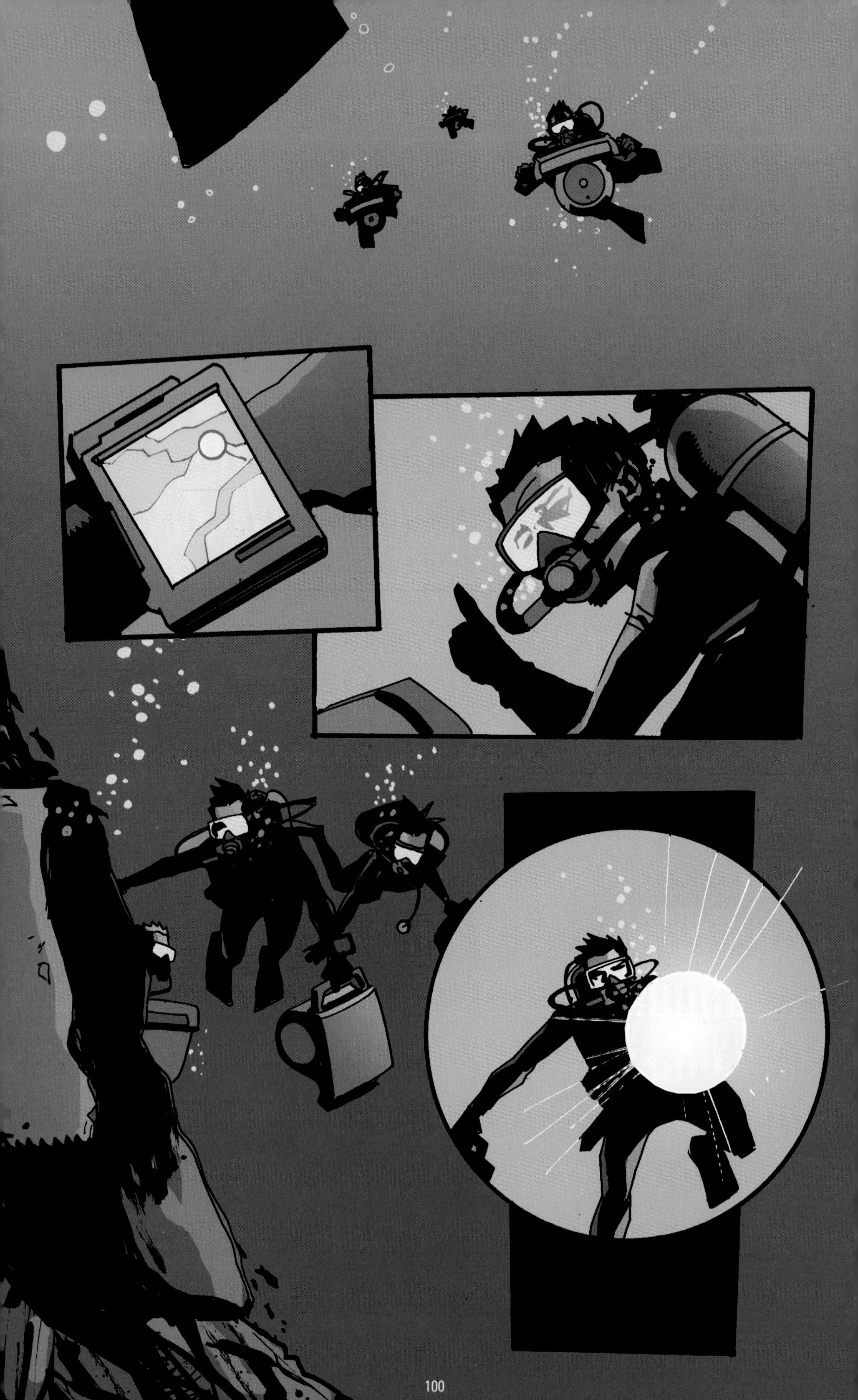

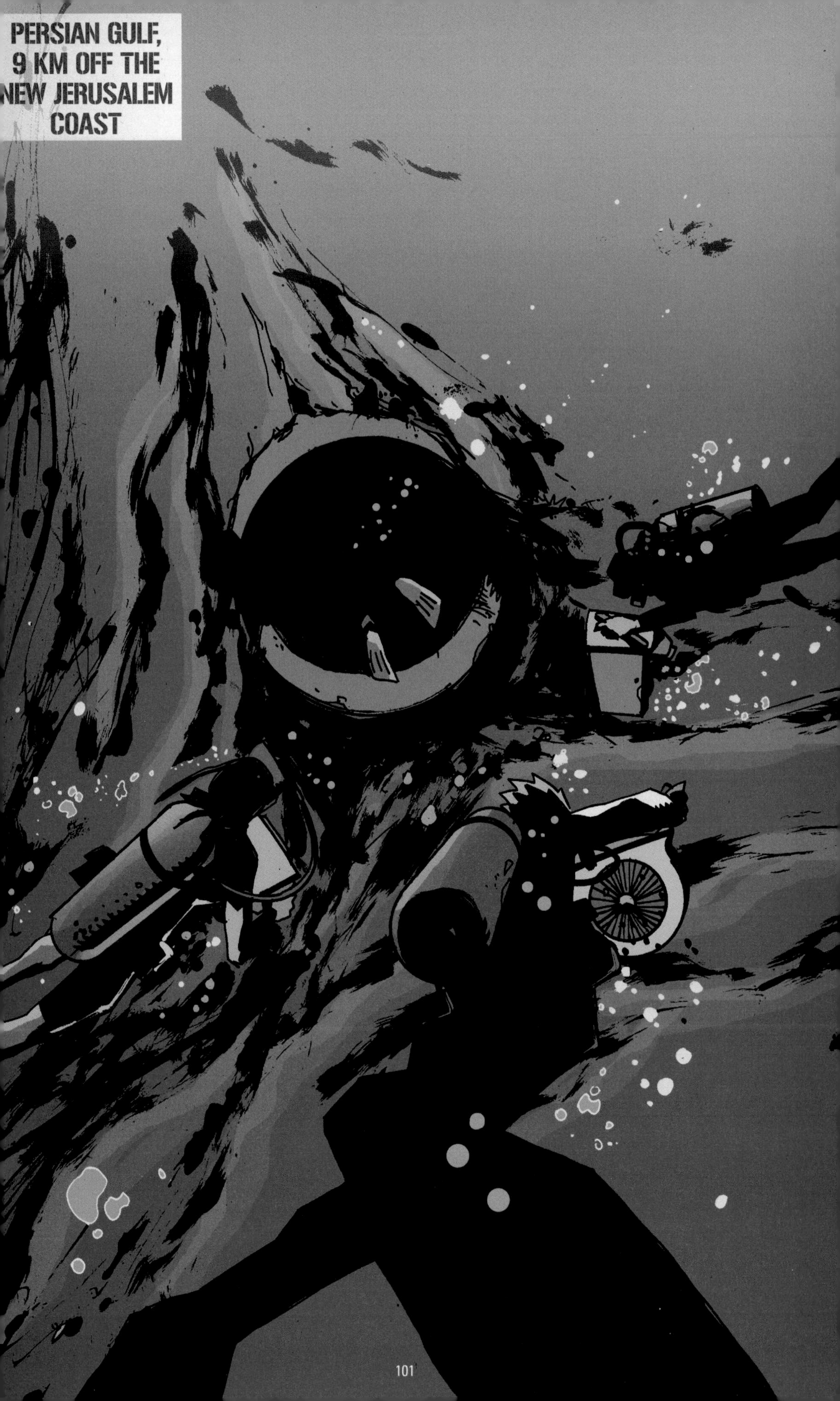
PERSIAN GULF, 9 KM OFF THE NEW JERUSALEM COAST

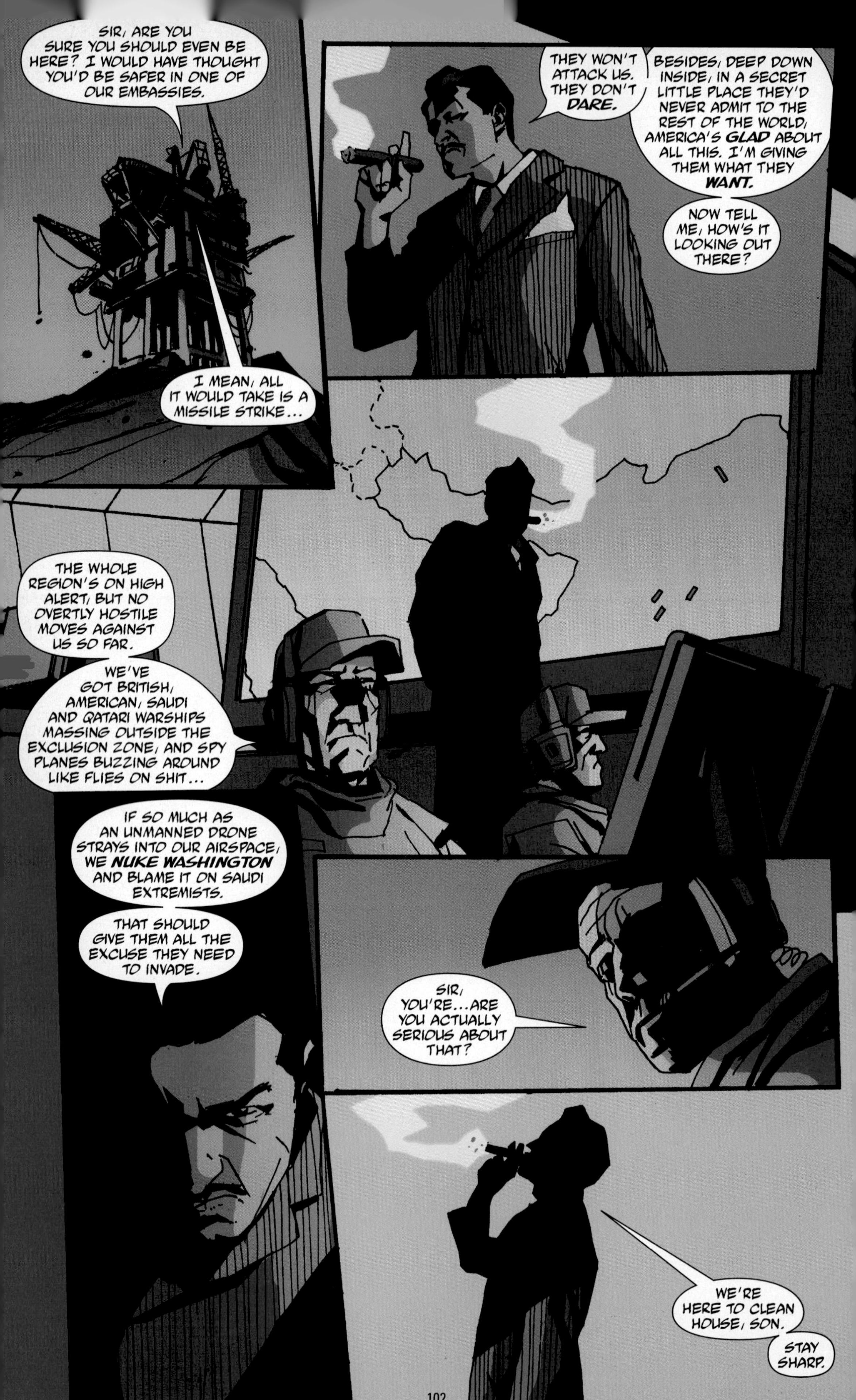
SIR, ARE YOU SURE YOU SHOULD EVEN BE HERE? I WOULD HAVE THOUGHT YOU'D BE SAFER IN ONE OF OUR EMBASSIES.
I MEAN, ALL IT WOULD TAKE IS A MISSILE STRIKE...
THEY WON'T ATTACK US. THEY DON'T DARE.
BESIDES, DEEP DOWN INSIDE, IN A SECRET LITTLE PLACE THEY'D NEVER ADMIT TO THE REST OF THE WORLD, AMERICA'S GLAD ABOUT ALL THIS. I'M GIVING THEM WHAT THEY WANT.
NOW TELL ME, HOW'S IT LOOKING OUT THERE?
THE WHOLE REGION'S ON HIGH ALERT, BUT NO OVERTLY HOSTILE MOVES AGAINST US SO FAR.
WE'VE GOT BRITISH, AMERICAN, SAUDI AND QATARI WARSHIPS MASSING OUTSIDE THE EXCLUSION ZONE, AND SPY PLANES BUZZING AROUND LIKE FLIES ON SHIT...
IF SO MUCH AS AN UNMANNED DRONE STRAYS INTO OUR AIRSPACE, WE NUKE WASHINGTON AND BLAME IT ON SAUDI EXTREMISTS.
THAT SHOULD GIVE THEM ALL THE EXCUSE THEY NEED TO INVADE.
SIR, YOU'RE...ARE YOU ACTUALLY SERIOUS ABOUT THAT?
WE'RE HERE TO CLEAN HOUSE, SON.
STAY SHARP.

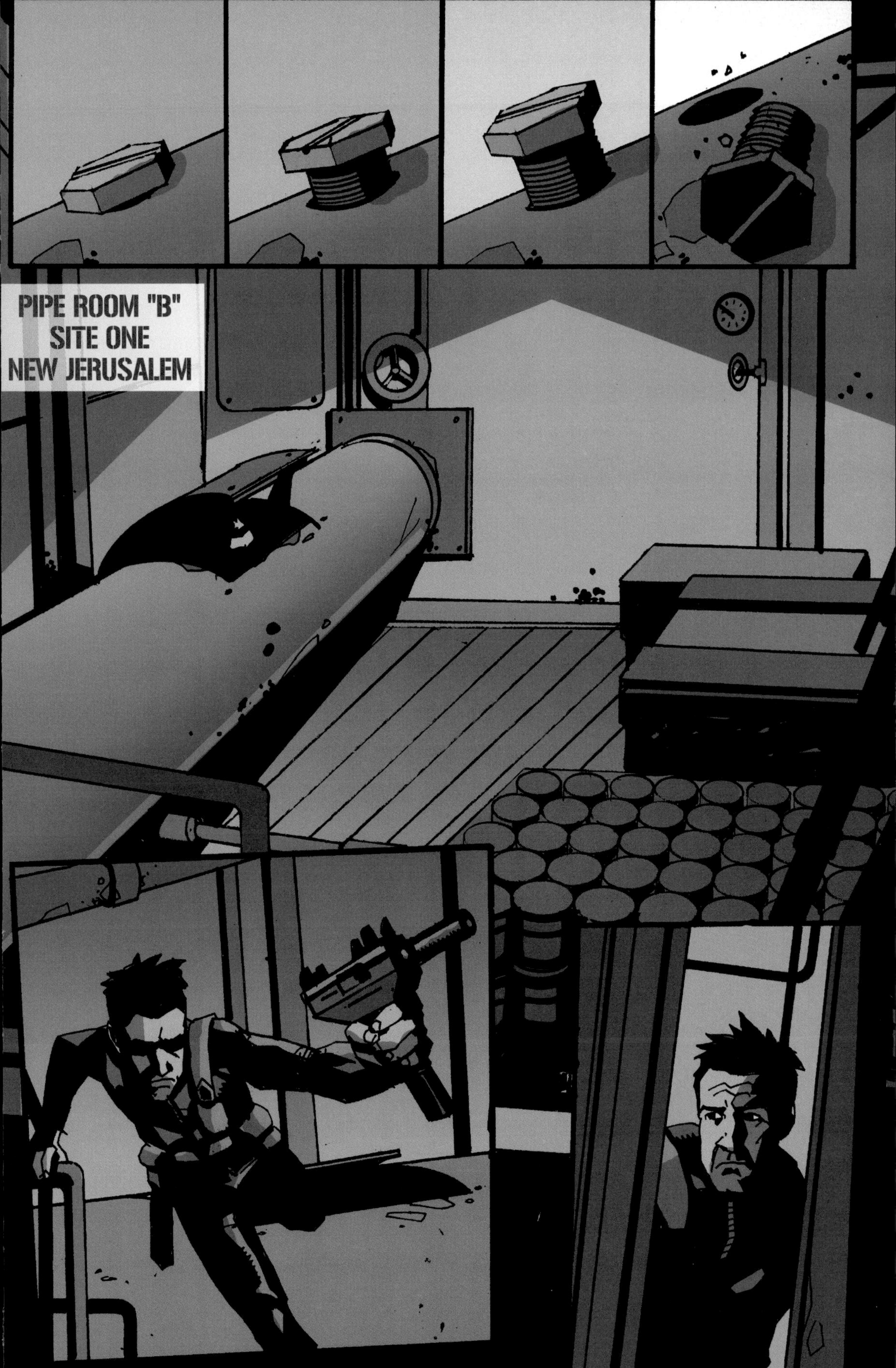
PIPE ROOM "B"
SITE ONE
NEW JERUSALEM

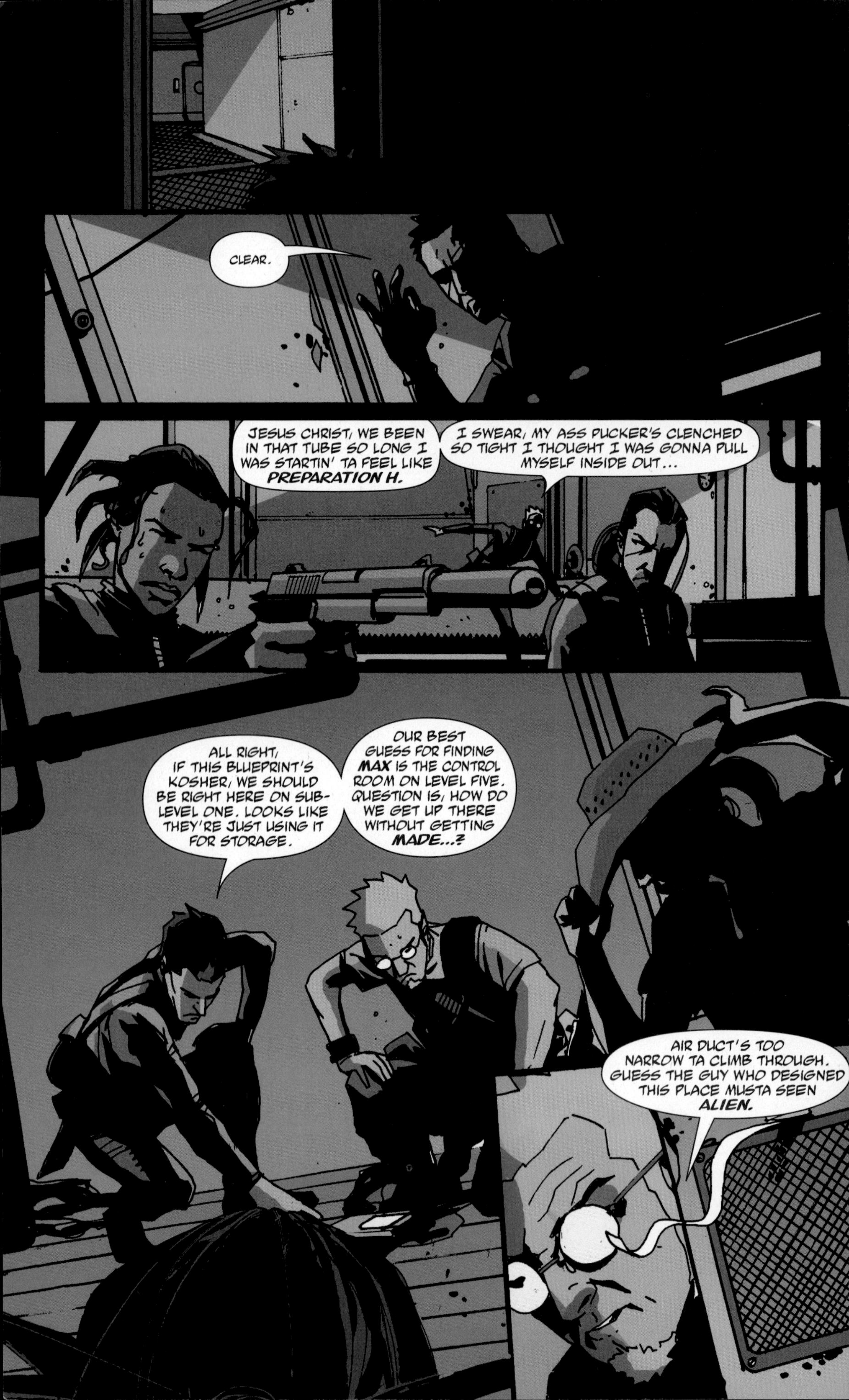
CLEAR.
JESUS CHRIST, WE BEEN IN THAT TUBE SO LONG I WAS STARTIN' TA FEEL LIKE **PREPARATION H.**
I SWEAR, MY ASS PUCKER'S CLENCHED SO TIGHT I THOUGHT I WAS GONNA PULL MYSELF INSIDE OUT...
ALL RIGHT, IF THIS BLUEPRINT'S KOSHER, WE SHOULD BE RIGHT HERE ON SUB-LEVEL ONE. LOOKS LIKE THEY'RE JUST USING IT FOR STORAGE.
OUR BEST GUESS FOR FINDING **MAX** IS THE CONTROL ROOM ON LEVEL FIVE. QUESTION IS, HOW DO WE GET UP THERE WITHOUT GETTING **MADE...?**
AIR DUCT'S TOO NARROW TA CLIMB THROUGH. GUESS THE GUY WHO DESIGNED THIS PLACE MUSTA SEEN **ALIEN.**

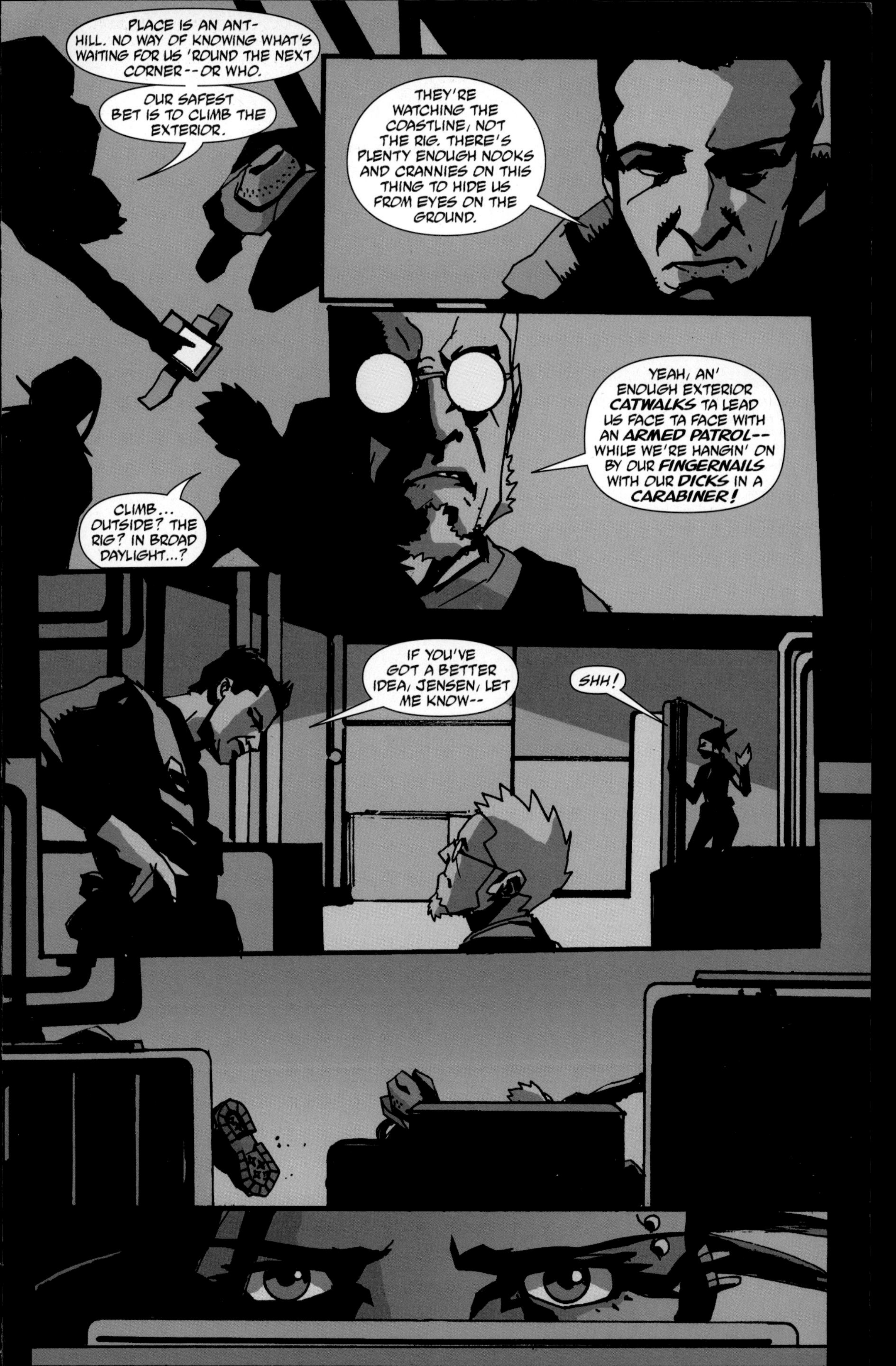
PLACE IS AN ANT-HILL. NO WAY OF KNOWING WHAT'S WAITING FOR US 'ROUND THE NEXT CORNER--OR WHO.
OUR SAFEST BET IS TO CLIMB THE EXTERIOR.
THEY'RE WATCHING THE COASTLINE, NOT THE RIG. THERE'S PLENTY ENOUGH NOOKS AND CRANNIES ON THIS THING TO HIDE US FROM EYES ON THE GROUND.
CLIMB... OUTSIDE? THE RIG? IN BROAD DAYLIGHT...?
YEAH, AN' ENOUGH EXTERIOR **CATWALKS** TA LEAD US FACE TA FACE WITH AN **ARMED PATROL**--WHILE WE'RE HANGIN' ON BY OUR **FINGERNAILS** WITH OUR **DICKS** IN A **CARABINER!**
IF YOU'VE GOT A BETTER IDEA, JENSEN, LET ME KNOW--
SHH!

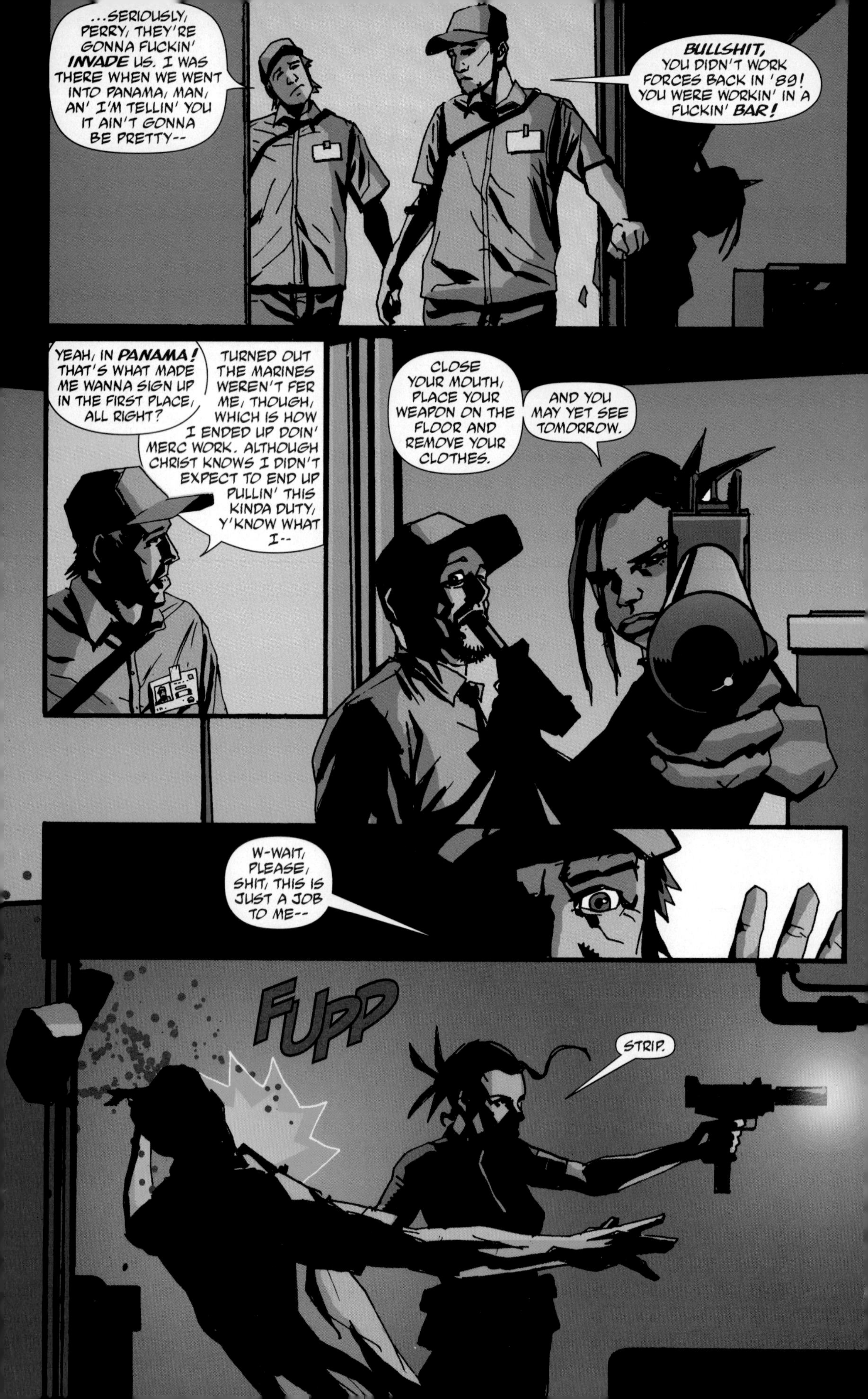
...SERIOUSLY, PERRY, THEY'RE GONNA FUCKIN' INVADE US. I WAS THERE WHEN WE WENT INTO PANAMA, MAN, AN' I'M TELLIN' YOU IT AIN'T GONNA BE PRETTY--
BULLSHIT, YOU DIDN'T WORK FORCES BACK IN '89! YOU WERE WORKIN' IN A FUCKIN' BAR!
YEAH, IN PANAMA! THAT'S WHAT MADE ME WANNA SIGN UP IN THE FIRST PLACE, ALL RIGHT?
TURNED OUT THE MARINES WEREN'T FER ME, THOUGH, WHICH IS HOW I ENDED UP DOIN' MERC WORK. ALTHOUGH CHRIST KNOWS I DIDN'T EXPECT TO END UP PULLIN' THIS KINDA DUTY, Y'KNOW WHAT I--
CLOSE YOUR MOUTH, PLACE YOUR WEAPON ON THE FLOOR AND REMOVE YOUR CLOTHES.
AND YOU MAY YET SEE TOMORROW.
W-WAIT, PLEASE, SHIT, THIS IS JUST A JOB TO ME--
FUPP
STRIP.

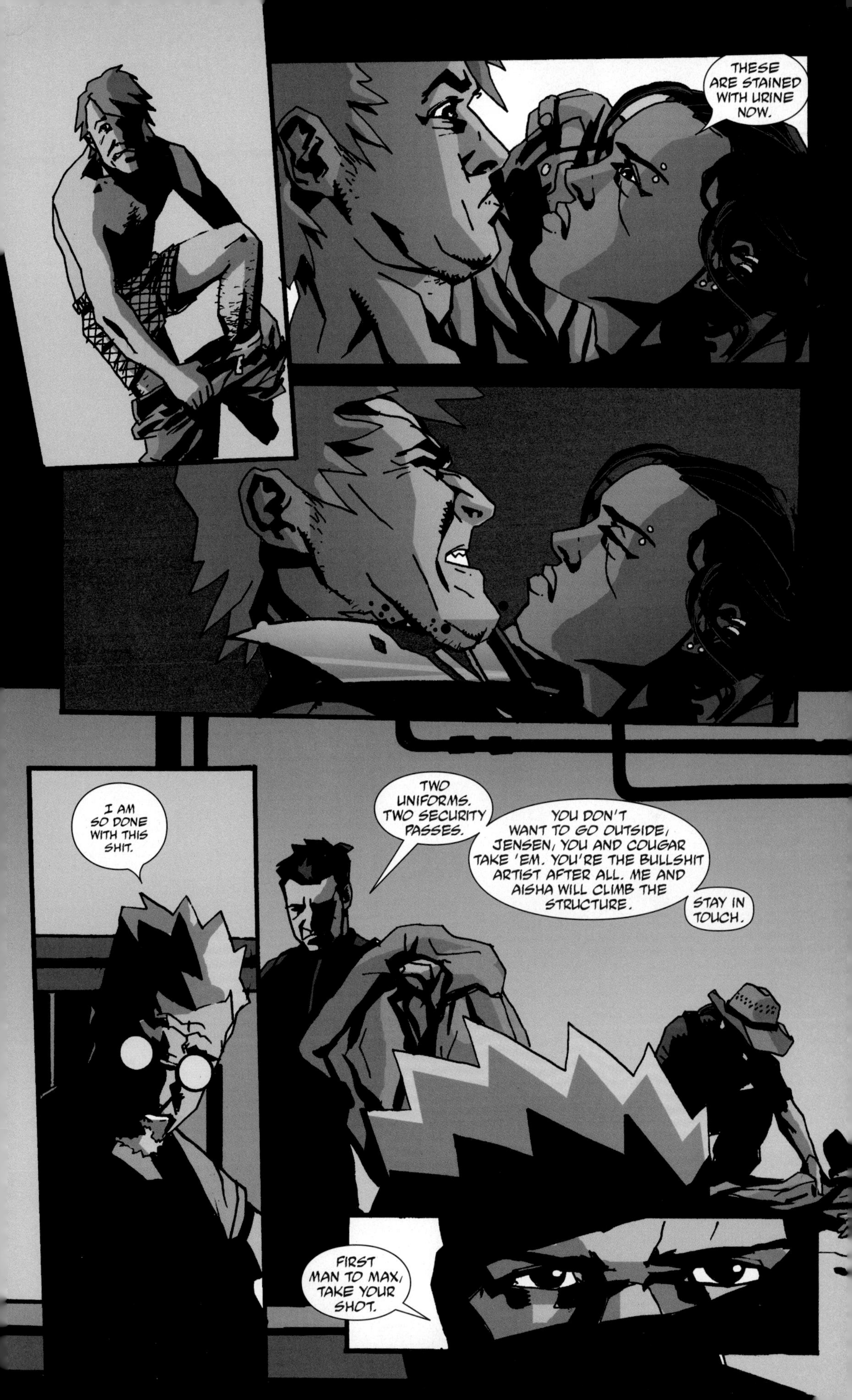
THESE ARE STAINED WITH URINE NOW.
I AM SO DONE WITH THIS SHIT.
TWO UNIFORMS. TWO SECURITY PASSES.
YOU DON'T WANT TO GO OUTSIDE, JENSEN, YOU AND COUGAR TAKE 'EM. YOU'RE THE BULLSHIT ARTIST AFTER ALL. ME AND AISHA WILL CLIMB THE STRUCTURE.
STAY IN TOUCH.
FIRST MAN TO MAX, TAKE YOUR SHOT.

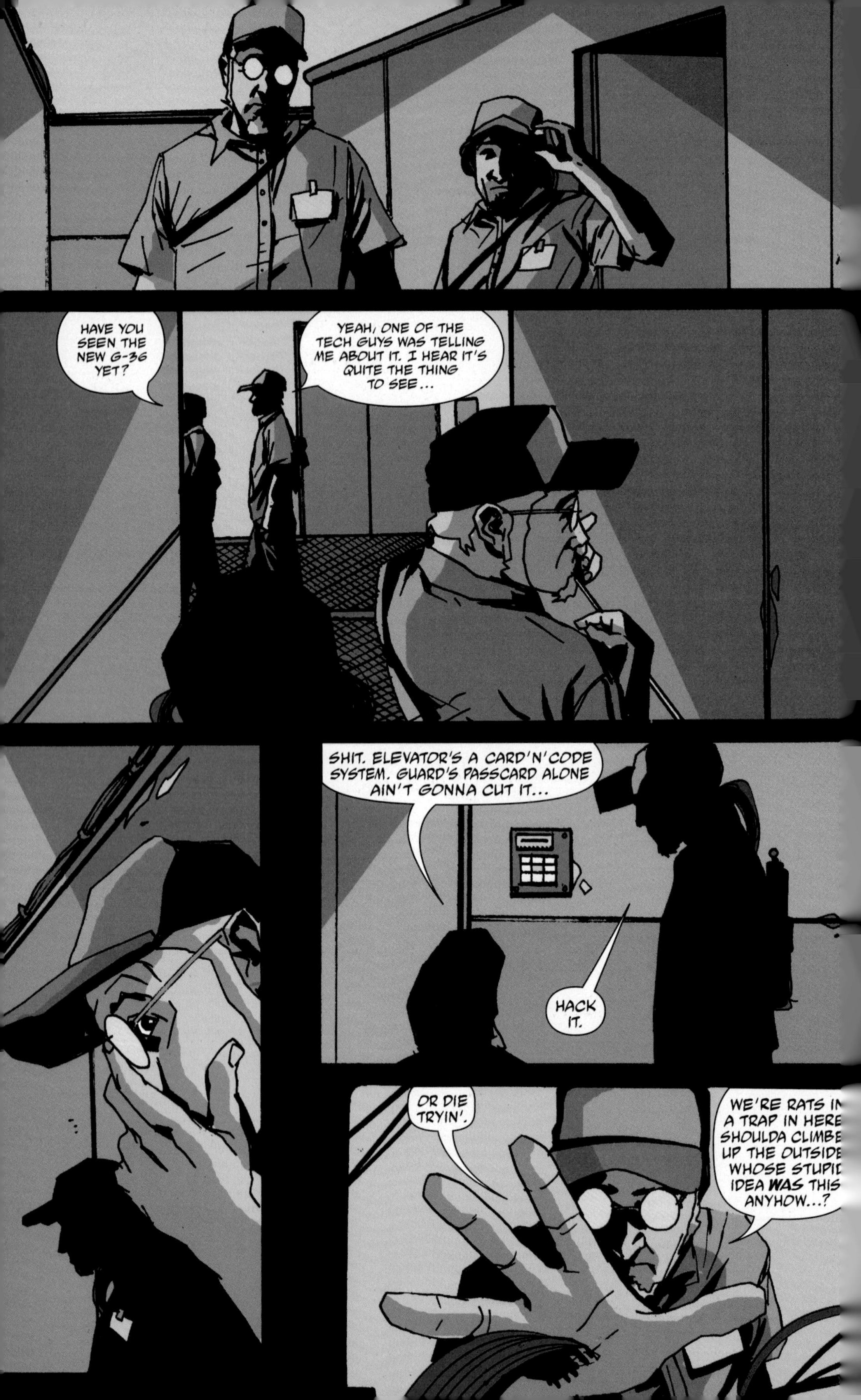
HAVE YOU SEEN THE NEW G-36 YET?
YEAH, ONE OF THE TECH GUYS WAS TELLING ME ABOUT IT. I HEAR IT'S QUITE THE THING TO SEE...
SHIT. ELEVATOR'S A CARD'N'CODE SYSTEM. GUARD'S PASSCARD ALONE AIN'T GONNA CUT IT...
HACK IT.
OR DIE TRYIN'.
WE'RE RATS IN A TRAP IN HERE SHOULDA CLIMBE UP THE OUTSIDE WHOSE STUPID IDEA **WAS** THIS ANYHOW...?

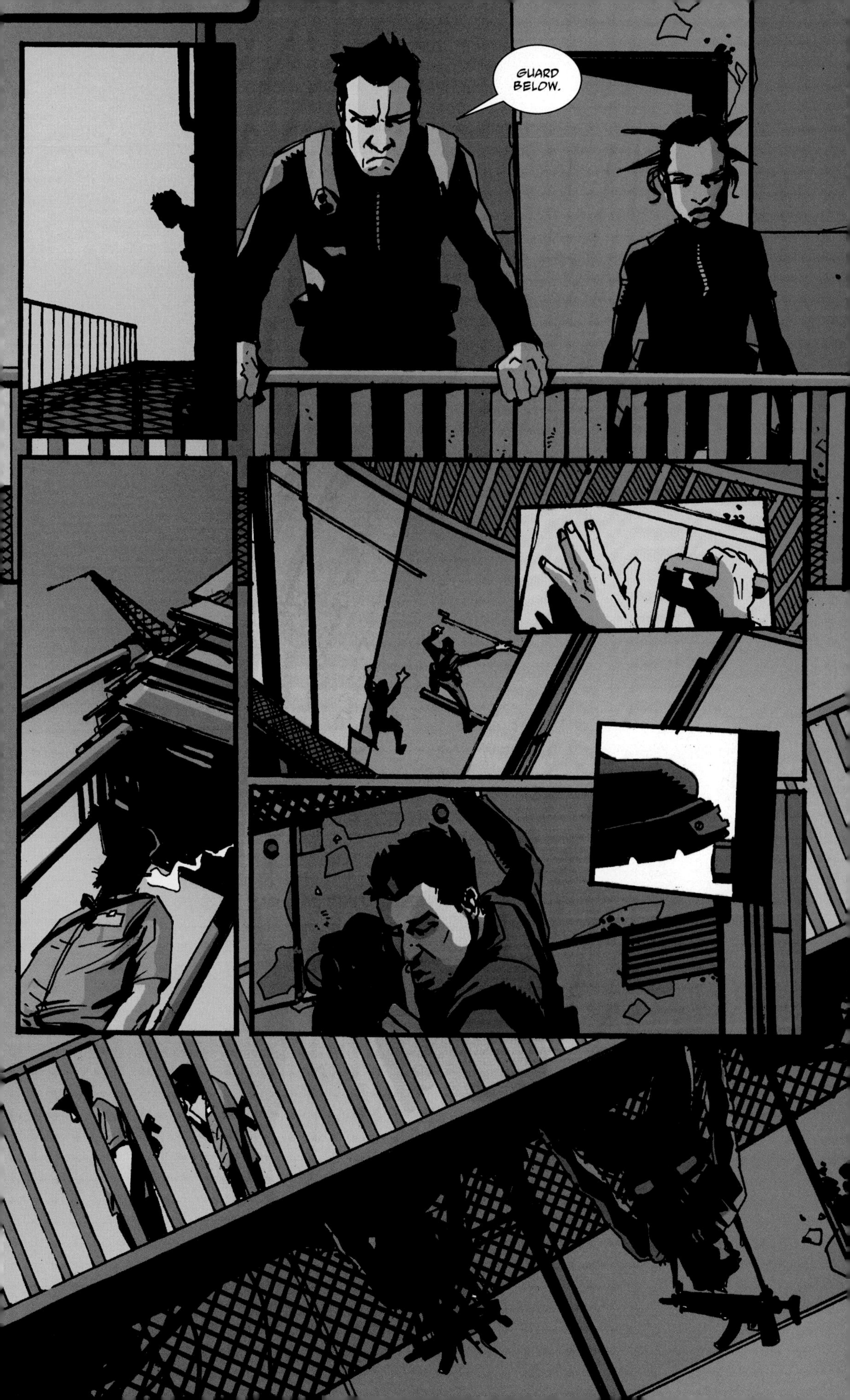
GUARD BELOW.

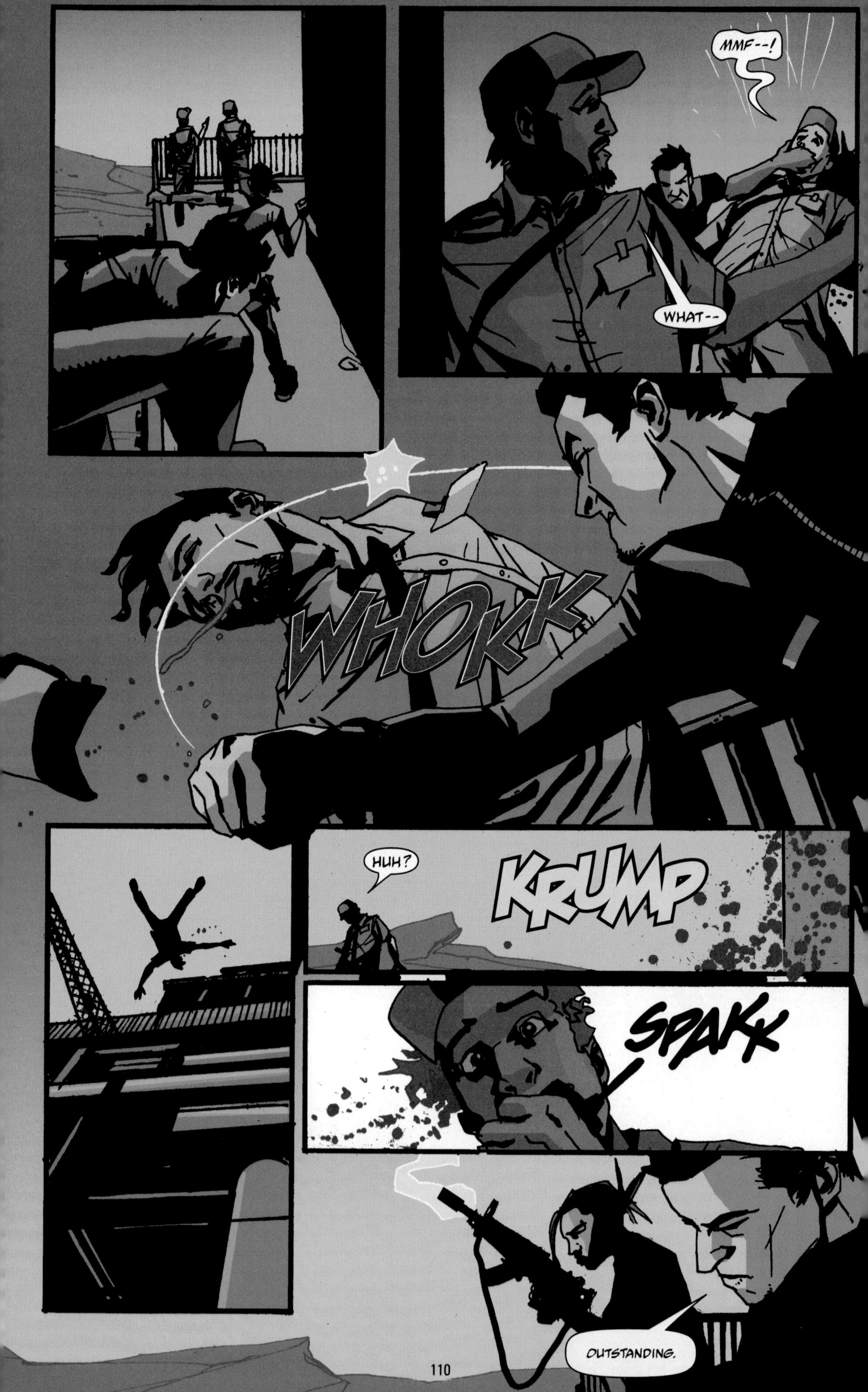
MMF--!
WHAT--
WHOKK
HUH?
KRUMP
SPAKK
OUTSTANDING.

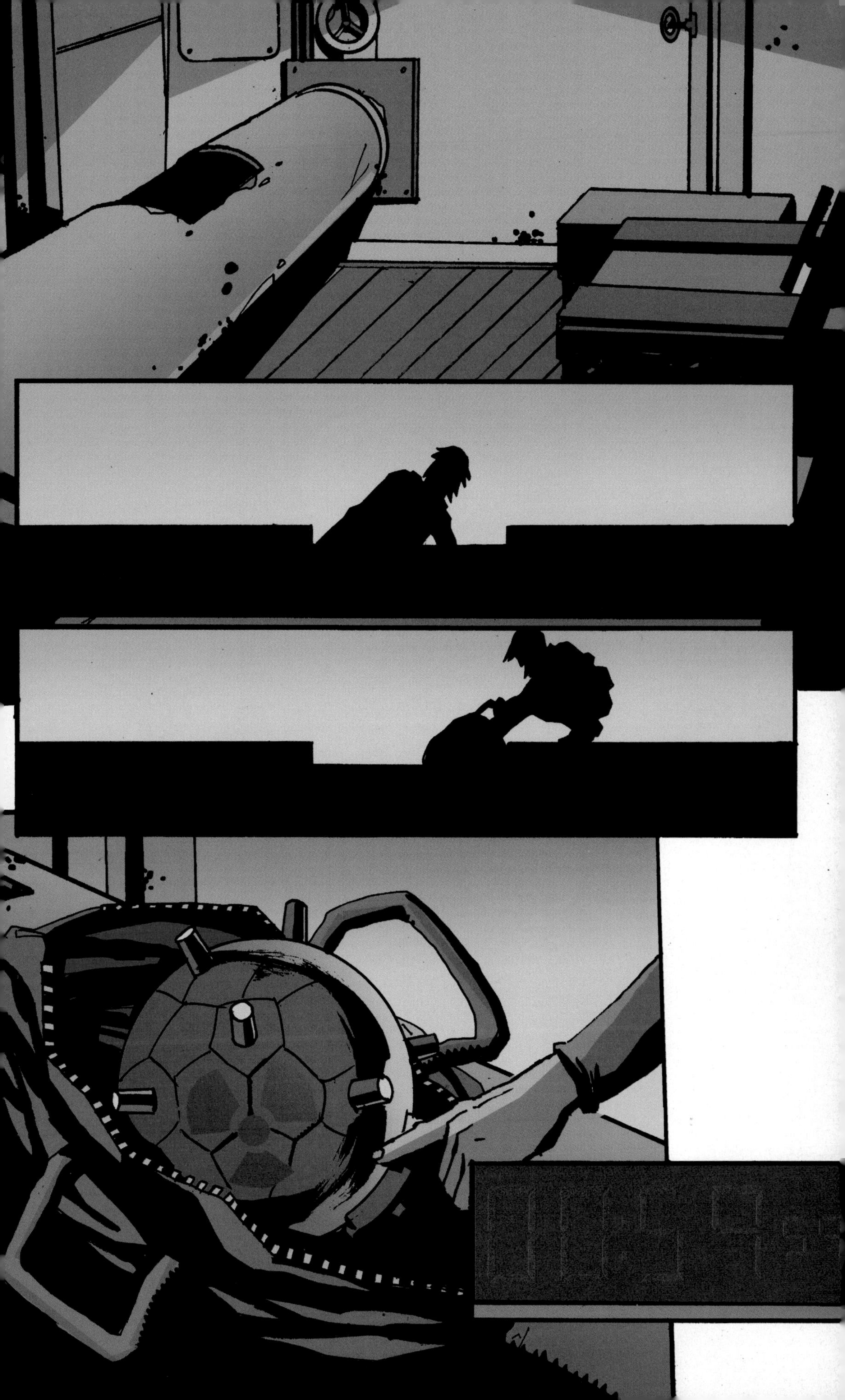

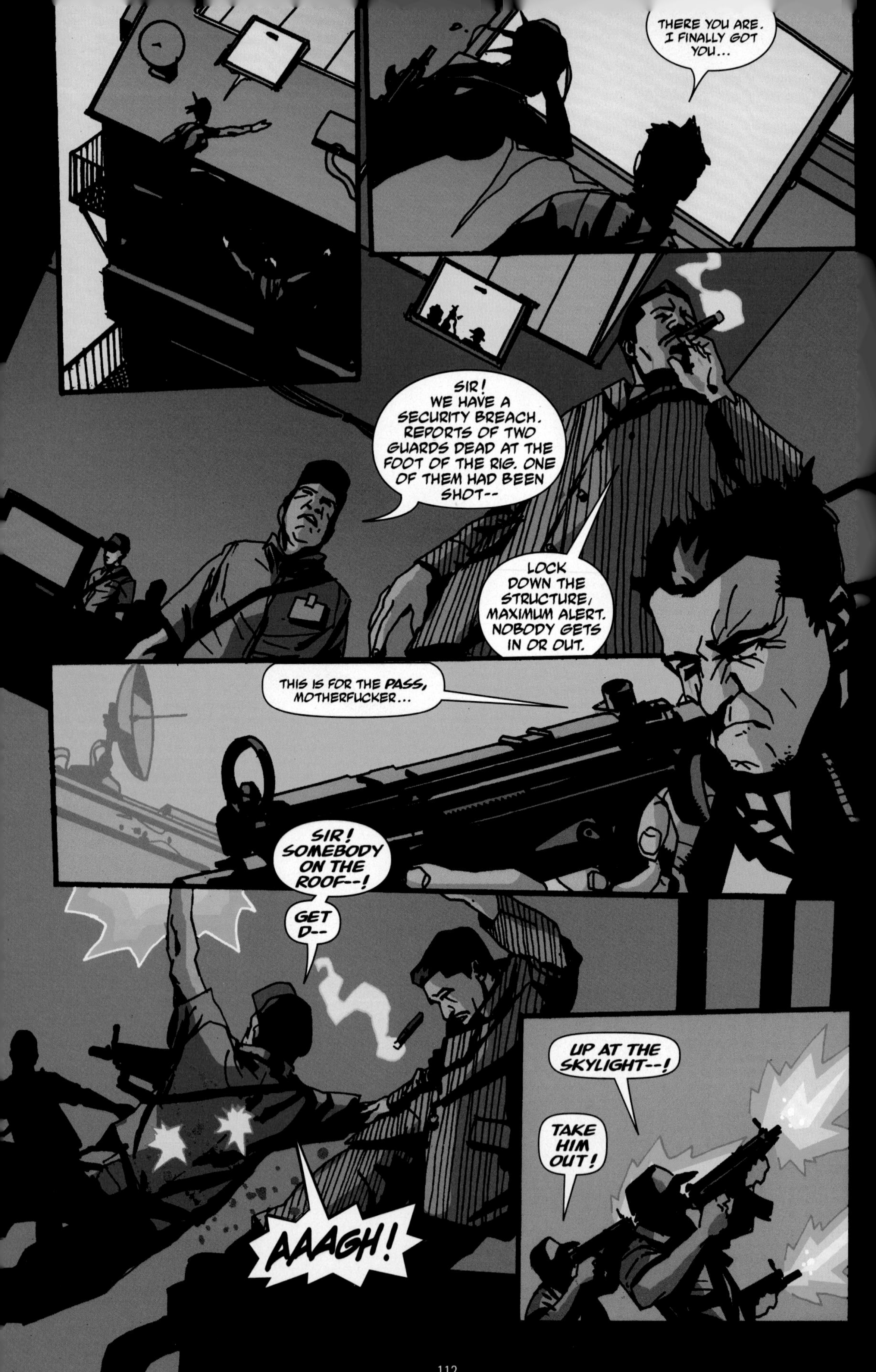
THERE YOU ARE. I FINALLY GOT YOU...
SIR! WE HAVE A SECURITY BREACH. REPORTS OF TWO GUARDS DEAD AT THE FOOT OF THE RIG. ONE OF THEM HAD BEEN SHOT--
LOCK DOWN THE STRUCTURE, MAXIMUM ALERT. NOBODY GETS IN OR OUT.
THIS IS FOR THE PASS, MOTHERFUCKER...
SIR! SOMEBODY ON THE ROOF--!
GET D--
AAAGH!
UP AT THE SKYLIGHT--!
TAKE HIM OUT!

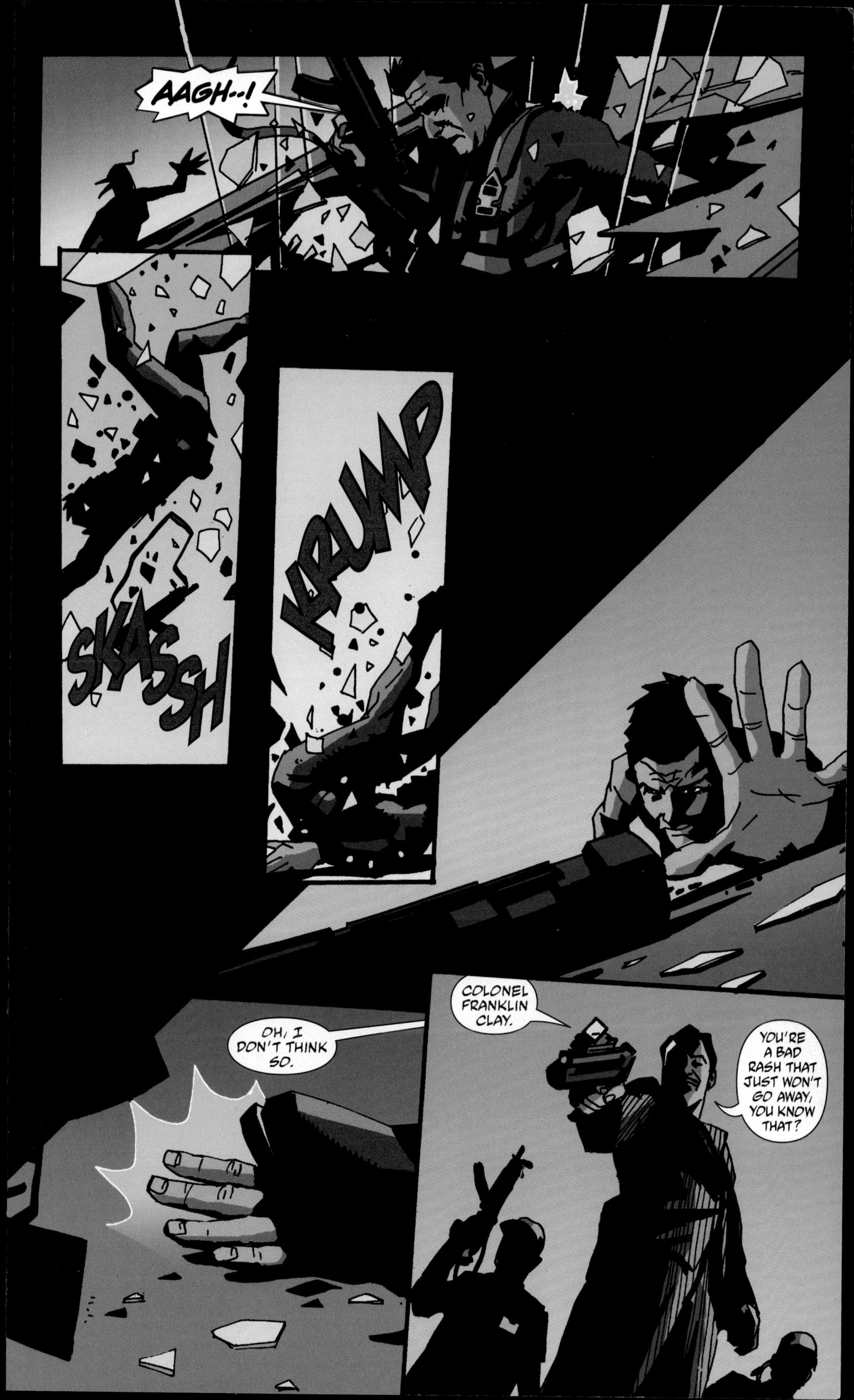
AAGH--!
SKASSH
KRUMP
OH, I DON'T THINK SO.
COLONEL FRANKLIN CLAY.
YOU'RE A BAD RASH THAT JUST WON'T GO AWAY, YOU KNOW THAT?

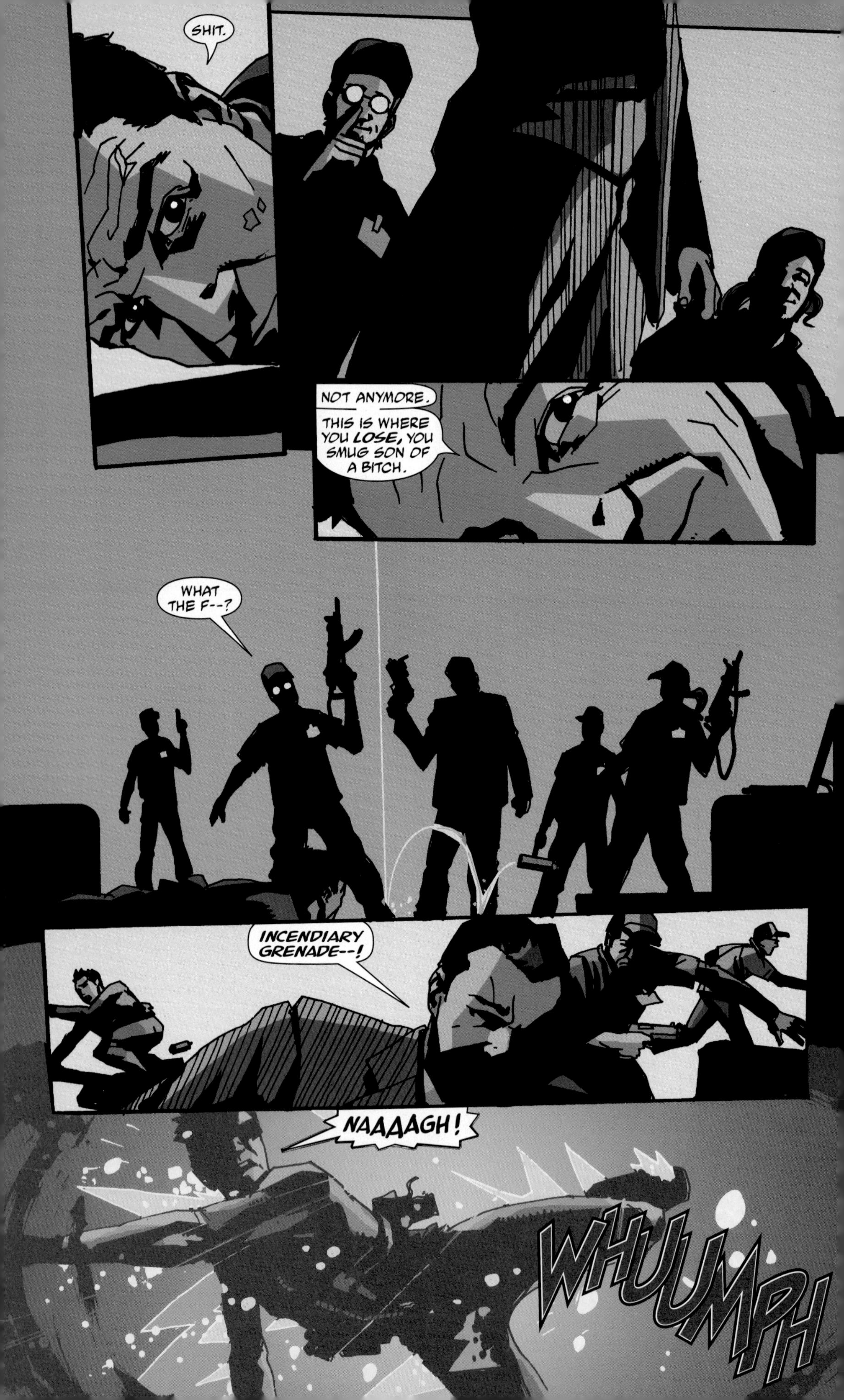
SHIT.
NOT ANYMORE.
THIS IS WHERE YOU LOSE, YOU SMUG SON OF A BITCH.
WHAT THE F--?
INCENDIARY GRENADE--!
NAAAAGH!
WHUUMPH

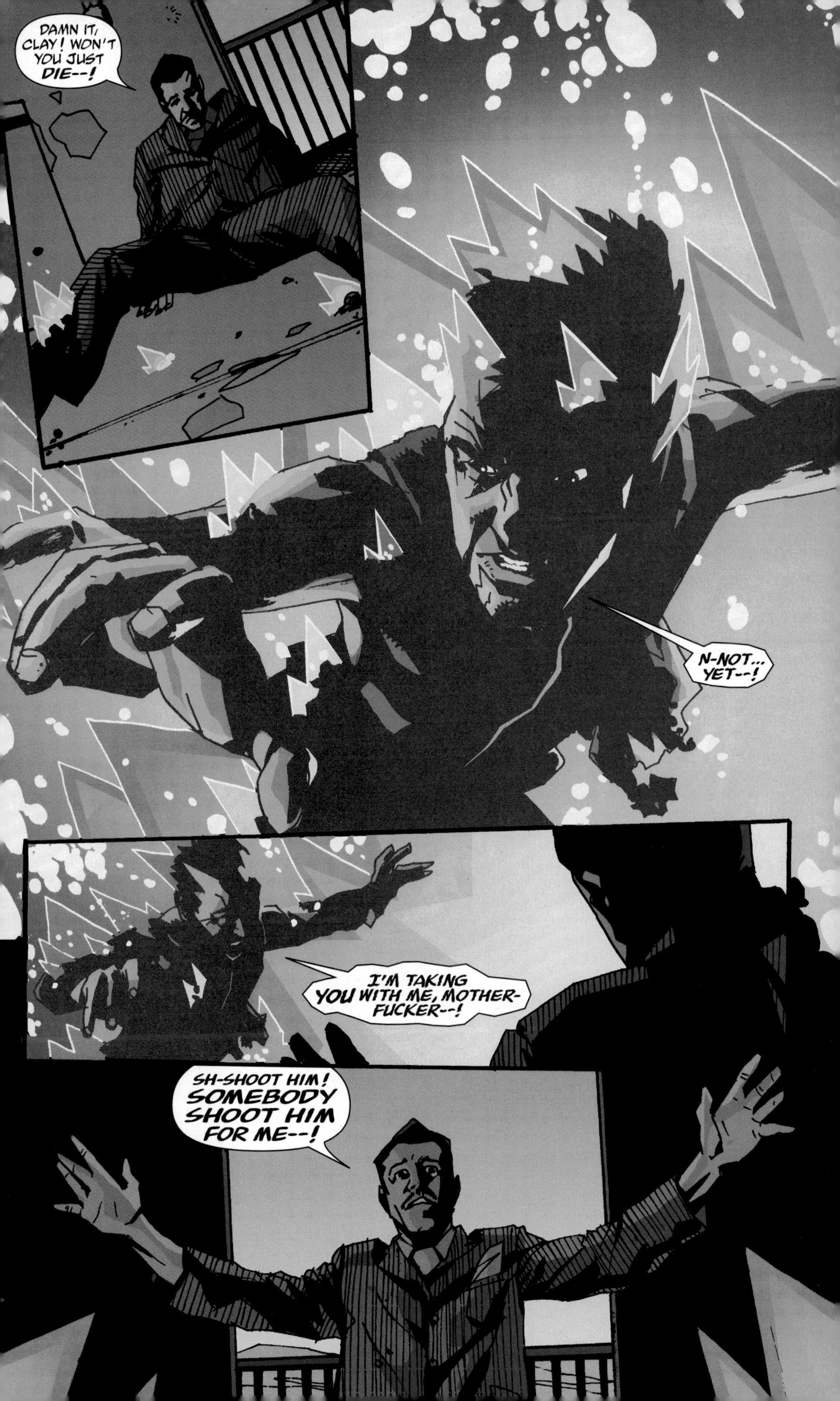
DAMN IT, CLAY! WON'T YOU JUST DIE--!
N-NOT... YET--!
I'M TAKING YOU WITH ME, MOTHER-FUCKER--!
SH-SHOOT HIM! SOMEBODY SHOOT HIM FOR ME--!

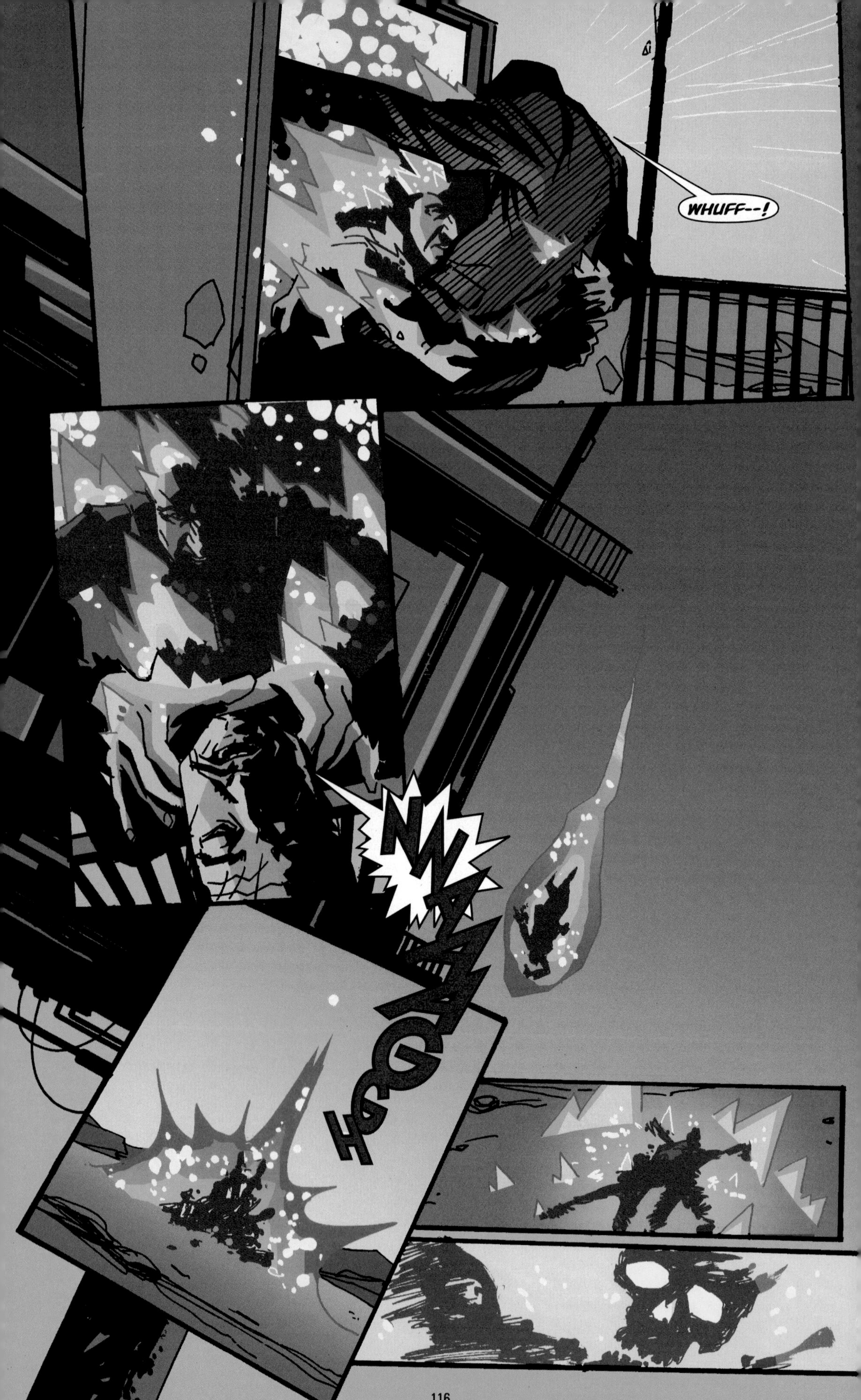
WHUFF--!
NNAAAGGH

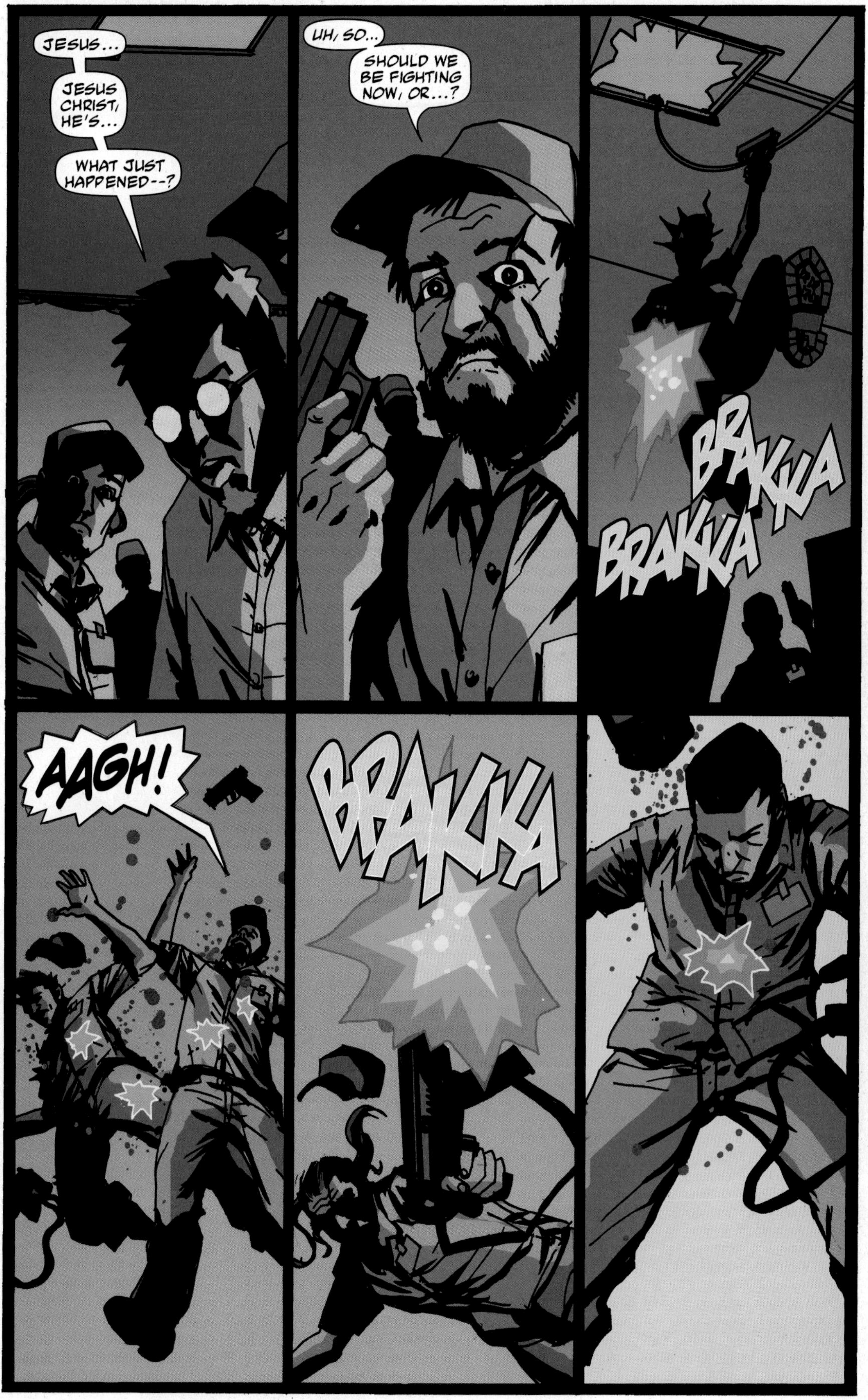

JESUS...
JESUS CHRIST, HE'S...
WHAT JUST HAPPENED--?
UH, SO...
SHOULD WE BE FIGHTING NOW, OR...?
BRAKKA
BRAKKA
AAGH!
BRAKKA

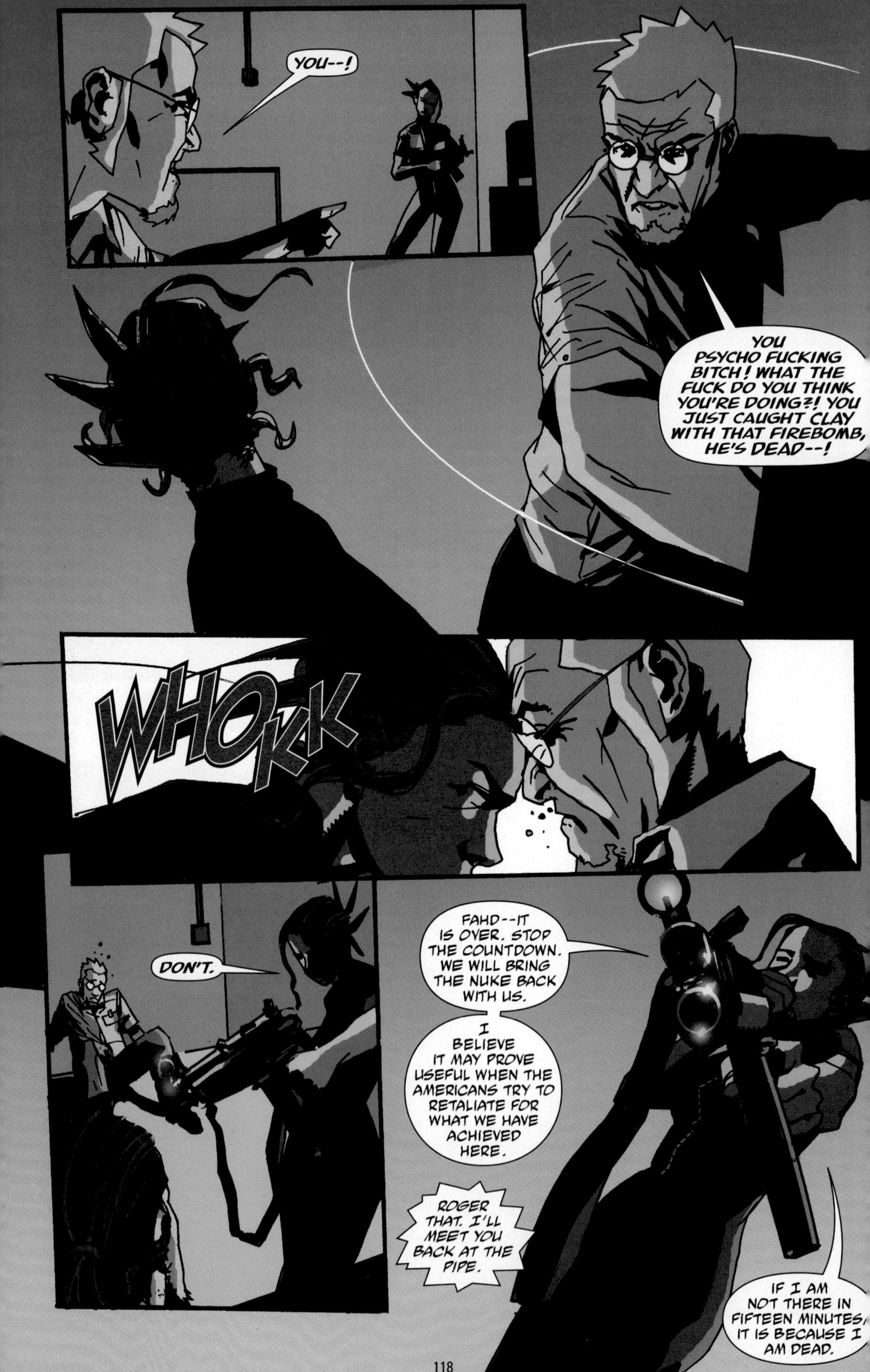
YOU--!
YOU PSYCHO FUCKING BITCH! WHAT THE FUCK DO YOU THINK YOU'RE DOING?! YOU JUST CAUGHT CLAY WITH THAT FIREBOMB, HE'S DEAD--!
WHOKK
DON'T.
FAHD--IT IS OVER. STOP THE COUNTDOWN. WE WILL BRING THE NUKE BACK WITH US.
I BELIEVE IT MAY PROVE USEFUL WHEN THE AMERICANS TRY TO RETALIATE FOR WHAT WE HAVE ACHIEVED HERE.
ROGER THAT. I'LL MEET YOU BACK AT THE PIPE.
IF I AM NOT THERE IN FIFTEEN MINUTES, IT IS BECAUSE I AM DEAD.

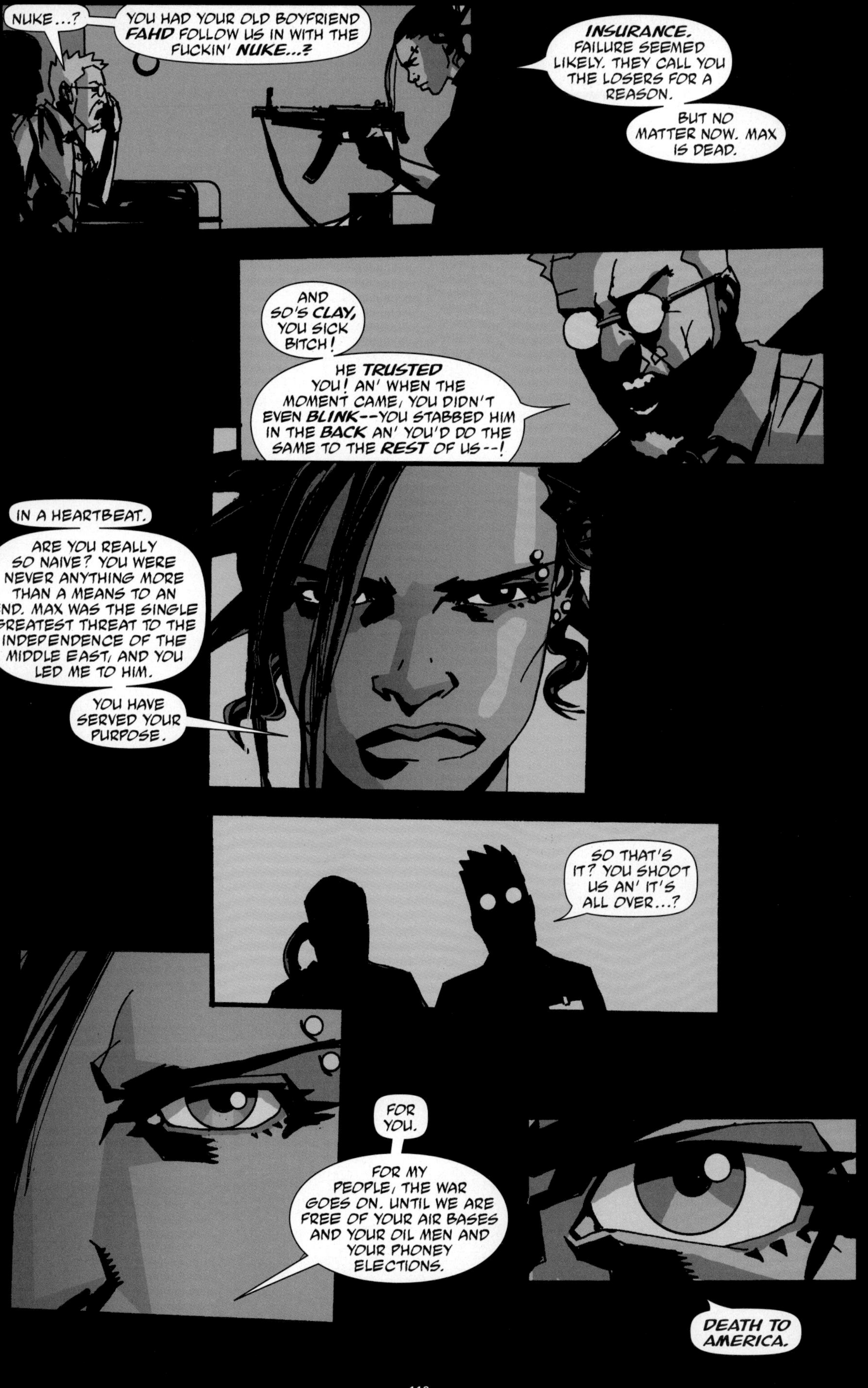
NUKE...?
YOU HAD YOUR OLD BOYFRIEND FAHD FOLLOW US IN WITH THE FUCKIN' NUKE...?
INSURANCE. FAILURE SEEMED LIKELY. THEY CALL YOU THE LOSERS FOR A REASON.
BUT NO MATTER NOW. MAX IS DEAD.
AND SO'S CLAY, YOU SICK BITCH!
HE TRUSTED YOU! AN' WHEN THE MOMENT CAME, YOU DIDN'T EVEN BLINK--YOU STABBED HIM IN THE BACK AN' YOU'D DO THE SAME TO THE REST OF US--!
IN A HEARTBEAT.
ARE YOU REALLY SO NAIVE? YOU WERE NEVER ANYTHING MORE THAN A MEANS TO AN END. MAX WAS THE SINGLE GREATEST THREAT TO THE INDEPENDENCE OF THE MIDDLE EAST, AND YOU LED ME TO HIM.
YOU HAVE SERVED YOUR PURPOSE.
SO THAT'S IT? YOU SHOOT US AN' IT'S ALL OVER...?
FOR YOU.
FOR MY PEOPLE, THE WAR GOES ON. UNTIL WE ARE FREE OF YOUR AIR BASES AND YOUR OIL MEN AND YOUR PHONEY ELECTIONS.
DEATH TO AMERICA.

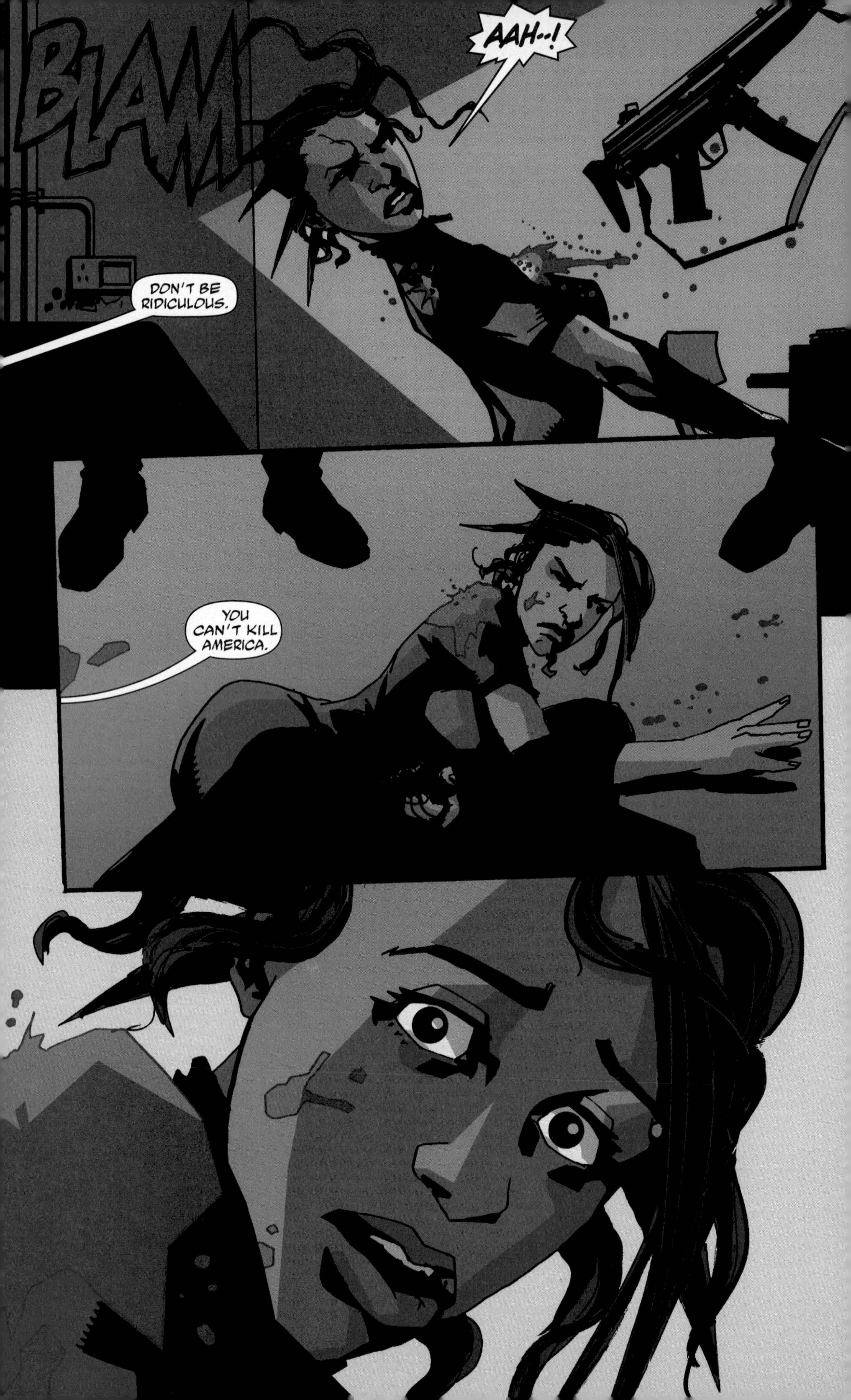
BLAM
AAH--!
DON'T BE RIDICULOUS.
YOU CAN'T KILL AMERICA.

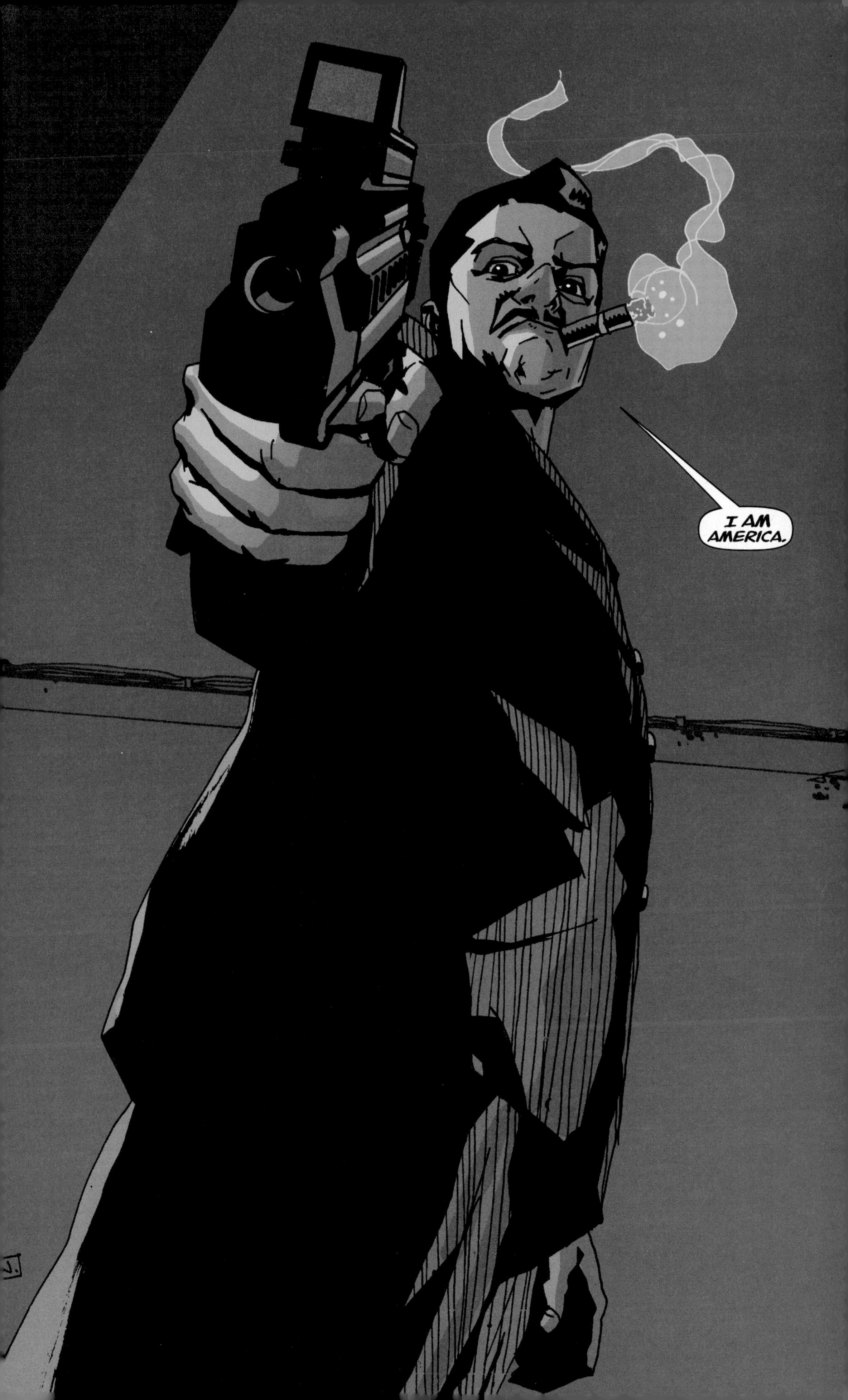
I AM AMERICA.

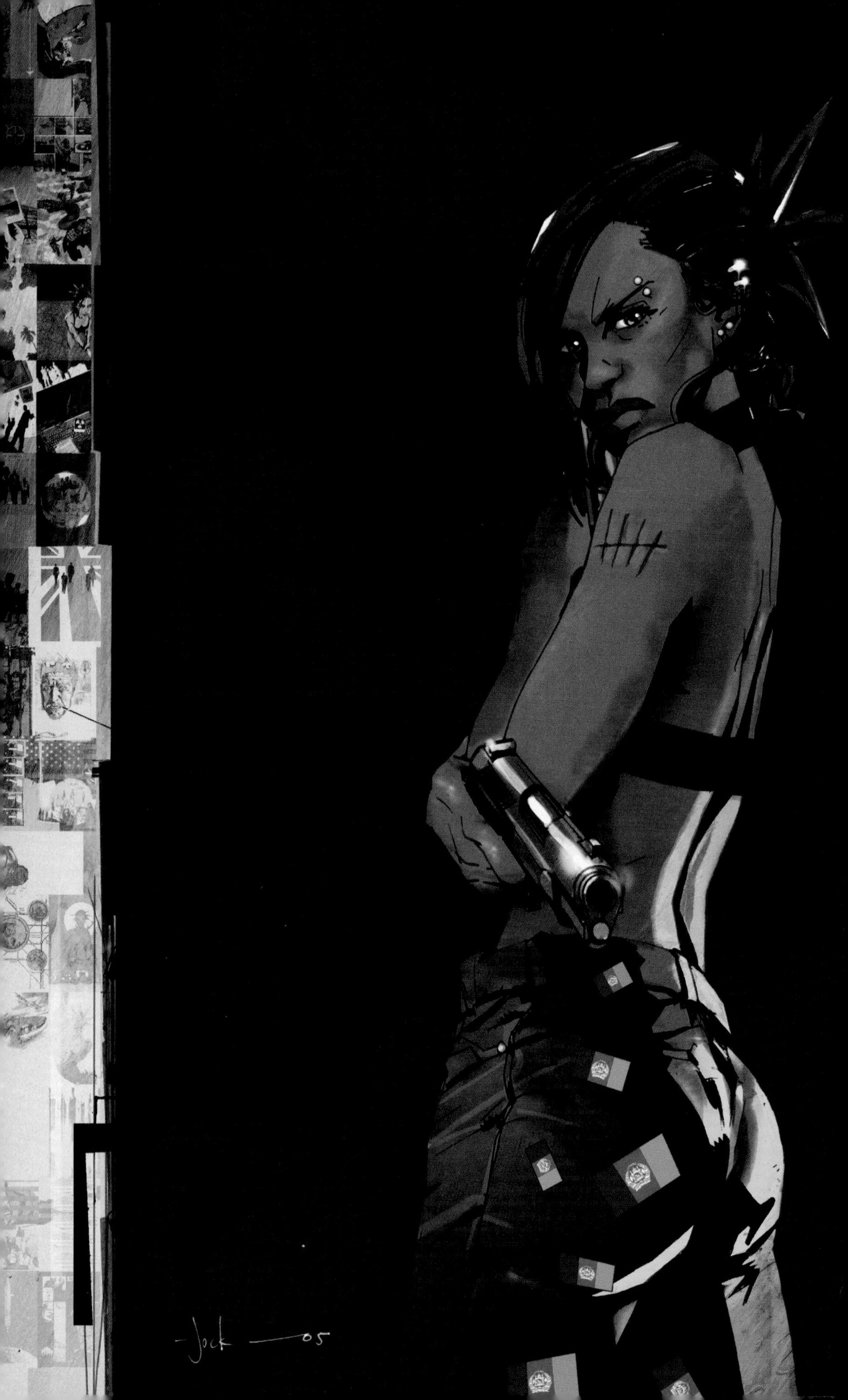
Jock 05

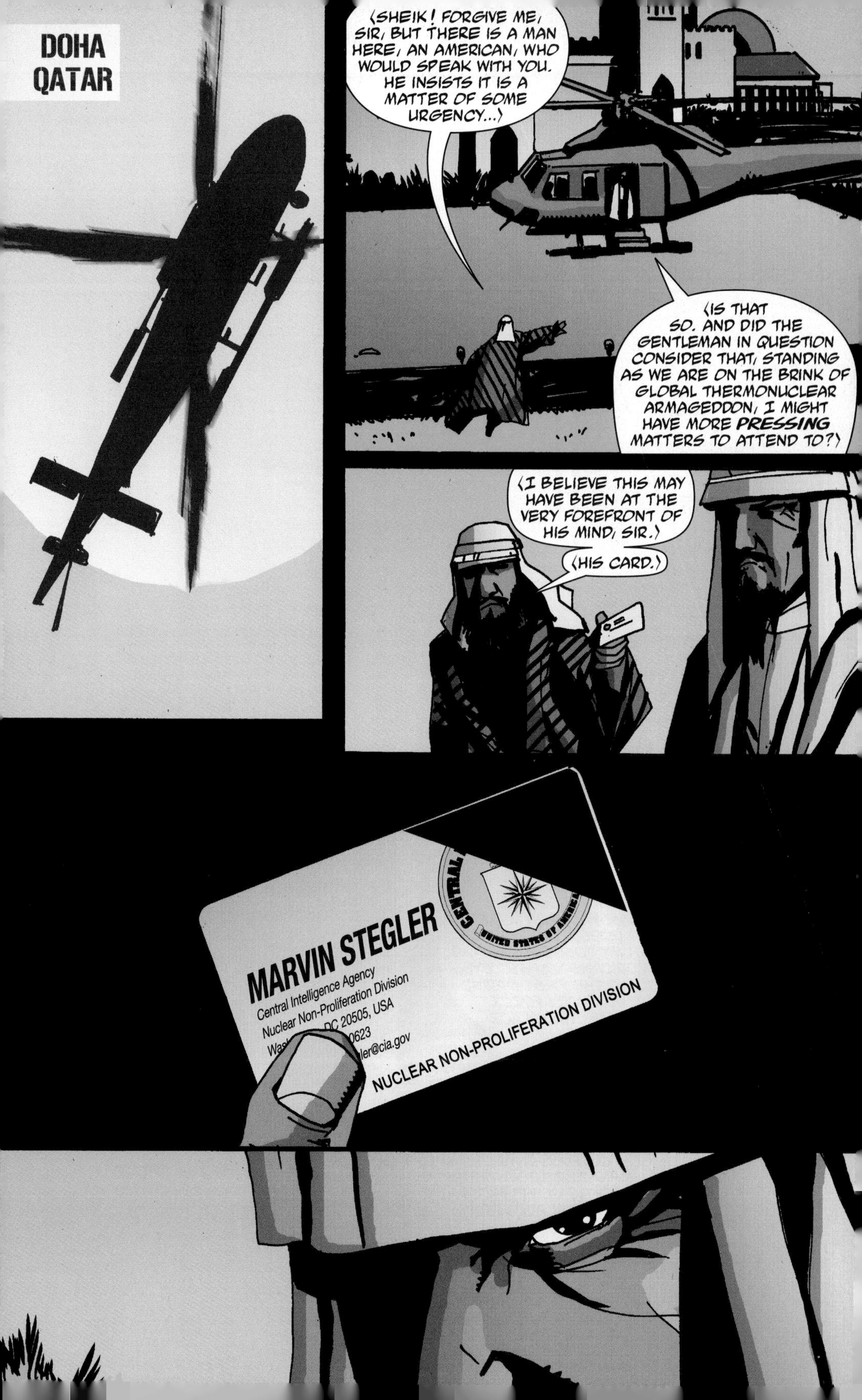
DOHA QATAR
⟨SHEIK! FORGIVE ME, SIR, BUT THERE IS A MAN HERE, AN AMERICAN, WHO WOULD SPEAK WITH YOU. HE INSISTS IT IS A MATTER OF SOME URGENCY...⟩
⟨IS THAT SO. AND DID THE GENTLEMAN IN QUESTION CONSIDER THAT, STANDING AS WE ARE ON THE BRINK OF GLOBAL THERMONUCLEAR ARMAGEDDON, I MIGHT HAVE MORE PRESSING MATTERS TO ATTEND TO?⟩
⟨I BELIEVE THIS MAY HAVE BEEN AT THE VERY FOREFRONT OF HIS MIND, SIR.⟩
⟨HIS CARD.⟩
MARVIN STEGLER
Central Intelligence Agency
Nuclear Non-Proliferation Division
DC 20505, USA
NUCLEAR NON-PROLIFERATION DIVISION

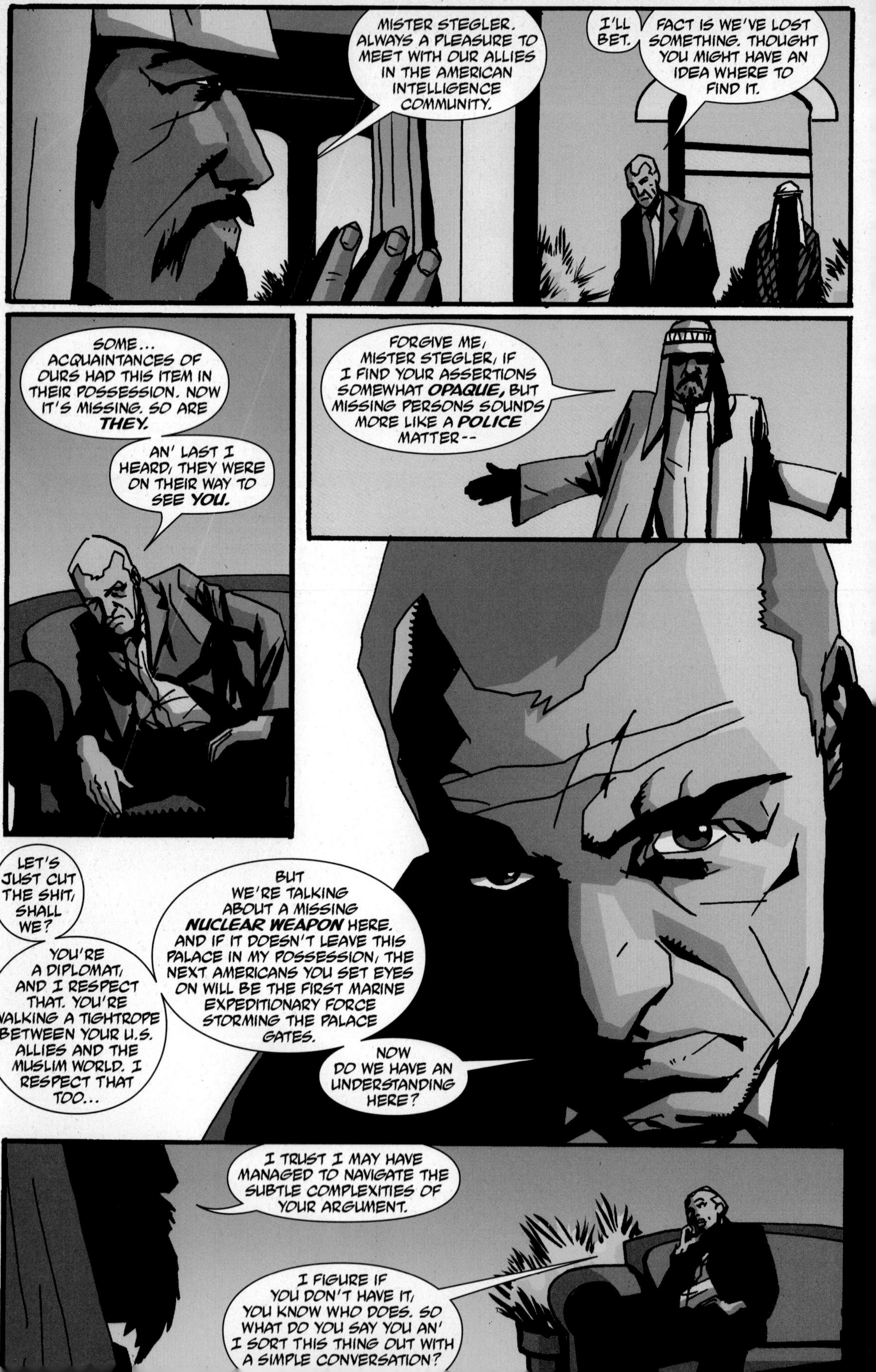
MISTER STEGLER. ALWAYS A PLEASURE TO MEET WITH OUR ALLIES IN THE AMERICAN INTELLIGENCE COMMUNITY.
I'LL BET.
FACT IS WE'VE LOST SOMETHING. THOUGHT YOU MIGHT HAVE AN IDEA WHERE TO FIND IT.
SOME... ACQUAINTANCES OF OURS HAD THIS ITEM IN THEIR POSSESSION. NOW IT'S MISSING. SO ARE THEY.
AN' LAST I HEARD, THEY WERE ON THEIR WAY TO SEE YOU.
FORGIVE ME, MISTER STEGLER, IF I FIND YOUR ASSERTIONS SOMEWHAT OPAQUE, BUT MISSING PERSONS SOUNDS MORE LIKE A POLICE MATTER--
LET'S JUST CUT THE SHIT, SHALL WE?
YOU'RE A DIPLOMAT, AND I RESPECT THAT. YOU'RE WALKING A TIGHTROPE BETWEEN YOUR U.S. ALLIES AND THE MUSLIM WORLD. I RESPECT THAT TOO...
BUT WE'RE TALKING ABOUT A MISSING NUCLEAR WEAPON HERE. AND IF IT DOESN'T LEAVE THIS PALACE IN MY POSSESSION, THE NEXT AMERICANS YOU SET EYES ON WILL BE THE FIRST MARINE EXPEDITIONARY FORCE STORMING THE PALACE GATES.
NOW DO WE HAVE AN UNDERSTANDING HERE?
I TRUST I MAY HAVE MANAGED TO NAVIGATE THE SUBTLE COMPLEXITIES OF YOUR ARGUMENT.
I FIGURE IF YOU DON'T HAVE IT, YOU KNOW WHO DOES. SO WHAT DO YOU SAY YOU AN' I SORT THIS THING OUT WITH A SIMPLE CONVERSATION?

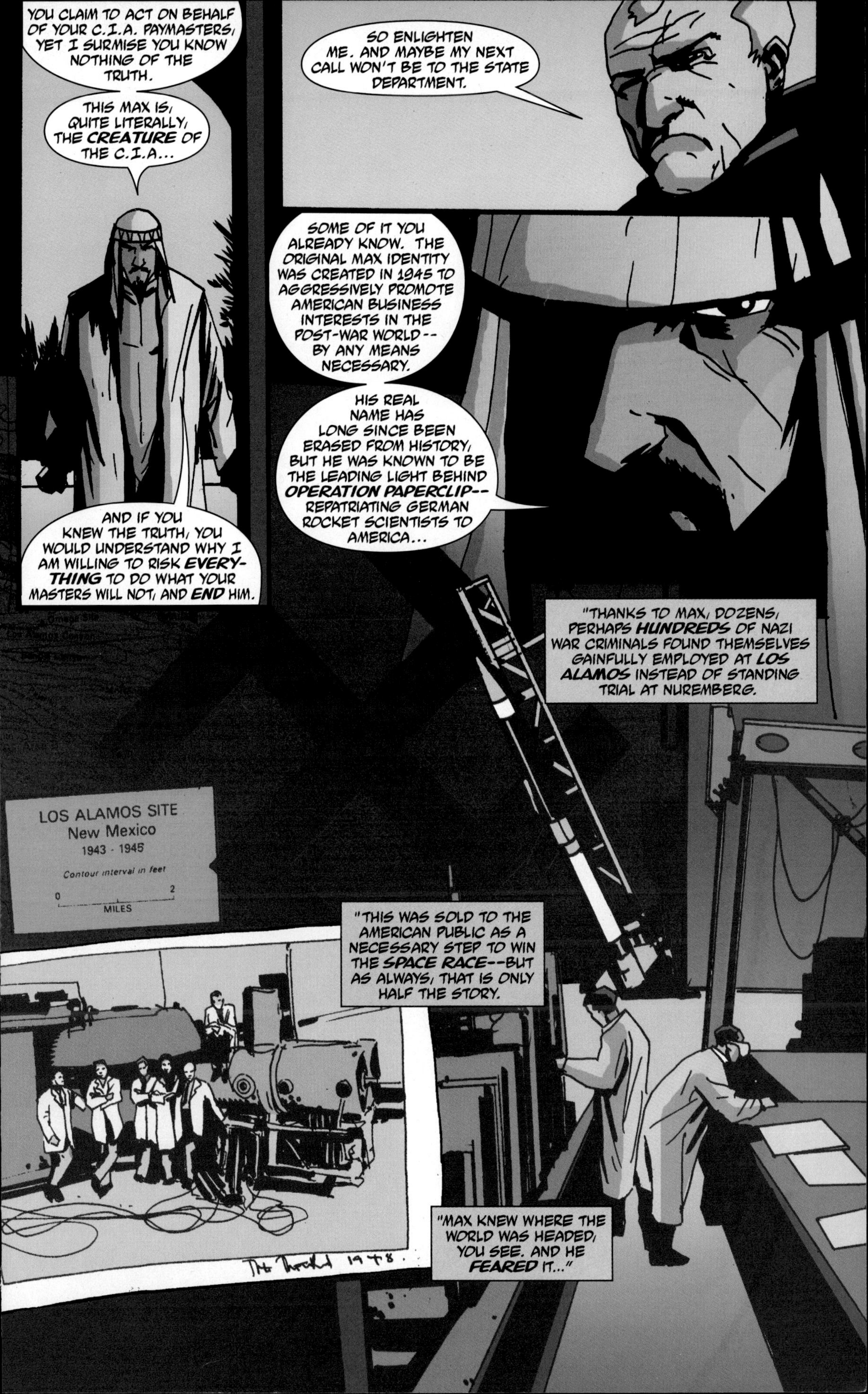
YOU CLAIM TO ACT ON BEHALF OF YOUR C.I.A. PAYMASTERS, YET I SURMISE YOU KNOW NOTHING OF THE TRUTH.
THIS MAX IS, QUITE LITERALLY, THE CREATURE OF THE C.I.A...
SO ENLIGHTEN ME. AND MAYBE MY NEXT CALL WON'T BE TO THE STATE DEPARTMENT.
AND IF YOU KNEW THE TRUTH, YOU WOULD UNDERSTAND WHY I AM WILLING TO RISK EVERYTHING TO DO WHAT YOUR MASTERS WILL NOT, AND END HIM.
SOME OF IT YOU ALREADY KNOW. THE ORIGINAL MAX IDENTITY WAS CREATED IN 1945 TO AGGRESSIVELY PROMOTE AMERICAN BUSINESS INTERESTS IN THE POST-WAR WORLD-- BY ANY MEANS NECESSARY.
HIS REAL NAME HAS LONG SINCE BEEN ERASED FROM HISTORY, BUT HE WAS KNOWN TO BE THE LEADING LIGHT BEHIND OPERATION PAPERCLIP-- REPATRIATING GERMAN ROCKET SCIENTISTS TO AMERICA...
"THANKS TO MAX, DOZENS, PERHAPS HUNDREDS OF NAZI WAR CRIMINALS FOUND THEMSELVES GAINFULLY EMPLOYED AT LOS ALAMOS INSTEAD OF STANDING TRIAL AT NUREMBERG.
LOS ALAMOS SITE
New Mexico
1943 - 1945
Contour interval in feet
0 2
MILES
"THIS WAS SOLD TO THE AMERICAN PUBLIC AS A NECESSARY STEP TO WIN THE SPACE RACE--BUT AS ALWAYS, THAT IS ONLY HALF THE STORY.
"MAX KNEW WHERE THE WORLD WAS HEADED, YOU SEE. AND HE FEARED IT..."

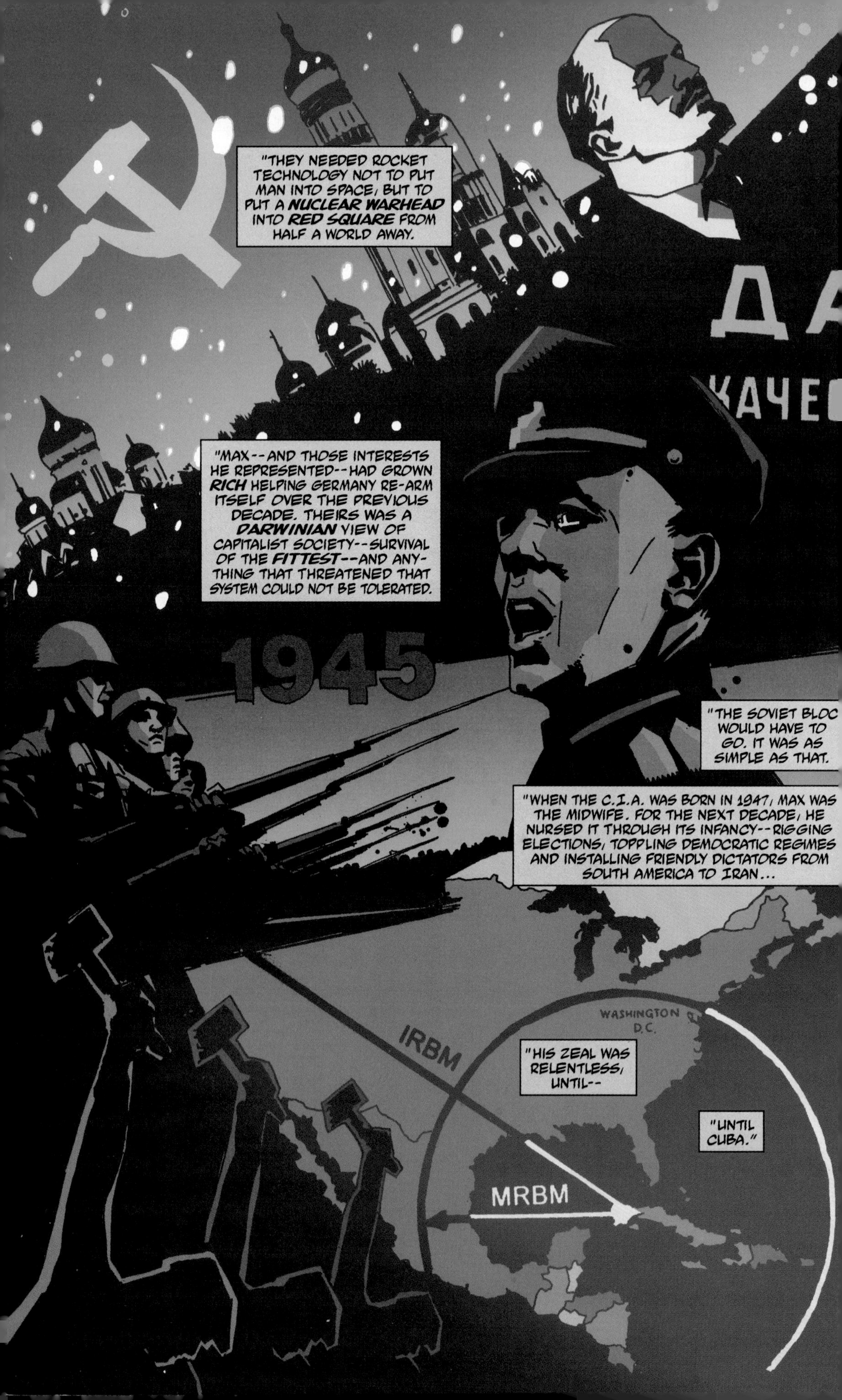
"THEY NEEDED ROCKET TECHNOLOGY NOT TO PUT MAN INTO SPACE, BUT TO PUT A NUCLEAR WARHEAD INTO RED SQUARE FROM HALF A WORLD AWAY.
ДА
КАЧЕ
"MAX--AND THOSE INTERESTS HE REPRESENTED--HAD GROWN RICH HELPING GERMANY RE-ARM ITSELF OVER THE PREVIOUS DECADE. THEIRS WAS A DARWINIAN VIEW OF CAPITALIST SOCIETY--SURVIVAL OF THE FITTEST--AND ANY-THING THAT THREATENED THAT SYSTEM COULD NOT BE TOLERATED.
1945
"THE SOVIET BLOC WOULD HAVE TO GO. IT WAS AS SIMPLE AS THAT.
"WHEN THE C.I.A. WAS BORN IN 1947, MAX WAS THE MIDWIFE. FOR THE NEXT DECADE, HE NURSED IT THROUGH ITS INFANCY--RIGGING ELECTIONS, TOPPLING DEMOCRATIC REGIMES AND INSTALLING FRIENDLY DICTATORS FROM SOUTH AMERICA TO IRAN...
WASHINGTON D.C.
IRBM
"HIS ZEAL WAS RELENTLESS, UNTIL--
"UNTIL CUBA."
MRBM

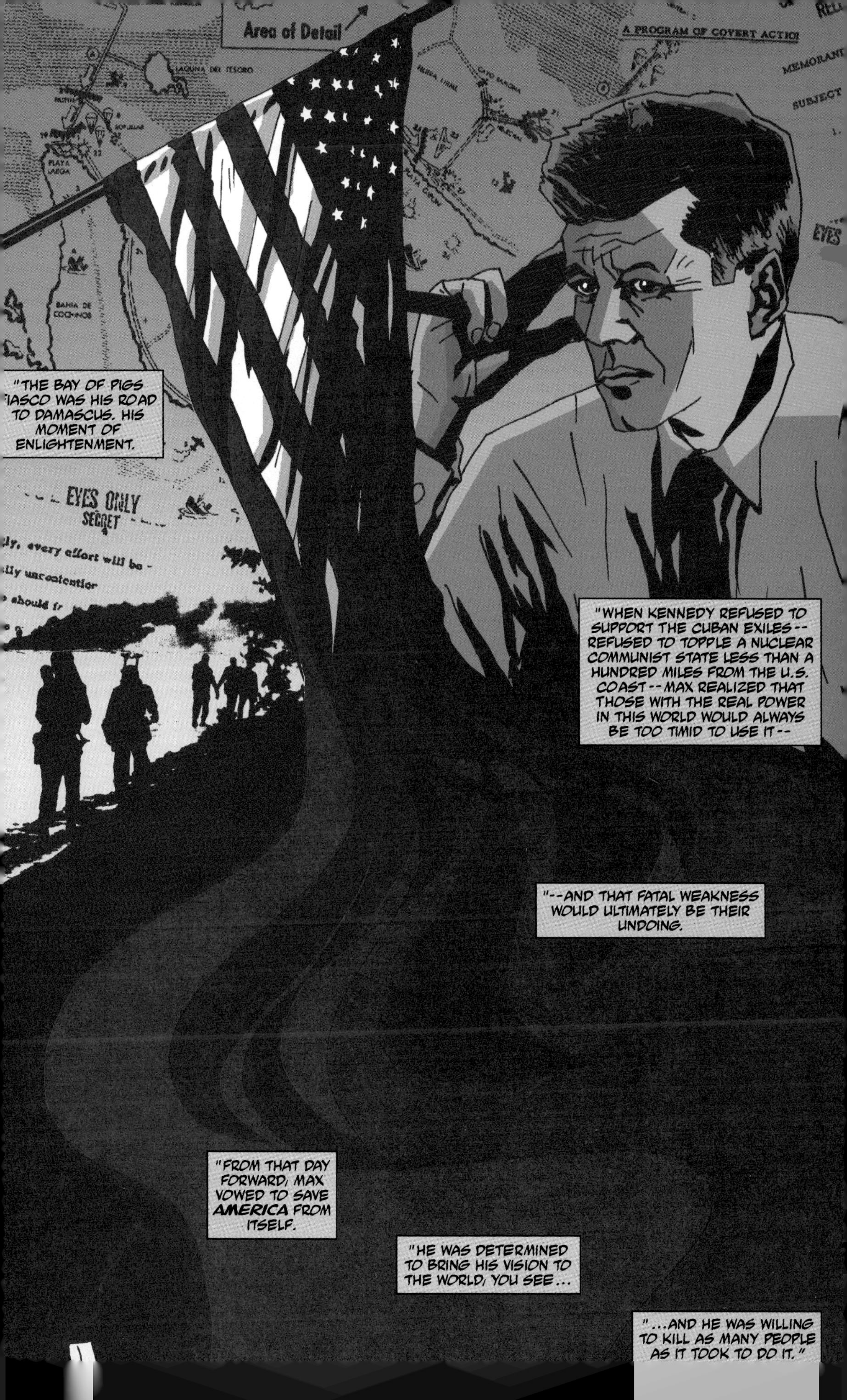

Area of Detail
A PROGRAM OF COVERT ACTIO
"THE BAY OF PIGS FIASCO WAS HIS ROAD TO DAMASCUS. HIS MOMENT OF ENLIGHTENMENT.
EYES ONLY
SECRET
"WHEN KENNEDY REFUSED TO SUPPORT THE CUBAN EXILES-- REFUSED TO TOPPLE A NUCLEAR COMMUNIST STATE LESS THAN A HUNDRED MILES FROM THE U.S. COAST--MAX REALIZED THAT THOSE WITH THE REAL POWER IN THIS WORLD WOULD ALWAYS BE TOO TIMID TO USE IT--
"--AND THAT FATAL WEAKNESS WOULD ULTIMATELY BE THEIR UNDOING.
"FROM THAT DAY FORWARD, MAX VOWED TO SAVE AMERICA FROM ITSELF.
"HE WAS DETERMINED TO BRING HIS VISION TO THE WORLD, YOU SEE...
"...AND HE WAS WILLING TO KILL AS MANY PEOPLE AS IT TOOK TO DO IT."

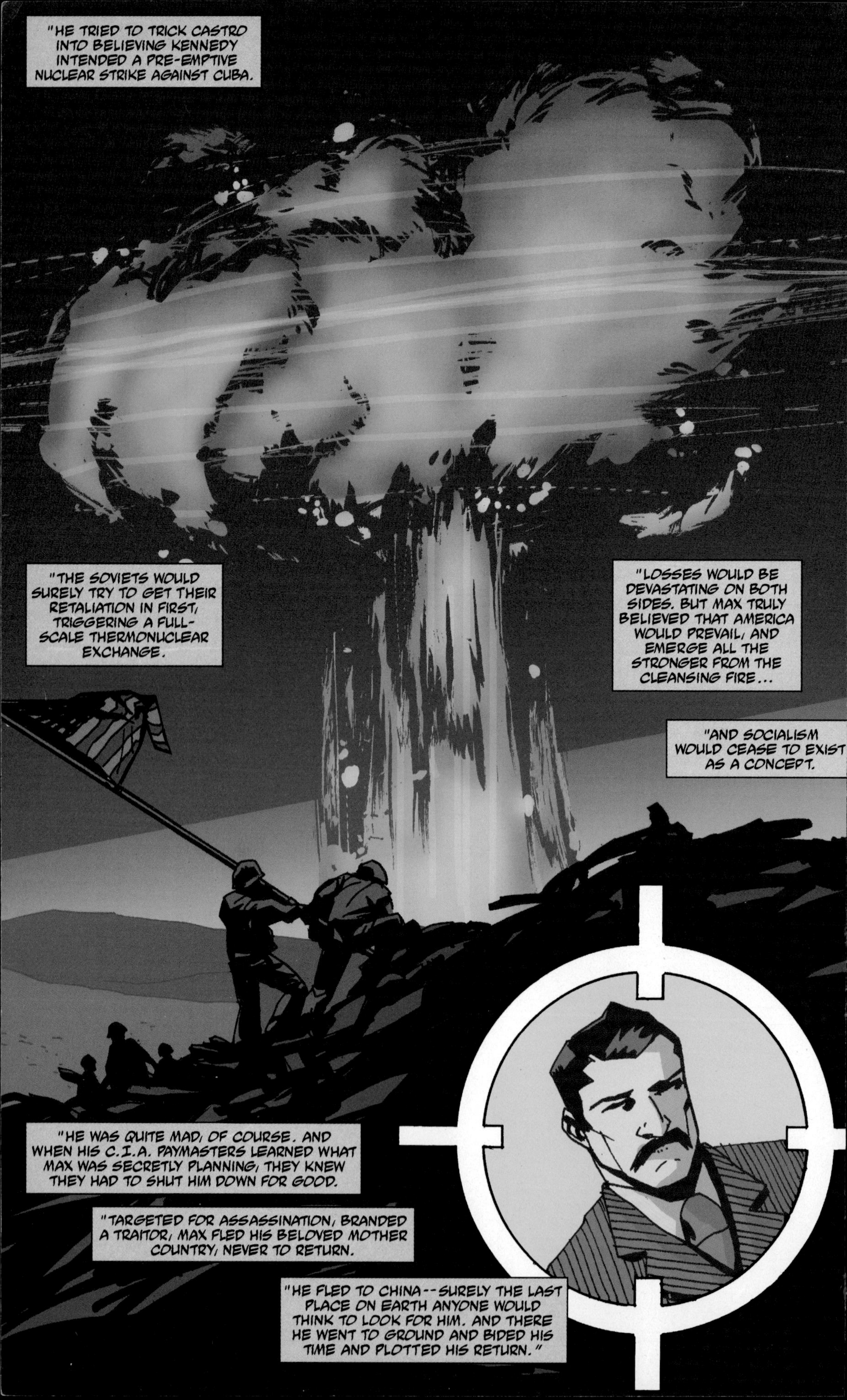
"HE TRIED TO TRICK CASTRO INTO BELIEVING KENNEDY INTENDED A PRE-EMPTIVE NUCLEAR STRIKE AGAINST CUBA.
"THE SOVIETS WOULD SURELY TRY TO GET THEIR RETALIATION IN FIRST, TRIGGERING A FULL-SCALE THERMONUCLEAR EXCHANGE.
"LOSSES WOULD BE DEVASTATING ON BOTH SIDES. BUT MAX TRULY BELIEVED THAT AMERICA WOULD PREVAIL, AND EMERGE ALL THE STRONGER FROM THE CLEANSING FIRE...
"AND SOCIALISM WOULD CEASE TO EXIST AS A CONCEPT.
"HE WAS QUITE MAD, OF COURSE. AND WHEN HIS C.I.A. PAYMASTERS LEARNED WHAT MAX WAS SECRETLY PLANNING, THEY KNEW THEY HAD TO SHUT HIM DOWN FOR GOOD.
"TARGETED FOR ASSASSINATION, BRANDED A TRAITOR, MAX FLED HIS BELOVED MOTHER COUNTRY, NEVER TO RETURN.
"HE FLED TO CHINA--SURELY THE LAST PLACE ON EARTH ANYONE WOULD THINK TO LOOK FOR HIM. AND THERE HE WENT TO GROUND AND BIDED HIS TIME AND PLOTTED HIS RETURN."

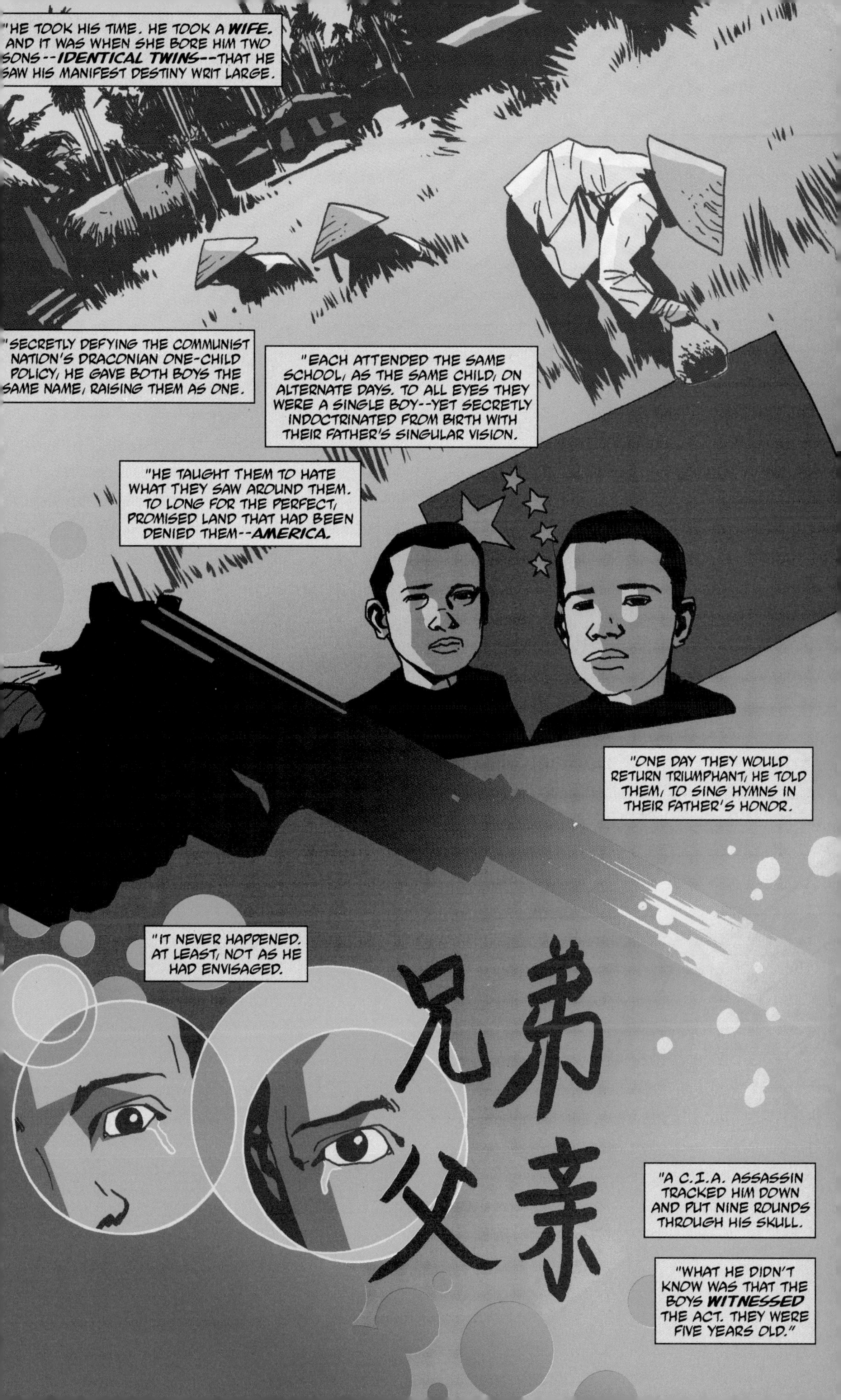
"HE TOOK HIS TIME. HE TOOK A **WIFE.** AND IT WAS WHEN SHE BORE HIM TWO SONS--**IDENTICAL TWINS**--THAT HE SAW HIS MANIFEST DESTINY WRIT LARGE.
"SECRETLY DEFYING THE COMMUNIST NATION'S DRACONIAN ONE-CHILD POLICY, HE GAVE BOTH BOYS THE SAME NAME, RAISING THEM AS ONE.
"EACH ATTENDED THE SAME SCHOOL, AS THE SAME CHILD, ON ALTERNATE DAYS. TO ALL EYES THEY WERE A SINGLE BOY--YET SECRETLY INDOCTRINATED FROM BIRTH WITH THEIR FATHER'S SINGULAR VISION.
"HE TAUGHT THEM TO HATE WHAT THEY SAW AROUND THEM. TO LONG FOR THE PERFECT, PROMISED LAND THAT HAD BEEN DENIED THEM--**AMERICA.**
"ONE DAY THEY WOULD RETURN TRIUMPHANT, HE TOLD THEM, TO SING HYMNS IN THEIR FATHER'S HONOR.
"IT NEVER HAPPENED. AT LEAST, NOT AS HE HAD ENVISAGED.
弟兄
亲父
"A C.I.A. ASSASSIN TRACKED HIM DOWN AND PUT NINE ROUNDS THROUGH HIS SKULL.
"WHAT HE DIDN'T KNOW WAS THAT THE BOYS **WITNESSED** THE ACT. THEY WERE FIVE YEARS OLD."

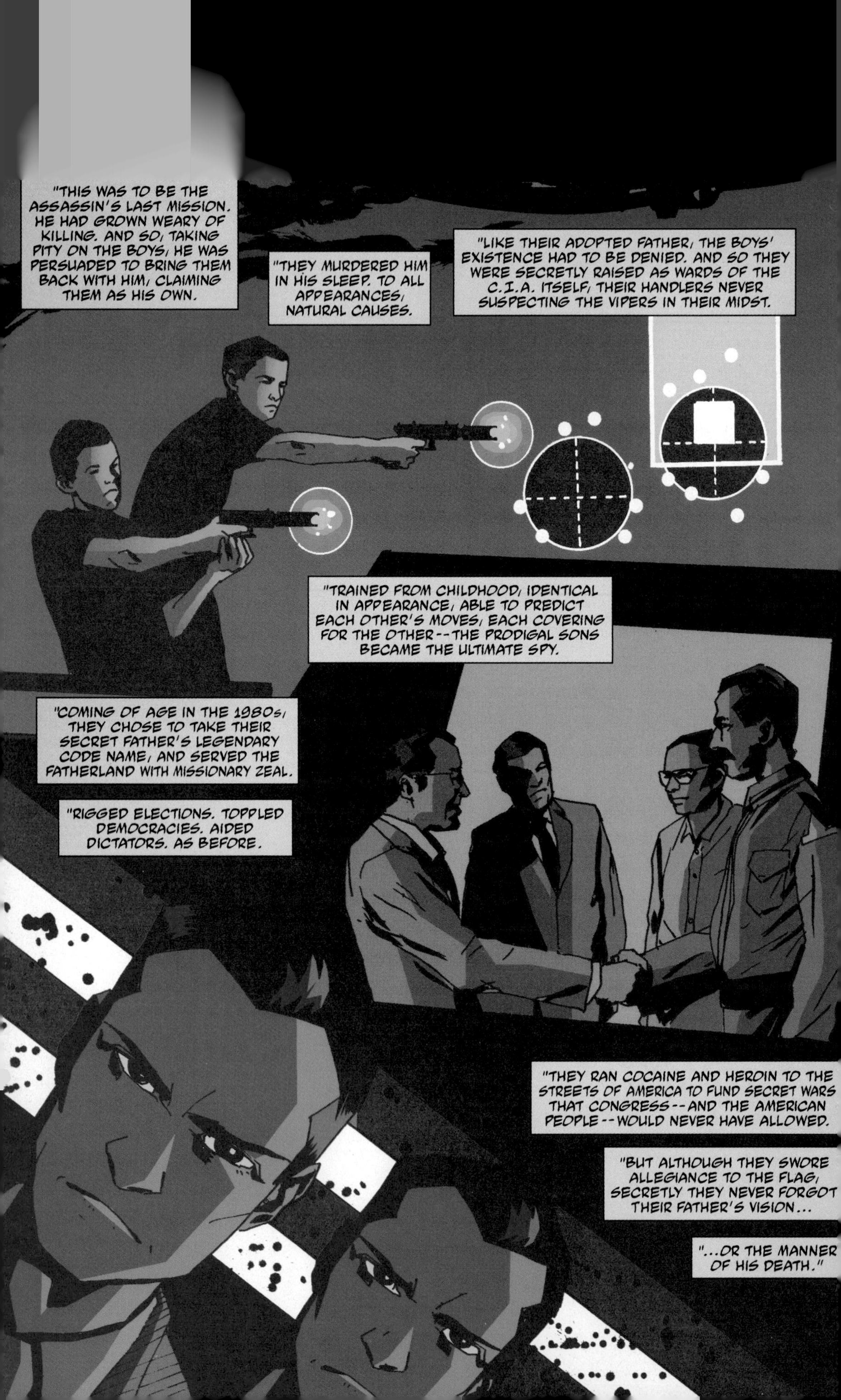
"THIS WAS TO BE THE ASSASSIN'S LAST MISSION. HE HAD GROWN WEARY OF KILLING. AND SO, TAKING PITY ON THE BOYS, HE WAS PERSUADED TO BRING THEM BACK WITH HIM, CLAIMING THEM AS HIS OWN.
"THEY MURDERED HIM IN HIS SLEEP. TO ALL APPEARANCES, NATURAL CAUSES.
"LIKE THEIR ADOPTED FATHER, THE BOYS' EXISTENCE HAD TO BE DENIED. AND SO THEY WERE SECRETLY RAISED AS WARDS OF THE C.I.A. ITSELF, THEIR HANDLERS NEVER SUSPECTING THE VIPERS IN THEIR MIDST.
"TRAINED FROM CHILDHOOD, IDENTICAL IN APPEARANCE, ABLE TO PREDICT EACH OTHER'S MOVES, EACH COVERING FOR THE OTHER--THE PRODIGAL SONS BECAME THE ULTIMATE SPY.
"COMING OF AGE IN THE 1980s, THEY CHOSE TO TAKE THEIR SECRET FATHER'S LEGENDARY CODE NAME, AND SERVED THE FATHERLAND WITH MISSIONARY ZEAL.
"RIGGED ELECTIONS. TOPPLED DEMOCRACIES. AIDED DICTATORS. AS BEFORE.
"THEY RAN COCAINE AND HEROIN TO THE STREETS OF AMERICA TO FUND SECRET WARS THAT CONGRESS--AND THE AMERICAN PEOPLE--WOULD NEVER HAVE ALLOWED.
"BUT ALTHOUGH THEY SWORE ALLEGIANCE TO THE FLAG, SECRETLY THEY NEVER FORGOT THEIR FATHER'S VISION...
"...OR THE MANNER OF HIS DEATH."

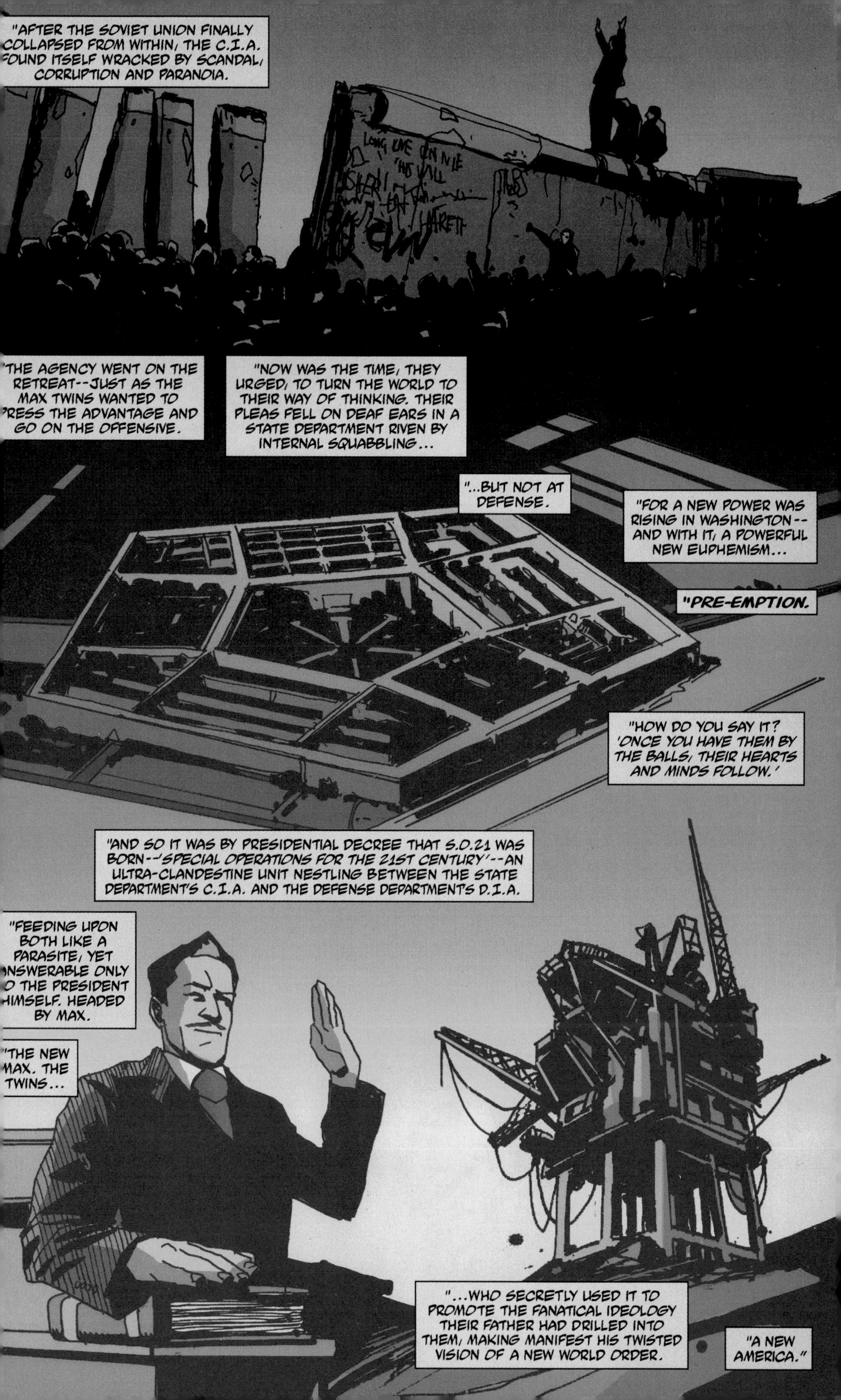

"AFTER THE SOVIET UNION FINALLY COLLAPSED FROM WITHIN, THE C.I.A. FOUND ITSELF WRACKED BY SCANDAL, CORRUPTION AND PARANOIA.
"THE AGENCY WENT ON THE RETREAT--JUST AS THE MAX TWINS WANTED TO PRESS THE ADVANTAGE AND GO ON THE OFFENSIVE.
"NOW WAS THE TIME, THEY URGED, TO TURN THE WORLD TO THEIR WAY OF THINKING. THEIR PLEAS FELL ON DEAF EARS IN A STATE DEPARTMENT RIVEN BY INTERNAL SQUABBLING...
"...BUT NOT AT DEFENSE.
"FOR A NEW POWER WAS RISING IN WASHINGTON--AND WITH IT, A POWERFUL NEW EUPHEMISM...
"PRE-EMPTION.
"HOW DO YOU SAY IT? 'ONCE YOU HAVE THEM BY THE BALLS, THEIR HEARTS AND MINDS FOLLOW.'
"AND SO IT WAS BY PRESIDENTIAL DECREE THAT S.O.21 WAS BORN--'SPECIAL OPERATIONS FOR THE 21ST CENTURY'--AN ULTRA-CLANDESTINE UNIT NESTLING BETWEEN THE STATE DEPARTMENT'S C.I.A. AND THE DEFENSE DEPARTMENT'S D.I.A.
"FEEDING UPON BOTH LIKE A PARASITE, YET ANSWERABLE ONLY TO THE PRESIDENT HIMSELF. HEADED BY MAX.
"THE NEW MAX. THE TWINS...
"...WHO SECRETLY USED IT TO PROMOTE THE FANATICAL IDEOLOGY THEIR FATHER HAD DRILLED INTO THEM, MAKING MANIFEST HIS TWISTED VISION OF A NEW WORLD ORDER.
"A NEW AMERICA."

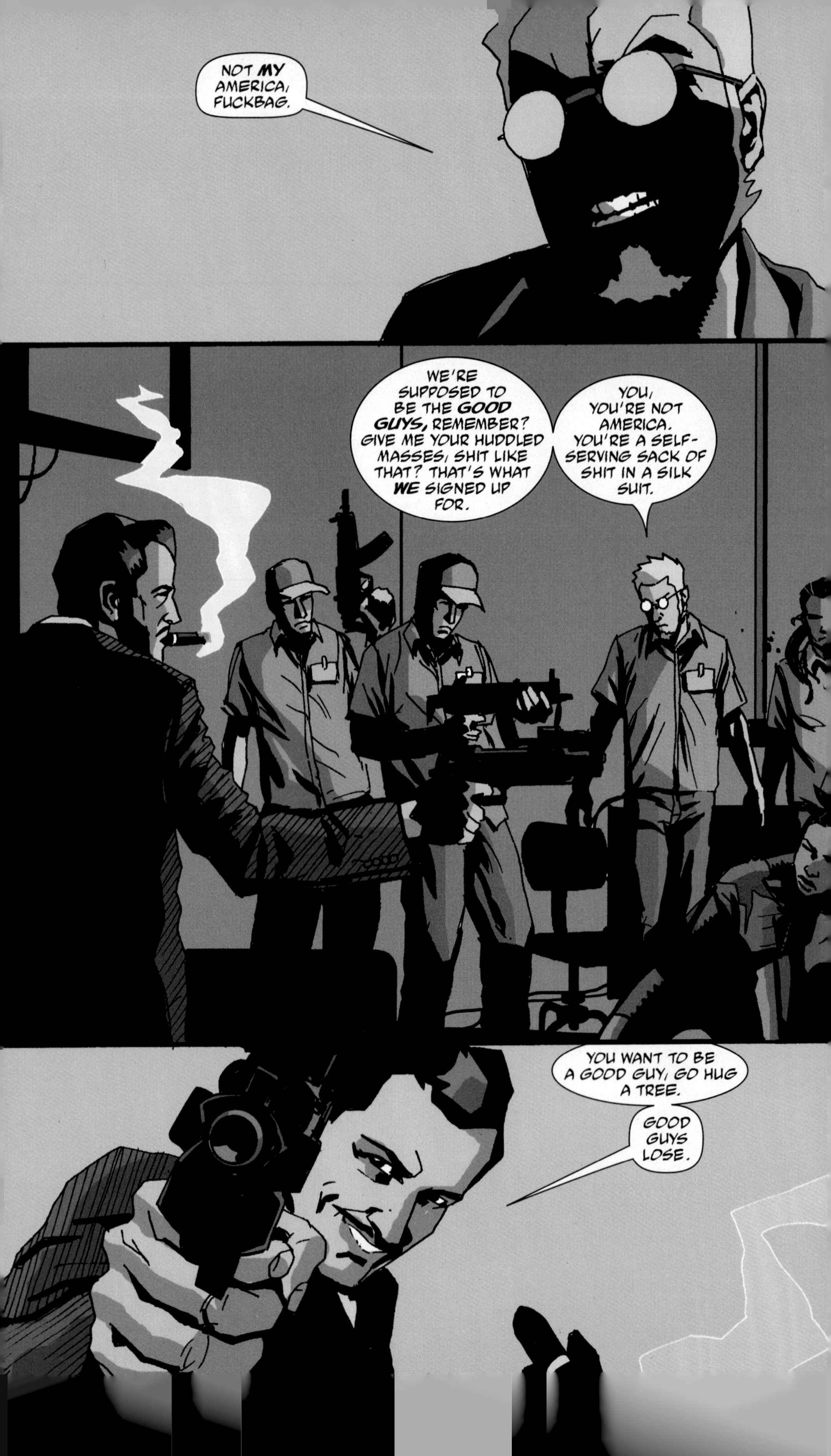
NOT MY AMERICA, FUCKBAG.
WE'RE SUPPOSED TO BE THE GOOD GUYS, REMEMBER? GIVE ME YOUR HUDDLED MASSES, SHIT LIKE THAT? THAT'S WHAT WE SIGNED UP FOR.
YOU, YOU'RE NOT AMERICA. YOU'RE A SELF-SERVING SACK OF SHIT IN A SILK SUIT.
YOU WANT TO BE A GOOD GUY, GO HUG A TREE.
GOOD GUYS LOSE.

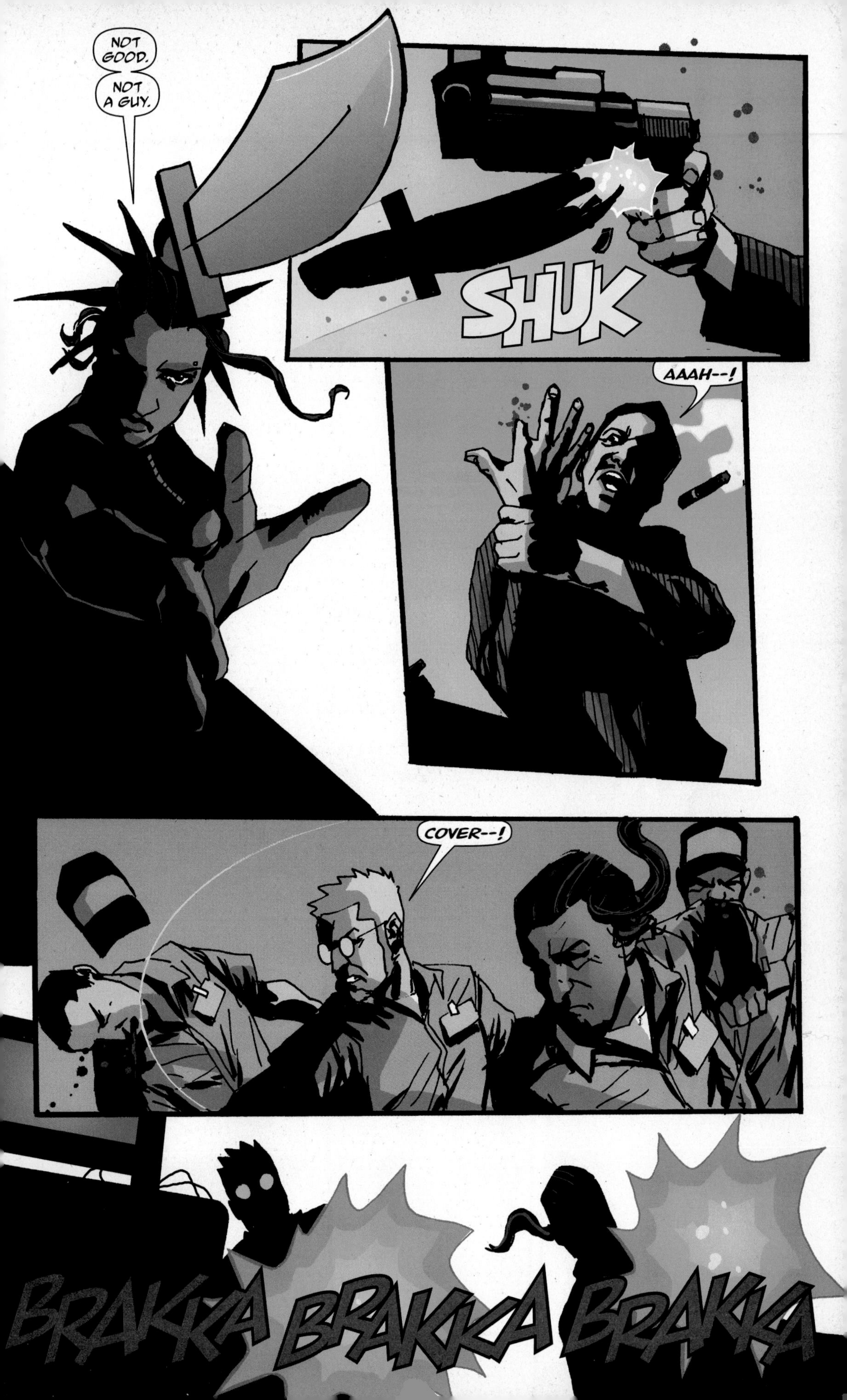
NOT GOOD.
NOT A GUY.
SHUK
AAAH--!
COVER--!
BRAKKA BRAKKA BRAKKA

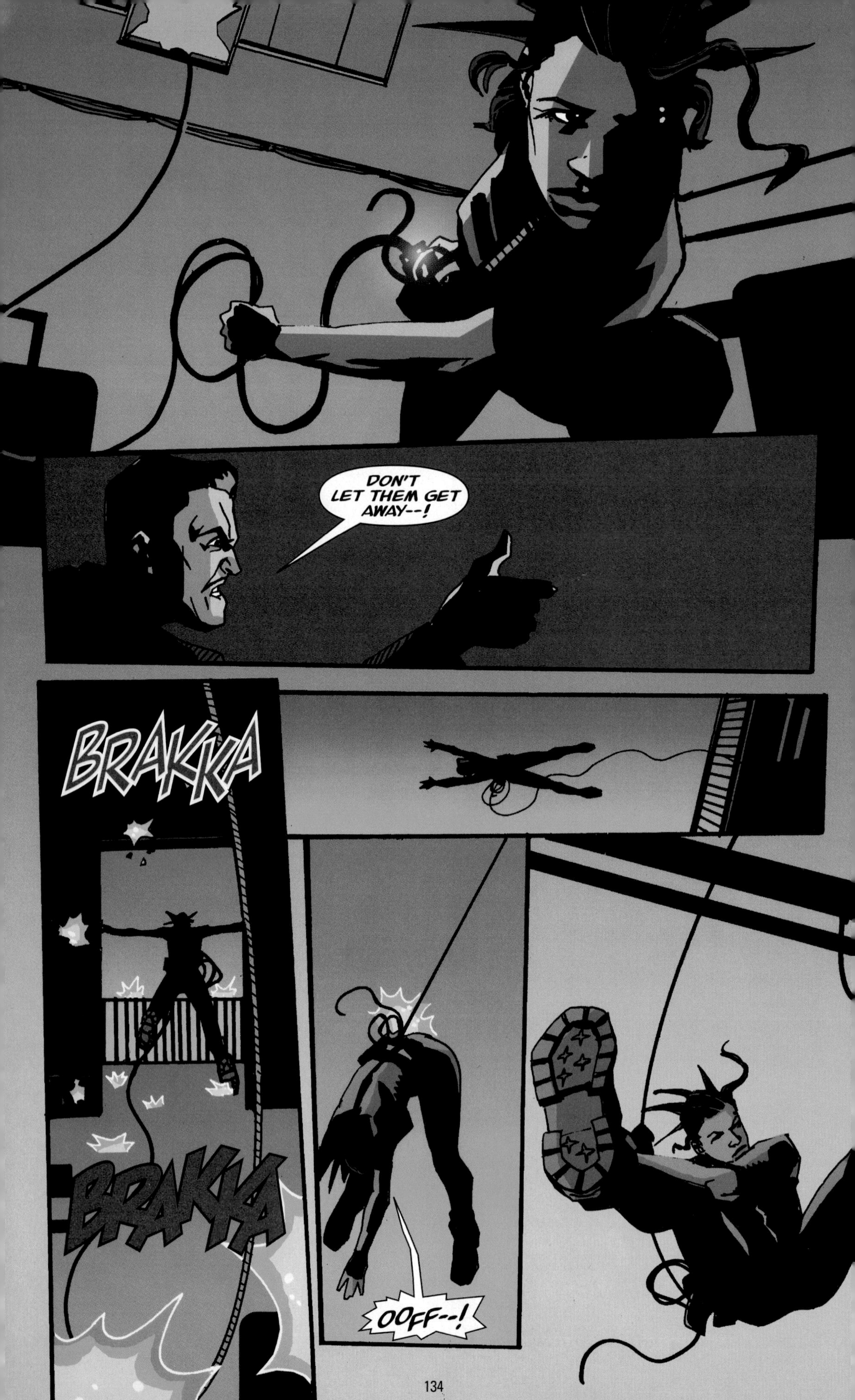
DON'T LET THEM GET AWAY--!
BRAKKA
BRAKKA
OOFF--!

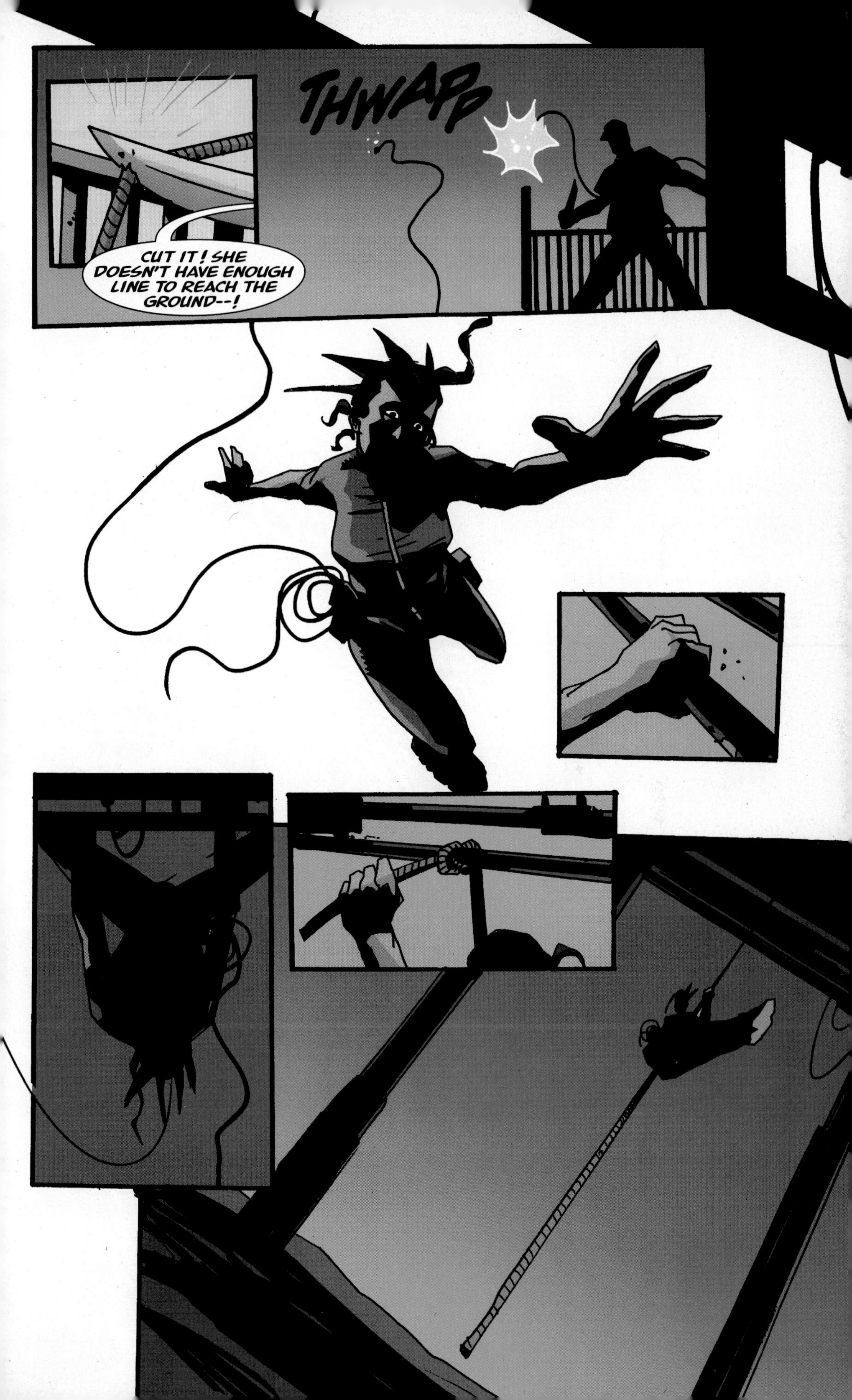
THWAPP
CUT IT! SHE DOESN'T HAVE ENOUGH LINE TO REACH THE GROUND--!

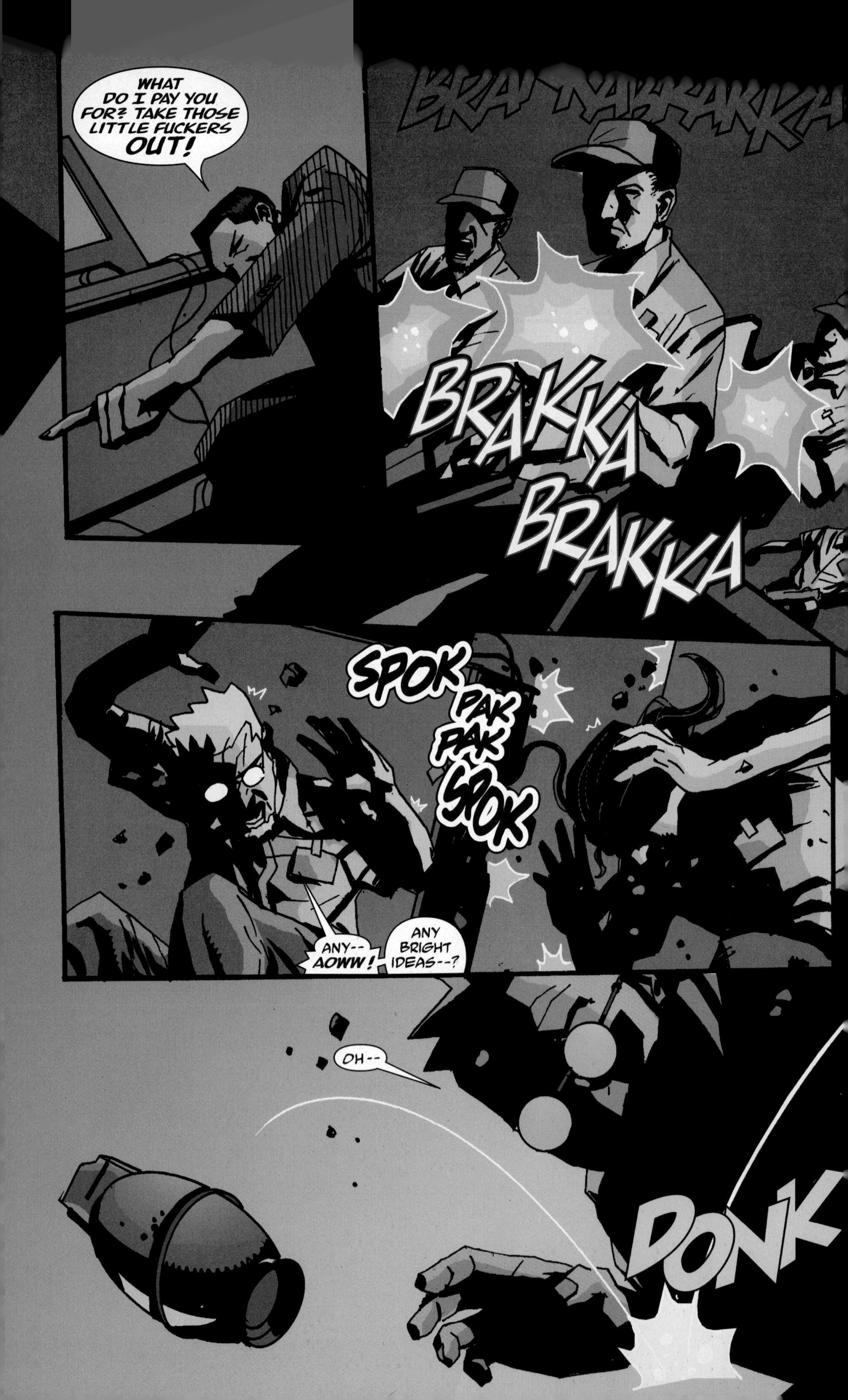
WHAT DO I PAY YOU FOR? TAKE THOSE LITTLE FUCKERS OUT!
BRAKKA BRAKKA
SPOK PAK PAK SPOK
ANY-- AOWW!
ANY BRIGHT IDEAS--?
OH--
DONK

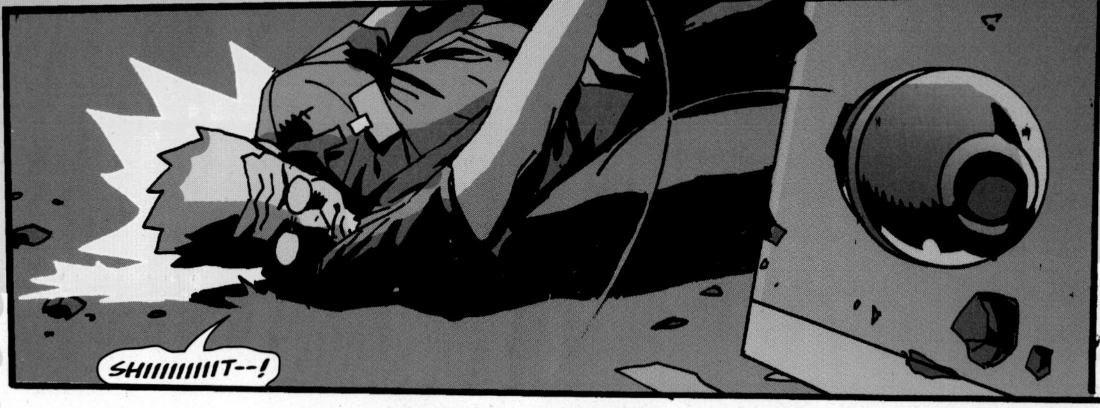
SHIIIIIIIIT--!

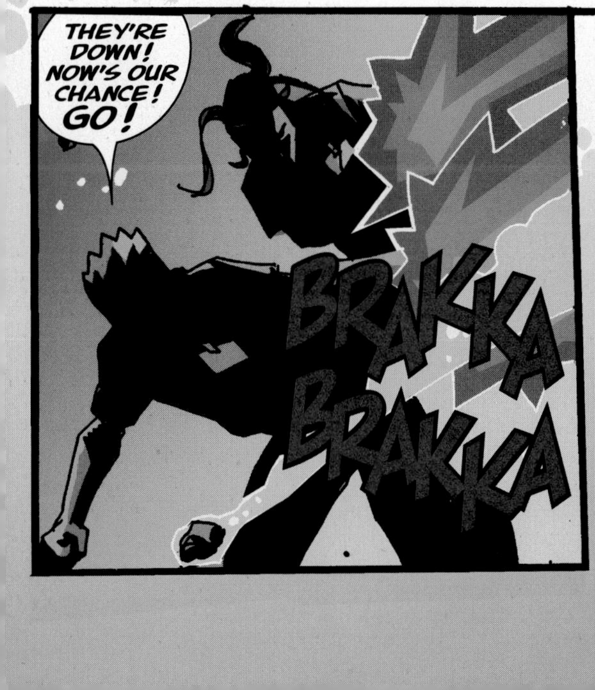
THEY'RE DOWN! NOW'S OUR CHANCE! GO!
BRAKKA BRAKKA

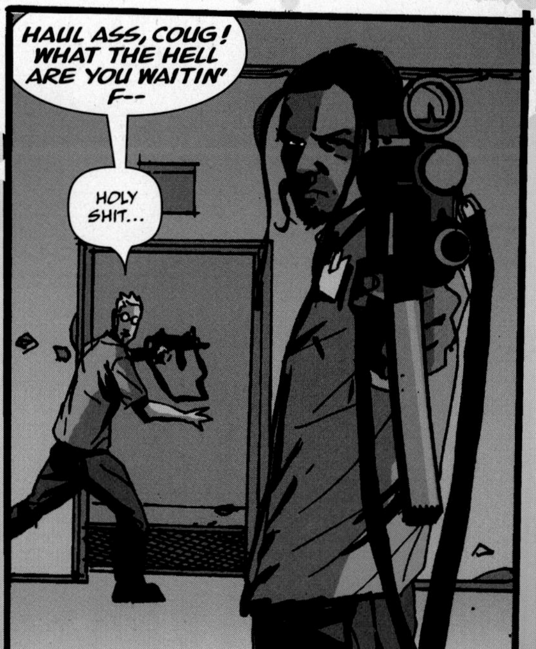
HAUL ASS, COUG! WHAT THE HELL ARE YOU WAITIN' F--
HOLY SHIT...

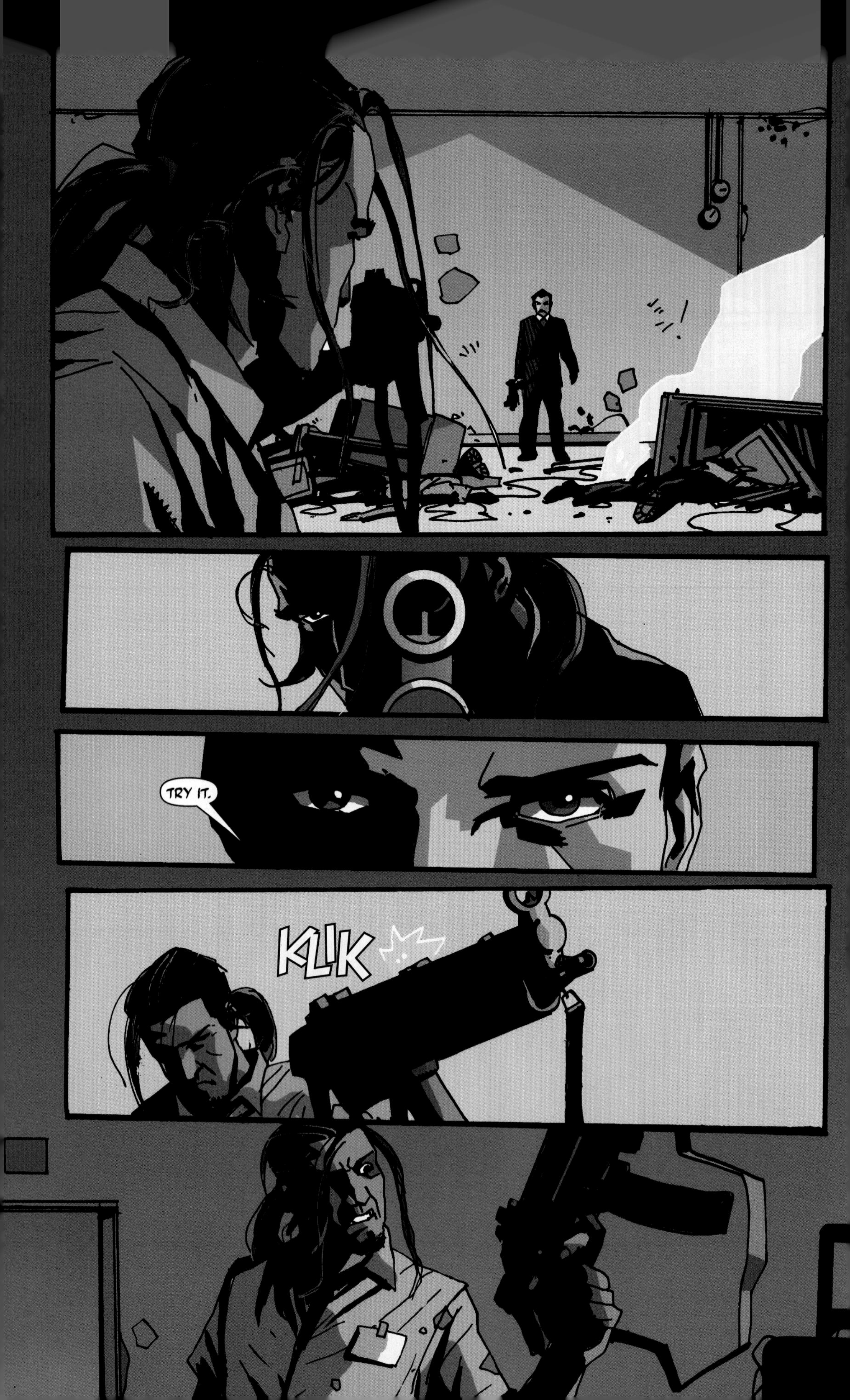
TRY IT.
KLIK

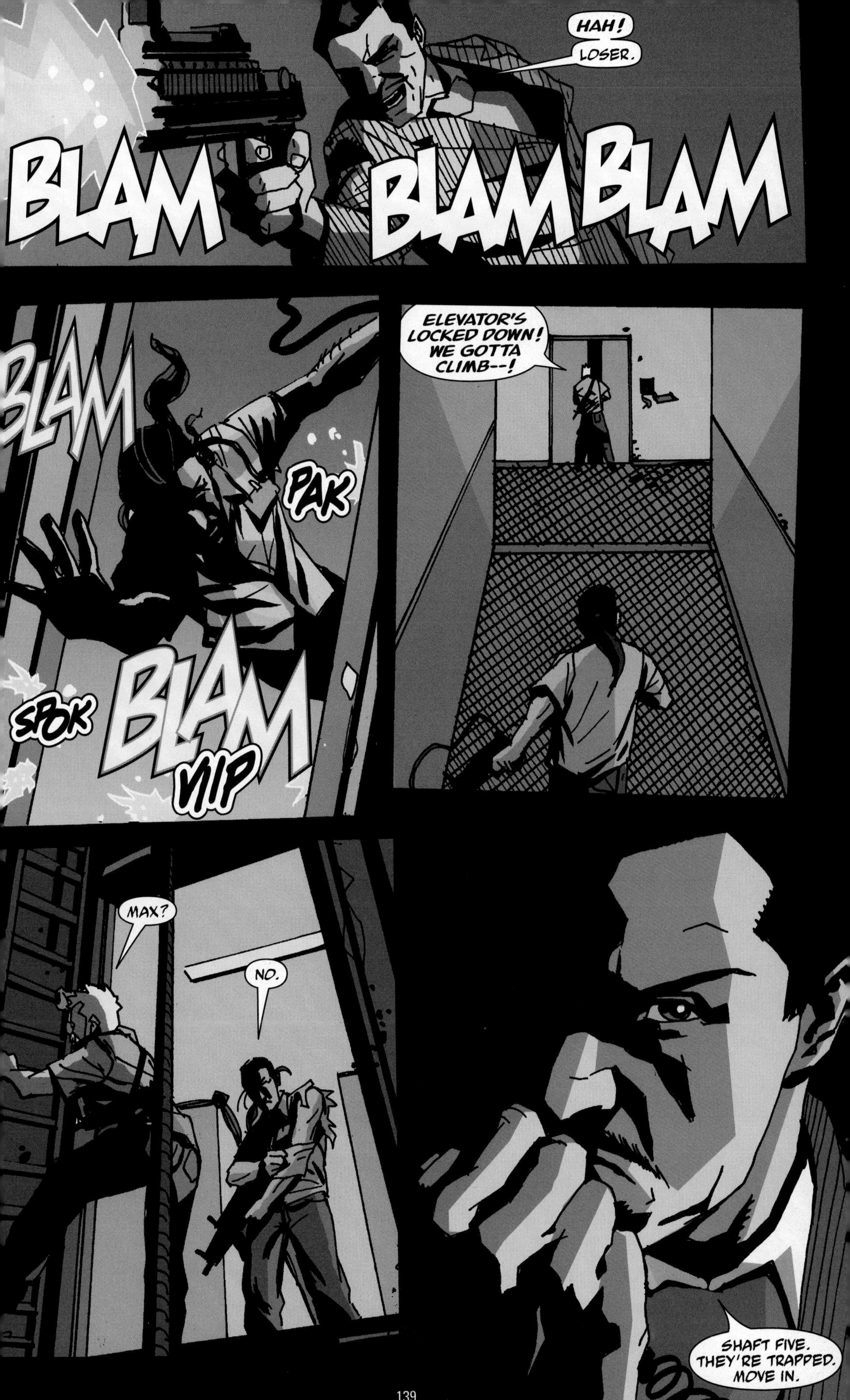
HAH!
LOSER.
BLAM
BLAM BLAM
BLAM
PAK
SPOK
BLAM
VIP
ELEVATOR'S LOCKED DOWN! WE GOTTA CLIMB--!
MAX?
NO.
SHAFT FIVE. THEY'RE TRAPPED. MOVE IN.

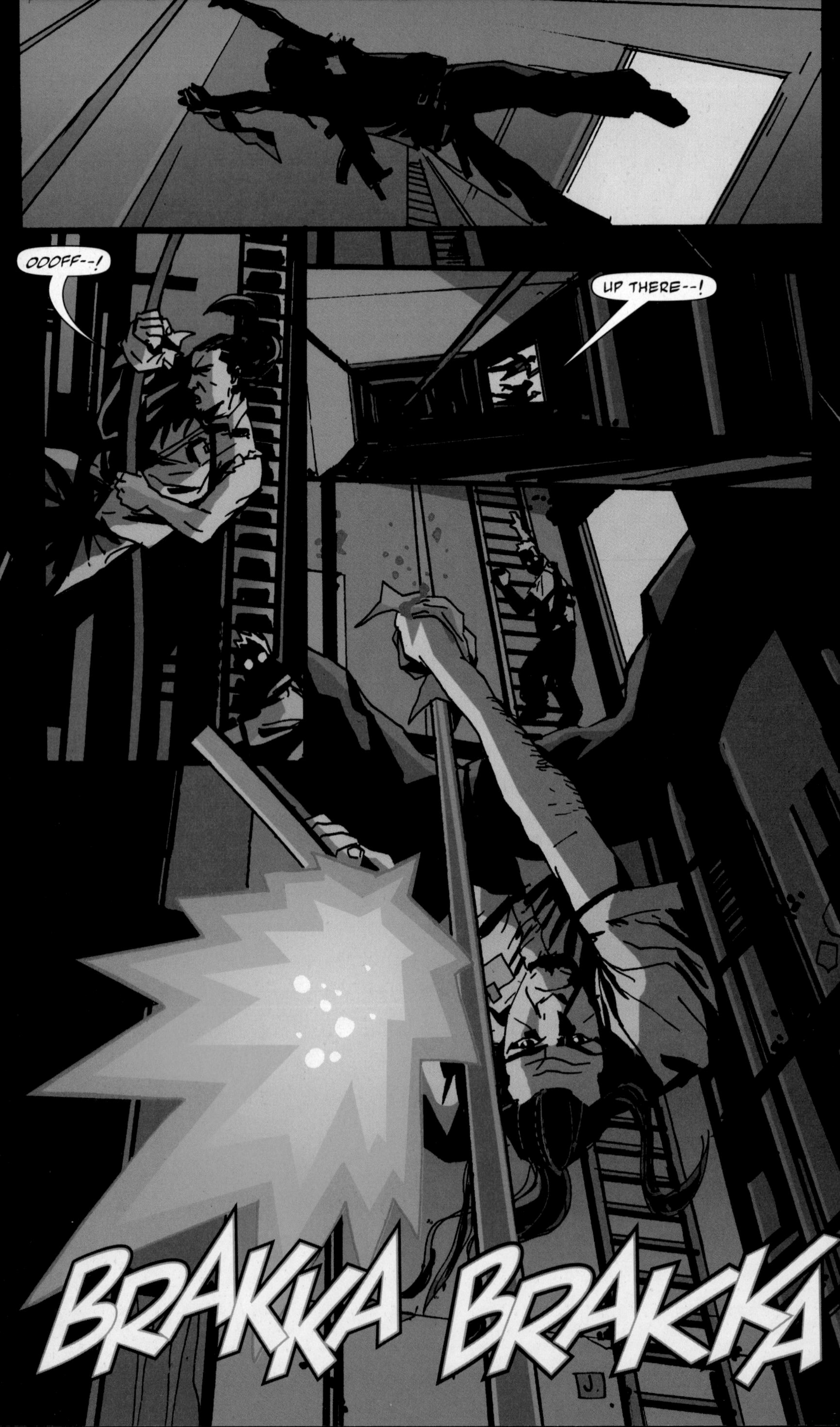
OOOFF--!
UP THERE--!
BRAKKA BRAKKA

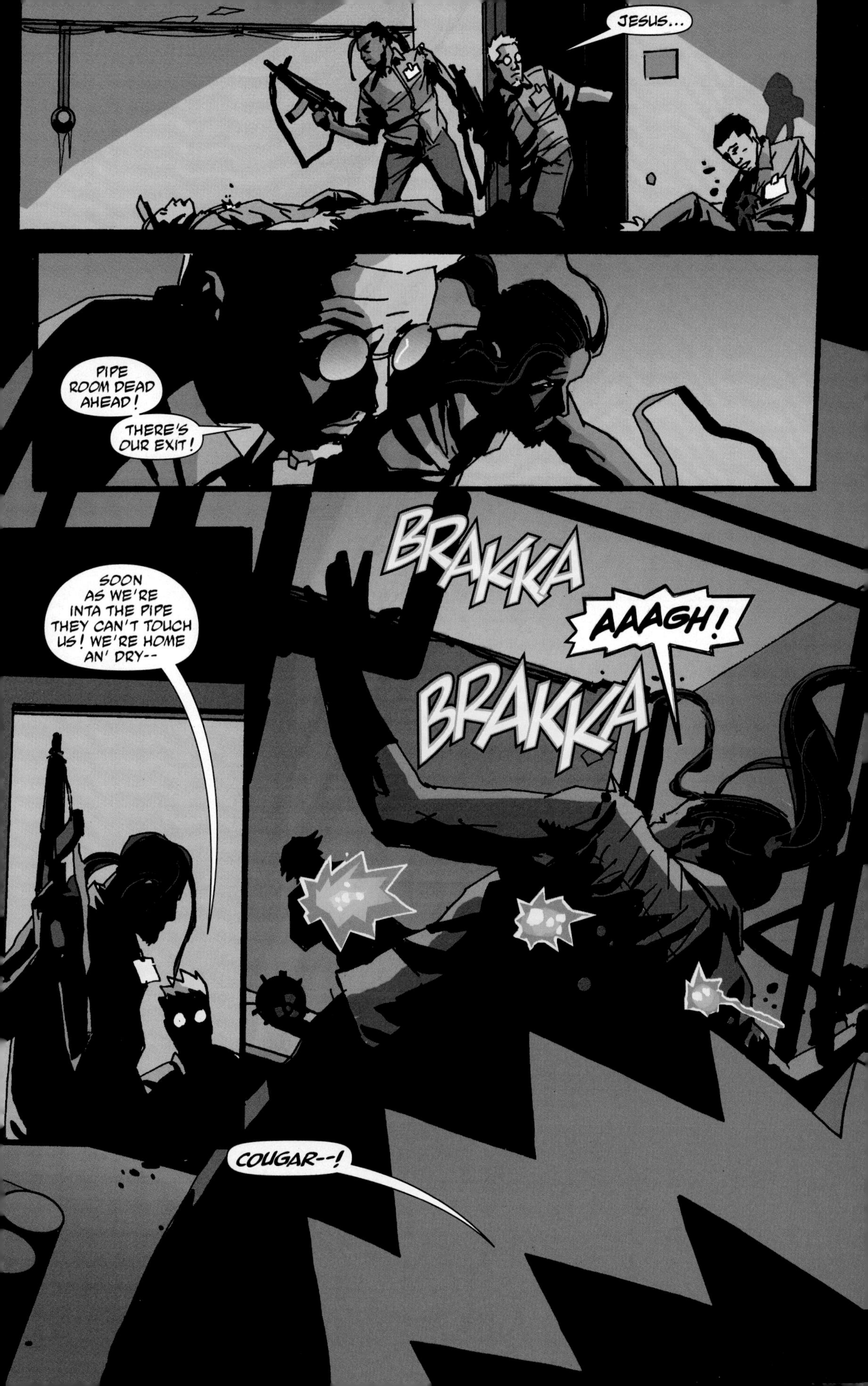
JESUS...
PIPE ROOM DEAD AHEAD!
THERE'S OUR EXIT!
BRAKKA
AAAGH!
BRAKKA
SOON AS WE'RE INTA THE PIPE THEY CAN'T TOUCH US! WE'RE HOME AN' DRY--
COUGAR--!

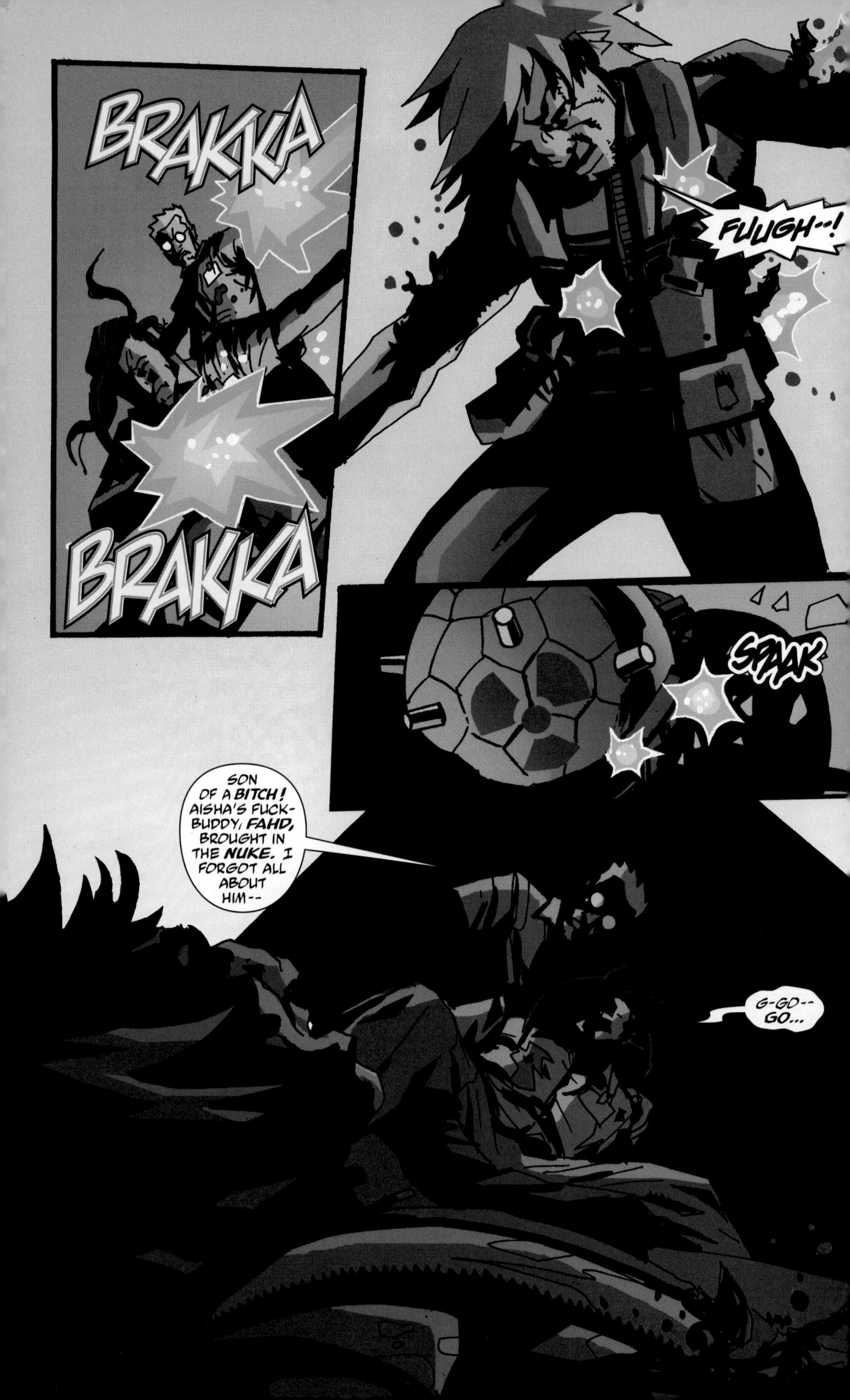
BRAKKA
BRAKKA
FUUGH--!
SPAAK
SON OF A BITCH! AISHA'S FUCK-BUDDY, FAHD, BROUGHT IN THE NUKE. I FORGOT ALL ABOUT HIM--
G-GO-- GO...

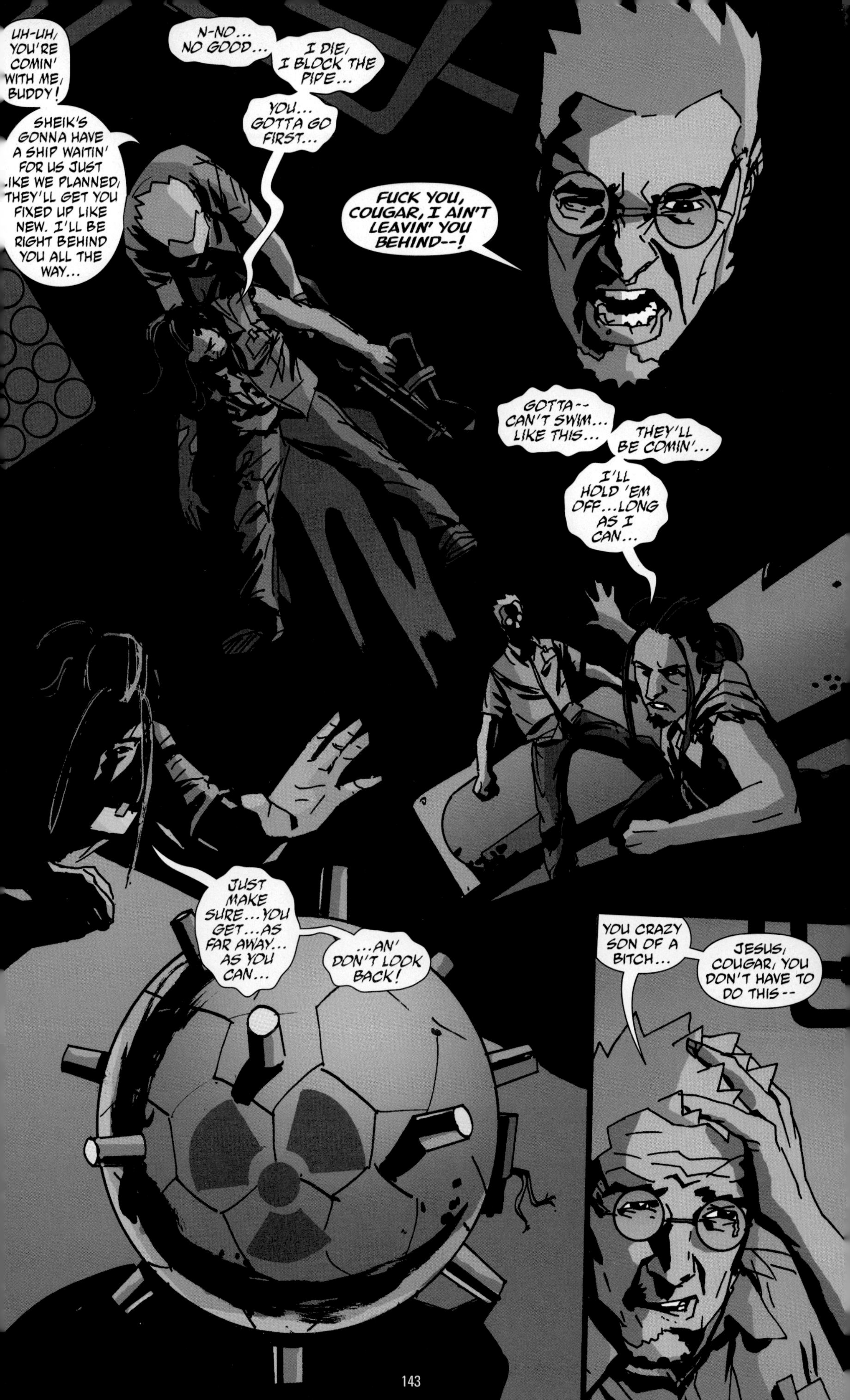
UH-UH, YOU'RE COMIN' WITH ME, BUDDY!
SHEIK'S GONNA HAVE A SHIP WAITIN' FOR US JUST LIKE WE PLANNED, THEY'LL GET YOU FIXED UP LIKE NEW. I'LL BE RIGHT BEHIND YOU ALL THE WAY...
N-NO... NO GOOD...
I DIE, I BLOCK THE PIPE...
YOU... GOTTA GO FIRST...
FUCK YOU, COUGAR, I AIN'T LEAVIN' YOU BEHIND--!
GOTTA-- CAN'T SWIM... LIKE THIS...
THEY'LL BE COMIN'...
I'LL HOLD 'EM OFF...LONG AS I CAN...
JUST MAKE SURE...YOU GET...AS FAR AWAY... AS YOU CAN...
...AN' DON'T LOOK BACK!
YOU CRAZY SON OF A BITCH...
JESUS, COUGAR, YOU DON'T HAVE TO DO THIS--

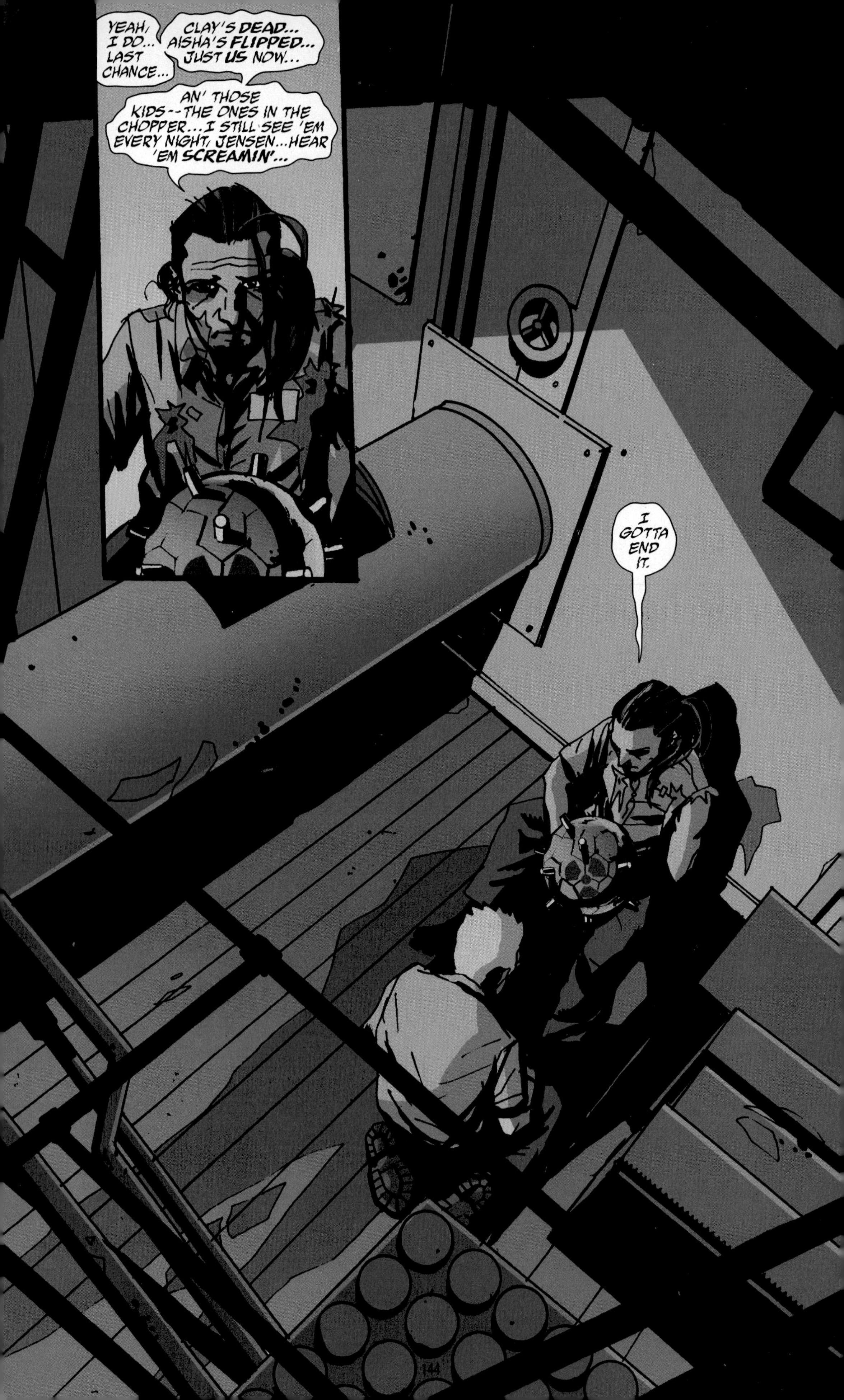
YEAH, I DO... LAST CHANCE...
CLAY'S DEAD... AISHA'S FLIPPED... JUST US NOW...
AN' THOSE KIDS--THE ONES IN THE CHOPPER...I STILL SEE 'EM EVERY NIGHT, JENSEN...HEAR 'EM SCREAMIN'...
I GOTTA END IT.

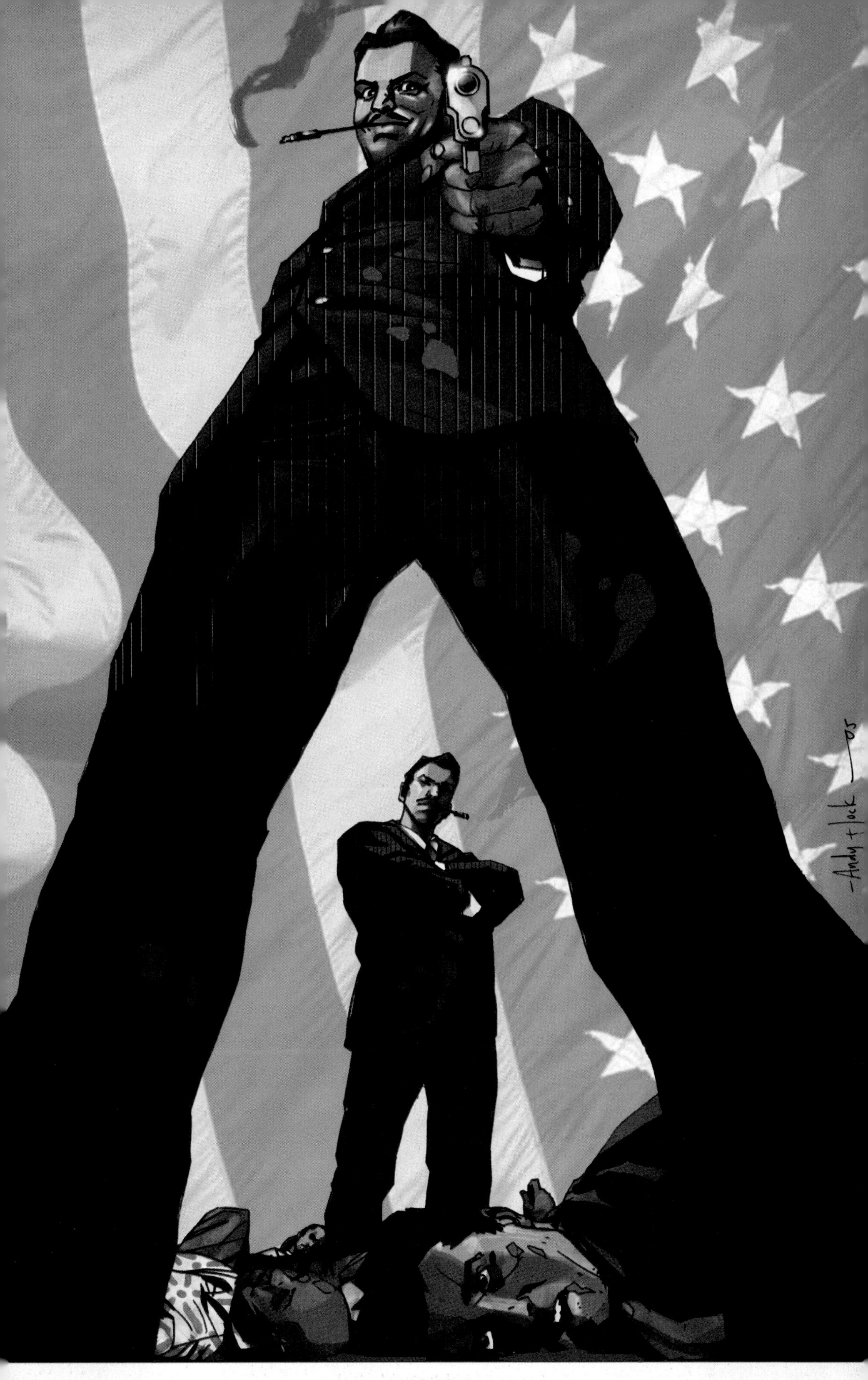

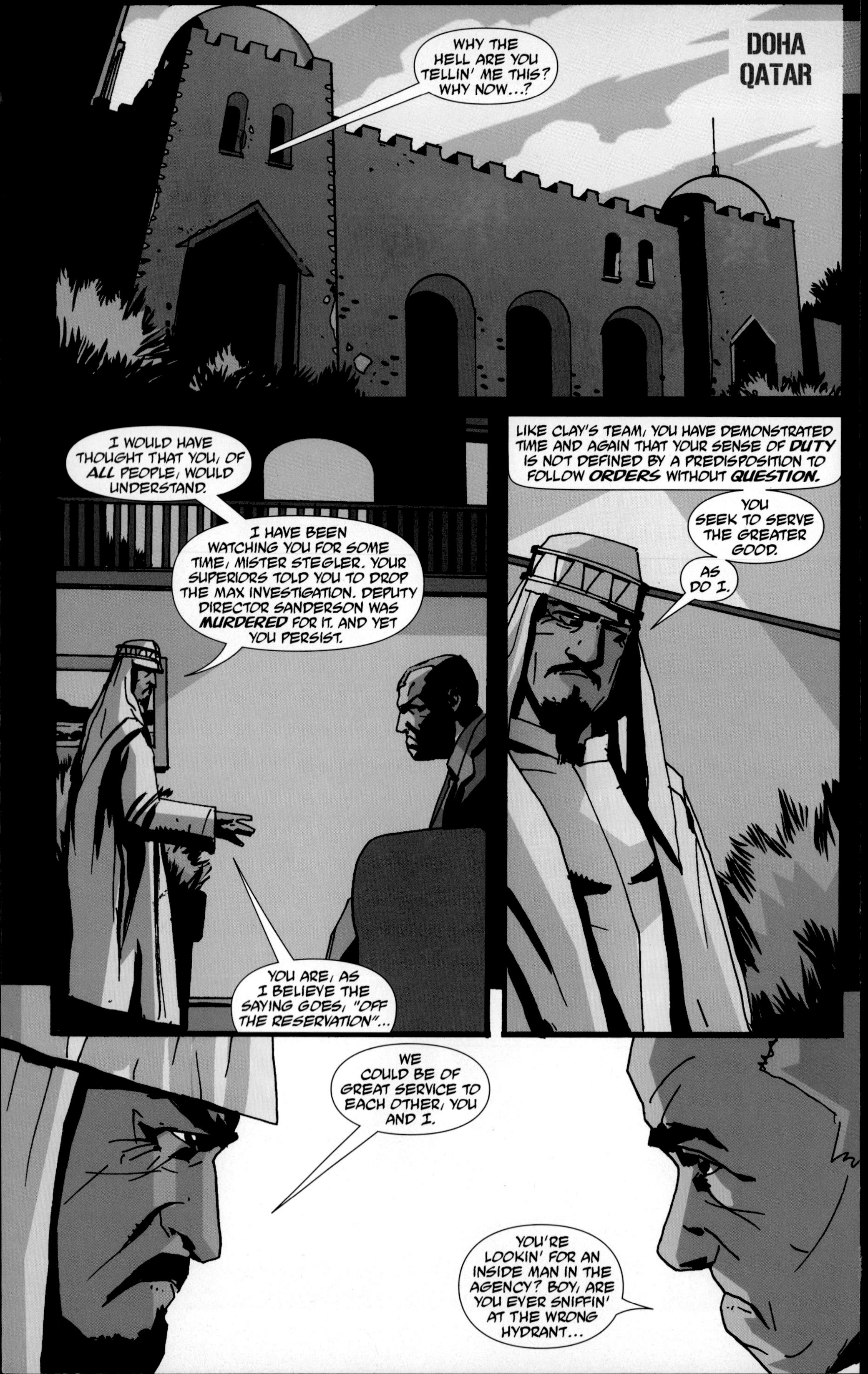
DOHA QATAR
WHY THE HELL ARE YOU TELLIN' ME THIS? WHY NOW...?
I WOULD HAVE THOUGHT THAT YOU, OF ALL PEOPLE, WOULD UNDERSTAND.
I HAVE BEEN WATCHING YOU FOR SOME TIME, MISTER STEGLER. YOUR SUPERIORS TOLD YOU TO DROP THE MAX INVESTIGATION. DEPUTY DIRECTOR SANDERSON WAS MURDERED FOR IT. AND YET YOU PERSIST.
YOU ARE, AS I BELIEVE THE SAYING GOES, "OFF THE RESERVATION"...
LIKE CLAY'S TEAM, YOU HAVE DEMONSTRATED TIME AND AGAIN THAT YOUR SENSE OF DUTY IS NOT DEFINED BY A PREDISPOSITION TO FOLLOW ORDERS WITHOUT QUESTION.
YOU SEEK TO SERVE THE GREATER GOOD.
AS DO I.
WE COULD BE OF GREAT SERVICE TO EACH OTHER, YOU AND I.
YOU'RE LOOKIN' FOR AN INSIDE MAN IN THE AGENCY? BOY, ARE YOU EVER SNIFFIN' AT THE WRONG HYDRANT...

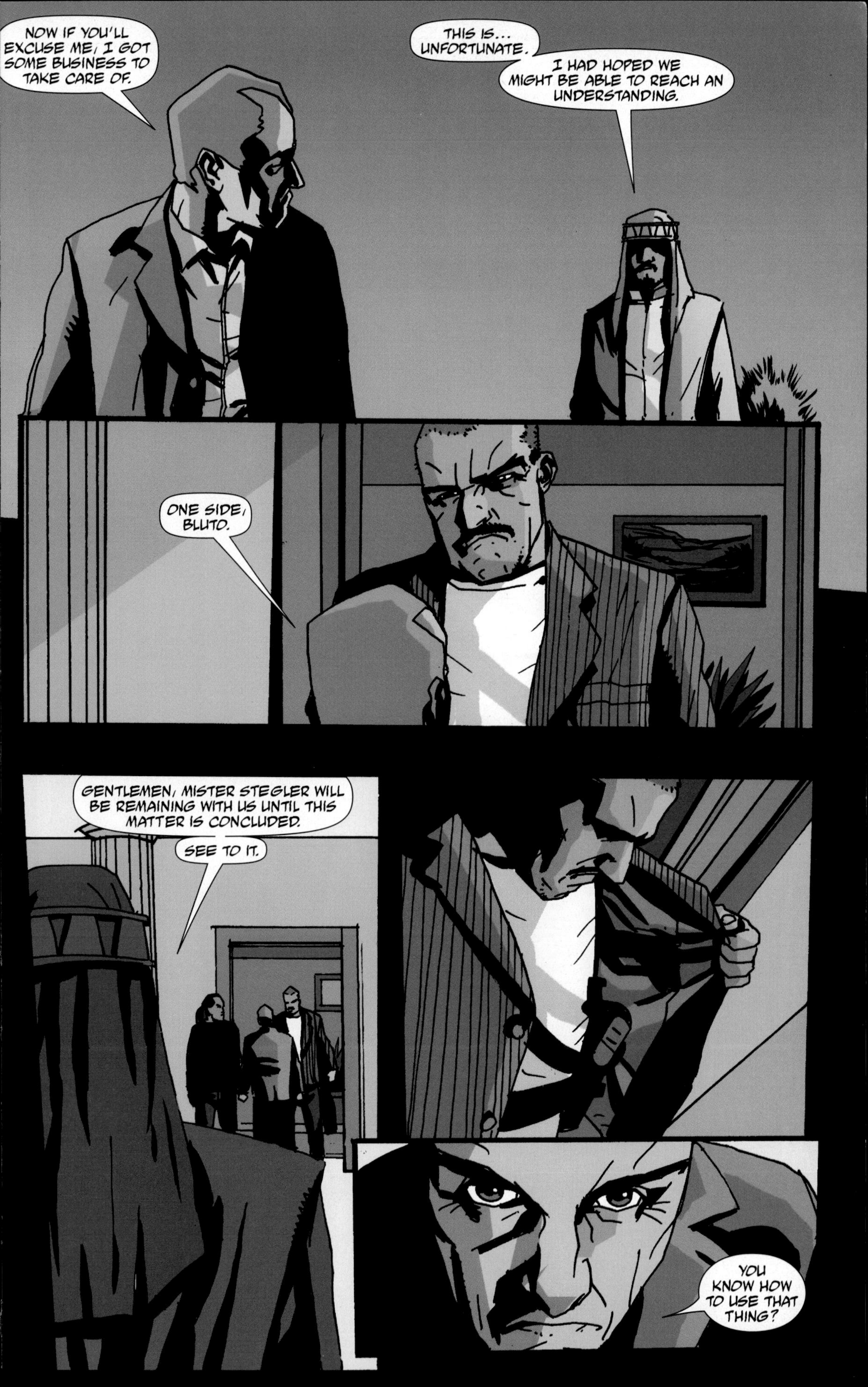
NOW IF YOU'LL EXCUSE ME, I GOT SOME BUSINESS TO TAKE CARE OF.
THIS IS... UNFORTUNATE.
I HAD HOPED WE MIGHT BE ABLE TO REACH AN UNDERSTANDING.
ONE SIDE, BLUTO.
GENTLEMEN, MISTER STEGLER WILL BE REMAINING WITH US UNTIL THIS MATTER IS CONCLUDED.
SEE TO IT.
YOU KNOW HOW TO USE THAT THING?

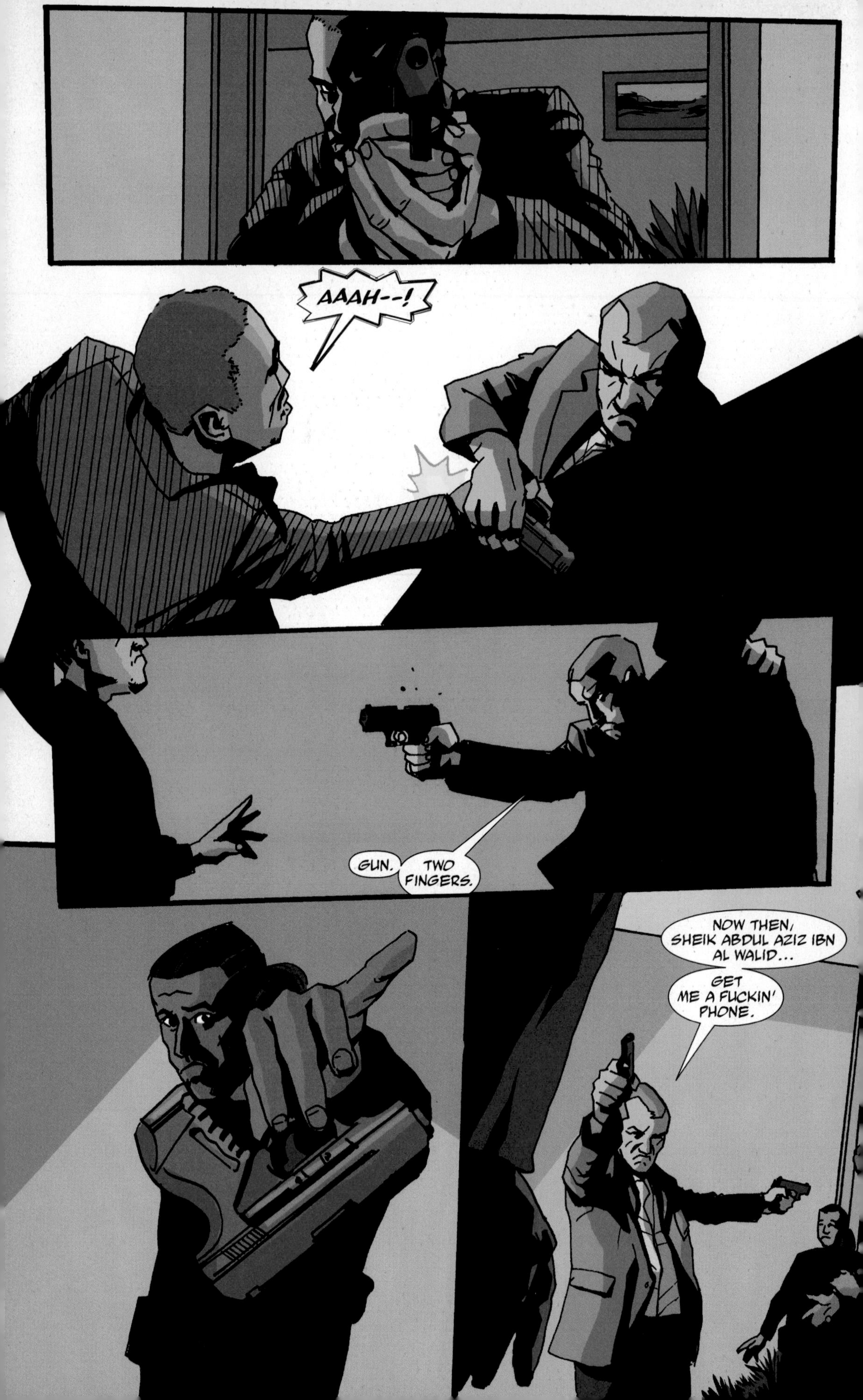
AAAH--!
GUN.
TWO FINGERS.
NOW THEN, SHEIK ABDUL AZIZ IBN AL WALID...
GET ME A FUCKIN' PHONE.

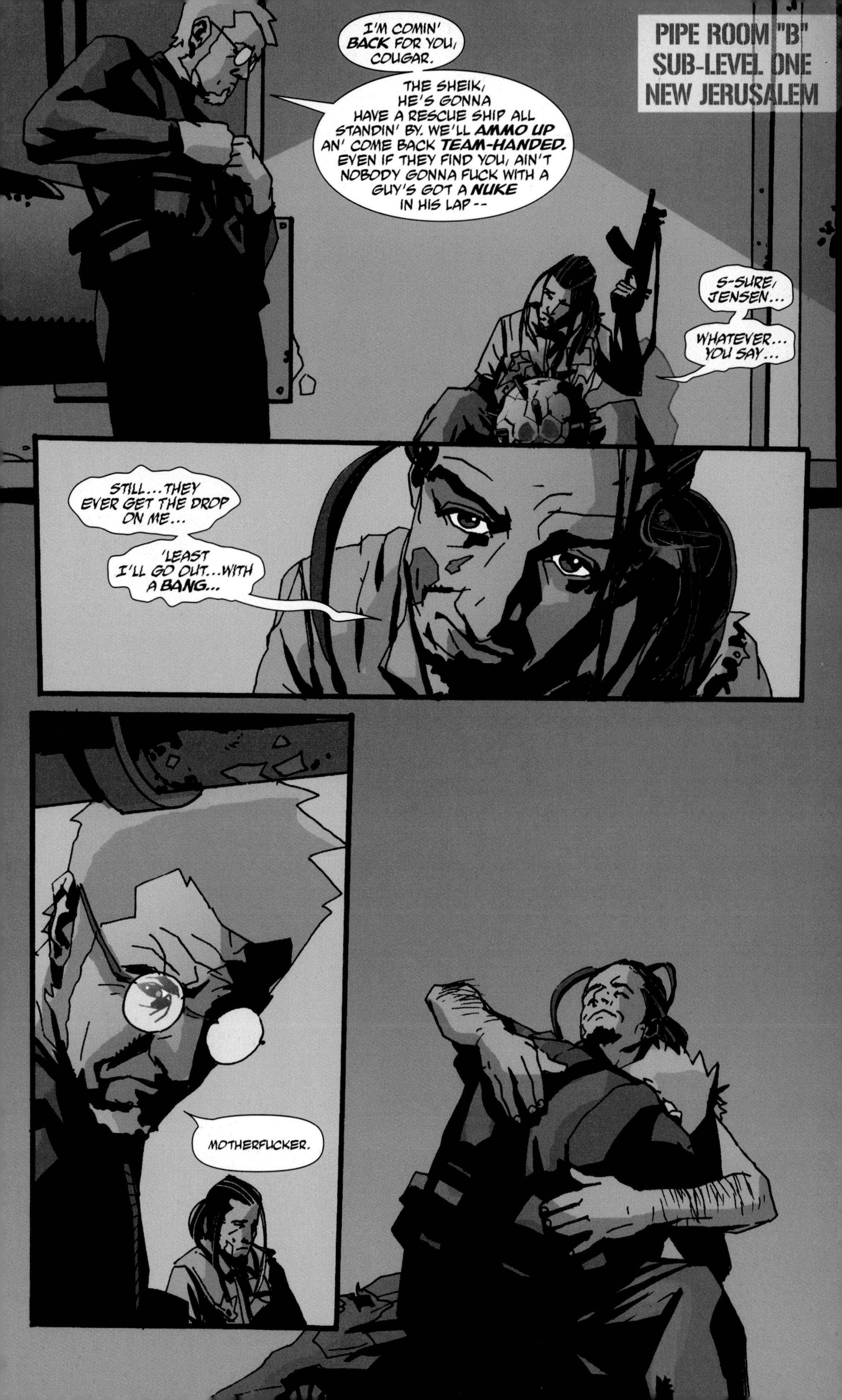
PIPE ROOM "B"
SUB-LEVEL ONE
NEW JERUSALEM
I'M COMIN' BACK FOR YOU, COUGAR.
THE SHEIK, HE'S GONNA HAVE A RESCUE SHIP ALL STANDIN' BY. WE'LL AMMO UP AN' COME BACK TEAM-HANDED. EVEN IF THEY FIND YOU, AIN'T NOBODY GONNA FUCK WITH A GUY'S GOT A NUKE IN HIS LAP --
S-SURE, JENSEN...
WHATEVER... YOU SAY...
STILL... THEY EVER GET THE DROP ON ME...
'LEAST I'LL GO OUT... WITH A BANG...
MOTHERFUCKER.

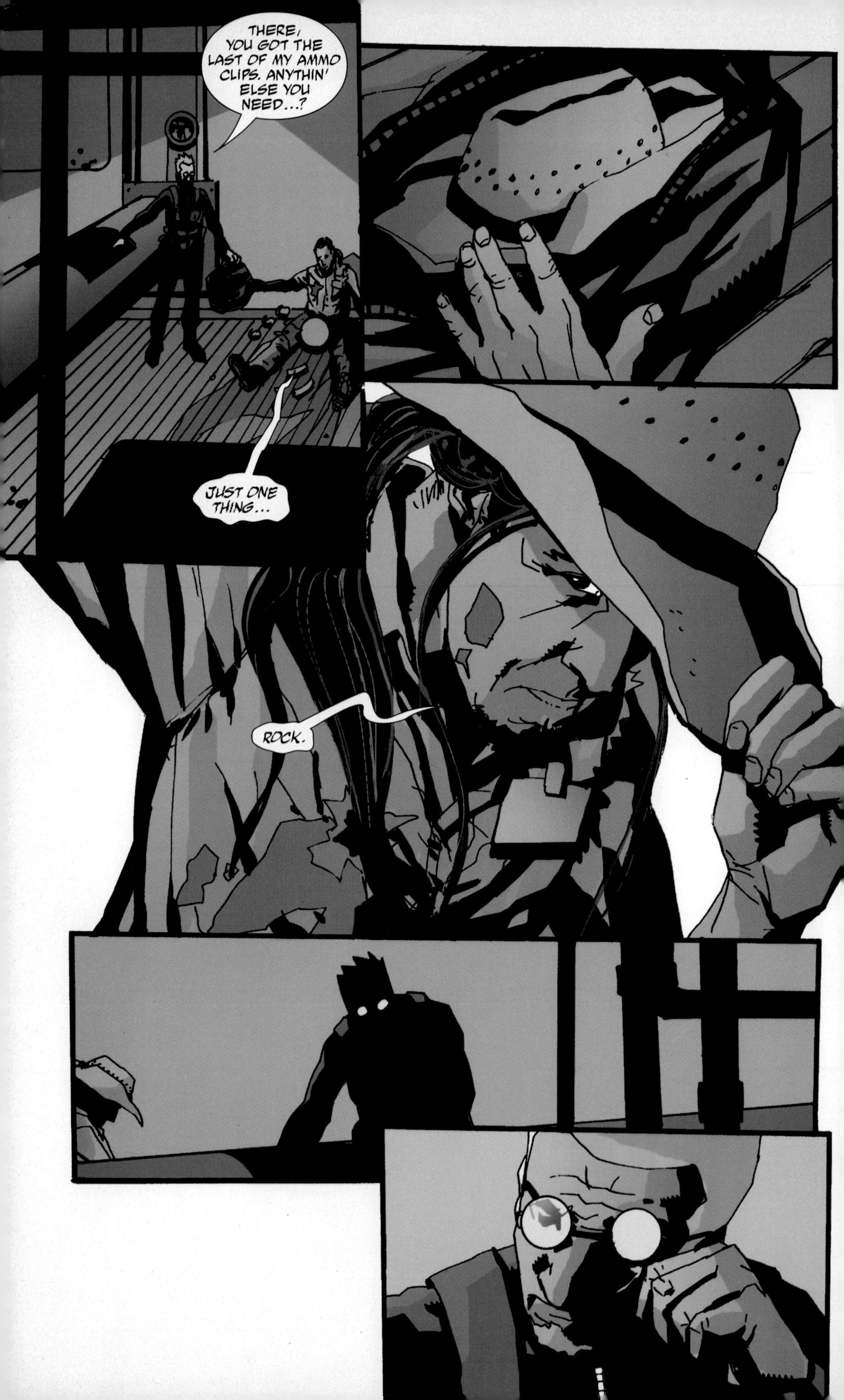
THERE, YOU GOT THE LAST OF MY AMMO CLIPS. ANYTHIN' ELSE YOU NEED...?
JUST ONE THING...
ROCK.

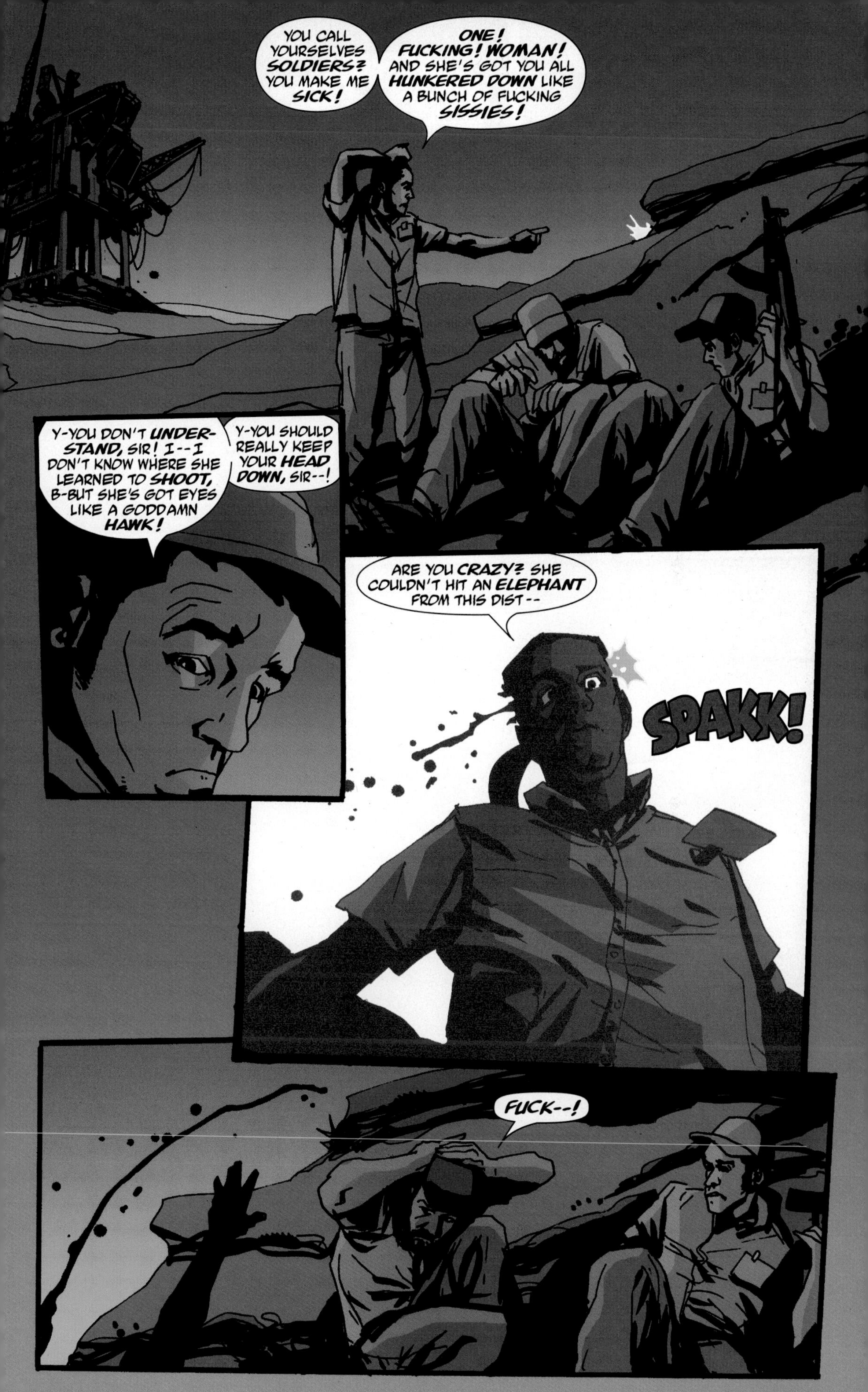
YOU CALL YOURSELVES SOLDIERS? YOU MAKE ME SICK!
ONE! FUCKING! WOMAN! AND SHE'S GOT YOU ALL HUNKERED DOWN LIKE A BUNCH OF FUCKING SISSIES!
Y-YOU DON'T UNDER-STAND, SIR! I--I DON'T KNOW WHERE SHE LEARNED TO SHOOT, B-BUT SHE'S GOT EYES LIKE A GODDAMN HAWK!
Y-YOU SHOULD REALLY KEEP YOUR HEAD DOWN, SIR--!
ARE YOU CRAZY? SHE COULDN'T HIT AN ELEPHANT FROM THIS DIST--
SPAKK!
FUCK--!

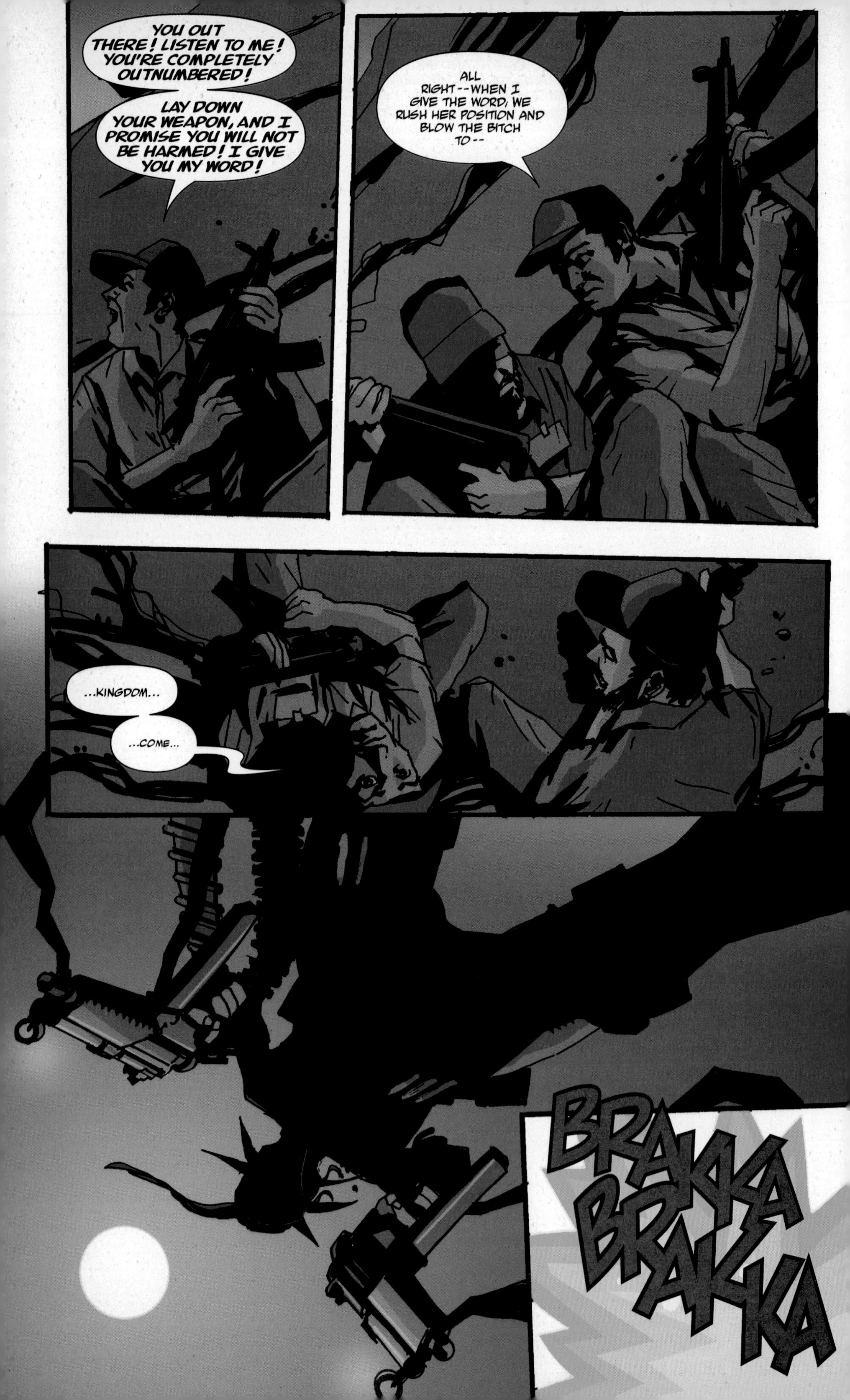
YOU OUT THERE! LISTEN TO ME! YOU'RE COMPLETELY OUTNUMBERED!
LAY DOWN YOUR WEAPON, AND I PROMISE YOU WILL NOT BE HARMED! I GIVE YOU MY WORD!
ALL RIGHT--WHEN I GIVE THE WORD, WE RUSH HER POSITION AND BLOW THE BITCH TO--
...KINGDOM...
...COME...
BRAKKA
BRAKKA
BRAKKA

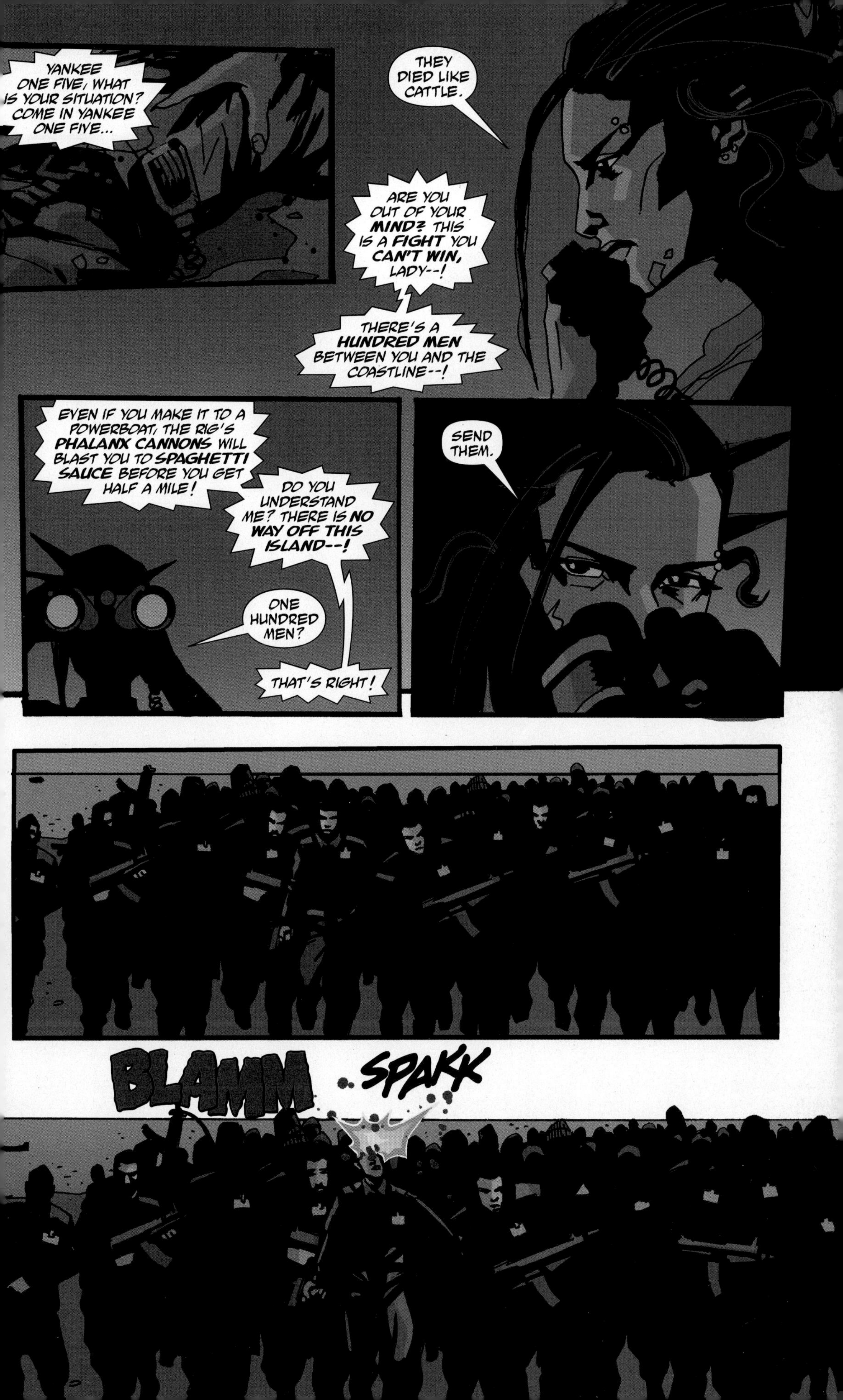
YANKEE ONE FIVE, WHAT IS YOUR SITUATION? COME IN YANKEE ONE FIVE...
THEY DIED LIKE CATTLE.
ARE YOU OUT OF YOUR MIND? THIS IS A FIGHT YOU CAN'T WIN, LADY--!
THERE'S A HUNDRED MEN BETWEEN YOU AND THE COASTLINE--!
EVEN IF YOU MAKE IT TO A POWERBOAT, THE RIG'S PHALANX CANNONS WILL BLAST YOU TO SPAGHETTI SAUCE BEFORE YOU GET HALF A MILE!
DO YOU UNDERSTAND ME? THERE IS NO WAY OFF THIS ISLAND--!
ONE HUNDRED MEN?
THAT'S RIGHT!
SEND THEM.
BLAMM
SPAKK

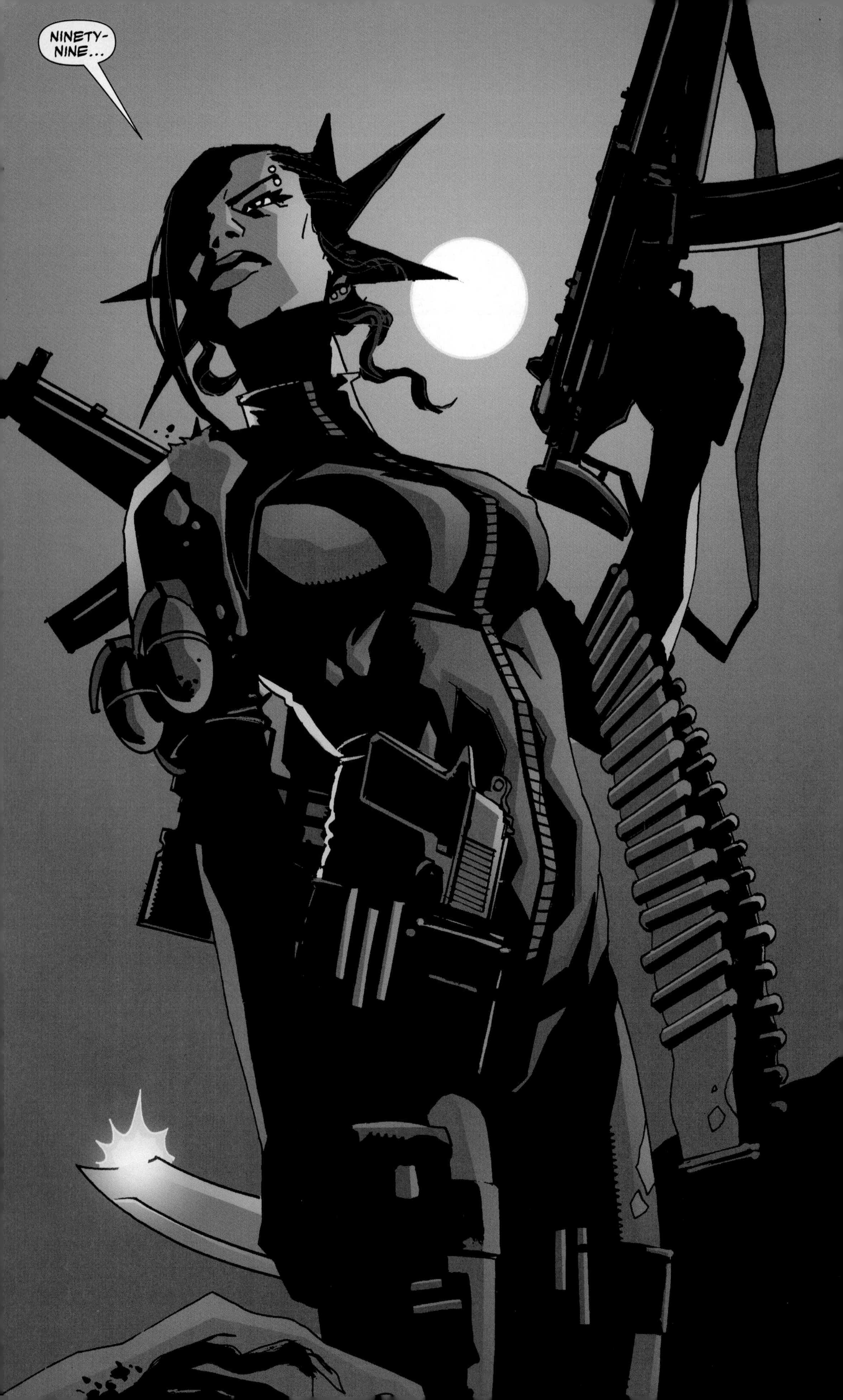
NINETY-NINE...

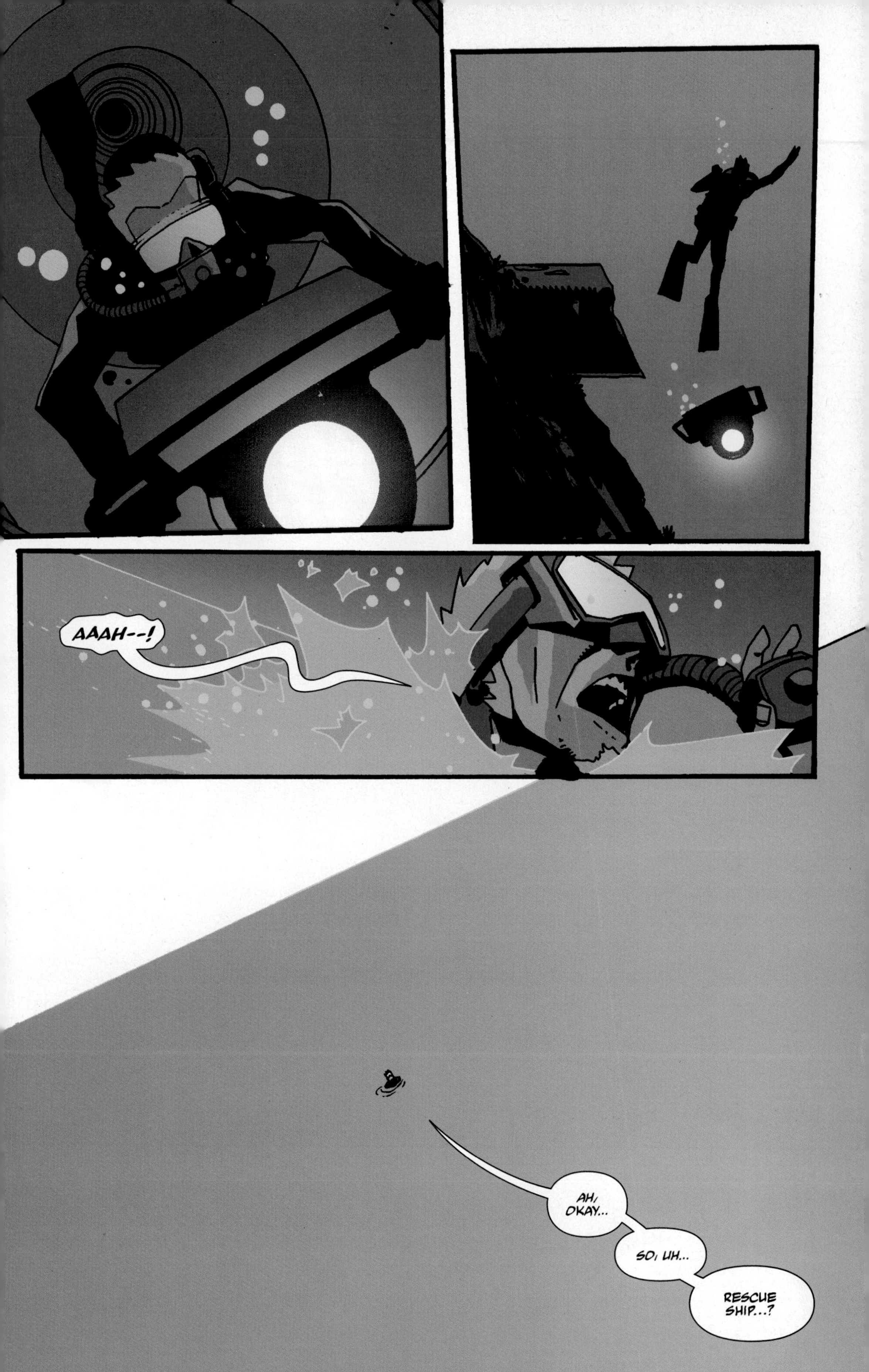
AAAH--!
AH, OKAY...
SO, UH...
RESCUE SHIP...?

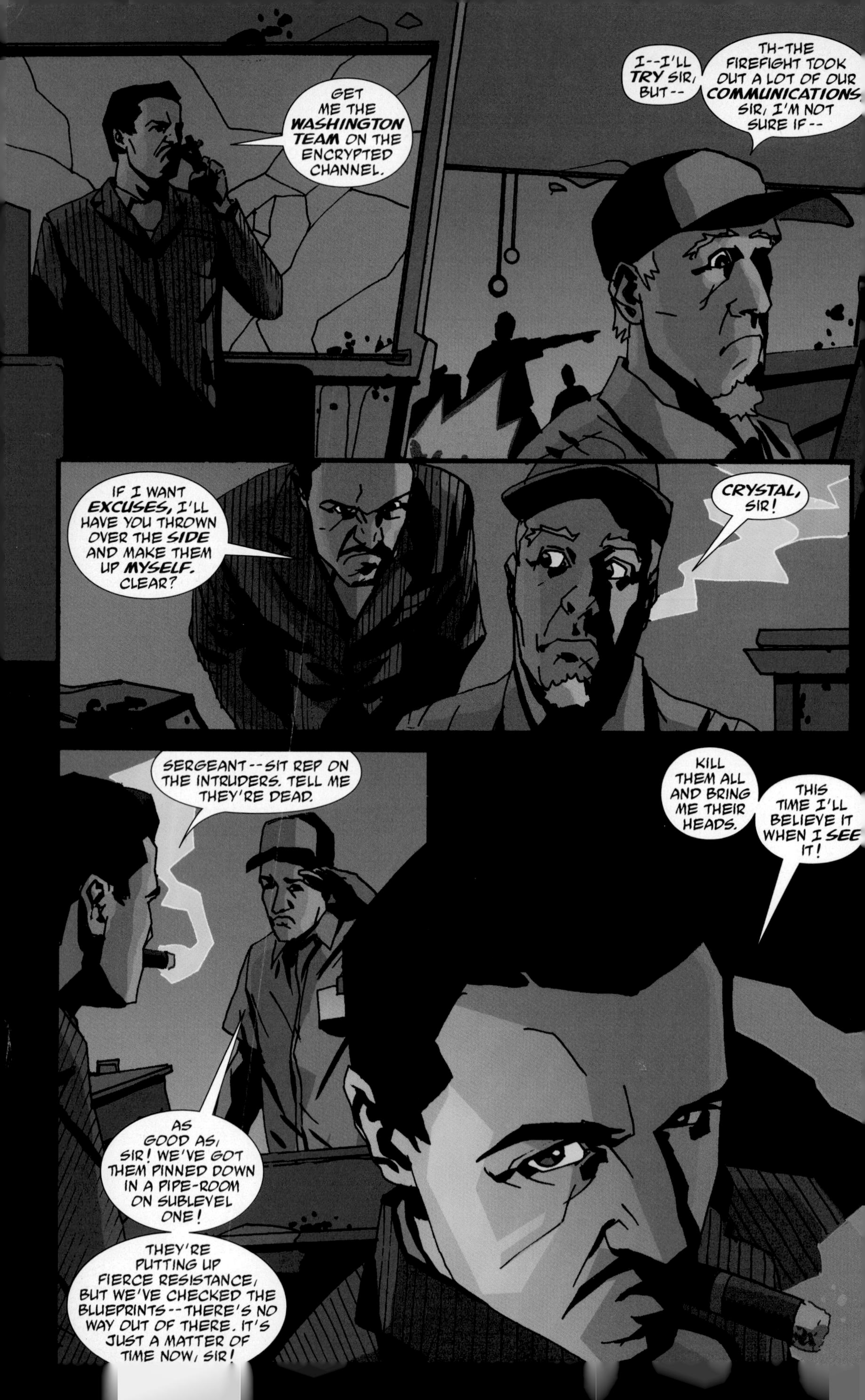
GET ME THE WASHINGTON TEAM ON THE ENCRYPTED CHANNEL.
I--I'LL TRY SIR, BUT--
TH-THE FIREFIGHT TOOK OUT A LOT OF OUR COMMUNICATIONS. SIR, I'M NOT SURE IF--
IF I WANT EXCUSES, I'LL HAVE YOU THROWN OVER THE SIDE AND MAKE THEM UP MYSELF. CLEAR?
CRYSTAL, SIR!
SERGEANT--SIT REP ON THE INTRUDERS. TELL ME THEY'RE DEAD.
AS GOOD AS, SIR! WE'VE GOT THEM PINNED DOWN IN A PIPE-ROOM ON SUBLEVEL ONE!
THEY'RE PUTTING UP FIERCE RESISTANCE, BUT WE'VE CHECKED THE BLUEPRINTS--THERE'S NO WAY OUT OF THERE. IT'S JUST A MATTER OF TIME NOW, SIR!
KILL THEM ALL AND BRING ME THEIR HEADS.
THIS TIME I'LL BELIEVE IT WHEN I SEE IT!

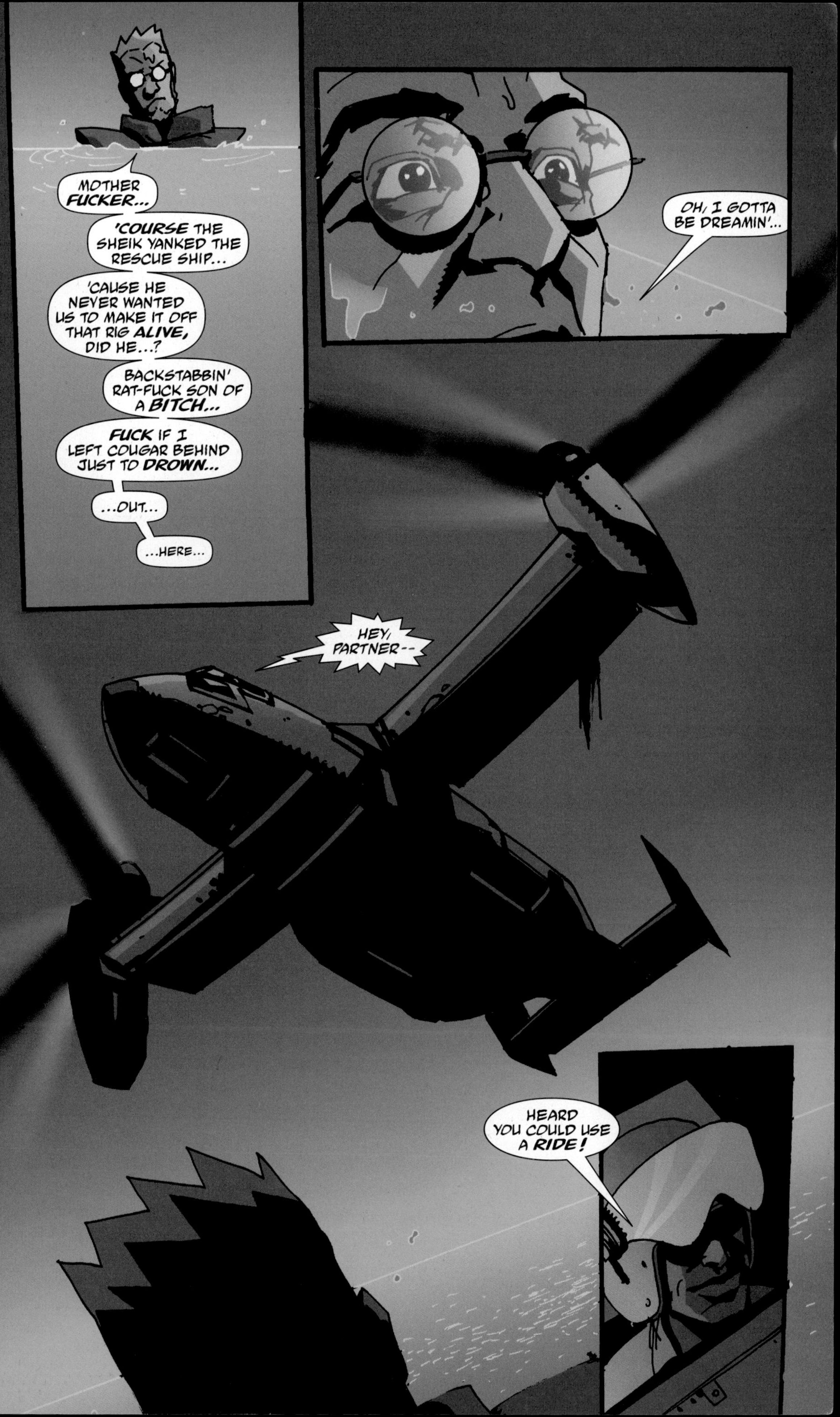
MOTHER FUCKER...
'COURSE THE SHEIK YANKED THE RESCUE SHIP...
'CAUSE HE NEVER WANTED US TO MAKE IT OFF THAT RIG ALIVE, DID HE...?
BACKSTABBIN' RAT-FUCK SON OF A BITCH...
FUCK IF I LEFT COUGAR BEHIND JUST TO DROWN...
...OUT...
...HERE...
OH, I GOTTA BE DREAMIN'...
HEY, PARTNER--
HEARD YOU COULD USE A RIDE!

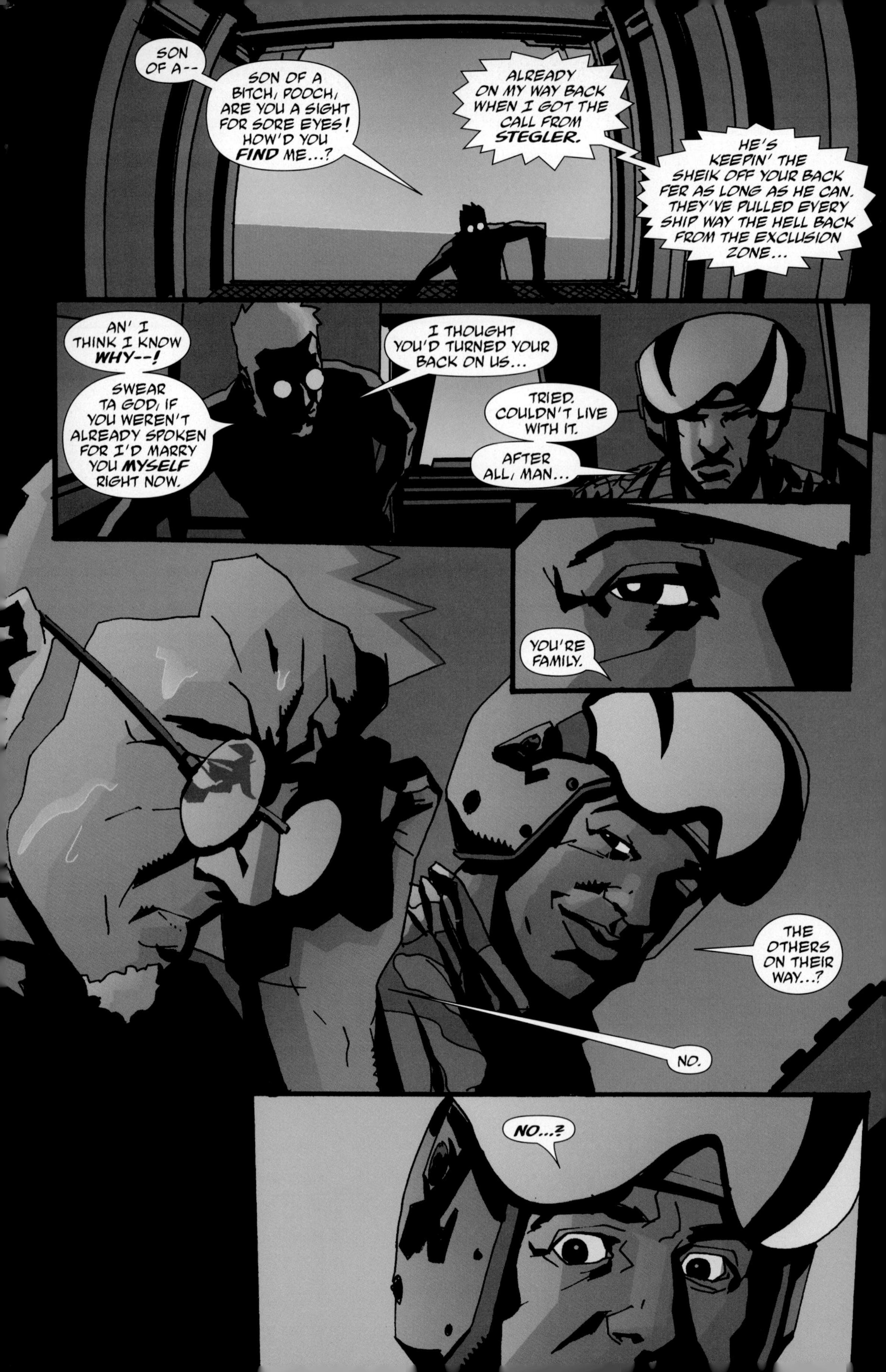
SON OF A--
SON OF A BITCH, POOCH, ARE YOU A SIGHT FOR SORE EYES! HOW'D YOU FIND ME...?
ALREADY ON MY WAY BACK WHEN I GOT THE CALL FROM STEGLER.
HE'S KEEPIN' THE SHEIK OFF YOUR BACK FER AS LONG AS HE CAN. THEY'VE PULLED EVERY SHIP WAY THE HELL BACK FROM THE EXCLUSION ZONE...
AN' I THINK I KNOW WHY--!
SWEAR TA GOD, IF YOU WEREN'T ALREADY SPOKEN FOR I'D MARRY YOU MYSELF RIGHT NOW.
I THOUGHT YOU'D TURNED YOUR BACK ON US...
TRIED. COULDN'T LIVE WITH IT.
AFTER ALL, MAN...
YOU'RE FAMILY.
THE OTHERS ON THEIR WAY...?
NO.
NO...?

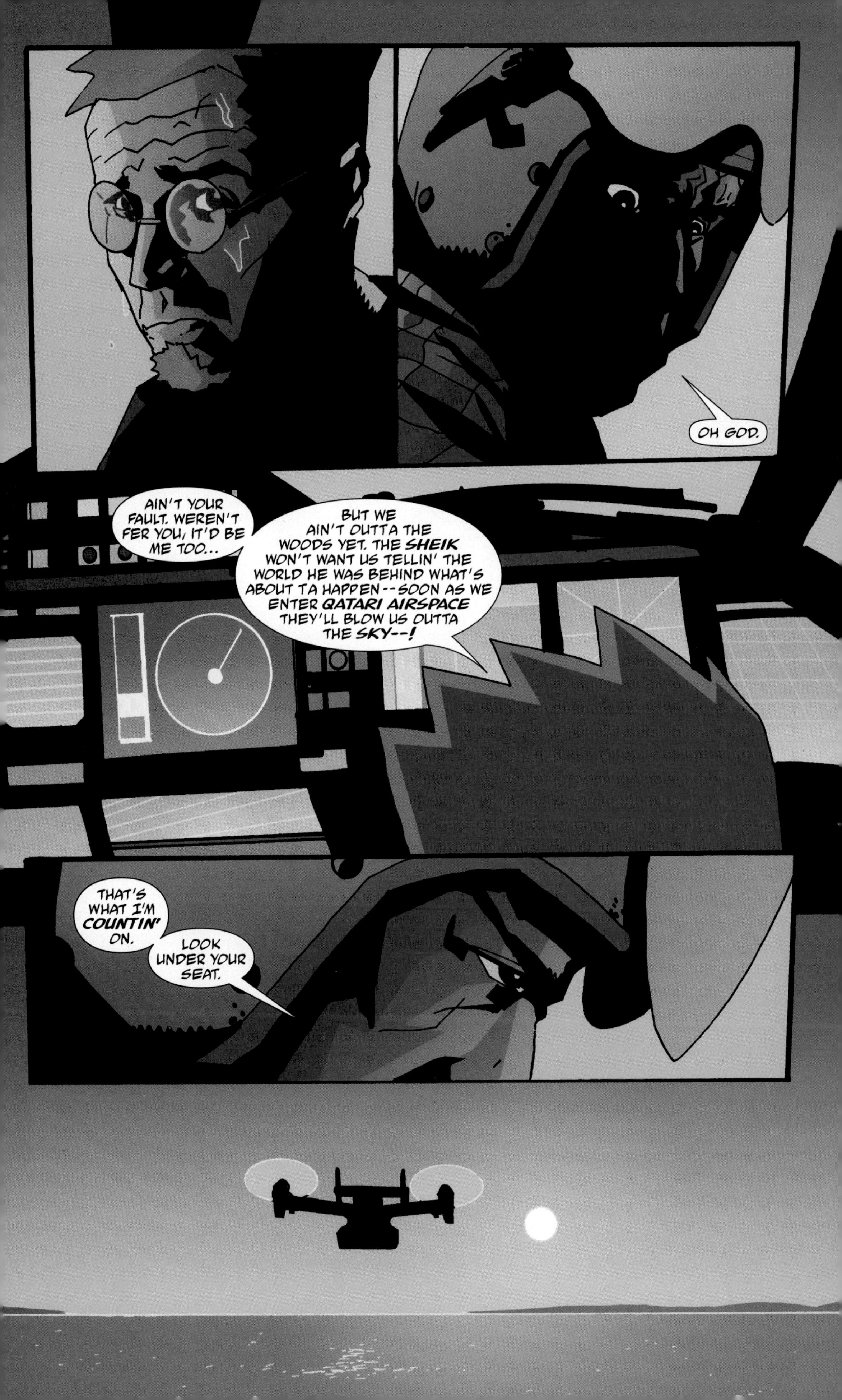
OH GOD.
AIN'T YOUR FAULT. WEREN'T FER YOU, IT'D BE ME TOO...
BUT WE AIN'T OUTTA THE WOODS YET. THE **SHEIK** WON'T WANT US TELLIN' THE WORLD HE WAS BEHIND WHAT'S ABOUT TA HAPPEN--SOON AS WE ENTER **QATARI AIRSPACE** THEY'LL BLOW US OUTTA THE **SKY--!**
THAT'S WHAT I'M **COUNTIN'** ON.
LOOK UNDER YOUR SEAT.

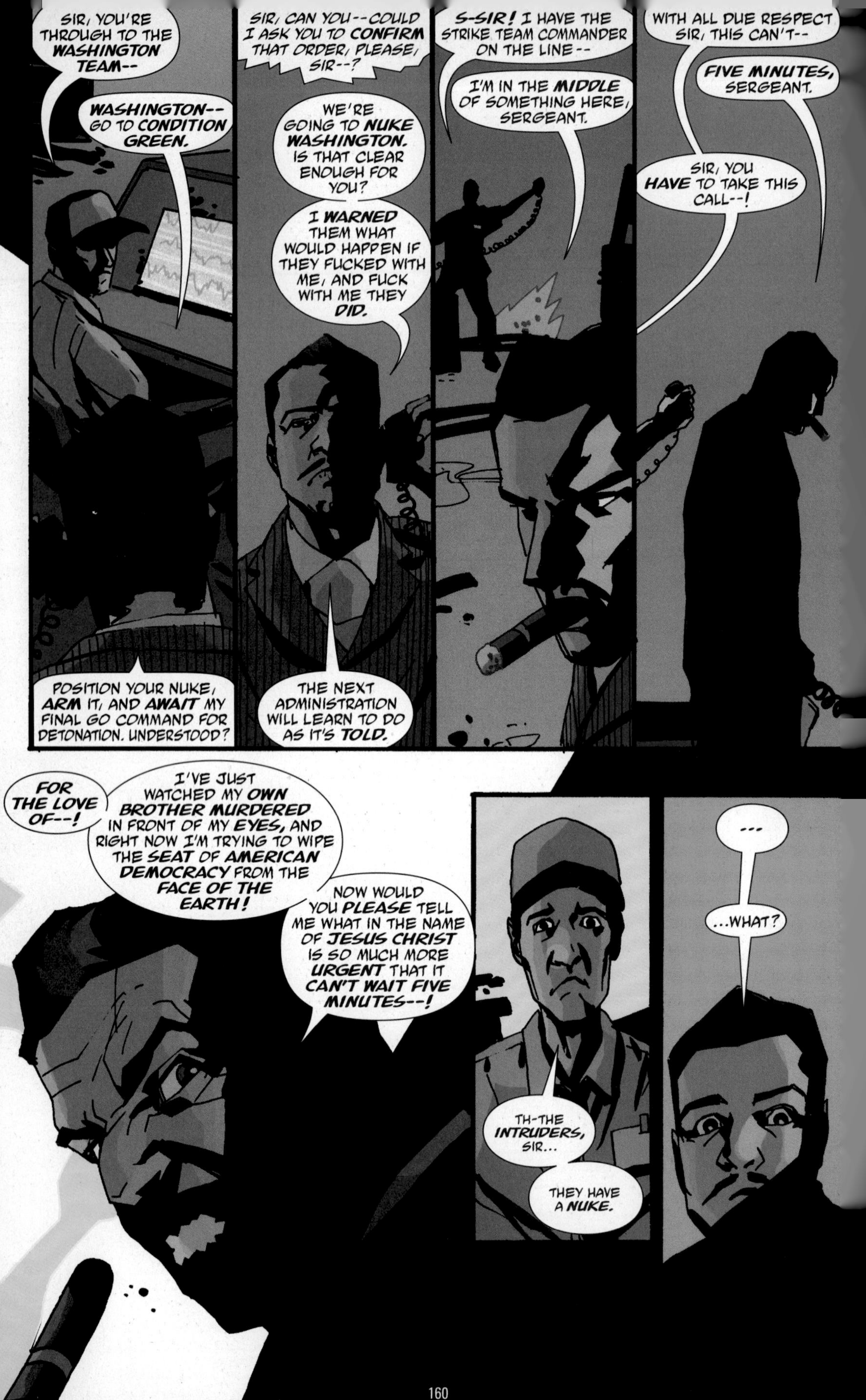
SIR, YOU'RE THROUGH TO THE WASHINGTON TEAM--
WASHINGTON-- GO TO CONDITION GREEN.
POSITION YOUR NUKE, ARM IT, AND AWAIT MY FINAL GO COMMAND FOR DETONATION. UNDERSTOOD?
SIR, CAN YOU--COULD I ASK YOU TO CONFIRM THAT ORDER, PLEASE, SIR--?
WE'RE GOING TO NUKE WASHINGTON. IS THAT CLEAR ENOUGH FOR YOU?
I WARNED THEM WHAT WOULD HAPPEN IF THEY FUCKED WITH ME, AND FUCK WITH ME THEY DID.
THE NEXT ADMINISTRATION WILL LEARN TO DO AS IT'S TOLD.
S-SIR! I HAVE THE STRIKE TEAM COMMANDER ON THE LINE--
I'M IN THE MIDDLE OF SOMETHING HERE, SERGEANT.
WITH ALL DUE RESPECT SIR, THIS CAN'T--
FIVE MINUTES, SERGEANT.
SIR, YOU HAVE TO TAKE THIS CALL--!
FOR THE LOVE OF--!
I'VE JUST WATCHED MY OWN BROTHER MURDERED IN FRONT OF MY EYES, AND RIGHT NOW I'M TRYING TO WIPE THE SEAT OF AMERICAN DEMOCRACY FROM THE FACE OF THE EARTH!
NOW WOULD YOU PLEASE TELL ME WHAT IN THE NAME OF JESUS CHRIST IS SO MUCH MORE URGENT THAT IT CAN'T WAIT FIVE MINUTES--!
TH-THE INTRUDERS, SIR...
THEY HAVE A NUKE.
...
...WHAT?

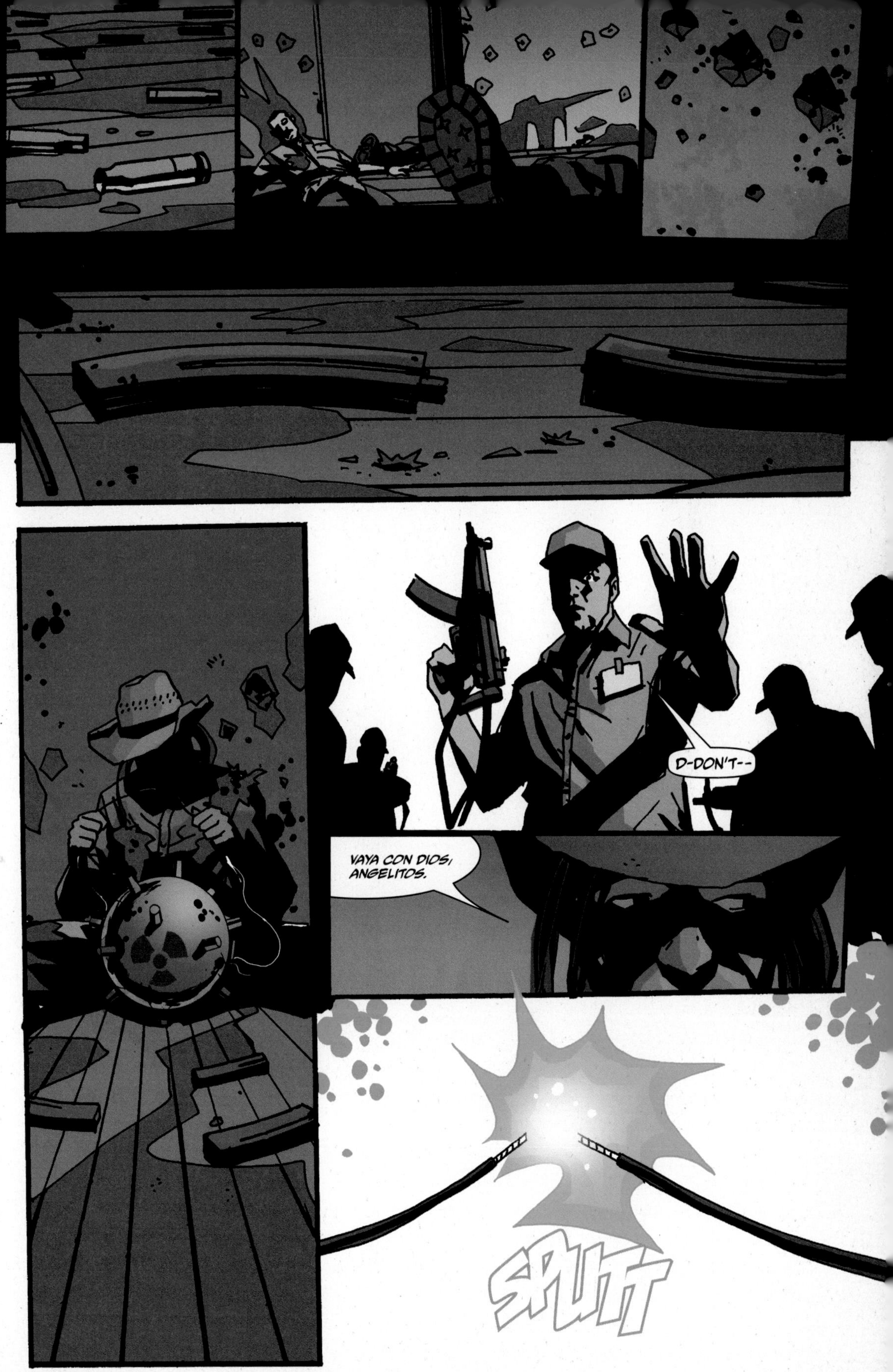
D-DON'T--
VAYA CON DIOS, ANGELITOS.
SPUTT

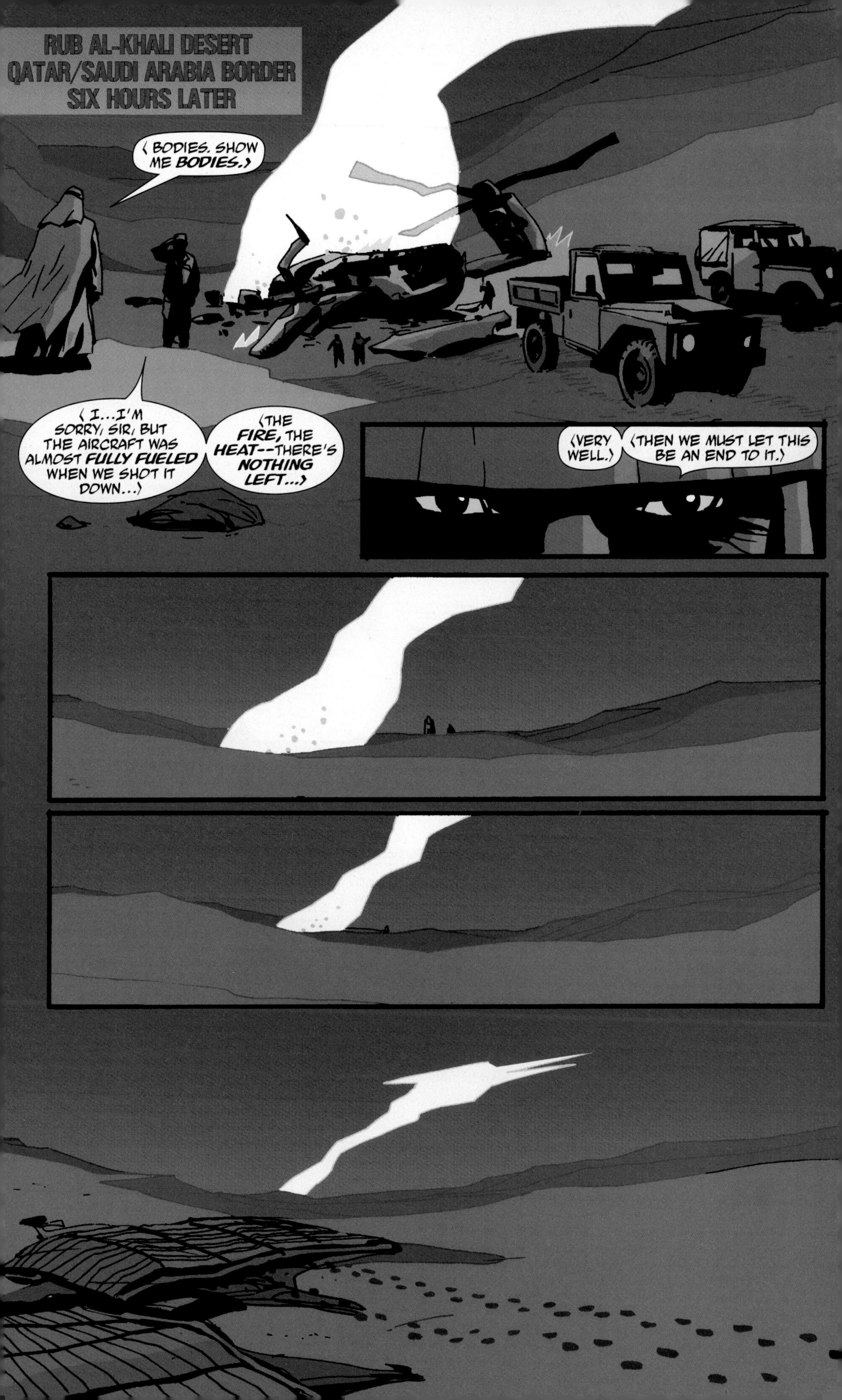
RUB AL-KHALI DESERT
QATAR/SAUDI ARABIA BORDER
SIX HOURS LATER
‹BODIES. SHOW ME BODIES.›
‹I...I'M SORRY, SIR, BUT THE AIRCRAFT WAS ALMOST FULLY FUELED WHEN WE SHOT IT DOWN...›
‹THE FIRE, THE HEAT--THERE'S NOTHING LEFT...›
‹VERY WELL.›
‹THEN WE MUST LET THIS BE AN END TO IT.›

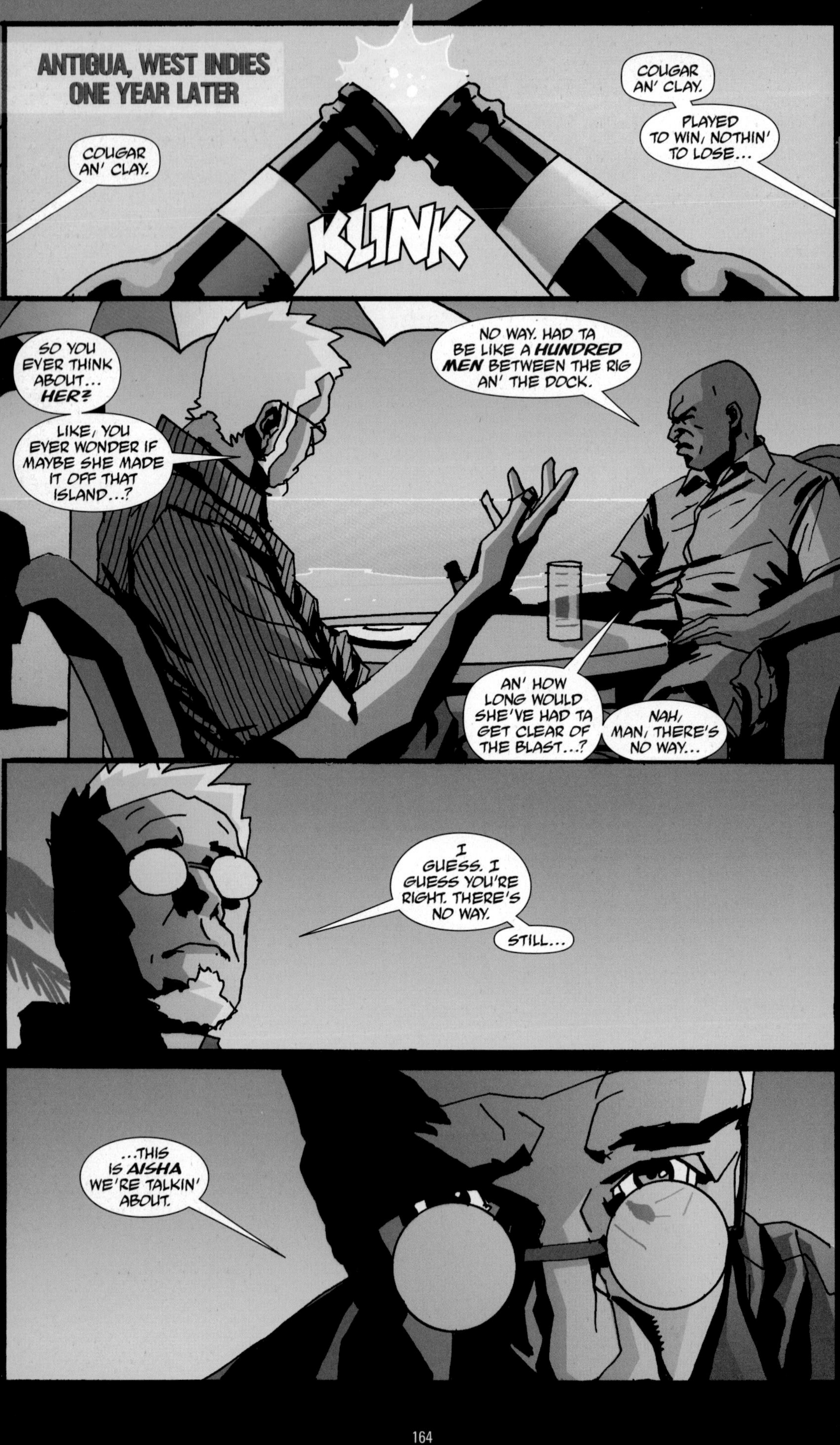
ANTIGUA, WEST INDIES
ONE YEAR LATER
COUGAR AN' CLAY.
COUGAR AN' CLAY.
PLAYED TO WIN, NOTHIN' TO LOSE...
KLINK
SO YOU EVER THINK ABOUT... HER?
LIKE, YOU EVER WONDER IF MAYBE SHE MADE IT OFF THAT ISLAND...?
NO WAY. HAD TA BE LIKE A HUNDRED MEN BETWEEN THE RIG AN' THE DOCK.
AN' HOW LONG WOULD SHE'VE HAD TA GET CLEAR OF THE BLAST...?
NAH, MAN, THERE'S NO WAY...
I GUESS. I GUESS YOU'RE RIGHT. THERE'S NO WAY.
STILL...
...THIS IS AISHA WE'RE TALKIN' ABOUT.

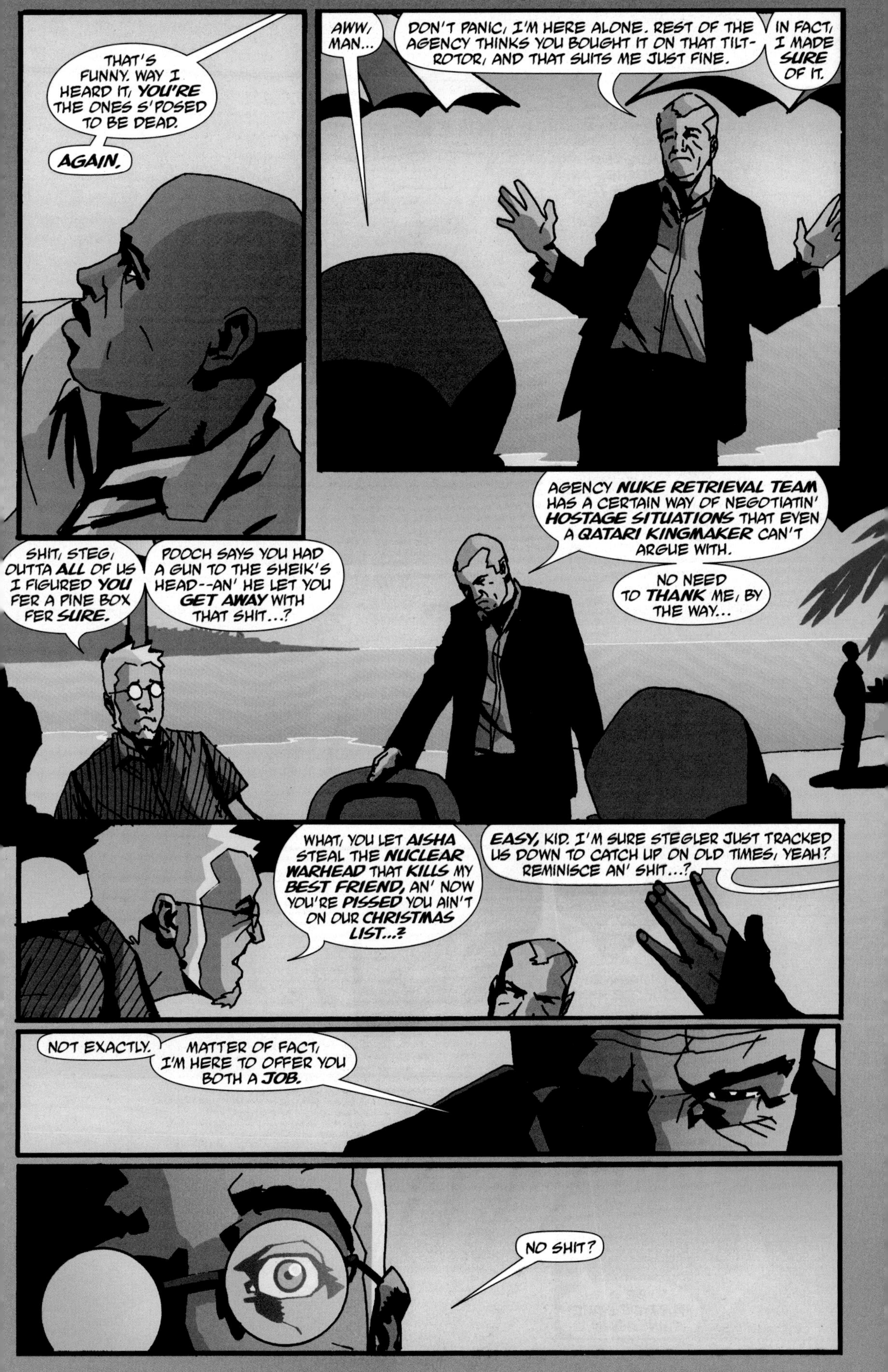
THAT'S FUNNY. WAY I HEARD IT, YOU'RE THE ONES S'POSED TO BE DEAD.
AGAIN.
AWW, MAN...
DON'T PANIC, I'M HERE ALONE. REST OF THE AGENCY THINKS YOU BOUGHT IT ON THAT TILT-ROTOR, AND THAT SUITS ME JUST FINE.
IN FACT, I MADE SURE OF IT.
SHIT, STEG, OUTTA ALL OF US I FIGURED YOU FER A PINE BOX FER SURE.
POOCH SAYS YOU HAD A GUN TO THE SHEIK'S HEAD--AN' HE LET YOU GET AWAY WITH THAT SHIT...?
AGENCY NUKE RETRIEVAL TEAM HAS A CERTAIN WAY OF NEGOTIATIN' HOSTAGE SITUATIONS THAT EVEN A QATARI KINGMAKER CAN'T ARGUE WITH.
NO NEED TO THANK ME, BY THE WAY...
WHAT, YOU LET AISHA STEAL THE NUCLEAR WARHEAD THAT KILLS MY BEST FRIEND, AN' NOW YOU'RE PISSED YOU AIN'T ON OUR CHRISTMAS LIST...?
EASY, KID. I'M SURE STEGLER JUST TRACKED US DOWN TO CATCH UP ON OLD TIMES, YEAH? REMINISCE AN' SHIT...?
NOT EXACTLY.
MATTER OF FACT, I'M HERE TO OFFER YOU BOTH A JOB.
NO SHIT?

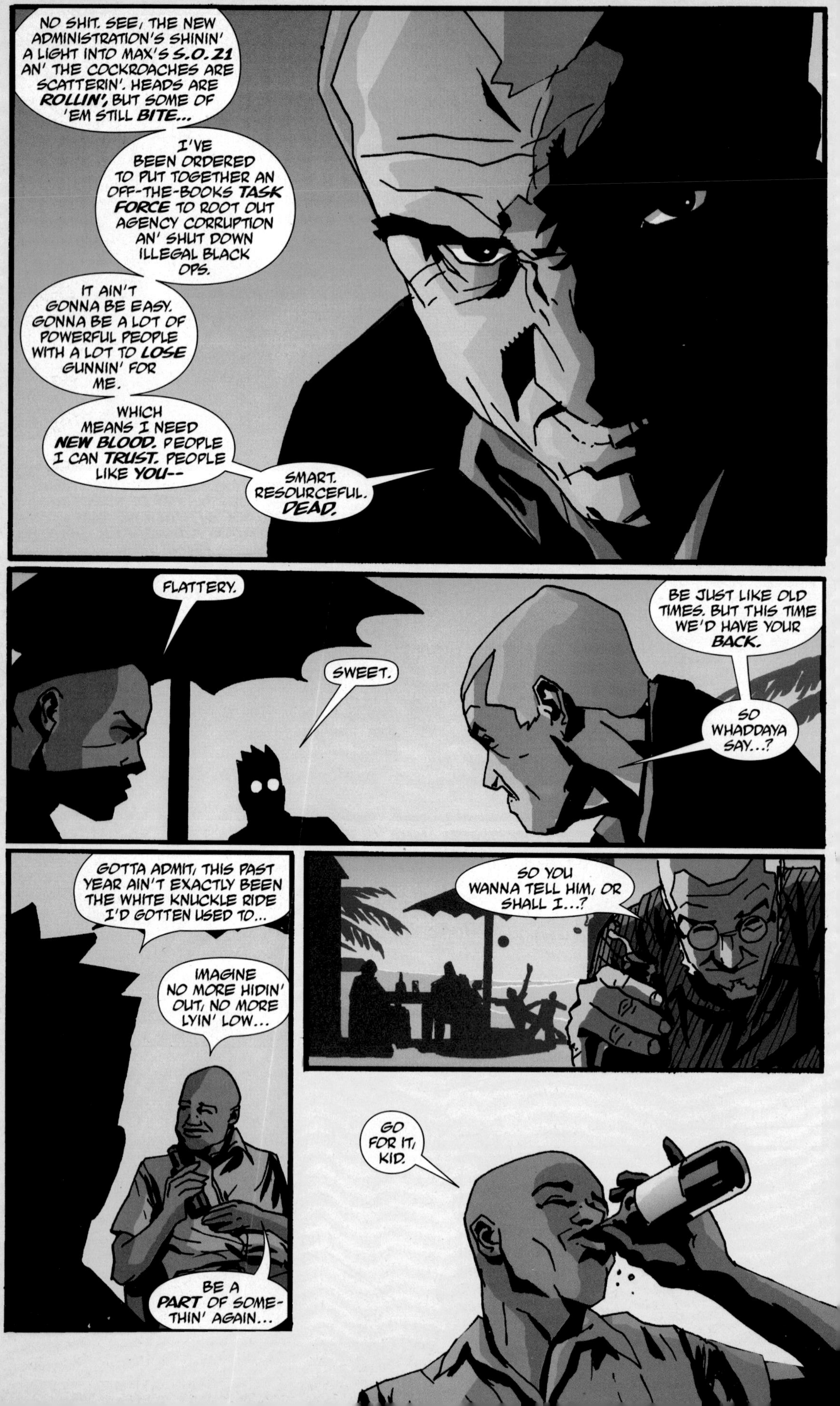
NO SHIT. SEE, THE NEW ADMINISTRATION'S SHININ' A LIGHT INTO MAX'S S.O.21 AN' THE COCKROACHES ARE SCATTERIN'. HEADS ARE ROLLIN', BUT SOME OF 'EM STILL BITE...
I'VE BEEN ORDERED TO PUT TOGETHER AN OFF-THE-BOOKS TASK FORCE TO ROOT OUT AGENCY CORRUPTION AN' SHUT DOWN ILLEGAL BLACK OPS.
IT AIN'T GONNA BE EASY. GONNA BE A LOT OF POWERFUL PEOPLE WITH A LOT TO LOSE GUNNIN' FOR ME.
WHICH MEANS I NEED NEW BLOOD. PEOPLE I CAN TRUST. PEOPLE LIKE YOU--
SMART. RESOURCEFUL. DEAD.
FLATTERY.
SWEET.
BE JUST LIKE OLD TIMES. BUT THIS TIME WE'D HAVE YOUR BACK.
SO WHADDAYA SAY...?
GOTTA ADMIT, THIS PAST YEAR AIN'T EXACTLY BEEN THE WHITE KNUCKLE RIDE I'D GOTTEN USED TO...
IMAGINE NO MORE HIDIN' OUT, NO MORE LYIN' LOW...
BE A PART OF SOME-THIN' AGAIN...
SO YOU WANNA TELL HIM, OR SHALL I...?
GO FOR IT, KID.

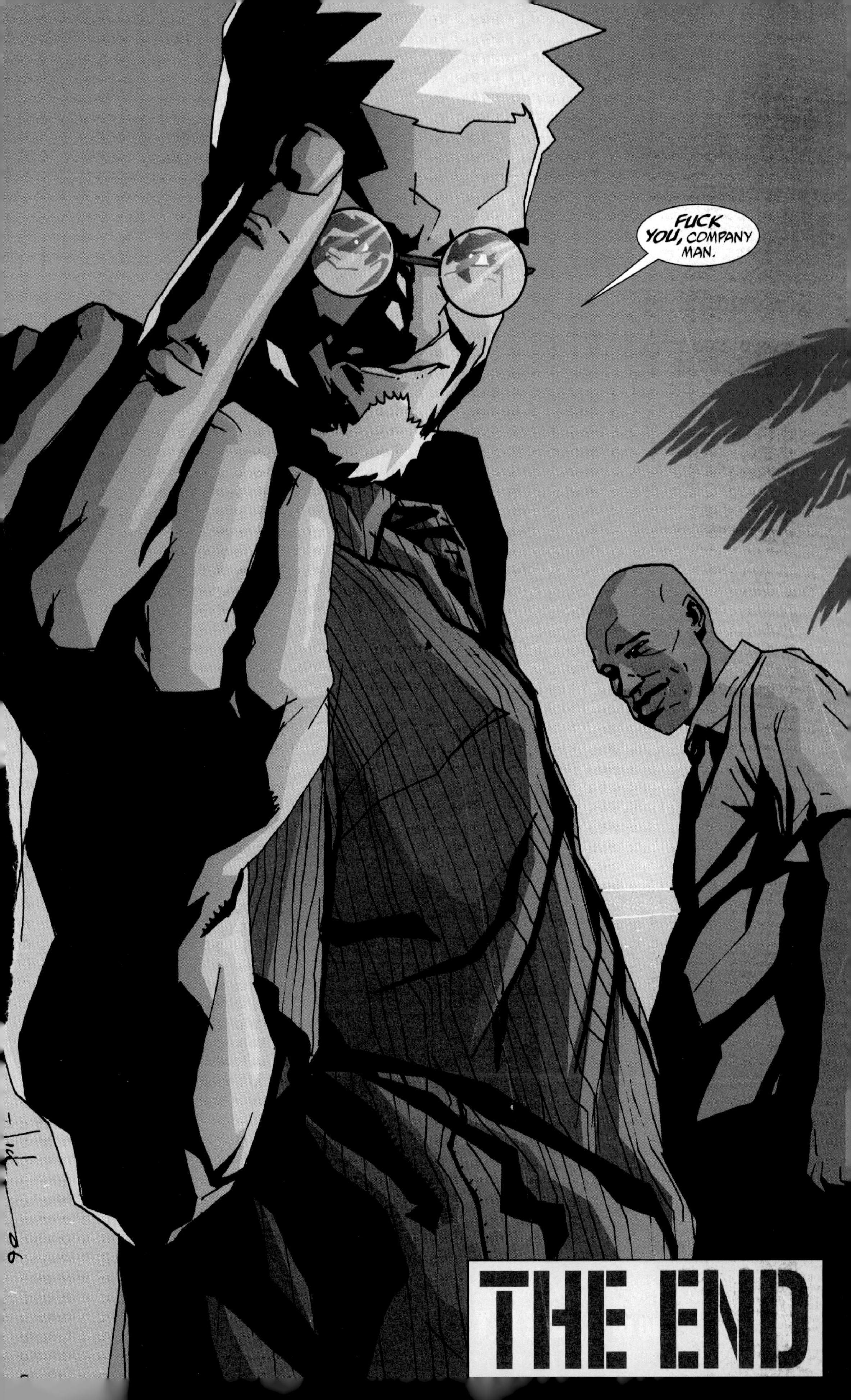
FUCK YOU, COMPANY MAN.
THE END